*Also in the Variorum Collected Studies Series:*

**ZSIGMOND PÁL PACH**
Hungary and the European Economy in Early Modern Times

**ANTONI MACZAK**
Money, Prices and Power in Poland, 16th–17th Centuries

**JERZY TOPOLSKI**
The Manorial Economy in Early-Modern East-Central Europe
Origins, Development and Consequences

**ALAIN DUCELLIER**
L'Albanie entre Byzance et Venise (Xe–XVe s.)

**SAMUEL H. BARON**
Explorations in Muscovite History

**JERZY KLOCZOWSKI**
La Pologne dans l'Eglise médiévale

**DIMITRI OBOLENSKY**
The Byzantine Inheritance of Eastern Europe

**ERIK FÜGEDI (Ed. J.M. Bak)**
Kings, Bishops, Nobles and Burghers in Medieval Hungary

**WLADIMIR VODOFF**
Princes et principautés russes, Xe–XVIIe siècles

**GUSTAVE ALEF**
Rulers and Nobles in 15th-Century Muscovy

**PASCHALIS M. KITROMILIDES**
Enlightenment, Nationalism, Orthodoxy
Studies in the Culture and Political Thought of Southeastern Europe

**MACHIEL KIEL**
Studies on the Ottoman Architecture of the Balkans
A Legacy in Stone

**MICHEL BALARD**
La Mer Noire et la Romanie génoise, XIIIe–XVe siècles

COLLECTED STUDIES SERIES

# Agrarian Development and Social Change in Eastern Europe, 14th–19th Centuries

Péter Gunst

# Agrarian Development and Social Change in Eastern Europe, 14th–19th Centuries

VARIORUM
1996

Published by VARIORUM
Ashgate Publishing Limited
Gower House, Croft Road,
Aldershot, Hampshire GU11 3HR
Great Britain

Ashgate Publishing Company
Old Post Road,
Brookfield, Vermont 05036
USA

ISBN 0–86078–598–X

**British Library CIP Data**
Gunst, Péter.
Agrarian Development and Social Change in Eastern Europe,
14th–19th Centuries. (Variorum Collected Studies Series; CS540).
1. Europe, Eastern–History. 2. Europe, Eastern–Social conditions.
3. Land use, rural–Europe, Eastern–History. I. Title.
947

**US Library of Congress CIP Data**
Gunst, Péter.
Agrarian Development and Social Change in Eastern Europe, 14th–19th
Centuries / Péter Gunst. p. cm. – (Collected Studies Series; CS540).
Includes index (cloth: alk. paper).
1. Agriculture–Economic aspects–Hungary–History. 2. Hungary–Social
Conditions. 3. Hungary–Economic conditions. 4. Hungary–Rural
Conditions. 5. Agriculture–Economic aspects–Europe, Eastern–History.
6. Europe, Eastern–Social conditions. 7. Europe, Eastern–Economic
conditions. 8. Europe, Eastern–Rural conditions. I. Title. II. Series:
Collected Studies; CS540.
HD1940. 5. G86 1996 96–2530
338. 1' 09439–dc20 CIP

The paper used in this publication meets the minimum requirements of the
American National Standard for Information Sciences – Permanance of Paper
for Printed Library Materials, ANSI Z39.48–1984. ∞ ™

Printed by Galliard (Printers) Ltd, Great Yarmouth, Norfolk, Great Britain
COLLECTED STUDIES SERIES C540

# CONTENTS

This volume contains x + 324 pages

# PREFACE

The twelve studies included in this volume result from a journey of exploration through the history of Eastern Europe, a journey undertaken over the past fee decades. I have been concerned with problems that were never properly acknowledged – What is 'Eastern European' about the development of Eastern Europe? What geographical area can be characterized as having an 'Eastern European' type of historical development? And where is Hungary to be situated within this area? Or is it outside it?

For my generation, the region said to be 'Eastern European' definitely meant Europe east of the River Elbe. The fact that after the Second World War this was approximately also the border of the area under Soviet influence, could not escape the attention of a young historian. This geographical conception was indeed a commonplace of post-1945 historical teaching and writing in this part of the world, but it was one that irritated me from the outset, because I would not have placed the development of Hungary (or Bohemia or Poland) within that scheme.

This 'irritation' became the source of these studies and lectures. The first one to be published appeared in 1974 in Hungarian; this was the first version of the paper appearing in German in this volume as Study III. It attracted general attention at the time, and stimulated similar efforts among several of my colleagues, the best known of whom is Jenö Szücs, whose excellent study of the topic was published in German and French as well. It was in fact preceeded, however, by the item published here as Study I, which had been initiated by American colleagues in 1973, but was only published a decade later, in 1984 in the United States.

Following these investigations, it is for me by now evident that there exists an in-between region, a 'Central Europe', between Eastern and Western Europe. This name does not derive from its geographical position, but from its historical development. In an area reaching from the Baltic countries, through Poland and Hungary, to Slovenia and Croatia, a basically Eastern European model of development was very early interrupted and changed into a Western European pattern. This was brought about by the economic, social and, not least, the military challenge of the Western European region, and above all by the economic and social achievements of masses of immigrant German peasants (and city dwellers). The most important factors in this were the disintegration of the village community system, the appearance of individual family taxation among the peasantry, and the withdrawal of the village community from its role in organizing the crop rotation system.

However, I do not want to hinder the reader looking through these studies. All the above is mentioned only to give some explanation to aid the understanding of how and why they were born.

PÉTER GUNST

*Budapest*
*March 1996*

# ACKNOWLEDGEMENTS

Grateful acknowledgement is made to the following persons, institutions and publishers for kindly permitting the reproduction of the studies included in this volume: Schenkman Books, Inc. (for study I); the University of California Press (II); the University of Cologne (III); Lothar Gall on behalf of the *Historische Zeischrift* (VI); the Akamémiai Kiadó és Nyomda Kft. (IX, X, XI).

## PUBLISHER'S NOTE

The articles in this volume, as in all others in the Collected Studies Series, have not been given a new, continuous pagination. In order to avoid confusion, and to facilitate their use where these same studies have been referred to elsewhere, the original pagination has been maintained wherever possible.

Each article has been given a Roman number in order of appearance, as listed in the Contents. This number is repeated in each page and is quoted in the index entries.

# I

# Some Characteristics of East European Economic and Social Development

## Data and Reflections

The appended chronological tables, statistics and diagrams give evidence of a certain time lag in general economic and agricultural development in rural society in Eastern Europe as compared to Western Europe and North America. The many reasons contributing to this phenomenon have remained obscure although they arise from the most characteristic features of economic, social and historical development in Eastern Europe. The first and most important factor we must consider is the interpretation of the Western European model as universal, obliging historians to prove that development outside of Western Europe followed the so-called universal pattern. Thus, in Eastern Europe historians depicted development at the turn of the eighteenth and throughout the nineteenth centuries as identical to that of the leading nations in Western Europe. Later, in the decades following the emancipation of serfs, historians of Eastern Europe began to describe quantitative and temporal peculiarities of their areas as due to a time lag. This backwardness was attributed to the effect of wars and the long reign of foreign, mostly nomadic conquerors–the Mongolians in Russia, the Turks in Hungary and in the Balkans. Historians of these countries realized only in the third period (see appendix, page 40) that essential differences in the bases of economic and social development predetermined the historical path of Eastern Europe. However, even today not all East European historians recognize these basic differences. For national pride often still demands the assumption that indigenous historical development must follow the Western European model, which was considered to be the classical one by the rigid, dogmatic interpretation of Marxist historical materialism in the 1950s. Thus historians in Eastern Europe often avoided the depicting of specific characteristics, emphasizing only general tendencies and imposing a developmental scheme that frequently did violence to the historical facts. For example, the concept of "second serfdom" was broadly and uniformly applied to widely differing phenomena in Eastern Europe.

Today, in considering the relation between Eastern and Western European developments, we proceed from the view that the economies of Western Europe, through foreign trade, greatly influenced Eastern Europe and its development, but that conditions created fundamental differences. A simple interpretation of historical sources would have demonstrated the difference in paths of development. For example, when the peoples of Eastern Europe adopted Christianity and founded their states, the lawgivers (who were mostly clergymen from Western Europe) applied their own conceptional systems identified by Latin names to structures of state organization, society and economics in the new Hungarian, Polish or Croatian states. It did not occur to them that they were using standardized Western European terms for quite different phenomena. Generations later, however, we find that in many documents corresponding colloquial names are noted beside the Latin terms.

## THE ASIATIC MODE OF PRODUCTION AND THE WEST

We now ask what caused the highly accelerated development in Western Europe, as compared to other parts of the world, and what were the consequences of this phenomenon for Eastern Europe? The following example will illustrate the problem at hand: the church frescos in Novgorod in the eleventh and twelfth centuries are almost identical, not only in technique but also in artistic conception, to those in Northern Italy of the same time. But if we compare sixteenth century Renaissance painting to Russian art of the same period, we discover an enormous difference. Painting in Russia does not seem to have developed either in technique or conception, while painting in Western Europe advanced dramatically. This example is valid for a broad spectrum of economic and social phenomena as well. Development in Western Europe did accelerate in these centuries, and this acceleration gave it the great advantage which has been characteristic of it since that time. Thus, in our opinion, it was not so much that Eastern Europe "deviated" from Western Europe in the fifteenth or sixteenth centuries, but that Western Europe had started on an expanded path of development centuries earlier. Why was this?

The first factor we must consider is the relation of the land to its inhabitants. At the beginning of the Middle Ages, population density was already much higher in Western Europe than in Eastern Europe. Consequently, the ever-increasing population in Western Europe stimulated intensive forms of development—at first principally in agriculture, but later in other sectors—dating especially from the time when strong state organizations were formed in Eastern Europe. While in Eastern Europe, land for cultivation was in limitless supply and nothing prevented the authorities from moving excess population to new land (in consequence of which for many centuries the old means of production were only copied but not improved or extended), the peasants of Western Europe had to intensify production in order that the same territory could support more and more people. It was this necessity that accelerated development in Western Europe.

But it is far less clear what enabled Western Europe to adopt its particular form of development. Summarizing briefly, it resulted from fusion of the technical, economic and juridical achievements of the classical world with those of the Germanic peoples, but this was not a simple amalgamation, since the essential achievements of the Greco-Roman world (primarily the system of private ownership of land and the economic and legal achievements thereof, and secondly technological advances) in essence superseded the Germanic system of common ownership of land. This was the case in Western Europe, especially in its central part, in northern Italy, in the present day areas of France, Western Germany, Belgium, Holland, Denmark and, to some extent, England.

The victory of the principle of private ownership in Western Europe stimulated the development of intensive methods of production which the growing population density made necessary. Private owners were able to retain at least a part of the surplus product. Communal ownership of land had been replaced by the openfield system, a form that retained many characteristics of common land although the land and the produce was actually divided among single families. Furthermore, the system of tribute was based primarily on the individual producer as taxpayer rather than upon the community. Production was greatly increased and the classical and Germanic achievements of technology and production, and later the technical innovations based on them, could be increasingly utilized. Furthermore, the Christian religion, especially Roman Catholicism, and the Roman legal system guaranteed the principle of private property.

But this principle did not gain ground in other parts of the world, including Eastern Europe. Even within the Roman Empire it succeeded only in the Western half, in the Greek city-states, in Italy, Gaul, etc., while the Eastern provinces maintained the system of the earlier empires of Persians, Hittites, etc. In Asia and even in the Balkans private property did not become general. Here the ancient Asiatic form of land ownership was maintained, respected even by the Roman conquerors. As a matter of fact the division of the Christian church was the demarcation line, since the Orthodox religion spread in those territories where the Asiatic form of land property remained.

The differences are fundamental. All the earlier civilizations of Asia and North Africa were based on common land ownership. All land belonged to the ruler and the peasants were taxed for the land they used, not as individuals but as members of village communities. Broadly speaking, a conglomeration of rural communities formed the state. The rural community, as the smallest unit of taxpayers and administration, guaranteed payment of the tax to the state administration, which in return for money collected, maintained systems necessary for production (such as irrigation canals) and maintained the army, and state and church apparatuses. Basic characteristics of this land community are the opposition of the rural community to the state, and the minimization of the independence and importance of the producing individual. For the individual in self-supporting rural communities, the outer world exists only as it affects the community in which he lives. This control of isolated rural communities (there were no industrial or trade centers at that time and the larger settlements were only administrative-military centers) was the basis of despotic systems. At the same time, the consequence of this system was extraordinary instability. For the rural community, after paying the taxes for which public utilities were maintained by the state administration, was quite indifferent to alterations of the larger political systems that caused whole empires to vanish and new ones to be born. Compared to territories where this social and production system did not exist, territories where it prevailed were disproportionately large, comprising Eurasia from the Mediterranean and the Balkans to China and Japan, as well as Africa. Although Greek civilization subjugated one part of this territory through the military expeditions of Alexander the Great, it did not change the basic foundations of these societies, and this system was maintained in the eastern provinces of the Roman Empire.

As we have seen, Greek society, first to establish private ownership of land, Roman society, and Western European societies after the migration period differed thoroughly from this so-called Asiatic social construction. When German peasants, among whom common ownership of land had prevailed, became part of the Western Roman Empire, they adopted private land ownership for the fields, but for the pastures and the woods they retained common ownership. The final result of the mutual interaction of classical society and Western European feudalism was the complete liquidation in Western Europe of the system of Asiatic rural communities. Although the system of rural communities undoubtedly once existed, the peasant came to personally own his fields and faced his landlord individually, delivering his fixed quota himself, or the more important part of it; as a result his farming directly increased his personal prosperity. The surplus product remaining in his possession provided incentives motivating development in Western Europe.

There were no such incentives to enlarge production under the Asiatic system of land ownership where lands were actually owned by the state and the individual village communities were the tax-paying units. The Russian chronicles portray the typical relationship between the princes and their escorts as representing, respectively, state power and the individual rural communities. Thus feudalism in Eastern Europe did not fundamentally alter the society, while in Western Europe feudalism incorporated the system of Roman law based on the liquidation of the system of common land ownership in rural communities, and thus reshaped the whole society. Throughout Eastern Europe, however, very strong central rulers dominated the nobility. Even in Hungary the king's powers were greater than that of his Western European counterpart. In much of Eastern Europe the feudal nobility composed an official military class which in many places and for many centuries could not inherit property, a circumstance which increased its subjection to the central ruler.

Of course the Asiatic system of land ownership was not identical everywhere. It must suffice here to make some limited general comparisons. In Russia and in the Balkans, especially in Romania, and in the Eastern territories of Poland before the emancipation of the serfs, the peasants were essentially slaves that could be bought and sold independently of the land. Only in those territories of Eastern Europe where Christianity was introduced by the Western church, in Poland, Hungary and Croatia, was this situation ameliorated. Since in most of Eastern Europe land could not be passed automatically from father to son even among the nobility, economic incentives were lacking and careless work and soil exhaustion were encouraged. At the same time the Asiatic form of land ownership served to centralize power to an extent seen only in Asia and in Northern Africa where the Asiatic system of land ownership, perpetuated from the Pharaohs to the Turkish Sultans and the Arabian Caliphs, preserved despotic autocracies.

What is important for us is the fact that in Eastern Europe the Asiatic form of land ownership, and the economic and legal system of society based on it which was not reshaped by the Greco-Roman tradition, made a West European type of development impossible from the outset. A further factor of great importance was that in Western Europe production became more intensive, not only in agriculture but in every sector of economic life, which in turn affected agricultural development. It is easy to understand that the development of industry in Western Europe, accompanied by the formation of towns and their enlargement, and the removal of part of the population from agricultural production, created an ever larger market for agricultural products, a process which was accelerated both by the growing population pressure and by the decrease in the number of agricultural producers compared to the total population. This process was accelerated in the nineteenth and the twentieth centuries, but it began considerable earlier. Western European towns broke away quite soon from agriculture and became centers first of trade and then of industrial production. Industrial production was also undertaken in many agricultural districts and became one of the main means of subsistence for a great part of peasant population.

Both agricultural and nonagricultural economic development in Eastern Europe proceeded more slowly than it did in Western Europe. The seemingly limitless abundance of land (which is still characteristic of the European territory of Russia) assured the livelihood of the growing population and even inhibited the simplest technological changes in agriculture. Thus, in European Russia up to the mid-nineteenth century the two-field system of crop rotation was dominant and the three-field system was introduced only in those few places where, from the beginning of the nineteenth century, the population increased more rapidly. The abundance of land assured the population's livelihood even with a two-field rotation and, accordingly, primitive tools sufficed to cultivate the land. In much of the area leaving land fallow was possible, making fertilizing unnecessary, mitigating even a two-field rotation. In contrast, during the eighteenth century, three-field rotation was already widespread in Western Europe, and in many places (in England, Holland, Belgium, northern France and northern Italy) crop-rotation became established, especially near the larger towns, thus increasing both production and animal husbandry based on the resulting fodder crops. By the second half of the nineteenth century modern crop rotation prevailed throughout Western Europe, and the use of chemical fertilizer as well as new implements and machines gained ground while in Eastern Europe the primitive two- or three-field system of crop rotation was retained, and the soil continued to be tilled with home-made implements and without chemical fertilizers. In these territories, modern farming methods and new types of plants and animals could be introduced only on the largest estates where sufficient capital was available. But even these did not use all the improvements developed in the West. Combines, for example, were simply not necessary because of agricultural overpopulation.

*Towns in Eastern Europe*

In Eastern Europe nonagricultural sectors of the economy were slow to develop. For many thousands of years the town was only a settlement of a small number of people. Such medieval towns typical of Eastern Europe and mentioned in historical sources did not attain the economic or social role of towns in Western Europe where the town settlements belonging to the king, landlord or church developed from administrative units into centers of trade and industry, becoming not only junctions of long-distance trade but also centers within districts for internal exchange of domestic products and, later, industrial settlements. In such true towns in Western Europe, the inhabitants formed a special order within feudal society: the citizens. On the other hand, for many centuries Eastern European settlements preserved their original characteristics, which varied widely. The first settlements becoming big towns (though not true towns in the West European sense) were junctions of transcontinental trade routes, and this characteristic did not change until long-distance transit trade eventually lost its importance due to a change of routes. The inhabitants of these towns were generally not local people, but for the most part, foreign tradesmen—for example, in Russia they were not Russians but Varangians, Arabs, Greeks, Jews, etc.

Another Eastern European settlement type was the administrative center. Its nucleus was the emperor and his court, a feudal lord and his entourage, or a religious order. Typically, however, such centers did not provide permanent residences for the elites, but only occasional ones, consisting originally of camps of tents, and only later did they evolve into more solid settlements. Until the nineteenth century they remained administrative centers supplemented by trade and industrial activity, the only change being the enlargement of the population from simply the ruler's entourage and his household to the inclusion of a more modern officialdom.

A third type of settlement in Europe was in fact only an expanded village associated with large-scale development of animal husbandry. Comparatively early (from the fourteenth century on), there began a large-scale export of cattle from the vast pastures of Eastern Europe (from southern Scandinavia through Poland and the Ukraine to Hungary and Moldavia), first to the towns of northern and southern Germany and northern Italy. The inhabitants of these "market towns" were primarily occupied with agriculture, especially with stock-breeding. Later some industry also developed but agriculture did not cease, and up to the middle of the twentieth century industry was only a complementary activity. The inhabitants were almost all serf-peasants who differed from the serf-peasants of the small villages only in that they enjoyed a measure of independence vis-à-vis the administration. However, they did not have the juridical or social status of the town inhabitants in Western Europe.

These three types of towns (trade route junctions, administrative centers and market towns) were common throughout Eastern Europe until the nineteenth century. Not one of the three was a town in the West European sense. None were inhabited by townmen comparable to the citizens who formed a special stratum of society in Western Europe. The majority of their inhabitants lived by agriculture, and these settlements seemed to the West European visitor to be towns only because of some of their legal characteristics and their population density, although, in fact, such settlements were more like villages, being basically rural as opposed to true towns. There were, of course, some towns in Eastern Europe that paralleled those in Western Europe, but not many and they were not typical. Their inhabitants were usually miners or tradesmen of German origin who migrated from the West. In these towns, the pattern and construction of settlement, the economic and social structure, as well as outward appearance corresponded to contemporary towns in Western Europe, and their inhabitants, for the most part, enjoyed the same social status within the society of Eastern Europe as did the citizens of the time in Western Europe. These towns did not arise so much from local development as from the exploitation of newly opened mines of precious metals and copper. Since mining was not highly regarded in Eastern Europe, the rulers were obliged to import miners from the West. The towns such immigrants founded did not integrate themselves readily into the local socioeconomic system and consequently they remained isolated ethnically. When they later became junctions of long-distance trade routes, these towns began a process of reagrarianization, and their development ceased to keep pace with that of Western European towns.

The towns in Eastern Europe that developed in the nineteenth century because of industrialization also were isolated. Although local economic development necessitated the settling of towns in the modern economic-social sense, ethnically they were not integrated into the larger society for a long time since the great majority of workers were imported from abroad. Only the second or third generation of workers became assimilated in these districts. It is interesting to observe that, due to delay in the various stages of economic development, German (Swabian, Austrian), Croatian or Bohemian workers, Ukrainians and engineers and other specialists migrated in Eastern Europe. Thus there were Poles in the Ukraine, Hungarians in Romania, Ukrainians in Russia, in different periods.

Due to these various circumstances, in the twentieth century towns in Eastern Europe have continued to vary widely, and "town inhabitant" does not signify what it does in Western Europe. Statistics show that the majority of the inhabitants of these so-called towns have not abandoned agriculture. It is characteristic that in the Great Hungarian Plain, for instance, in the decades between the two world wars the overwhelming part of the population of "towns" having 20,000 to 60,000 inhabitants lived by agriculture. The appearance of a town provides evidence of the social composition of its inhabitants. Built primarily in the second half of the nineteenth century, there are still few one-story buildings; the streets are lined by traditional peasant houses; public utilities (water, sewage) and paved streets, etc., are nonexistent.

## ECONOMIC RELATIONS, EAST AND WEST

While the accelerated pace of economic development in Western Europe during the latter Middle Ages was not paralleled in Eastern Europe, there were important earlier economic, cultural, and even sometimes military, relations between the two areas. Thus the appearance in Eastern Europe of the town at the junction of long-distance trade routes was a result of relations with the West, even though this connection was not a close one and thus did not fundamentally influence the economy of Eastern Europe. The goods streaming from Asia, Arabia and the Arctic region into Western Europe through Eastern Europe did transform the life of the trading towns, where the inhabitants remained ethnically isolated for a long time. Western European influence was most visible in the realm of military life, caused by military conflicts which were felt by the beginning of the eleventh century. Arms were almost the only goods that occasionally were traded from Western to Eastern Europe at this time. This resulted because the technical development of Western Europe in weaponry became evident obliging East European armies (at least in the regions next to the Western boundaries) to take over the tactics of the West and import arms, usually together with Western soldiers, and later to import miners. By the thirteenth century the Hungarian and Polish armies adopted knightly military tactics and used corresponding weapons, while the armies of the Russian principalities and the Balkan countries consisted of light cavalry.

In the fourteenth century the growing economic development in Western Europe began to have more direct consequences for Eastern Europe, since the Western nations needed raw materials, agricultural products and metals that, before the discovery of the New World, could be supplied only by Eastern Europe. This demand stimulated advances in the mining of precious metal and copper in Hungary and other Eastern European countries from the fourteenth century on. Precious metals were exported either as ore or as coinage in exchange for consumer goods (arms, clothes, textiles, etc.) from Western Europe, articles that were highly desired by the Eastern European reigning classes. For example, "fashion" clothing for the upper classes was dictated by Western European standards from this time on. Thus there were increasingly great differences in dress between the common people and the higher ranks. While in Western Europe clothing styles of peasants and citizens directly followed that of the upper classes and new forms and materials spread relatively quickly, in Eastern Europe this process sometimes took centuries, and it did not proceed everywhere at the same rate or to the same degree. In Hungary and Poland, for instance, not only the aristocracy but the well-to-do or middle strata of the lesser nobility wore Western styles, while in the Balkans and in Russia the aristocracy and most of the nobility wore the traditional national costume.

Even more important than the demand by Western Europe for precious metals was the parallel one for agricultural products from the fourteenth century onward. The increasing urban population produced a need for food that Western Europe could no longer satisfy from its own production. The demand for meat in urban centers exceeded the supply of the rural hinterlands, and since this was a commodity that could be brought to market on its own feet, so to speak, it is not surprising that the export of cattle from Eastern Europe (Hungary, Poland, the Romanian principalities) into Western Europe developed so quickly from the second half of the fourteenth century onward. Livestock was Eastern Europe's first important agricultural export, and the settlement of market-towns was due to such trade.

Thus the first, and for a long time the most stable, economic relation between Western and Eastern Europe was based on mining precious metals and animal husbandry. Later it was augmented by trade in grain and, to some extent, lumber. The growing towns in Western Europe required a large quantity of grain, but for Eastern Europe producing grain was profitable only where delivery was feasible. From the fifteenth century on grain was grown only in regions which had satisfactory water-ways. Before the existence of the railroad, grain was exported from Eastern Europe only by eastern Germany, some districts of Poland, the Baltic countries, Denmark and southern Sweden. It is true that some parts of Hungary also increased grain production, but except for the directly adjacent lower Austrian towns and Vienna and the Western frontier zone, this production satisfied only the routine needs of the army. Grain production increased in Hungary only in the mid-nineteenth century when it could be exported by railway and by ship. Similarly, grain exports from central Russia and the Ukraine to Eastern Europe began on a large scale only after railroads were built.

These economic relations with Western Europe were not without consequences for the socioeconomic life of Eastern Europe. Demand on the part of Eastern European ruling classes for money coming into Eastern Europe, and the consumer goods of Western Europe that this money could buy, increased while prices in sixteenth century Western Europe were subject to inflation. But the sums owed to rulers by the Eastern European peasants as a result of delivery obligations could not be raised, because the economic level in Eastern Europe did not make it possible, forcing noblemen to join in production. They were already experienced in cattle trade since most export cattle were raised on large estates in areas where grain production or forest exploitation were labor-intensive processes. There was no alternative but to increase the number of the estates or manors managed by the landlords themselves and to start production on them by using the unpaid labor of the serfs. Manorial lands were cultivated, and the produce was transported to the markets by serfs using their own implements.

The increase of production for foreign markets brought with it mechanized farming, but worsened the situation of East European peasants. In their need for more large units of land, landlords dispossessed many peasants. Remaining peasants were frequently forced to render more labor and to suffer increasing legal regulations. The regions of German colonization, especially in eastern Germany, were typical examples. Thus the development of the manorial system was accompanied by a tightening of the bonds of the serfs to the soil which lasted from the end of the fifteenth century to the end of the eighteenth century, a period during which some areas of Eastern Europe joined in producing grain for West European markets.

A third period of Western European economic influence begins in the second half of the eighteenth century, brought about by the demands of the West European textile industry for wool from Eastern Europe, causing the development of sheep-breeding, at first on the estates of the landlords. Merimo sheep, which produce wool in great quantity, were imported from the West by the landlords. Wool could be transported more easily than grain and so the prosperity gained from wool spread to territories where that of grain did not. This was the last major influence of Western European development on Eastern Europe before the appearance of the railway.

Initially these effects were not felt throughout the Eastern European plain but only in regions such as the frontier zones on the West, Hungary, Poland, the Baltic and Croatia. It was these regions which had experienced other economic changes, as we have noted, since they were favored by their geographical location, and since Roman Catholicism and Roman law pertained. Naturally, peasants from Western Europe settled mainly in these territories, influencing local society. It must be remembered that the Western half of Hungary, Pannonia, briefly belonged to the Roman Empire and later was part of the empire of Charles the Great. Thus at the time of the formation of the Hungarian state, Western influence was already strong. This was true of Croatia, while in Poland, the Baltic countries and Bohemia, peasant settlers from Germany were the bearers of Western development. Consequently there emerged a "transitional" frontier zone in Eastern Europe comprising the Baltic states, Poland, the Czech-Moravian territories, Hungary and Croatia. Here Western European influence greatly altered the original structure. Thus, the Western form of the manor system could be found only in those countries. Although in other Eastern European countries socage spread legally (partly because in these countries labor was still the most important element of rent, and at that time had not been replaced by produce, let alone money), it was almost never made use of. In Romania and Central Russia, socage became more important only at the end of the eighteenth and the beginning of the nineteenth centuries, and often not even then. Rather, the money resources of the landlord were increased by securing monopolies, for example, the sale of meat in Hungary and the distilling of spirits in Hungary, in Romanian principalities and Poland primarily.

In the "transitional" regions the traditional rural communities lost their communal character. Peasants paid taxes individually to the landlords and to the state. There the emancipation of the serfs was directed toward individuals, unlike in Russia where the emancipation of the serfs was by imperial decree, and, if anything, even further strengthened the rural communities, since they were made responsible for paying off redemption fees. In Poland and Hungary all that remained of the traditional rural communities was the openfield system. The land used by the serfs was legally separated from the land used by the landlord and there was no possibility of decreasing the peasants' land, while in Russia and Romania the emancipation of the serfs involved the essential diminution of their property.

We must remember, too, that while in Poland, Hungary and East Central European and Baltic countries the towns and their citizens became more or less an independent social order, this was not the case in Russia and the Balkans. Although in the western portion of Eastern Europe the townfolk were ethnically isolated, they did slowly acquire independent functions within the socioeconomic system and, accordingly, were gradually assimilated by the local population. In Russia and the Balkans this did not happen; settlements having a town-like character did not become independent of the landlords until considerably later.

Thus Eastern Europe, due to the economic influence of Western Europe and the social effects of immigration from the West, was split into two parts. From the fourteenth century on, the transitional zone took a special path of development which was not followed by most of Eastern Europe. West European demands could not affect other parts of Eastern Europe until transportation became feasible, and with the exception of the coastline and areas along navigable rivers, this could only happen with the building of railroads. If we discount the effects of long-distance trade, which did not affect purely local economic-social conditions, continental Eastern Europe remained economically isolated until the period of railway building.

However, the military influence of Western Europe penetrated everywhere long before the building of railroads. Technical advances, heavy cavalry and the spread of firearms forced the Russian tsars to keep pace with military developments. At first it was sufficient to buy weapons, but later it became necessary (and proved cheaper when armies grew) to develop a defense industry modelled on that of Western Europe. This was the real intent of the industrial ambitions of Peter the Great. In Russia the building of ironworks, weapons factories and ships was possible only through the state and this predetermined the shape of Russia's industrial development. Economic development was still not advanced sufficiently to motivate manufacture in other areas of life, and so such industries were only rarely established. No wage laborers, only serfs, worked in the factories, since a social class of wage laborers did not exist. It may seem to the casual observer that factory enterprises developed in the East as they did in Western Europe, but the two cases were actually quite different. On the whole, the manufacturing situation in Eastern Europe resembles that of its town development. The manufacturing industry developed one-sidedly, responding to the state's orders, and serving only to supply the needs of the army. Its workers were mostly peasants, especially before the emancipation of the serfs. Until the mid-twentieth century, production of consumer goods remained within the confines of the guilds or home industry.

## SOME SPECIFICS OF THE SPLIT BETWEEN EASTERN AND WESTERN ZONES OF EASTERN EUROPE

Let us sum up the specific features of the socioeconomic structure of Eastern Europe in the first half of the nineteenth century. We must reemphasize the duality of this region: Eastern Europe was separated into two spheres. The western half, from Poland and the Baltic states to Croatia, was strongly influenced by West European economic, political and cultural developments. These influences were evident in the new system of market production formed, beginning in the fifteenth and sixteenth centuries, on the estates of the landlords. Peasants and burghers from Western Europe influenced development here. On the other hand, the eastern half, that is, Russia and the Balkan states, was influenced by West European economies only in the last decades and participated only recently in world trade. Here rural communities were maintained intact and towns had but an insignificant role. For the most part only primitive home-industry prospered, and the product-money relationship, due to slow industrial development of industry, existed on an extremely low level. As a result, in part, of these factors, these countries were governed quite differently. Tsarist politics took into consideration the enormous differences between the western parts of the empire (Poland and Baltic states) and Central Russia. The emancipation of the serfs, for instance, was carried out quite differently in these two regions of the Russian Empire.

The following are some of the specific features of the emancipation of the serfs in Eastern Europe, both those that distinguish the economic and the political structures of the two spheres, and those underscoring the unity of Eastern Europe. Among the latter is the effective role of the state in the emancipation of the serfs. Thus, the state brought about the emancipation and reforms from above despite the resistance of most of the ruling class, and the state financially idemnified the landlords after the emancipation.

In regard to the personal emancipation of the serfs, however, there were great differences between the Baltic states, Poland, Hungary and Croatia on the one hand, and the other parts of Eastern Europe on the other. In the transitional regions, personal freedom was granted to the serfs far earlier, under the Hapsburg Monarchy, for example, after the reforms of Joseph II, and even the quantity of the serfs tribute was regulated by the state. It only remained to determine the already legally distinct lands of the landlords and those of the serfs *(terra dominicalis–terra rusticalis).* The peasants, in some parts of these regions, were granted a part of the *terra dominicalis,* whether used by them or not. However, in Central Russia and in Romania, land was not divided into two distinct parts; all the land belonged to, and was theoretically used by, the landlords, and the land cultivated by the peasants could be diminished or taken from them at will, there being no legal obstacles, not even those of common law. For example the amount of land under peasant use was greatly reduced in both Romania and Russia after the emancipation of the serfs, partly because the newly built railroads made it possible and profitable to export great quantities of grain and the peasants could pay off the value of their lands by working in grain production.

In the transitional region emancipation of the peasants meant granting them their land as personal property that was personally redeemed in instalments, whereas in Russia and Romania the emancipation law provided only for the separation of the lands of the nobility from those of the rural communities, and it was the rural community that disposed of the land given to the peasants. Frequently the rural communities were strengthened since they were entrusted with the indemnification of the landlords. Thus we cannot speak of private ownership of the land by the peasants in these regions as long as rural communities existed.

Even after peasants were emancipated in the eastern zone of Eastern Europe there remained many feudal restrictions burdening the peasants, especially in Russia and Romania. The landlords' estates were cultivated by the peasants in socage and the peasants paid in instalments for the lands they received, while the rural communities guaranteed this payment. This method of payment was only partially and briefly manifested in Hungary and Poland, but in Russia and Romania it continued for a longer period, leading to violent peasant uprisings at the end of the nineteenth and the beginning of the twentieth centuries in Romania (1888 and 1907) and tsarist Russia (1905–06). The ruling classes were forced to carry out reforms (primarily to liquidate rural communities) bringing these countries closer to the Polish, Hungarian and Croatian models. The statistical data show that at the turn of the century 60 percent of the population of Hungary lived from agriculture while in the Balkan countries or in Russia the figure was nearly 80 percent. While in Hungary (ca. 1930) the proportion of agricultural workers to wage-earners was 50 percent, in Yugoslavia it was 57 percent as late as 1960, and in Romania 70 percent. The conclusions hidden in these statistical data are not only quantitative but very often qualitative, pointing to those essential differences that had long existed between the two regions of Eastern Europe.

From about the middle of the nineteenth century on the gap between these two regions began to close. Affected by the world market, the development of Eastern Europe, although retaining some characteristics (strong feudal remnants, etc.), turned towards the West, although it could only proceed slowly, and the quantitative indices of development were much retarded. Finally, Eastern Europe succeeded in breaking away from the pattern of development characterizing other parts of the world and followed that of Western Europe.

## CONCLUSION

We conclude with some comments concerning the recent developments in Eastern Europe:

### *Large-scale or small-scale production*

A copious polemic literature exists on the question whether small-scale production, primarily small-scale farming, is capable of development, and this question has a special significance for Eastern Europe. The general view in Eastern Europe has been that socioeconomical development was hindered solely by strong feudal remnants which existed even during the era of capitalism, first and foremost in large landed estates. There is doubtless some truth in this, but it would be incorrect to reduce the problem to this one factor. In the western frontier zones of Eastern Europe, in Hungary, Poland, Croatia and partly in Bohemia, during the development of the manorial system, it became evident that only large estates were capable of large-scale production. These large estates were also in a position to use the achievements of modern technology, i.e., new machinery, tools, fertilizers, etc. and, last but not least, the great advantages afforded by a modern division of labor. Later, when continental Eastern Europe joined the world market, the large estates of the landlords which remained in Russia and Romania after the emancipation of the serfs became the foremost promotors of agricultural production and modern agricultural techniques. Only these estates had the capital necessary to modernize production. Statistical data sometimes blur such differences between large-scale and small-scale production levels. For instance, the small quantity of chemical fertilizers employed in Eastern Europe for a unit of territory meant that while large estates used chemical fertilizers in the same quantity as in Western Europe, most of the country used no chemical fertilizers at all. One could easily cite many other examples.

Naturally, those who were politically antagonistic to the great estates saw them as the most important obstacles of development. This leads us to the next point.

*Land question*

Because in Eastern Europe, even in the mid-nineteenth century, industry was underdeveloped and the vast majority of the population was employed in agriculture, the land question had special significance. Most of the inhabitants remained peasants. But when, from the eighteenth century on, because of advances in medicine and hygiene, etc., the population gradually increased, the land question became acute. Since most land belonged to the landlords, the increasing peasant population was obliged to subsist on the same limited territory, leading to increasing subdivision of the land and to the impoverishment of great masses of peasants. In Western Europe, which followed partially German traditions, the problem was solved by primogeniture. The eldest son of a peasant family indemnified his sisters and brothers with money and they then either emigrated or became wage earners, first in agriculture and later in industry. But industrial development in Eastern Europe was so slow and ineffectual that the superfluous population was bound to agriculture. The inheritance of land among the peasants was based upon the principle of proportionate distribution, and the result was that more and more peasants had very small land holdings, forcing them to resort to seasonal work on the large estates of the landlords for which they were paid in grain, thus earning a bare living. This ever-growing population could not imagine a life outside the context of the traditional peasant existence. Therefore, their goal remained obtaining enough land to be self-sufficient. In the second half of the nineteenth century some emigrated, mainly to North America, and this delayed the outburst of social antagonisms. But when, after the First World War, emigration was no longer possible, the only hope that remained for the increasing millions was that they secure land at home.

We may say that the land question in Europe as a sociopolitical problem is a typically East European symptom (and, of course, it was found wherever development occurred at the level determined by the Asiatic form of land ownership). In Western Europe the peasant dilemma manifested itself differently. The number of people in agricultural production continuously decreased, while profitable enterprises grew and more and more capital was needed to run them. The excess agricultural population obtained work in the rapidly developing nonagricultural sectors of the economy, and the agrarian question therefore ceased to dominate the peasant world. In Eastern Europe, as well as in other parts of the world, the ever-growing millions who were bound to agriculture had no recourse but to break up large estates in the most radical way (no matter how intensively they were producing). These masses (and perhaps even the politicians speaking for them) did not always realize that this could be but a temporary solution.

The real problem was, in fact, not so much the large estates as the slow development of the nonagrarian sectors of the economy. This was a severe problem in Bulgaria and Serbia where the landlords disappeared in the course of the nineteenth century and only rural communities remained. The original ruling class was driven away by the Turks; later the Turkish landlords were expelled, and then landlord system collapsed. Thus in Bulgaria, at the beginning of the 1920s there were no more landlord estates to be divided, leading to peasant revolts where the poorer ones attempted to divide among themselves the property of the richer peasants. Peasants in Bulgaria and Serbia, who had only a few hectares of independent land, had a much lower standard of living than even the landless agricultural proletarians of Eastern Prussia. Thus, because of the very slow development of the nonagrarian sectors of the economy, the land question continued to be the central problem of Eastern Europe.

### *The special features of industrial development*

Industrial development in Eastern Europe not only started later and developed more slowly than in Western Europe, but its function in the economy was also peculiar in many ways. From the outset industrial development has been not only a question of economics but of foreign policy. For instance, from the end of the seventeenth century states developed industry first in those branches which had military importance. Technologically advanced factories were established, without exception, only in those sectors. And when, from the nineteenth century on, industrial development began in other regions as well, uneven development occurred. The organization and construction of industry was frequently in conflict with coexisting primitive home industry (in the Balkans or Russia, for example, where rural needs for industrial products were generally satisfied by home industry and urban needs by modern industry. Furthermore, typically in the Western frontier zone of Eastern Europe, industrial development proceeded rapidly and affected economic life deeply but produced not for the small home market but mainly for export. The domestic market was kept very small. In Hungary and Poland those branches of industry developed first (heavy industry, machine industry, etc.) that satisfied the demands of Western Europe, while the demands of the local population were met by primitive small-scale or home industry. In Hungary, for instance, most light industrial production (shoes, textiles, etc.) are exported while domestic consumption of the same products is barely half or a third of that of Western Europe, and the same pattern prevails in heavy industry. Both heavy industry and light industry in these countries are produced mainly for export, just as the large estates produced for the agricultural export market. In contrast, while all the branches of industry in Western Europe have a tremendous export, nonetheless their production was based on domestic consumption, especially in its first phases.

*The role of the state*

The state played a special role in the industrial development of Eastern Europe. Developing industry, obtaining markets for agricultural products, and making infrastructural investments (building railways and roads, channeling rivers, etc.) required enormous capital which had not been accumulated in Eastern Europe as it had in Western Europe. Thus the state secured the capital partly by raising loans abroad and guaranteeing their payment, and partly by direct state investments. In Eastern Europe the state, from the outset, took a more active and direct part in economic development than it did in Western Europe. Although from the seventeenth century on West European states also exerted an increasing influence on economic life, except for the decades following the Great Depression (1929/32) they did so only indirectly, primarily regulating foreign trade. In Eastern Europe, from the time of Peter the Great, the direct and effective economic activity of the state has remained one of the characteristics of economic development.

## Appendix Data

## I. HISTORICAL ANTECEDENTS

### *I. 1 Peasant risings in Europe*

| | |
|---|---|
| France | 1358 |
| England | 1381 |
| Hungary | 1514 |
| Germany | 1524–26 |
| Lithuania | 1525–28 |
| Ukraine | 1591–96 |
| Austria | 1595–97 |
| Russia | 1606–07 |
| Little-Poland | 1630 |
| Bohemia | 1680 |

### *I. 2 The abolition of the right of free removal of the serfs*

| | |
|---|---|
| Bohemia | 1487 and 1497 |
| Latvia | 1491 |
| Poland | 1493, 1520 and 1543 |
| East-Prussia | about 1500 |
| Holstein | about 1500 |
| Hungary | 1514 |
| Estonia | the middle of the XVIth century |
| Russia | 1592 |
| Valachia | 1595 |
| Schleswig | about 1600 |
| Kurland | 1617 |
| Moldavia | 1646 |

### *I. 3 Regulation of the socage by the state*

| | |
|---|---|
| Hungary | 1767 |
| Silesia | 1771 |
| Lower Austria | 1772 and 1846 |
| Bohemia | 1775 |
| Moravia | 1775 |
| Styria and Carinthia | 1778 |
| Croatia | 1780 |
| Galicia | 1786 and 1846 |
| Livland | 1804 |
| Latvia | 1804 |

I



| | |
|---|---|
| Estonia | 1804 and 1856 |
| Moldavia | 1805 |
| Kurland | 1817 |
| Roman principalities | 1831–1833 |
| Polish Kingdom | 1835 and 1847 |
| Russia (only on state estates) | 1837–1841 |

*I. 4 Abolition of serfdom*

| | |
|---|---|
| East-Prussia | 1804 |
| Prussia | 1807, 1811 and 1850 |
| The Grand Duchy of Poznan | 1807, 1823 and 1850 |
| Hungary | 1848, 11th April |
| Galicia | 1848, 15th May |
| German Empire | 1848, 7th September |
| Russia | 1861 |
| Romania | 1864, 14th August |

## II. SOME INDICES OF GENERAL ECONOMIC DEVELOPMENT

*II.1 Percentage of total population dependent on, or of manpower engaged in, agriculture*

| | *1850* | *1900* | *1930* | *1950* | *1960* |
|---|---|---|---|---|---|
| Great Britain | 28 | 12 | 8 | 7 | 6 |
| Belgium | 50 | 24 | 18 | 13 | 9 |
| Denmark | 54 | 41 | 29 | 24 | 18 |
| Norway | 70 | 44 | 37 | 22 | 18 |
| Netherlands | | 34 | 23 | 18 | 12 |
| Austria | | | 31 | 25 | 20 |
| Czechoslovakia | | | 33 | 25 | 21 |
| Hungary | | 58 | 51 | 48 | 37 |
| Romania | | | 71 | 74 | 67 |
| Bulgaria | | | 71 | 69 | 55 |
| Yugoslavia | | | 74 | 73 | 50 |
| Greece | | | 50 | 49 | 48 |
| USSR (incl. Asian parts) | | | | 45 | 40 |

*II.2 Railway system (km)*

| | *1850* | | *1896–97* | |
|---|---|---|---|---|
| | for 100.000 people | for 100 $km^2$ | 100.000 people | 100 $m^2$ |
| England | 39.3 | 3.4 | 86.0 | 10.8 |
| Germany | 16.6 | 1.1 | 91.0 | 8.8 |

| | | | | |
|---|---|---|---|---|
| Hungary | 1.7 | 0.1 | 86.6 | 4.8 |
| Polish Kingdom | – | – | 29.3 | 2.9 |
| Romania | – | – | 46.3 | 2.2 |
| Serbia | – | – | 25.3 | 1.2 |
| Bulgaria | – | – | 29.0 | 1.0 |
| Russia | 1.0 | 0.01 | 33.3 | 0.8 |

*II.3 National income for one person* (in dollars, 1937)

| | |
|---|---|
| Great Britain | 440 |
| Germany | 340 |
| Czechoslovakia | 170 |
| Hungary | 120 |
| Poland | 100 |
| Romania | 81 |
| Yugoslavia | 80 |
| Bulgaria | 75 |

*II.4 The value of industrial products for one person* (in dollars, 1938)

| | |
|---|---|
| Great Britain | 140 |
| Germany | 132 |
| Czechoslovakia | 57 |
| Hungary | 26 |
| Poland | 21 |
| Romania | 12 |

*II.5 The contribution of agriculture to national income*

| | *1913* | *1938* |
|---|---|---|
| Czechoslovakia | 33 | 23.2 |
| Hungary | 41.8 | 36.5 |
| Poland | ? | 39 |
| Romania | 60.2 | 53.2 |
| Yugoslavia | 58.0 | 53.6 |
| Bulgaria | 71.4 | 63.3 |

## III. LEVEL OF AGRICULTURAL PRODUCTION

*III.1 The comsumption of chemical fertilizers (pure agent kg/ha) 1936–1938*

| | |
|---|---|
| Holland | 311.0 |
| Germany | 100.0 |
| Hungary | 2.0 |

| | |
|---|---|
| Yugoslavia | 1.0 |
| Bulgaria | 1.8 |
| Romania | 0.2 |

*III.2 The average wheat-crop (q/ha)*

| | *1909/13* | *1925/29* | *1935/38* | *1965/68* |
|---|---|---|---|---|
| Great Britain | 21.2 | 22.6 | 22.5 | 39.1 |
| Holland | 23.5 | 30.2 | 29.6 | 44.3 |
| Czechoslovakia | | 17.1 | 17.5 | 27.1 |
| Austria | 13.7 | 15.1 | 16.5 | 30.0 |
| Hungary | 14.3 | 13.4 | 14.3 | 23.6 |
| Poland | 12.4 | 12.3 | 11.9 | 22.3 |
| Romania | 12.9 | 9.2 | 10.2 | 18.5 |
| Yugoslavia | 10.5 | 11.8 | 11.9 | 23.3 |
| Bulgaria | 6.2 | 10.2 | 13.6 | 26.3 |
| Russia (USSR) | 6.9 | 7.5 | 9.3 | 12.1 |
| Latvia | 11.8 | 11.1 | 12.4 | ? |
| Lithuania | 10.4 | 11.5 | 11.6 | ? |
| Estonia | 11.0 | 10.3 | 10.8 | ? |
| Greece | | 6.6 | 9.0 | 16.5 |

*III.3 Mechanization in agriculture about 1900*

| | *hectares for one steam-operated threshing-machine* | *hectares for one sowing-machine* |
|---|---|---|
| Hungary | 945 | 153 |
| Romania | 1194 | 437 |
| Bulgaria | 15600 | 9400 |
| Germany | 111 | 170 |

*III.4 The productivity of agriculture*

(manpower. European average in 1931–35 = 100%)

| | |
|---|---|
| Denmark | 323 |
| Germany | 191 |
| Hungary | 75 |
| Bulgaria | 55 |

| | |
|---|---|
| Romania | 53 |
| Yugoslavia | 43 |

## IV. AGRARIAN POPULATION AND LAND PROPERTY

### *IV.1 Land and manpower in Europe*

(Approximate man-land ratio = hectares per man)

| | *1900* | *1930* | *1950* | *1960* |
|---|---|---|---|---|
| British Isles | 11 | 13 | 14 | 18 |
| Belgium | 3 | 3 | 5 | 7 |
| Czechoslovakia* | 4 | 5 | 7 | 10 |
| Poland** | 6 | 5 | 6 | 7 |
| Hungary | 5 | 5 | 5 | 6 |
| Romania | 6 | 4 | 4 | 5 |
| Bulgaria | 6 | 4 | 3 | 3 |
| Yugoslavia*** | 5 | 4 | 4 | 6 |
| Albania | 7 | 5 | 4 | 4 |
| Greece | 12 | 9 | 8 | 7 |
| Europe USSR | 9 | 8 | . . . | 16 |

The new Eastern European countries, created after the First World War, sometimes have territories of different level. A few examples for that:

| | | | | |
|---|---|---|---|---|
| *Czechoslovakia: | | | | |
| Czech. prov. | 4 | 5 | 8 | 11 |
| Slovakia | 5 | 5 | 5 | 9 |
| **Poland: | | | | |
| West | 7 | 7 | 14 | 14 |
| East | 6 | 4 | 5 | 5 |
| South | 3 | 3 | 4 | 4 |

| ***Yugoslavia | *1900* | *1953* | *1961* |
|---|---|---|---|
| Slovenia | 4 | 5 | 7 |
| Croatia | 4 | 5 | 6 |
| Vojvodina | 6 | 6 | 7 |
| Old Serbia | 5 | 3 | 4 |
| Kosmet prov. | 4 | 3 | 3 |
| Bosnia-Hercegovina | 6 | 5 | 5 |
| Montenegro | 10 | 7 | 8 |
| Macedonia | 7 | 5 | 6 |

I



*IV.2 Manpower needed and available in the agriculture (in 000s)*

*England and Wales*

| | *available* | | *needed* | |
|---|---|---|---|---|
| | *1924* | *1942* | *1924* | *1942* |
| all the farms | 1061 | 1008 | 830 | 821 |
| - 50 acres | 383 | 346 | 168 | 159 |
| over 50 acres | 678 | 662 | 661 | 662 |

*Bulgaria*

| | *available* | *needed* |
|---|---|---|
| all the farms | 2879 | 1527 |
| - 5 ha | 1523 | 582 |
| 5–15 ha | 1203 | 769 |
| over 15 ha | 171 | 176 |

*IV.3 Stratification of the peasants (serfs)*

*a) East-Prussia about 1800*

43.000 serfs with holding
55.000 agricultural workers

*b) Upper-Silesia 1858*

| | | *peasant farms* | *percent of peasant land* |
|---|---|---|---|
| – | 1.27 ha | 36.23 | 5.01 |
| 1.27 | 7.65 ha | 44.59 | 31.58 |
| 7.65 | 76.5 ha | 19.18 | 63.41 |

*c) Galicia*

(percent of peasant farms)

| *dimension (ha)* | *1819* | *1847–59* |
|---|---|---|
| -1.6 | 19.4 | 27.2 |
| 1.6 - 2.9 | 15.8 | 16.7 |
| 2.9 - 5.8 | 25.4 | 29.3 |
| 5.8 - 1.6 | 26.9 | 23.4 |
| over 11.6 ha | 12.5 | 3.4 |

*d) Grand Duchy of Poznań, 1859*

(percent of peasant farms)

| *dimension (ha)* | *percent* |
|---|---|
| 1.3 | 23.16 |
| 1.3 - 7.7 | 30.85 |
| 7.7 - 76.6 | 42.48 |

| | |
|---|---|
| 76.6 – 153.2 | 1.01 |
| over 153.2 ha | 2.50 |

*e) Russian Poland 1859/63*
(percent of peasant farms)

| | |
|---|---|
| – 5.38 ha | 39 |
| 5.38 – 12.56 ha | 39 |
| over 12.56 ha | 22 |
| have-not peasants | 40% |

*f) Moravia before 1848*

| | |
|---|---|
| having full holding | 7699 |
| " 3/4 " | 4375 |
| " 1/2 " | 25906 |
| " 1/4 " | 25616 |
| Gartner | 19462 |
| Häusler | 71080 |
| Häusler | 14677 |

*g) Proportion of the cotters*
(before 1848, compared to the whole number of peasants)

| | |
|---|---|
| Lower-Austria | 46.6% |
| Styria | 60.8% |
| Moravia | 63.4% |

*h) Hungary about 1848*

| | |
|---|---|
| Serfs with holding | 624132 fam. |
| cotters | 913962 fam. |

*i) Croatia about 1848*

| | |
|---|---|
| Have-not peasants | 11% |

*j) Slovenia about 1848*

| | |
|---|---|
| Have-not peasants | 38% |

*IV.4 Distribution of land property about 1900*
*a) Hungary 1895*

| | *Proportion of the* | |
|---|---|---|
| | *farms* | *land* |
| 0–5 ha | 53.4 | 5.8 |
| 5–100 ha | 45.5 | 46.5 |
| 100–1000 ha | 0.8 | 15.4 |
| over 1000 ha | 0.2 | 32.3 |

*b) Romania 1899*

| | Proportion of the farms | Proportion of the land |
|---|---|---|
| 0–5 ha | 77.2 | 25.9 |
| 5–10 ha | 18.2 | 14.7 |
| 10–100 ha | 4.0 | 11.1 |
| over 100 ha | 0.6 | 48.3 |

*c) Poland between 1892–1970 (% of the estates)*

| *region* | *year* | *– 5 ha* | *5–20 ha* | *20–100 ha* | *over 100 ha* |
|---|---|---|---|---|---|
| Grand Duchy of Poznań | 1907 | 67.80 | 24.88 | 6.34 | 0.98 |
| Polish Kingdom* | 1892 | 38.85 | 52.77 | 7.36 | 0.94 |
| Galicia | 1892 | 79.6 | 18.8 | 1.1 | 0.5 |

* Russian Poland: 0,08 % dwarfs

*d) Bulgaria 1899*

| | Proportion of the farms | Proportion of the land |
|---|---|---|
| 0–10 ha | 67.3 | 49.0 |
| 10–100 ha | 32.6 | 44.5 |
| over 100 ha | 0.1 | 6.5 |

*IV.5 Construction of land property in the 1930 years*

| | *Hungary* | | *Romania* | | *Yugoslavia* | | *Bulgaria* | | *Czechoslovakia* | |
|---|---|---|---|---|---|---|---|---|---|---|
| | 1 | 2 | 1 | 2 | 1 | 2 | 1 | 2 | 1 | 2 |
| -2/resp. 3/ha | 71.5 | 10.9 | 52.1 | 12.8 | 33.8 | 6.5 | 27.0 | 5.3 | 26.3 | 1.06 |
| 2–5 ha | 12.5 | 9.2 | 22.9 | 15.2 | 34.0 | 21.5 | 36.1 | 24.7 | 43.8 | 13.9 |
| 5–50 ha | 15.1 | 33.5 | 24.2 | 39.8 | 31.8 | 62.4 | 36.8 | 68.4 | 29.0 | 41.2 |
| 50–100 ha | 0.4 | 5.5 | 0.4 | 4.5 | 0.3 | 3.2 | 0.1 | 1.6 | 0.4 | 3.7 |
| 100–500 ha | 0.4 | 17.2 | 0.3 | 10.6 | 0.1 | 2.8 | – | – | 0.5 | 39.6 |
| over 500 ha | 0.1 | 23.7 | 0.1 | 17.1 | 0.0 | 3.6 | – | – | | |
| the sum of below 50 ha | 99.1 | 53.6 | 99.2 | 67.8 | 99.6 | 90.4 | 99.9 | 98.4 | 99.1 | 66.7 |

1 = proportion of farms

2 = proportion of land

# II

# Agrarian Systems of Central and Eastern Europe

The particular features of East European agricultural development cannot be understood without first expanding our horizons geographically and chronologically. The regional scope of research must include continental Russia and especially Western Europe, while chronological boundaries must extend far back in time to encompass important agrarian developments that came about prior to the sixteenth century. Moreover, nonagrarian sectors of the economy in general, and the development of towns in particular, must be considered if we are to explain the characteristic features of agrarian development in the different zones of Eastern Europe.

The development of Western Europe in a world perspective has to be considered first, because this specific type of development eventually became, in whole or in part, a model to be achieved by the rest of the world. In other words, the rest of the world was obliged to follow the evolutionary course of Western Europe. From this perspective, one of the main characteristics of East European development is that this region was the earliest and the quickest to follow Western Europe and the first to adopt its technical and social achievements.

Why did the development of Western Europe, compared to the rest of the world, "accelerate" onto a separate and peculiar road? What is the essence of West European development, and how did this unique phenomenon come about? The first fact to consider is the relationship between the land and its population. Western Europe (here meaning the areas of Northern Italy, France, Western Germany, Switzerland, Belgium, Holland, Denmark, and England) was much more densely populated in the early Middle Ages than were most other parts of the world, and certainly more than Eastern Europe. This population density constantly pressed for more intensive forms and modes of development, at first only in connection with agriculture, but increasingly in other sectors of the economy as well. Whereas in Eastern Europe the great quantity of arable land and the ease of population resettlement resulted in a repetition of traditional structures of production from one century to another, in Western Europe the peasants were obliged to ensure that a limited amount of land would be capable of supplying the needs of an increasing population. The development of Western Europe was thus accelerated by the force of intensification.

What made this intensification possible in the West? In my view, it was the fortunate amalgamation of the ancient world of Greece and Rome on the one hand with the Celtic and Germanic cultures on the other. This was no simple mixing, but a complex process of unification by which the economic, legal, and technical achievements of the ancient world actually swallowed up the Celto-German system based on common property of land, while at the same time taking over certain achievements from the Celtic and Germanic peoples. The development of agriculture was based on landowners' feudal estates formed from Roman villas, new techniques and technologies such as three-field rotation and the asymmetrical heavy plow with coulter and mouldboard (or what the French call *charrue*), and a new economic and social system of individual plots and villeinage. The villeinage and plot system continued to grow from the sixth century onward, until between the eighth and tenth centuries the village of villeins became dominant. Significantly, this system was based on a principle of private property supported by the Christian Church. This victory of the ancient Greek principle of private property ultimately enabled Western Europe to adopt more intensive methods, once its increasing population reached the critical point.[1]

The principle of private property led the producer to take a personal interest in increasing his production. The larger part of surplus production remained in the possession of the producer. The former system of land commune agriculture gave way to a new system in which, despite remaining communal features stemming from the three-field system, the product now became the property of certain families. The fact that taxation was no longer based on the community but on individual taxpayers was a fundamental change. The attraction of surplus production was thus very great, and peasant society became interested in technical innovations, which naturally demanded more labor than had the earlier methods. The system of private property was guaranteed by the Roman way of Christianity and by the receptivity of society to Roman legal practice.

This system of private ownership was not, however, dominant in other parts of the world, including Eastern Europe. Even within the Roman Empire it made its way only toward the West: to the Greek *polis*, to Italy, and partly to Gaul. It did not show up in Asian territories, or even in the Balkans. The explanation for this variation can be found in relative population densities. Whereas in Western Europe the population of Roman origin was relatively dense and exceeded the Celtic and Germanic populations, in the Balkans the case was different. The influx of Slavic peoples into the Balkans far outnumbered the surviving population of Byzantine origin, so Byzantine legal relations could not play the same role in the Balkans that Roman law played in the West. In Greek colonies, the Greek social order was achieved only in those places where local population did not exceed Greek population. In the villages of Northern Africa and Asia Minor, by contrast, the previous form of land property and the social order based on it remained unchanged. The split of the Christian Church can be considered the approximate demarcation line, with the Eastern type of land property remaining preponderant in the zone where the Orthodox Church prevailed. In any case, the Church never attained a social position in the East comparable to the role of the Church in the West, instead always remaining subordinate to the ruling power.[2]

Other agrarian civilizations of the world were generally based on common land property. Above the little village communities there stood the joining units of state power—more simply clans, tribes, and rulers—who appeared as the owners of the land, and in whose person the common property in land was exemplified. To the ruler belonged all of the land, which was not used by peasants individually, but through village and land communes. The village community, being the smallest taxing and administrative unit, guaranteed taxes for the state machinery. In this system it was the village that faced the state, while the individual was of little interest. These village communities were isolated from one another and from changes that occurred in the political sphere, which explains in part the permanence of the system.[3]

Greek society, which for the first time treated land as private property, differed entirely from this social structure, as would the Roman and West European societies that followed.[4] The western part of the Roman Empire had a social system based on private property, which the Germanic peasants were unable to change; instead they adopted it, at least as far as tillage plots were concerned, though grazing lands and forests remained common property. The system of livestock inheritance, which up to that time had not been known in this part of the Roman Empire, now came to dominate. The result of the interaction of these two systems was feudalism in Western Europe, which meant the abolition of land communes. Instead the peasant possessed the land individually, and likewise faced the landlord as an individual. The peasant performed his services, or the larger part of them, alone.[5] The surplus resulting from increased production remained mostly the property of the peasant, and this encouraged him to greater efforts. The result was one of the most important differences between West and East, namely that West European societies were more dynamic.[6]

By contrast, the system of communal fields and village communities led to an economic and social stasis wherever it was practiced. The intensification of production was not encouraged within this system, for it did not pay the peasant well to produce more. The relatively despotic system of power did not present an opportunity for the individual producer to keep surplus product for himself. This was the situation in Eastern Europe, as seen in the early Russian chronicles. There we get a characteristic picture of village communities being exploited in the most primitive way by tax collectors in the name of rulers and their escorts, who represent state power.[7]

This also explains why the structure of feudal society in Eastern Europe differed from that of Western Europe. In Western Europe the prevalence of Roman legal practice, the early breakup of common landed property, and the German system of single inheritance (primo- or ultimate geniture) enabled vassalage to penetrate into society. Throughout Eastern Europe, by contrast, an extraordinarily strong central power prevailed over a dependent nobility. Even in Hungary state organization was much more homogeneous than in Western Europe. The structure of East European society was therefore not as deep nor its legal structure as complex as in Western Europe. The feudal nobility of continental Eastern Europe had always been a kind of service nobility, long unable to achieve hereditary tenure (in Russia, for example, until the reforms of Peter the Great), and was therefore subordinated to the ruler.[8]

Social systems based on communal land are not uniform in every way. It is not known, in fact, why in one case the system takes on a despotic character while in another case more democratic forms appear. In the case of the Slavic tribes, despotic power became dominant rather early. The point is that in Eastern Europe as a whole the possibility of a West European type of development was precluded by the collective form of land property, by the despotic system of rule built on land communes and village communities, and by the economic and legal order of the whole society. It is evident that in such societies socioeconomic changes could only originate from above. Not only was the majority of the ruling class often against reforms, but the village communities were largely indifferent as well. This was certainly true of the reforms of Ivan IV and Peter the Great, and of the struggle for liberation of the serfs in Russia and the Romanian principalities.

There was a long period in Eastern Europe when Western social forms were assumed outwardly but did not penetrate into society. Such was the case with the adoption of West European legal terminology by societies that lacked the real legal content on which the terms were based. It is essential to stress that the tardiness and superficiality of such borrowing was due not only to the communal land system, but also to the fact that this system had not been affected by the ancient influences of Greece and Rome, as had Western Europe. It is true that Christianity spread and Roman legal practice appeared in Eastern Europe, which in that sense can be said to have followed the West European pattern with a delay. But the time difference is not what is essential here. In Eastern Europe even the slightest remains of any classical tradition were missing; as a result, social mechanisms that embodied this tradition in Western Europe in the period of migrations did not exist to spur a revival in the East.

The relative abundance of land and the system of village communes, as well as the complete lack of Graeco-Roman traditions resulted in the fact that Eastern Europe developed on other tracks and at a considerably slower pace than did Western Europe. Production did not need to be intensified, as land was plentiful. It is illustrative that in most parts of Russia even in the middle of the nineteenth century the two-field system was still dominant, and it was in large areas supplemented by yet more primitive cultivation methods such as slash-and-burn agriculture.[9] The development of nonagrarian sectors of the East European economy was correspondingly slow.

In Western Europe intensification of production characterized not only agriculture but every sector of the economy. This is fundamental, because the development of agriculture was greatly influenced by the other sectors. West European towns, whether their origin was Roman, Celtic, or later, soon developed from their initial role as centers of administration (royal, ecclesiastical, or manorial) into a new role as trade centers. The settlement of towns was rather dense, reaching some 7 to 10 percent of total population by the thirteenth and fourteenth centuries. These towns became not only junctures for long-distance trade, but also the forum for the internal exchange of products within certain districts and, later, industrial settlements. West European towns therefore had a great influence on agriculture. The towns became markets for local agricultural products, thus making the town–village relationship the driving force behind agricultural commodity production. The connection between town and village changed, as the town gave an impulse to the development of agriculture and to the village itself. Meanwhile, in accordance with their role in the division of labor, the inhabitants of the towns created a special social order of their own.

The East European town did not play the same economic role as that of Western Europe. Various types of towns in Eastern Europe long preserved their original character. Many towns were way points for long-distance trade, primarily engaged in transshipping goods toward Western Europe from distant points. Most of the inhabitants in this type of town were not of local origin but were foreign merchants: in Russia the Varangians or Arabs, for example, and in the Balkans the Greeks, Jews, or Armenians. A second group of towns were the military and administrative centers; here the primary occupation of local populations was to provide services for those centers. The characteristics of these East European centers did not change over time, except that the rulers and heads of church, along with their escorts, were later replaced by soldiers and civil servants.[10]

The third type of town in Eastern Europe was in fact nothing but a bigger village, serving the goals of long-distance agricultural trade. Its development in Eastern Europe was due to the fourteenth-century development of large-scale cattle exports toward Western Europe from the region stretching from South Sweden through the Polish lowlands to Moldavia and to the Carpathian basin. Apart from the fact that certain of these market towns later received urban privileges or became industrial towns, their formation was otherwise connected with agricultural production, principally with delivering cattle to foreign markets. Such market towns were primarily collection points that failed to generate any autonomous economic drive. Wherever the breeding of cattle served export purposes, this sort of settlement came into being: on the Polish plains and in the Ukraine, Moldavia, and Hungary.[11]

These three types of towns were characteristic of Eastern Europe, though none could be called a real town in the West European sense, since these places were not inhabited by citizens creating a separate order in feudal society. Most of the inhabitants were engaged in agriculture. What turned them into towns, aside from certain features of their legal status, was the fact that to the eyes of West European observers their very size gave them an urban appearance.

True, there were also towns in the West European sense of the word to be found in Eastern Europe. These were towns in which the population consisted mostly of merchants or miners, migrants from the West, mainly of German origin. The structure of settlement, the economic and social organization, and the outlook of the towns created by these people met the requirements of a West European town, and the inhabitants usually possessed the social status accorded town dwellers in the West as well. But these towns were not characteristic of Eastern Europe, arising only in part from local conditions. Rather, they were developed in order to extract ores. Mining was undeveloped in the region, so rulers imported miners. As a consequence these towns did not fit into the local socioeconomic structure, and even ethnically remained strangers for centuries. By the time such towns assimilated, they had already begun to decline, as their character became more agrarian and their development stopped. Furthermore, these Western-type towns did not form as dense a network and did not account for such a considerable part of the entire population in Eastern as in Western Europe. These towns remained largely isolated from the East European peoples, just as Greek towns had done in ancient Northern Africa and Asia Minor.

Socioeconomic structure differed not only in the town but also in the village. In most parts of Eastern Europe the peasants remained more or less serfs (bondsmen) until a late date. Communal land property, the system of domination based on it, and the dependent status of the village peasant were closely connected. The situation was different only where Christianity had been spread by the Western Church: the Baltic area, Poland, Hungary, Bohemia, Croatia, and Slovenia. Elsewhere in Eastern Europe the peasants belonged to the property of the rulers, landowners, or boyars. Under the influence of Christianity the slavery-like features of the system were restrained, but the peasants themselves remained personally enserfed. The members of the village communities had mutual responsibilities for each other, and this primitive relationship prevailed into the twentieth century. Apart from their nominal legal status, the peasants had essentially the same destiny. The masses of Russian peasants were, for example, either slaves or serfs (holop), and sources referred to them as equivalent to cattle. Another form of serf was the *tcheliadj,* who was distinguished from the free peasant (smerd), but the blood-payment that was to be paid in case they were killed was the same.[12]

The position of the ruling classes in Eastern Europe also differed from the West European version. In what may more properly be called Central Europe—Hungary, Croatia, Bohemia, and Poland—the foundations of feudal society were laid by the foreign, mainly German feudal aristocracy that had spread Christianity and become the military base of the ruling families. In Hungary these aristocratic families of foreign origin quickly amalgamated with the tribal leadership and became an organic part of the feudal aristocracy. Similar processes took place in Poland and Bohemia where the number of foreign families was greater than in Hungary. In Croatia and Slovenia foreign families predominated in the aristocracy. The course of development in Croatia was further complicated by a feudal aristocracy of Hungarian origin that played an important role.

The crowds of foreign aristocrats and their military retinue entering this region modified the original form of tribal proprietorship. The landed properties became feudal estates very soon in Hungary, Poland, and especially Bohemia, which was part of the Holy Roman Empire. Estates became inheritable in the same way as had happened in Western Europe. The structure of the ruling class, the connection between ruler and certain strata of nobility followed behind the West European pattern by one or two centuries.

Still, the feudal system did not develop here in as complicated a form as in France and Germany. Towns did not take part in the feudal assemblies that arose, leaving the aristocracy and large landowners so dominant as to become stronger than the royal power itself. The most extreme case, the "Polish Republic of Nobility," became a regime of the high aristocracy.

Further east, for many centuries the ruler remained the sole theoretical owner of land, especially in Russia. The majority of the Russian nobility, and also the Romanian and Serbian nobilities, were servitors who received land only for the period of their services and whose land could not automatically be inherited by their descendants. A smaller part of the nobility consisted of the tribal or clannish aristocracy, the boyars, most of whom were in the direct service of the monarch or territorial ruler. In Russia and the Balkans feudal parliaments never came into being, so power was not divided between the rulers and the estates. The first great nationwide assembly of the nobility in Russian history occurred in 1549, but it was more a royal council than a "States General" and was never of much importance. The same was true of the very limited assemblies of nobles in Romania.[13]

Thus in Eastern Europe society was of a different character than in

Western Europe. The fact that peasants were treated like serfs for so long was an enormous obstacle to the intensive development of the economy. Because lands belonging to the nobilities were for a long period not hereditary meant that they were subject to extortion rather than more careful, rational exploitation. Paradoxically, the communal form of village property facilitated such a superficial form of control. The internal coherence of the village allowed lords to exploit it without having to consolidate ownership rights. Aristocracies were not obliged to consolidate as self-conscious classes. This made it more difficult for them to counterbalance central power in Russia and the Romanian principalities. This does not mean, of course, that these states never fell apart, but in such cases the petty local monarchs exercised the same despotic power as had the rulers of the big empires. Power was divided only geographically, not socially. The lack of West European feudal property in land caused the absence of real feudal features in the East; most notably, it precluded the development of a broadly based, relatively independent feudal nobility.

In other words, after the tenth century, Eastern Europe began to divide into distinct zones. Those parts closest to the West had to adapt in order to fight on more equal terms with their more advanced neighbors. Weapons were a commodity from Western Europe that altered society somewhat, for skilled personnel as well as armaments needed to be imported, much as would happen later in the case of miners. Hungarian, Bohemian, and Polish armies changed over rather quickly to the military tactics of feudal Europe, while the assimilation of armed men coming into these countries from the West sped the transformation toward a modified form of feudalism. This contact created an intermediary area, partly Eastern, with some Western traits; but Western influence still remained fairly shallow.

## THE FORMATION OF AN EAST CENTRAL EUROPEAN ECONOMIC AND SOCIAL ZONE

In the fourteenth century, West European economic development and expansion led to the establishment of closer economic connections with the region nearest to it. This is why at least some parts of Eastern Europe were compelled to adopt elements of the Western model of development quite early. We cannot speak about the influence of Western Europe in other parts of the world in this period, for relations with the Middle East and Asia were limited to a low-volume exchange of a few commodities over long distances. Not until a later phase, following the so-called age of discoveries, would this type of trade relation take on a qualitatively new form.

The Western economic impact on East Central Europe made itself felt from the very start in raw agricultural products and ores. The latter could be purchased in these centuries only from East Central Europe. The surge of copper and precious metal mining in Hungary, Bohemia, and Silesia is explained by this demand. Precious metals were exported to the West either in raw form or as coins; in return, consumption goods and articles such as dresses, textiles, and arms were imported. The technical achievements of West European development created a good market for these articles among members of the ruling class. This is the period, after all, when Western fashion began to conquer the world, and when the sumptuary habits of the people and the noble aristocracy in Eastern Europe began to differ from each other. The prosperity of the mining industry brought miners with new techniques into the region, created mining settlements and towns, and marked the beginning of a new type of social development.

Similar to the demand for precious metals and copper, yet greater and longer lasting in its importance, was the demand for agricultural products that began in the fourteenth century. The growth of towns and the increase in population produced a demand for food products that could not be satisfied by West European supplies alone. The demand for meat, especially, could no longer be met from nearby areas. At the same time meat was the product that could be delivered relatively easily on its own legs to the markets. In the fourteenth century cattle exports began to take place from a wide area. This marked the beginning of the development of market towns in Eastern and Central Europe.

From the next century onward a new feature was included with the former two: an increasing demand for grain and timber. The demand for grain from Dutch towns, to which it could be delivered by water, exerted an influence everywhere. From the end of the fourteenth century this influence spread over England, Denmark, and Southern Sweden on one side, and East German, Polish, and Baltic areas on the other.[14] As a matter of fact, until the appearance of railways there would not be any way of delivering grain in large quantities to Western Europe from other East European areas. Only after the construction of the railway network could Russian, Hungarian, and Romanian grain appear on the Western markets.

At this point the effects of Western Europe's dynamic geographical expansion become important to our theme. We can witness an eastern as well as western migration from the territory called Western Europe. The peasants of the overpopulated areas settled in huge waves in the as yet uninhabited North Flemish territories, and colonization towards the east spread with a surprising velocity. This was facilitated by a fact not usually mentioned in this connection, namely the German system of inheritance by which the land could be inherited by only one successor. The oldest or youngest son thus received the entire inheritance, leaving the other successors the choice of remaining there to serve, or migrating to begin cultivation of a new piece of land.

This system of succession provided the German peasants with greater mobility than other peasants in Eastern Europe and facilitated their migrations. As a result of population growth, colonization by German peasants had reached the Elbe-Saale-Czech forest line in about the eleventh century, and by the thirteenth century their colonization had spread from Silesia to Poland and Hungary. In the other direction the German peasants very successfully inhabited Holland, soon even reclaiming areas from the sea. Such colonization activity meant not only the migration or expansion of a population to uninhabited areas, but also the transplantation of an economic and social system. The German peasants settling between the Elbe-Saale and the Oder Germanized and practically absorbed the earlier inhabitants. However, in the territories east of the Oder, there were not enough German peasants to achieve such results. Thus in the Baltic region there appeared mixed settlements of peasant and town citizens.

Colonization of this sort was supported by the Polish, Czech, and Hungarian kings, because they expected their income to increase by it. In return the settlers were allowed to maintain their social and economic order, as well as their personal freedom, which had previously been unknown in these territories. Where the Germans settled in masses, the advantages of this socioeconomic order soon became clear for the Czech, Hungarian, and Polish peasants. The settlers introduced more advanced agricultural techniques and technologies: the asymmetric, partly iron heavy plow; the three-field system; individual plots; horse yoking; and better animal husbandry, which allowed permanent stabling. Of even more importance, however, were the personal freedom of the peasant, the freer communal system of the German village, which was limited to the use of special commons, and more advantageous tax conditions.

Within a few centuries the colonization by German peasants reached its eastern limit. Settlements in Russia in the eighteenth century no longer brought about the significant effects that had occurred east of the Oder since the twelfth century. While the German villages in

Bukovina and Russia in the eighteenth century kept their own social order, including personal freedom and lighter services than their Russian counterparts, their population was too small to exert any substantial influence on the surrounding areas.

In Polish, Baltic, and Bohemian territories, however, the appearance of numerous German villages reshaped the structure of the local societies. In Silesia at the end of the thirteenth century there were 200 so-called villages under German law, and by the mid-fourteenth century the number had risen to 1200, with 120 towns of the same kind. In Great Poland, where a "privilege" consisted of several villages, the number of privileges grew from 164 in the mid-fourteenth to about a thousand by the early fifteenth century. By the turn of the sixteenth century, 153 towns under German law had also come into being. In the territories of the archbishopric of Gnezno, for example, 215 settlements under German law were founded between the years 1285 and 1512. We also know that at the time of the first partition of Poland in 1772 there were 73 towns and 96 villages under German law around Lemberg and altogether 650 such settlements in Galicia.[15]

In time, of course, the population of the villages under German law dissolved rather easily into the native population. This was not the case with towns, however, so it is easier to determine the eastern border of these settlements. In the northern part of the continent, towns under German law were found from Stettin to Königsberg; these took the law of Lubeck (niederdeutsches Recht) as their basis. In the central zone, towns based on the law of Magdeburg (flämmisches Recht) were founded in Eastern Galicia along a line through Brest, Lublin, Radom, Sandom, and Lemberg. In the south the law of Nuremberg (oberdeutsches Recht) prevailed in the German towns of Bohemia, Moravia, and Hungary to the line of the Carpathians. The eastern border of German settlements of large numbers is approximately the Memel line, running from Brest up the Bug. To the north we usually find towns such as Riga and Dorpat, but no network of village settlements as extensive as those in the central and southern regions.[16]

Large-scale colonization by the German peasants cemented the already existing processes leading to the gradual strengthening of certain Western elements of the economic and social system in this part of Europe. A few places in this area had belonged to the Roman Empire and later to the empire of Charlemagne, so in these places the ancient traditions had left traces. It is not by chance that Hungary and Bohemia were influenced by the Roman rather than Greek Church so that the Western form of Christianity triumphed. Besides the representatives of the Church, military men soon appeared, invited by the rulers of those countries. They protected the power of the king against pagan rebels in Hungary, for example. The Hungarian tribes did not find the Carpathian basin deserted at the time of their colonization, for there were ethnic groups with Western-style social and economic structures inhabiting the area west of the Danube, which had belonged to Charlemagne's empire. The effect of these peasant folk groups upon the development of Hungarian society is undeniable. The conquering Hungarians settled not upon empty or depopulated land in the trans-Danubian area, but into an existing agrarian society that had previously been saturated by Western structures. Italian, French, and Southern German influence played a role in this area later, exerted partly by the Church and partly by feudal military elements. This divergence in Hungary between western trans-Danubia and the eastern plains gives an example of how certain state formations could incorporate two types of structure from the start. But it also proves the role played by ethnic groups living in the western half in forming the socioeconomic order of Hungarian folk society, and it shows that this has been an important and manifest advantage to the country for centuries.

In Hungary, Bohemia, Croatia, and Slovenia, Roman law had a deeper effect than in Poland or the Baltic states. The role of the classical Mediterranean tradition was about the same in Croatia and Slovenia as in Hungary. In Bohemia there was the added influence of the Celtic *oppidum* culture, whose effect could still be felt after the Slavic colonization.[17] Thus the societies and economies of these areas had many Western or Western-like structural elements even before the arrival of German settlers. These elements had not, however, prevailed. It was the German peasants and townsmen who accounted for the relatively quick and strong success of Western patterns of development in Central Europe.[18]

Later on, unfortunately, the matter of German colonization became an issue of national politics throughout the region. The ideological positions that resulted either preached the superiority of German culture, or totally denied any significant role for German colonization. The fact was, though, that for certain peoples of Eastern Europe, those who came to form a distinct East Central European culture, the achievement of Western social and economic development materialized in the form of settlements inhabited by German peasants. The stress here is not so much on the German peasants who migrated into the area, but on the Western-style social structures that spread and were maintained.

This had a great effect on the Hungarian, Czech, and Polish peasants who were in contact with the greatest number of German settlers. Especially Polish, but also Hungarian historical sources bear witness to the process by which peasants began to follow German law (called *hospes* or "guest" law in Hungary). After a period of time the colonists could not be distinguished from other peasants who lived according to German law. In the thirteenth and fourteenth centuries began the process of unification of different strata of the peasantry, first in Bohemia, then Hungary, then Poland. Parallel to this process was the spread of production techniques and technologies introduced by the settlers. The fact that a great number of towns under German law came into being with the aid of the territorial rulers served to accelerate and deepen the process and contributed to the formation of a new social structure with Western features in Hungary, Croatia, Bohemia, Poland, and the Baltic countries.[19]

Of course East Central Europe showed important differences from the West, as well, which must be pointed out. In these countries the delicate structure of feudal society found in Western Europe never existed. The role of the towns was not as great or as important, except in Bohemia, and in fact the rise of towns did not really reshape society as it had in Western Europe. Commodity production, and with it the money economy, had not penetrated to the extent it had in the West. Central power remained much stronger, and there was an essential difference in the social position of the nobility. Still it is true that this part of Eastern Europe broke away socially from the rest of Eastern Europe as well. Peasants faced their lords individually, they supplied services individually, the solidarity of the village community vanished, the land commune system of redistribution ceased and the land was given permanently to individual farmers (although the village community reserved a certain role in connection with the field rotation system). On the whole, the same basic system of private land property spread as among the peasants of Western Europe.

## THE INTRODUCTION OF THE MODERN WORLD MARKET

By the time these processes had completely unfolded and transformed society, a new type economic impact from Western Europe was being felt in the form of greatly increased demand for grain. From the second half of the fifteenth century the demand for grain in towns of the Netherlands gradually increased. The Low Countries, being by the sea coast, profited from their advantageous position by importing grain in large quantities, while their own agriculture concentrated on more valuable products such as meat and dairy foods. A world agricultural market came into existence.

The Dutch demand for grain made itself felt all around the Baltic Sea, where navigable streams facilitated the delivery of grain to the sea. At a distance of one or two days' journey from both sides of the great Elbe, Oder, and Vistula Rivers, large-scale production of grain commenced. This produced relations between Western Europe and the western zone of Eastern Europe that were more organic than had previously been imaginable. Direct economic influence was exerted over these places. The economic relations of previous centuries between these two parts of Europe now became more and more tightly woven. In the fifteenth century a number of everyday articles, such as textiles and utensils, appeared among the nobilities of Hungary, Bohemia, and Poland. As a result, this part of East Central Europe was also attached to the West financially.

The price revolution of the sixteenth century gave a new impetus to these economic ties, and at the same time determined for a long period to come the economic and social relations in the western belt of Eastern Europe. The nobility of the region was very badly hit by the price revolution because its profits were no longer enough to maintain the living standard to which it was accustomed. The difficulties arose from the fact that the economies of these countries could not keep up with the economic development of Western Europe. Western imports rose in price faster than domestic ones, and the terms of trade shifted against the East Central European exports.

The nobility could no longer increase its income by raising peasant dues, especially not where they had been established earlier by tradition. Land rent in kind could not be increased either; the grain production capacity of the peasant economies was too limited. The nobility needed money, but where nobles attempted to raise the burden of the peasants, the peasants sooner or later rebelled (as in Transylvania in 1437 when the Church increased its tax by demanding it in hard currency retroactive for three years). The nobility was obliged to look for new sources of income, which meant suitable new ways of exploiting the peasants or new economic activities.

A different solution presented itself in each area according to the economic conditions, but the widening of economic activities among the nobility was characteristic of all areas and led to the establishment of direct connections between the nobility and economic life. The nobility had earlier been engaged in the cattle trade and had excluded the direct producers, the peasants, from a share of the profits. In the period of the price revolution the nobility now quickly joined the new business of grain export and, even more importantly, became engaged in direct grain production as well.[20]

All along the rivers flowing into the Baltic Sea the nobility became active in growing grain. Many places already had enough cultivable land, while others had the possibility for increasing their available land. The nobility began building individual grain-producing estates wherever feasible. The heart of these estates consisted of the smaller plots of land previously used by nobles for securing their own provisions. These plots existed in some form or other in most areas, though not to the same extent as two or three centuries earlier. Where there was not enough land, peasants' lands were wholly or partially expropriated, and land became much more concentrated in noble hands. In Poland and Hungary the nobles rarely had to resort to such measures because of the low density of land use; further west, in Mecklenburg or parts of Brandenburg, for example, a denser population and the resultant land shortage led nobles simply to drive the peasants away from their small plots (Bauernlegen). Especially after the mid-seventeenth century, self-managed grain production farms were established in this way by the nobles. From the beginning of the eighteenth century up to the first decades of the nineteenth, we find increasing numbers of such self-managed farms alongside the major rivers in the great region between the Elbe and the Vistula. Thus, as a result of the direct economic impact of Western Europe, the large manorial farm came into being.[21]

The formation of these large manorial farms entailed serious social consequences by reshaping peasant conditions. Besides the land itself, large-scale production also required labor power and equipment in quantities that the nobility had not before possessed. The nobility lacked the necessary financial means to engage sufficient numbers of paid workers for large-scale grain production. Instead they came upon another solution: they began gradually to increase the socage services of the peasantry. In part of Prussia and the region between the Elbe and the Oder, where the nobility was scrambling to secure enough labor to grow and deliver grain to the markets, socage services grew from one and two up to five or even six days out of the week. This meant in practice that a peasant household had to hire outside labor either to meet its own needs or to fulfill the manorial demands of socage. This increasing burden of socage services prevented any possible development of peasant economies, making it simply impossible for the peasants to develop their own lands.

The increase of socage burdens led in certain cases to legal consequences as well. The free migration of peasants and the ability to abrogate their contract had to be stopped, that is, they had to be deprived of the important right they had obtained as a result of the German colonization. In many places the free movement of peasants was banned, as in the eastern part of Poland or in the Baltic states. The bondage of the peasant to the person of the noble was the actual sine qua non for the adequate functioning of large-scale grain production based on socage services everywhere in Eastern Europe where there existed market possibilities. In other areas of Eastern Europe peasants had to be tied to the seigneur because the great amount of empty land tempted peasants to migrate, and the nobles would have been deserted and left without taxpaying subjects. This was the case in Russia. The limitation of the rights and personal freedom of peasants forced them practically into the status of slaves. In places the peasants' right to inherit had been abolished, and the seigneur gained the power to make important decisions about their lives, such as marriage.

The most extreme utilization of peasant labor resulted in Poland, Brandenburg, and Prussia, and also in part of Bohemia—everywhere, that is, where grain production found good markets as a result of the continuous and permanent increase of West European demand. In these areas the system of manorial large-scale production based on the utilization of corvée labor power and equipment of the peasants was established.[22] This type of development, however, was only characteristic of areas where there existed suitable market and delivery opportunities. This zone of grain-producing farms based on socage services included the eastern part of Germany, Polish and some Latvian territories, and the district of Livonia. The situation was somewhat different in Bohemia and Hungary and in the regions further south, as well as in the huge areas east of the Polish and Hungarian borders.

But Bohemian development was not identical to Polish or Baltic patterns because Bohemia had already become much more Westernized. In Bohemia German colonization had proved to be very successful as a society-shaping process. Characteristic of this were the formation of a substantially free peasant society, wide diffusion of the asymmetric heavy plow and a three-field system, and fixed taxation obligations for the peasants. The social position of the peasants in Bohemia (German settlers and their Slavic partners equally) was established on the basis of *deutsches Recht*. A great number of towns were built as a consequence of colonization: Czech silver played a determining role in the European economy in the thirteenth and fourteenth centuries, and colonization by miners began relatively early. To this day it is not known what caused the large-scale development of commodity production and the money economy conditions that occurred before the German colonization, yet it is an undoubtable fact that Czech town development was unique in Eastern Europe. While Poland and Hungary had a loose network of towns that lay rather far from one another, the Czech towns lay only one or two days' journey apart. This dense network of towns provided a large internal market for agricultural goods, not only for one or two articles but for a whole range of products from grain, fruits, and milk to meat and fish.

In Bohemia, as in Western Europe, the internal basis for the development of agricultural production had been laid and this development could therefore take intensive forms. Here, too, manorial farming existed, and nobles tried to increase their income by means of grain production, but the large-scale production consisted here primarily of barley and hops (components of beer) instead of wheat and rye. Another important form of manorial commodity production was the creation of fish ponds. Fish is a delicate commodity that decays easily; delivering it is no easy task, and to deliver it over great distances in the Middle Ages was quite impossible. It is evident that the large-scale development of fish ponds was due to the high standard of Bohemian town development from the fifteenth century on. Artificial fish breeding is a labor intensive branch of production, so the socage burdens of the peasants significantly increased in the sixteenth to seventeenth centuries in Bohemia.

Peasant economies became part of commodity production in Bohemia. The peasants themselves became connected with money circulation, which was made possible by the significant network of towns. The great number of towns limited exploitation by landowners, for the peasants' moving into town was a real and everyday danger in spite of legal restrictions. The general economic and social development of Bohemia thus included a number of West European elements that made this region totally different from the rest of East Central Europe and raised Bohemian development to the same quality as that of Western Europe. (It must be added, though, that Bohemian development had been, as it later turned out, one of the weakest among the West European socioeconomic systems.) Simply put, beginning in the thirteenth century the quality of Bohemian development bore the ubiquitous marks of a West European type of development and had a share in it.[23]

The situation was quite different in Hungary because the main river of the Carpathian basin, the Danube, did not enable that country to join the European grain trade. Thus, large manorial grain-producing estates did not come into being in Hungary in the sixteenth and seventeenth centuries as in Germany or Poland. There existed a sporadic local demand for grain, especially during the Turkish-Hungarian wars. After that the system of forts running through the middle of the country as a result of the Turkish occupation produced a market for grain. This, however, failed to reform economic life permanently. The Hungarian nobility therefore had to choose another way to increase its income.

One way the Hungarian nobility increased its income was through various trade monopolies, especially on wine and spirit sales and the right to run a mill or butcher shop. The inhabitants of villages in Hungary were obliged to drink only the wine of the nobles for six months of the year. This was not, as a matter of fact, wine made by the nobles; the majority of what was sold by force by the landowners to the peasants had been made by the peasants themselves, then had been delivered in the form of services to the nobles and the church. The greater part of the income of landlords consisted of income from licensing spirits, mills, and other such monopolies. This was the road taken by the nobles to raise their incomes until the second half of the eighteenth century. Even then, however, the grain-producing manorial estates began to develop only in the western and northwestern regions of the country, in the very regions where grain could easily be transported to nearby Austrian or Bohemian towns. Within the larger eastern part of the country, grain production began only in the second half of the nineteenth century, after the construction of the railway network.

The Hungarian nobility naturally participated in the animal trade as well. An increasing part of its income came from this, as well as from the licensing of inns, mills, and butcher shops. Large manorial farms based on socage services first took shape only in the second half of the eighteenth century. In spite of the statute declaring the so-called terrestrial tie of the peasants, manorial estates based on socage service did not stabilize before the eighteenth century. This statute withdrew the peasants' right to move from one place to another and plunged them into serfdom following the 1514 peasant revolution. But elements of free movement again appeared in Hungarian society during the sixteenth century. The reaction of 1514 proved therefore premature; the nobility could not make use of bound corvée labor. Even the peasant revolt itself originated from rivalry between the nobility and the wealthiest elements of the peasantry which dealt with the animal trade and mostly inhabited market towns. While in the second half of the fifteenth century royal power supported the development of market towns, at the turn of the sixteenth century it was the nobility that came out on top and cruelly liquidated its rival. This was the intent of the terrestrial tie and eternal serfdom. Its ultimate result, however, only emerged in the middle of the eighteenth century, when large manorial grain farms came into being in the western part of the country.[24]

Nor did large grain-producing farms arise in the continental regions further to the east. Nobles in Russia, Eastern Poland, Moldavia, and Wallachia had no other choice than to take the same path as the Hungarian nobility, namely to make use of alcohol and other monopolies. These regions fell outside the reach of the European grain markets, because grain could not yet be transported from these areas. Only after the Treaty of Adrianople, which in 1829 opened the gates of the Bosporus to Russian trading ships, could large-scale grain production finally begin in earnest.[25] Soon after, train connections were established, which meant that the whole of Eastern Europe could finally join the world grain trade.

During the sixteenth to eighteenth centuries Eastern Europe became permanently bifurcated: in the smaller western zone, big manorial farms based on socage and grain production appeared, while in the larger zone to the east, a society based on taxation and rent took shape. The features of this society that hindered development were even stronger than those of the socage system, because they were combined with the mutual responsibility system of village communities. The parasitic nature of this eastern system determined the relationship between the nobility and the peasantry in Russia and the Romanian principalities.

We must take into consideration though that a completely clear picture of either zone of Eastern Europe cannot be drawn. The big manorial farm based on socage is generally characteristic of Poland and Bohemia, yet there remained areas unsuitable for transporting grain, especially in Poland, where manors were not established. There the nobility increased its income by means of seignorial monopolies. At the same time there existed districts within the eastern belt which for some reason were able to join in the grain trade, so that manorial grain-producing economies with their consequent socage burdens could be formed. Thus for example in Moldavia the possibility of manorial grain production was greater than in Wallachia; and again in some Hungarian regions in the sixteenth to seventeenth centuries the socage system also appeared for a few decades. This, however, did not change the position of the regions as a whole, which preserved their character as shaped by more permanent conditions.

## THE NINETEENTH CENTURY

An important new feature in the socioeconomic position of Eastern Europe and in the development of agriculture was the agrarian boom that appeared in the whole East European region at the turn of the nineteenth century. Over two decades, in the age of the Napoleonic wars, this boom left undeniable marks on the agrarian development of both zones of Eastern Europe. For the western sphere it brought about the significant strengthening of manorial grain-producing farms. The manorial economy, using socage and the tools of the serfs, now appeared all over in areas where the effects of the grain boom had not shown up earlier because of the distance from markets. The permanently enlarged armies and their garrisons produced an important market for grain and fodder production and for the products of animal breeding. The quick construction of a network of roads to satisfy army demands at the turn of the nineteenth century also contributed to the economic expansion, as these roads were also utilized for trade purposes. The continental embargo further strengthened the military boom, yielding favorable conditions for the production of sugar beets and tobacco. The diffusion of potato production, especially in the Baltic area, contributed to an increase in the distillation of spirits, while the towns of the district produced a market for manorial dairy farming.[26]

One new economic effect of Western Europe reaching the continental parts of Eastern Europe, including inner Russia, appeared forcefully during the last three decades of the eighteenth century in the form of a strong demand for wool. West European, Austrian, Czech, and German textile industries began to demand increasing quantities of wool, which was all the more important for Russia because it was easier to transport wool than grain. As a result, the demand for wool produced a boom in places where this had never before occurred. Sheep farming spread quickly, and different Western ovine species appeared rather early. Even in continental parts of Russia as well as in Hungary and Poland, manors in regions far from the markets could now join in wool production.

Far-reaching consequences followed. Under the conditions of the wool boom a change of species soon took place on the sheep farms of the bigger estates, with the goal of acclimatizing Western ovine races. These animals, however, were kept differently than the traditional species. In Hungary and Poland, and in parts of Bohemia and Russia, the Western-type merino sheep were fed with cultivated fodder. This brought about the introduction of new forms of vegetation and new production techniques. On the most developed manorial sheep farms the Western species of sheep that were bred on a wide scale were usually foddered, while sheep runs had become only an accessory element in feeding sheep. Fodder plants were either imported directly from Western Europe or they came in indirectly, via Austria or Bohemia. The new fodder plants were cultivated in a field system especially established for this purpose, with the help of the then modern English, French, or Dutch tools. Hired labor was often used instead of socage services, because dependent peasants were not trusted to deal with the expensive new tools.

As a consequence of this process in the western sphere of Eastern Europe, the second and third decades of the nineteenth century brought signs of the great difference in production techniques between big farms on one hand and peasant economies on the other. The farms of the richest landowning aristocrats represented an enclave within East European agriculture in the first half of the nineteenth century comparable to that of the modern industry established by West European firms in the colonies a century later. On a few farms of a few great landowners we can find the most modern production techniques and technologies of the age: new plows, sowing machines, drainage, rotations system instead of the old field system, new and previously unknown fodder plants, stabled animal breeding, acclimatization of new animal species, and in places the hiring of wage laborers. These farms stood up to the modern English, French, and Dutch farms of their age. But there were only a few such farms belonging to a few great landowners, and this was more of a luxury or an expensive passion than a good business. Moreover, these same great landowners operated the more traditional grain farms on most of their land, cultivating with unpaid socage labor. These manorial initiatives did not mean a breakthrough in the agriculture of the whole region, therefore, as they did not significantly diffuse modern production techniques and technology. Agricultural production was carried out all over Eastern Europe largely in the old form, with the old means. This was also the case on the majority of estates belonging to the great landowning aristocrats; in reality the new means could only be introduced by the richest aristocrats on only a few model farms. The basic reason for this was the lack of capital in the whole region, which resulted in the inability of the nobles and the peasants to improve their technology.

The difference between continental Eastern Europe and East Central Europe was that in Hungary, Poland, and the Baltic lands there were to be found such modern farms among the richest feudal proprietors, and slow modernization among the less rich landowners had also started, while in continental Eastern Europe even the great landowning aristocracy was not able to develop its economy in comparable proportions. The general lack of capital, the extremely long distance from the market, and the lack of technical knowledge prevented this.[27] In Hungary, for example, in the regions lying west and northwest of the Danube there were a few big farms in every county that represented the new and the modern, at least in a few respects. In Russia, on the other hand, even in provinces of a regency scale there were hardly even one or two to be found. The difference in this regard is not just quantitative, it is qualitative, and it reflects perfectly the differences between the two major regions of Eastern Europe.[28]

In many ways the situation was different in Bohemia. Here the general level of development of the economy, and especially the urbanization essential for the development of agricultural production, was at a higher level. The beneficial effect of this advanced level presented itself in greater agricultural production as well as in the socioeconomic conditions of the peasantry. In the whole region, Bohemia alone produced a strong and increasing internal market for agricultural goods, while everywhere else most commercialized agricultural goods were merely exported. The presence of this internal market promoted the balanced development of agriculture. The usual case in Eastern Europe was that only those branches of agriculture developed which found markets abroad. In Hungary cattle breeding and quality wine production developed first, then from the second half of the eighteenth century grain production, and in the first half of the nineteenth century sheep farming. In Poland grain production and a few branches of animal breeding developed. Similarly the Baltic lands became involved in grain, and potatoes were also grown for the distillation of spirits. In Bohemia, however, every branch of agriculture developed proportionally. Along with grain, fodder plants were also grown on the arable land; all branches of animal breeding were practiced; hops and barley were grown for beer; and from the first half of the nineteenth century, sugar beets were grown as well. Here no single leading branch of large-scale production, as in Hungarian or Polish estates, ever dominated. At the same time the developmental gap between peasants' and landlords' farms was not as great as, for example, in Hungary. The peasant economies kept pace with modern production technologies, whose use was not limited to big manors.

The social position of the peasantry was also different in Bohemia. In the early seventeenth century the resistance of the estates had been crushed, and following the peasant revolt of 1680 the nobles could no longer use peasant socage to the same extent as before. During the eighteenth century the peasant-supporting measures of the court in Vienna were enforced in Bohemia, thereby changing significantly the social position of the peasantry. The high level of town development played a primary role in this area as well. The dense network of towns enabled peasants to settle in cities, and this opportunity was so widely taken that the demands of the landlords were automatically limited. Agrarian development in Bohemia took the West European path, in fact, in every respect, so that at the turn of the nineteenth century there was no difference at all between Austrian, Bavarian, and Bohemian agricultural conditions. Bohemia, in fact, belonged more to Western Europe.

Let us summarize the essence of what characterized the social and economic situations of the peasantry in the two zones of Eastern Europe by the middle of the nineteenth century. A substantial German colonization of this region beginning in the thirteenth century had resulted in a growth of the population density, which in turn led to a general intensification of agricultural systems. The economic influence of Western Europe then produced a demand in the nearby western zone of Eastern Europe for grain and later wool, making conditions favorable for the growth of large grain-producing farms. These farms were cultivated with socage labor and with the tools of the peasants. At first only in spots, but by the mid-nineteenth century all over the region, modern techniques such as three-field rotation and tools such as the asymmetric heavy plow became dominant, particularly on the large manorial farms. By the turn of the nineteenth century the cultivation of fallow land had begun in some areas, yielding potatoes in Poland's most developed places, and potatoes and maize in Hungary. Meanwhile the peasant's methods of cultivation and the peasant economy itself had not changed qualitatively. Peasants still used traditional tools and traditional forms, though by the mid-nineteenth century the three-field system had replaced the two-field system almost everywhere.

In other words, despite advances, the western part of Eastern Europe (i.e., Central Europe) still lacked a sufficiently high population and urban density to support full agricultural modernization. Only Bohemia was an exception. By the early nineteenth century a certain degree of modernization had occurred in the technology of the large landowners who grew grain for export, but these enclaves of modern economic production did not transform the peasant economies, nor even the great majority of big farms, which were still based on socage service. The peasant economy, serving the small internal market, stayed at its traditional level of production technique, unchanged and unmodernized. The peasantry of this region was cultivating the land in the same manner as the West European peasantry had been doing in the fifteenth and sixteenth centuries.

But even the production pattern that has just been described was not characteristic of the zone lying farther to the east, especially not for the inner Russian regions. In this continental portion of Eastern Europe the pressure of the population was not strong, agricultural export was not significant until the late nineteenth century, and the internal market was not even as developed as, for example, in Poland. Here we cannot speak of the spread of the asymmetric heavy plow or about the dominant role of the three-field system; for here the two-field system was dominant, and the more extensive forms of cultivation played an important role.[29] Peasant production remained at its earlier level, and the income of the nobility grew not as a result of self-managed manors, but as a result of the use of various noble monopolies, first among them being the distillation and sale of alcoholic spirits. When the export possibilities for agricultural products finally arose, in the nineteenth century, the production capabilities of the nobles' self-managed farms, based on peasant labor, proved unable to exceed the standard of the peasant economies.

While in the western sphere of Eastern Europe the big farms of the great landowners created enclaves of modern agricultural production, this did not occur on the continental side even after railroads had brought international trade to the rural agricultural region as far as the Urals. Only after the liberation of the serfs did such a process begin in the eastern zone. In the whole of Eastern Europe the strong role of the state was elemental in the liberation of the serfs. This meant that the power of the state had to impose liberation of the serfs against the stubborn resistance of the majority of the land-controlling class. Furthermore, the state played a dominant role everywhere in securing financial compensation for the nobility, due to the low economic level of society and the lack of capital of the peasantry.

Precisely the low standard of economy and the great lack of capital of these societies explains why serf liberation and the creation of capitalist conditions took place in agriculture by reforms from above. In continental Eastern Europe—Russia, Romania, as well as in Serbia and Bulgaria—the preconditions of capitalism were so weakly formed that these countries could not wait decades or centuries for their development. Here, too, the military challenge had to be calculated. The example of greater Russia proves what role the military interests of the empire played in the abolition of serfdom. The state itself thus quickened the process, though it was not capable of creating capitalist conditions at once.

The nobility was compensated for the liberation of the serfs in both zones of Eastern Europe, making the level of economic development at the time of liberation most influential. The precondition of liberation was in every case a certain amount of commodity production and the existence of money circulation in agriculture. In this respect there were essential differences between the continental and western parts of Eastern Europe. Hungary, Poland, the Baltic lands, and Bohemia joined world trade earlier and more powerfully, and goods and money played a much greater role in agriculture than was the case in Russia and some of the Balkan countries. Emancipation therefore occurred not only earlier, but in several respects differently than in the east. In Croatia, Hungary, Bohemia, and the western and central parts of Poland, peasants could keep a rather large part of the land in their own use; the compensation did not mean that the peasant had to compensate for his freedom by giving up his land. Here even the various forms of labor compensation were not long-lasting, and the changeover to a capitalist type of farming took place rather early.[30]

There were other differences as well. In Poland, Bohemia, and Hungary the serfs were no longer as subservient as in Russia and Romania. The quantity of services to be performed had been limited by the state. The only question to be decided in 1848 was thus whether the peasants should also receive a share of the landlords' land (terra dominicalis, as opposed to terra rusticalis in law). In Russia the debate was about whether peasants still regarded as virtual slaves should be freed in person, and whether the liberated serfs should then receive any share in the land whatsoever. In the Romanian principalities, too, the issue was whether or not the freed serfs should get any land, and if so, how much. The land in this eastern zone, as a matter of fact, had not been legally divided into two parts, so in principle all the land belonged to the nobility. Although peasants had used the land, the owners could still take it away, change it, or reduce its size, unhindered by legal obstacles or customary law. In the same way, the person of the serf could be bought, sold, or pawned quite independently of the land.

In Russia and Romania the liberation of the serfs took place after these areas had joined international trade, namely at about the same time as the construction of railway networks. This created the possibility for the peasants to produce goods. The relative backwardness of the region meant that the peasants did not have enough money. This was one reason why the landowners were compensated with land and services.

Compensation by services included cultivation of the landlords' land in socage even after the liberation, land lease against labor service, and sale of peasant labor for a period of years in advance. All these forms of service resulted from the fact that the peasantry was chronically impecunious. This eventually spread usury into villages and caused the deterioration of the peasants' conditions.[31]

One result of the general shortage of money was that by liberating the serfs the state strengthened village communes throughout the eastern zone. In Russia these communes were made responsible for the correct settlement of the redemption of the peasants: if someone failed to pay, the village community had to pay instead. In the case of Romania the village community had to guarantee implementation of the labor duties of peasants. Communal lands and villages prevailed long after this type of liberation of the serfs had taken place. In vast areas of Russia the system of redivision of land by the community also existed. This all hindered the capitalist development of agriculture a great deal, and because the peasants were practically tied to the land communities, it also meant a blockage to the development of industry. The systematic and equalizing redivision of the land, the principle of solidarity among members of the village community, and the binding of superfluous labor power to the agricultural land—none of this could be adjusted to capitalist conditions.[32]

In the second half of the nineteenth century, in the decades of the grain boom and the following grain crisis, the peasant economies of Poland, Bohemia, and Hungary developed significantly. The three-field system changed to a more advanced rotation system, and the technique of plowing improved with the introduction of factory-produced iron plows that could be pulled by a pair of horses. These plows became widely available by the end of the century. The iron harrow, the sowing machine, and the scythe also contributed to the development of cultivation. Machine threshing was predominant by the end of the century in the peasant economies. During the grain crisis there began the rapid development of animal breeding in peasant households. The changeover to stalling and the acclimatization of western types of cattle, swine, and sheep followed the big farms with a delay of only one or two decades. The development of cooperatives made dairy farming profitable for peasant holdings, especially in Bohemia. The development of animal breeding started a new wave of investment in which farm buildings were constructed; new machines such as grinders were purchased and installed on the peasant farms. Increased breeding also changed the use of arable land, as the cultivation of fodder plants gained ground against the extensive raising of grain in plowed fields. The proportion of hoed and industrial plants such as sugar beet, maize, and potato also increased. As a result of all this the productivity of the peasant economies increased dramatically, while the great capitalist farms characteristic of Bohemia, but also found in parts of Poland and Hungary, surpassed the peasant economies in every way and rivaled the most advanced German or Dutch farms. This is reflected in the average yields of the more important crops, which approached French or Bavarian levels.[33]

These patterns hold true for the whole western belt of Eastern Europe, yet variations are worth noting. Western Poland, being part of imperial Germany and thereby protected by its tariffs, achieved a much higher level of agricultural development than the part of the country belonging to the tsarist empire, a difference that is still, in fact, apparent today. Bohemia's high level of industrialization and urbanization created a significant internal market that exerted an extremely strong demand on agricultural production. The gap between the large estates and the peasant holdings was not nearly as great as in Poland or Hungary, for the peasant farms operated at quite a high level. Agricultural production in Bohemia matched the most advanced German districts and surpassed that of France; only a few areas in Europe did better, those being Belgium, Holland, and industrialized parts of France and northern Italy. It is an important factor that Bohemian industrial development, like that of German Poland, absorbed excess labor from agriculture and allowed thereby for a relatively egalitarian development of peasant agriculture.

Such was not the case in Hungary. Industrial development there was insufficient to absorb the quantity of agricultural labor that was released. Emigration did reduce somewhat the excess labor power, but not enough to stop the sharpening social differences. The real wage of agricultural labor was decreasing at the turn of this century due to the grain crisis, which along with increasing unemployment caused a few tense decades. By this time the agrarian society of Hungary had been significantly proletarianized due to the principle of equal inheritance. Since industry could not absorb the agrarian labor, about half the agricultural population consisted of totally destitute agrarian proletarians or dwarf holders who subsisted by wage labor. The shortage of land meant that peasant landholders were proportionally fewer, and the agrarian proletariat proportionally greater, than in Russia. The poverty stricken agrarian strata were the "agrosocialists" of the turn of the century, whose movements took the form of harvest strikes, and who calmed down only in 1907 when the protective tariffs of the Austro-Hungarian Monarchy were raised. Under the protection of these duties

Hungarian agriculture then attained a favorable position in the markets of the monarchy, which enabled agricultural wages to rise.

The situation was completely different in Russia and the Balkans. In Russia the redemption sums paid to landlords, along with taxes, placed such a heavy burden on the peasants that they were not able to invest in farms. The system of redivision of lands also prevented accumulation and investment. Meanwhile the settlement of liabilities forced the peasants to increase production on the land. By the end of the nineteenth century this exploitive farming, still based on the wooden plow, thorn-harrow, and other medieval tools, ended in a series of bad harvests and famines. The government reduced the burdens somewhat, but kept the land communes and the system of paying debts in labor. Peasants suffered usury and such hardships that the revolutionary situation brought on by the Russo-Japanese war spread revolt among the peasants like wildfire. Usury was even worse in Romania, where peasants sold their labor to landlords in advance, or traded it for land. The big landowners did not cultivate the land themselves, but signed usurious contracts with tenant farmers. The situation sometimes became unbearable, leading to the bloody revolts of 1888 and 1907.

These turns of events were caused mainly by the insufficient development of money and trade conditions and the consequent inability of the peasants to settle their debts. The simultaneous growth of the peasant population in the nineteenth century caused a relative overpopulation of the land. For the first time in Russian history it was impossible to increase tillage to match population growth. Considering the burdens of the peasantry, any increase in agricultural production could only have been attained through intensive methods. Such intensification could not be effected through accumulation and investment because of a shortage of peasant capital and because of the long survival of the land communes, which lasted until 1907. The famines that arose regularly around the turn of the century (there were twelve bad harvests in Russia between 1891 and 1914) marked the crisis in the system. Finally the peasant revolts of 1905 to 1907 in Russia and Romania washed away the roadblocks preventing development along the Polish or Hungarian path. This created the possibility of accelerating the capitalist development of agriculture.[34]

## CONCLUSION

The whole of Eastern Europe was divided rather early into two unequal parts by the economic relationships that tied them to Western Europe.

In the territories lying geographically nearer Western Europe the influence of Roman law made for a more private, less communal form of peasant property. Large-scale colonization took place continuously after the twelfth century, giving strong impulse to the socioeconomic development of private peasant property in agriculture. This process allowed peasants to be less dependent on lords. Population density contributed considerably to the development of agricultural techniques and technology. The attraction of West European markets beginning in the fifteenth century led to the creation of great manorial farms that produced commodities using socage labor (hence, the notion of a "second serfdom"). These great manors spearheaded the modernization of agriculture after the eighteenth century and served as examples for peasant holdings as well. After the liberation of the serfs the transformation of peasant holdings was quick.

This zone spreading from Finland and Estonia through Latvia and Lithuania, the western part of Poland, Hungary, Croatia, and Slovenia can actually in a historical sense be called "Middle Europe." This is a transitional area where West European and East European influences mixed with one another, creating at places dominant Eastern features moderated by Western influences, and at other places the reverse. Given their social and economic structures, Bohemia and Austria did not belong to this Middle Europe, but constituted the least developed line of Western Europe. Regions to the east of Middle Europe, on the other hand, developed on a different basis altogether.

The region lying to the east of the line between the Baltics, Lithuania, and the Carpathians entered West European markets only very slowly. Outside markets exerted an influence on agricultural production only in the late nineteenth century when railways facilitated large-scale exports. The landowners in these areas, lacking money, derived an income from the alcohol monopoly, taxes, rents, and other activities outside the productive sphere. Peasants belonged to the landowners as personal property, particularly in Russia. Peasants lived within a system of land communes and village communities that lasted into the twentieth century. Thus, both from the top and bottom there were strong forces that prevented agricultural modernization. Lords had little direct interest in it, and peasant communities were bound by traditional institutions highly resistant to any individual initiative or change. The great amount of land and sparse population did not demand intensive techniques, so production remained extensive instead. Even the three-field system was not in preponderance in the mid-nineteenth century. Production techniques remained at a rather low level on peasant farms and on manorial estates alike.

The fact that the nonagrarian sectors of the economy were underdeveloped up to the end of the nineteenth century also contributed to the survival of traditional agricultural methods in the eastern zone. Industry, trade, and urbanization were undeveloped, so that those who lived from this sector were nearly as much in servitude as were the peasants. From the late seventeenth century the state took important steps to develop industry and towns but this was limited mostly to the military realm and was never in organic relation to the rest of the economy. West European military techniques meant an inescapable challenge for Russia, so tsarist policy strived to create a military equilibrium, especially under Peter I. The modernization that resulted had no real effect on the economy as a whole, though, because manufacture was limited to military needs and was carried out by serfs. The direct economic impact of Western Europe on the vast territories of continental Eastern Europe did not appear until late in the nineteenth century. Characteristically for the inflexible rigidity of the whole society, it took an immense military defeat to shock tsarist absolutism into carrying out any of the most necessary modernization, even in the military sector. And because only the most necessary changes were made, continental Eastern Europe had to suffer yet other shocks before finally opening itself to the world market. Even then, the opening was never completed.

## NOTES

1. See A. I. Shevelenko, "O tipologii genezisa feodalisma," *Voprosy Istorii,* no. 1 (1971), 97–107; Aleksandr R. Korsunski, *Gotskaia Ispania* (Moscow: University of Moscow, 1969); Perry Anderson, *Passages from Antiquity to Feudalism* (London: NLB, 1978), pp. 128–142; Péter Gunst, *Einige Probleme der wirtschaftlichen und sozialen Entwicklung Osteuropas* (Köln: University of Köln, 1977), pp. 8–10. On plows see Marc Bloch, *French Rural History* (Berkeley and Los Angeles: University of California Press, 1966), pp. 50–53.

2. This prevailed typically in the case of the Russian Church which was at last degraded to a mere government office by the reforms of Peter I in 1721. It was the situation in the case of the Romanian principalities, too. This is shown excellently in Dimitrie Cantemir, *Descrierea Moldovei* (Bucharest: Cartea Românească, 1923), pp. 173–177. [The original Latin text was written in 1715.] He pointed out that the ruling power could keep the Church in total subjection only in Russia and Moldavia. For the social position of the Church in Kievan Russia, see Andrzej Poppe, "Le prince et l'église en Russie de Kiev depuis la fin

du Xe siècle et jusqu'au début de XIIe siècle," *Acta Poloniae Historica* 20 (1969): 95–119; and Iaroslav N. Shchapov, *Knazheskie ustavi i cerkov' v drevnei Rusi XI–XIV vv.* (Moscow: Academy of Sciences, 1972), pp. 13–21. This raises the question about the difference between the religious doctrines of Eastern and Western Europe. What role did the distinctive split in Western Christianity play? In the Orthodox Church, of course, there was never a Reformation.

3. This statement is valid for the early period of Russian history and the foundation of the Russian state. Soviet historiography differed from this standpoint for a long time and in connection with early Russian development emphasized that it had developed qualitatively together with the Western European feudal system. The most outstanding representative of this tendency is Grekov. But even in Grekov's work the data support my opinion in several respects. Compare with Boris D. Grekov, *Kievskaia Rus'* (Moscow: Academy of Sciences, 1949), and B. D. Grekov, *Krest'iane na Russi s drevnieishikh vremen do XVII veka* (Moscow: Academy of Sciences, vol. 1, 1952; vol. 2, 1954). In the newer studies of the last decade, Soviet historians have been increasingly disposed to recognize that Kievan Russia did not belong to a Western type of society. The outstanding representatives of this tendency are Y. A. Kirilov, "Predposylki perehoda vostochnogo slavianstva k feudalismu," *Voprosy Istorii* no. 3 (1969), 90–104; Aleksandr L. Shapiro, "O prirode feodal'noi sobstuennosti na zemliu," *Voprosy Istorii,* no. 12 (1969), 57–72; Igor I. Froianov, "Kievskaia Rus'," in *Ocherki sotsialno-ekonomicheskoi istorii* (Leningrad: University of Leningrad, 1974); Mikhail B. Sverdlov, "Iz istorii sistemy nalogo-oblozhenia v Drevnei Rusi," in Lev V. Cherepnin and Iaroslav N. Shchapov, eds., *Vostochnaia Evropa v Drevnosti i Sredneivekovie* (Moscow: Academy of Sciences, 1978), pp. 144–150; Igor I. Froianov, "Kievskaia Rus'," in *Ocherki sotsialno-politicheskoi istorii* (Leningrad: University of Leningrad, 1980). For similar development of the Romanian principalities see Henri H. Stahl, *Traditional Romanian Village Community: The Transition from the Communal to the Capitalist Mode of Production in the Danube Region* (Cambridge: Cambridge University Press, 1980), pp. 37–42, 129–158, and 216. There are a great number of studies dealing with village communities and the despotism based on them. I mention here only those, besides the standard works of Haxthausen, Kowalewski, Maine, etc., which were theoretically the most useful in the course of my studying this problem. See Karl Polanyi, *Dahomey and the Slave Trade: An Analysis of an Archaic Economy* (Seattle: University of Washington Press, 1966); Karl Polanyi, *Primitive, Archaic and Modern Economies* (Garden City, N.Y.: Anchor Books, 1968); Karl Polanyi, *The Great Transformation* (Boston: Beacon, 1968); Maurice Godelier, *Sur les sociétés précapitalistes* (Paris, 1970); Henri Mendras, *Sociétés paysannes* (Paris: Armand Colin, 1976); Eric Wolf, *Peasants* (Englewood Cliffs, N.J.: Prentice Hall, 1969); Aleksandr V. Tschajanow (Chaianov), *Die Lehre von der bauerlichen Wirtschaft* (Berlin: P. Parey, 1923); Teodor Shanin, ed., *Peasants and Peasant Societies* (Harmondsworth: Penguin, 1971); J. M. Potter, M. N. Diaz, G. M. Foster, eds., *Peasant Society: A Reader* (Boston: Little, Brown, 1967). On the concrete forms of Eastern despotism, for China see Étienne

Balazs, "La propriété foncière en Chine," in *Atti del Primo Congresse Internazionale di Diritto Agrario,* vol. 2 (Milan, 1955) and John L. Buck, *Land Utilization in China,* vols. 1–3 (Chicago: University of Chicago Press, 1937). For the Indian village community see the classical Baden H. Baden-Powell, *The Indian Village Community* (London: Longmans, Green, 1896) and *The Land Systems of British India,* vols. 1–3 (Oxford: Clarendon, 1892). See also Eric J. Hobsbawm, *Introduction to Karl Marx's Pre-capitalist Economic Formations* (New York: International Publishers, 1965).

4. For Greek society and the formation of private ownership see Attila Ágh, *Labyrinth in the Mode of Production Controversy* (Budapest: Institute for World Economy, 1980); Ferenc Tőkei, *Antike und Feudalismus* (Budapest; Akadémiai Kiadó, 1977) and *Zur Theorie der Geschichtsformen* (Budapest: Akadémiai Kiadó, 1977).

5. There is a good description of the Western European village community in Karl S. Bader, *Rechtsformen und Schichten der Liegenschaftsnutzung im mittelalterlichen Dorf* (Vienna: Böhlau, 1973).

6. For the whole problem—among others—see Gunst, *Einige Probleme,* pp. 13–14, and Péter Gunst, "Some Characteristics of East European Economic and Social Development: Data and Reflections," in Irene P. Winner and Thomas G. Winner, eds., *The Peasant and the City in Eastern Europe: Interpenetrating Structures* (Cambridge, Mass.: Schenkman, 1984), p. 18; Anderson, *Passages,* pp. 182–196; Aleksandra D. Liublinskaia, "Tipologia rannego feodalizma v Zapadnoi Evrope i problema romano-germanskogo sinteza," *Srednie Veka* 31 (1968): 9–44.

7. See Sverdlov, "Iz istorii sistemy nalogo-oblozhenia," pp. 144–150; Igor I. Froianov, "Froianov's Study," in *Problemy istorii feodalnoi Rossii* (Leningrad: University of Leningrad, 1971); Mikhail B. Sverdlov, "M. B. Sverdlov's Study," *Problemy istorii feodalnoi Rossii*; Jerome Blum, *Lord and Peasant in Russia from the Ninth to the Nineteenth Century* (Princeton: Princeton University Press, 1961), pp. 24–42; Lev. V. Cherepnin, "Iz istorii formirovania klassa feodalnozavisimogo krest'ianstva na Rusi," *Istoricheskie Zapiski* 20 (1956), 234–264.

8. Blum, *Lord and Peasant,* pp. 70–74, 92, 135–148, and 168–170. For Poland, see S. Smolka, *Uwagi o pierwotnym ustroju społecznym Polski Piastowskiej* [Observations on the Original Social Structure of Poland in the Age of Piasts] (Krakow, 1881).

9. For Eastern European, especially Russian, land use systems, see the volumes of *Ezhegodnik po agrarnoi istorii vostochnoi Evropi,* from 1959. The volumes of the series contain studies of this problem based on good source material. Compare with Blum, *Lord and Peasant,* pp. 22–23, 166, 328, and 336–339.

10. Russian towns are the most typical in this respect. See A. I. Nikitskii, *Istoria ekonomicheskogo byta Velikago Novgoroda* (Moscow, 1892); Kesniia N. Serbina, *Ocherki iz sotsialno-ekonomicheskoi istorii russkogo goroda* (Moscow: Academy of Sciences, 1951); M. V. Tihomirov, *Drevnierusskie goroda* (Moscow, 1956); A. M. Saharov, "O termine 'gorod' v istochnikah XVI v.," in *Obshchestvo i gosudarstvo feodal'noi Rossii: Sbornik statiei* (Moscow, 1975), pp. 62–66; Witold Hensel, *An-*

*fänge der Städte bei den Ost- und Westslawen* (Bautzen; Domowina-Verlag, 1967); Aleksander Gieysztor, "Aux origines de la ville slave: Ville de grands, ville d'état aux IX$^{e}$-XI$^{e}$ siècles," *Cahiers Bruxellois* 12 (1967), 97–106; T. Lalik, "Recherches sur les origines des villes en Pologne," *Acta Poloniae Historica* 3 (1960), 101–131; Jiři Kejř, "Nad počátky našich měst" [The Beginning of the Bohemian Towns], *Československý Časopis Historický* no. 3 (1976), 377–401; Nikolai Todorov, "The Balkan Town in the Second Half of the 19th Century," *Études Balkaniques* no. 2 (1969), 31–50; Nikolai Todorov, "Balkanskii gorod XV–XIX vv. v sostave osmanskoi imperii" [The Balkan Town of the 15th–19th Centuries in the Ottoman Empire], *Études Balkaniques,* no. 4 (1971), 28–54; Nikolai Todorov and N. Sofia, eds., *La ville balcanique XV$^{e}$–XIX$^{e}$ siècles* (Bucharest: International Association for the Study of Southeastern Europe, 1980); Bistra A. Tsvetkova, *Proutshvania na grodskoto stopanstvo prez XV–XVI vek* [Studies of Town Economy in Bulgaria in the 15th–16th Centuries] (Sofia: Nauka i Izkustvo, 1972).

11. For this form of settlement, which is typical in the Eastern European countries, see Akademie der Wissenschaften der DDR, Zentralinstitut für Geschichte, Arbeitskreis für Haus- und Siedlungsforschung, *Protokoll der* 15 *Jahrestagung in Weimar vom* 16.*bis* 19. *Juni* 1974 (Berlin, 1975). For the Hungarian market towns see Vera Bácskai, *Magyar mezővárosok a XV. században* [Hungarian Market Towns in the 15th Century] (Budapest: Akadémiai Kiadó, 1965); Péter Gunst, "Der ungarische Bauernaufstand von 1514," in Peter Blickle, ed., *Historische Zeitschrifte* Beiheft 4 (1975), 62–83. For Russia see Anatolii P. Gritskevich, *Chastnovladel'cheskie gorody Belorussii v XVI–XVII vv.* (Minsk: Nauka i tekhnika, 1975); and Anatolii P. Gritskevich, *Sotsialnaia borba gorozhan Belorussii: XVI–XVIII vv.* (Minsk: Nauka i tekhnika, 1979).

12. For the various strata of the Russian peasantry, and the whole question, see Grekov, *Krest'iane na Russi,* vols. 1 and 2, which are still used although they have been criticized severely for about twenty years. See also Blum, *Lord and Peasant,* pp. 27–28, 45–56; Cherepnin, "Iz istorii formirovania," pp. 234–264; Sverdlov, "Study"; A. A. Zhimin, *Holopi na Rusi: s drevneishih vremen do konca 15 v.* (Moscow, 1973).

13. For Russia and for the Russian nobility, see Blum, *Lord and Peasant,* pp. 32–35, 38–42, 74, 80–85, 140–143, and 150–151. See also Henryk Lowmianski, "O proizhozhdenii russkogo boiarstva," in Lev. V. Cherepnin, ed., *Vostochnaia Evropa v Drevnosti i Srednevekove* (Moscow: Academy of Sciences, 1978), pp. 93–100. For Poland, see Eugen O. Kossmann, "Die polnischen liberi als herzogliche Heermannen," *Vierteljahrschrift für Sozial-und Wirtschaftsgeschichte* (1968), 182–192. On the assemblies of the Romanian principalities, see P. P. Panaitescu, "La grande assemblée du pays, institution du régime féodal en Moldavie et Valachie," in *Nouvelles Étude d'Histoire,* vol. 3 (Bucharest: Editura Academiei, 1965).

14. For the development of the European division of labor in the thirteenth to fifteenth centuries, see Marian Małowist, *Wschód a zachód Europy w XIII–XIV. wieku* [Eastern and Western Europe in the 13th–14th Centuries] (Warsaw: Państwowe Wydawn, 1973); Michael M. Postan, "Economic Relations Between Eastern and Western Europe," in Geoffrey Barraclough, *Eastern and Western*

*Europe during the Middle Ages* (London: Thames and Hudson, 1970), pp. 125–174; Barbara Krzemieńska and Dušan Třeštík, "Wirtschaftliche Grundlagen der frühmittelalterlichen Staates in Mitteleuropa: Böhmen, Polen, Ungarn im 10–11. Jahrhundert," *Acta Poloniae Historica* 40 (1979): 5–31.

15. For German colonization see H. F. Schmid, "Das deutsche Recht in Polen," in Albert Brackmann, ed., *Deutschland und Polen: Beitrage zu ihren geschichtlichen Beziehungen* (Munich: R. Oldenburg, 1933), pp. 64–80; Walter Schlesinger, "Die geschichtliche Stellung der mittelalterlichen deutschen Ostbewegung," *Historische Zeitschrift* 183 (1957) 517–542; Rudolf Kötzschke, "Die Anfänge des deutschen Rechtes in der Siedlungsgeschichte des Ostens," *Berichte über die Verhandlungen der Sächsischen Akademie der Wissenschaften zu Leipzig* 93:2 (1941); František Graus, "Deutsche und slawische Verfassungsgeschichte?" *Historische Zeitschrift* 197 (1963): 279–305; Benedykt Zientara, "Foreigners in Poland in the 10th–15th Centuries: Their Role in the Opinion of the Polish Medieval Community," *Acta Poloniae Historica* 29 (1974): 5–28; Władysław Rusinski, "Deutsche Siedlungen auf polnischem Boden im 16–18. Jahrhundert: Mythen und Wirklichkeit," *Acta Poloniae Historica* 47 (1983): 209–257; Eugen O. Kossmann, "Zur Geschichte der Polnischen Bauern und ihrer Freiheit," *Historische Zeitschrift* 205 (1967): 15–45.

16. Max Sering and Constantin von Dietze, eds., *Agrarverfassung der deutschen Auslandssiedlungen in Osteuropa* (Berlin; F. Vahlen, 1939), pp. 14–18.

17. I refer to those Celtic settlements, not only in Bohemia, which were not exclusively villages. The number of inhabitants and the quantity of industrial production in these places were early signs of urbanization in a period of European development preceding and independent of Roman influence.

18. František Graus, "Origines de l'état et de la noblesse en Moravie et en Bohême," *Revue des Études Slaves* 51 (1961), 43–58, and František Graus, *Dějiny venkovského lidu v Čechach v době předhusitské,* 2 (Prague: Czechoslovak Academy, Historical Sections, 1957): 114–118.

19. For the economic and social importance of the German colonization in this region see Kossmann, "Zur Geschichte," pp. 15–45; Heinz Stoob, "Die Ausbreitung der ausländischen Stadt im östlichen Mitteleuropa: Untersuchungen zu einer Kartenfolge im Atlas Östliches Mitteleuropa," *Zeitschrift für Ostforschung* 10 (1961), 25–84; Ilona Bolla, *A jigilag egységes jobbágyosztály kialakulása Magyarországon* [Formation of the Class of Copy-holders Unified by Law in Hungary] (Budapest: Akadémiai Kiadó, 1983); Kazimierz Tymieniecki, *Historia chłopów polskich* [History of Polish Peasantry] (Warsaw: Państowe Wydawn, 1965) 1: 132–147; Valentyn M. Fomenkova, "Polozhenie krest'ian v Polshe vo vtoroi polovine XIII i XIV vv.," in *Uchenie Zapiski Instituta Slavianovedienia* (Moscow: Academy of Sciences, 1956); Gunst, "Einige Probleme," pp. 33–35; Stanisław Trawkowski, "W sprawie roli kolonizacji niemckiej w przemianach kultury materialnej na ziemiac polskich w XIII wieku" [To the Real Role of German Colonization in Polish Material Culture in the 13th Century], *Kwartalnik Historii Kultury Materialnej* 8 (1960), 183–207.

20. For the position of nobility and its consequences, see Jerzy Topolski,

*Narodziny kapitalizmu w Europie x XIV–XVII wieku* [The Birth of Capitalism in Europe in the 14th–17th Centuries] (Warsaw: Państwowe Wydawn. Naukowe, 1965); Topolski, "La reféodalisation dans l'économie des grands domaines en Europe Centrale et Orientale: XVI$^{e}$–XVIII$^{e}$ siècles," *Studia Historiae Oeconomicae* 6 (1972), 51–63; Topolski, "Grand domaine et petites exploitations, seigneurs et paysans en Pologne au Moyen Âge et dans les Temps Modernes," in Péter Gunst and Tamás Hoffmann, eds., *Grand domaine et petites exploitations en Europe au Moyen Âge et dans les Temps Modernes* (Budapest: Akadémiai Kiadó, 1982), pp. 209–227; Anderson, *Passages,* pp. 257–264; Witold Kula, *Théorie economique du système féodale* (Paris: Mouton, 1970), pp. 50–68; Ferenc Maksay, "Gutswirtschaft und Bauernlegen in Ungarn im 16. Jahrhundert," *Vierteljahrschrift für Sozial- und Wirtschaftsgeschichte* (1958), 37–61; Zsigmond P. Pach, *Die ungarische Agrarentwicklung im 16–17. Jahrhundert: Abbiegung vom westeuropäischen Entwicklungsgang* (Budapest: Akadémiai Kiadó, 1964); Vera Zimányi and Gyula Benda, "Grand domaine et petite exploitation en Hongrie: XIII$^{e}$–XVIII$^{e}$ siècles" in Gunst and Hoffmann, eds., *Grand domaine et petite exploitations,* pp. 142–153; Hartmut Harnisch and Gerhard Heitz, "Feudale Gutswirtschaft und Bauernwirtschaft in den deutschen Territorien: Eine vergleichende Analyse unter besonderer Berücksichtigung der Marktprodktion," in Gunst and Hoffmann, eds., *Grand domaine et petites exploitations,* pp. 9–32.

21. A full discussion of this problem is worked out and summarized by Anderson, *Passages,* 246–264. See also Pach, *Die ungarische Agrarentwicklung*; Johannes Nichtweiss, *Das Bauernlegen in Mecklenburg: Eine Untersuchung zur Geschichte der Bauernschaft und der zweiten Leibeigenschaft in Mecklenburg bis Beginn des 19. Jahrhunderts* (Berlin: Rütten and Loening, 1954). For Poland see Stanisław Śreniawski, *Uwlaszczenie chłopów w Polsce* [Expropriation of the Peasants in Poland] (Warsaw: Państwowe Wydawn. Naukowe, 1956); Leonid Żytkowicz, "The Peasant's Farm and the Landlord's Farm in Poland from the 16th to the Middle of the 18th Century," *Journal of European Economic History,* no. 1 (1972), 135–154.

22. For the restriction of free migration and other rights of peasantry in these countries, see György Székely, "Földesuri törekvések a jobbágyság költözési jogának felszámolására Magyarországon-Kelet-európai tipusu társadalmi folyamat az 1514 előtti évtizedekben" [East European Social Process in the Decades before 1514: Efforts of the Landlords to Liquidate the Rights of the Peasants to Move in Hungary] *Agrártörténeti Szemle* 16 (1972), 261–264. For the situation in Russia, besides Grekov, *Krest'iane na Russi,* vols. 1 and 2, see Blum, *Lord and Peasant,* pp. 106–116, 247–249, and 253–268; and D. L. Pohilevich, "Pravo," pp. 50–66.

23. For Bohemia's development, see the data and interpretations in the following studies: Graus, *Dějiny venkovského*; Alois Mika, *Poddanýlid v Čechách v první polovině 16. století* [The Obliged Peasantry in Bohemia in the 16th Century] (Prague: Czechoslovak Academy, 1960); František Matejek, *Feudálni velkostátek a poddaný na Moravě s prihlednutim k přilehlému územi Sležska a Polska* (Prague: Czechoslovak Academy, 1959); Josef Valka, *Hospodářská politika feudálního velko-*

*statku na předbělohorské Moravě* [Economic Policy of the Great Domains in Moravia After 1620] (Brno: University of Brno, 1962); Josef Petrán, *Poddaný lid v Čechách na Prahu třicetileté války* (Prague: Czechoslovak Academy, 1964); Josef Koči, "Patent a zrušení nevolnictví v českých zemích," *Československý Časopis Historický* no. 1 (1969), 69–108.

24. See Gunst, "Der ungarische Bauernaufstand," pp. 62–76; Maksay, "Gutswirtschaft unds Bauernlegen," pp. 37–61; Pach, *Die ungarische Agrarentwicklung*; Zsigmond P. Pach, "Az 1514. évi parasztfelkelés és a 'második jobágyság'" [The Peasant Uprising of 1514 and the So-Called Second Serfdom in Hungary], in *Az MTA Filozófiai és Társadalomtudományi Osztályának Közleményei* (1972), pp. 231–257; Zsigmond P. Pach, "A kelet-európai 'Gutswirtschaft' problematikájához: robotmunka és bérmunka a földesuri majoságokon a XVI–XVII. századi Magyarországon" [To the Problems of East-European "Gutswirtschaft": Socage and Paid Work on the Landlord's Demesne in Hungary in the 16th–17th Centuries], *Agrártörténeti Szemle* (1971), 1–14; János Varga, *Typen und Probleme des bäuerlichen Grundbesitzes in Ungarn, 1767–1849* (Budapest: Académiai Kiadó, 1965); Varga, *Jobbágyrendszer Magyarországon a feudalizmus kései századaiban 1556–1767* [The System of Serfdom in Hungary in the Late Feudal Ages, 1556–1767] (Budapest: Akadémiai Kiadó, 1969). For development in the eighteenth century see Varga, *Jobbágyrendszer*; Imre Wellmann, *A magyar mezőgazdaság a XVIII. században* [Hungarian Agriculture in the 18th Century] (Budapest: Akadémiai Kiadó, 1979), pp. 67–121; Péter Gunst, "Die technische Entwicklung der ungarischen Landwirtschaft und die Hindernisse dieser Entwicklung," *Zeitschrift für Agrargeschichte und Agrarsoziologie* 23:1 (1975), 59–70.

25. For the position of the Romanian principalities, see Sergiu Columbeanu, "A havasalföldi majorsági földek kérdéséhez a XVIII. században és a XIX. század első felében" [The Manorial Lands in Wallachia in the 18th and First Half of the 19th Centuries], *Agrártörténeti Szemle* 14 (1971), 296–316; Sergiu Columbeanu, *Economia domeniului feudal din Ţara Românească in secolul al XVIII-lea.* (Bucharest: Editura Academiei, 1972); V. Mihordea, *Maîtres du sol et paysans dans les Principautés Roumaines au XVIII$^e$ siècle* (Bucharest: Editura Academiei, 1971); Demir M. Dragnev, *Selskoe choziaistvo feodalnoi Moldavii: konets XVII–nachalo XIX v.* (Kishinev: Moldavian Academy of Sciences, 1975); Ilie Corfus, *Agricultura Ţării Româneşti in prima jumătate a secolului al XIX-lea.* (Bucharest: Editura Academiei, 1969); Ioana Constantinescu, "Arendarea moşiilor în Moldova pînă la Regulamentul organic," *Studii şi Materiale de Istorie Medie* (Bucharest: Editura Academiei, 1973), pp. 259–267; Demir M. Dragnev and P. V. Sovetov, "Perestroika stuktury zemklevladienia v Moldavii XV–XVIII vv.," *Istoria SSSR* no. 1 (1968), 70–92; Şerban Papacostea, *Oltenia sub stăpinirea Austriacă: 1718–1739* [Oltenia under Austrian Rule] (Bucharest: Editura Academiei, 1971); Ilie Corfus, "Dreptul de stăpînire al clăcaşilor din Ţara Româneasca asupra pămîntului defrişat în perioada destrămării feudalismului," *Studii: Revista de Istorie* 2 (1970), 341–361; Daniel Chirot, *Social Change in a Peripheral Society: The Creation of a Balkan Colony* (New York: Academic Press, 1976).

26. Juhan Kahk, and Enn Tarvel, "Large Estates and Small Holdings in Estonia from the 16th to the 19th Centuries," in Gunst and Hoffmann, eds., *Grand domaine et petites exploitations,* pp. 365–375; Jan Rutkowski, *Historie gospodarcza Polski: do 1864 r.* [An Economic History of Poland to 1864] (Warsaw: Książkai Wiezda, 1953); A. E. Tobin, *Die Agrargesetzgebung Livlands im 19. Jahrhundert,* vol. 1 (Berlin, 1899), vol. 2 (Riga, 1911); Gyula Mérei, *Magyarország története 1790–1848* [The History of Hungary, 1790–1848] (Budapest: Akadémiai Kiadó, 1982), pp. 245–250, 264–276, 324–372.

27. For Russia, see Michael Confino, *Systèmes agraires et progrés agricole: L'assolement triennal en Russie aux XVIII^e-XIX^e siècles* (Paris: Mouton, 1969), pp. 230-253.

28. For the prosperity of wool at the turn of the eighteenth to nineteenth century and its influences on agricultural cultivation and the growth of a gap in productive equipment between the peasant's and landlord's farms in Eastern Europe, see Gunst, "Die technische Entiwicklung," pp. 61–63; Gunst, *Einige Probleme,* pp. 32–33; Blum, *Lord and Peasant,* pp. 326–344, 386–413.

29. Confino, *Systèmes agraires,* pp. 37–51, 109–115.

30. For the abolition of serfdom in the Eastern European countries see Emil Niederhauser, *A jobbágyfelszabaditás Kelet-Európában* [The Abolition of Serfdom in Eastern Europe] (Budapest: Akadémiai Kiadó, 1962); Emil Neiderhauser, "A jobbágyfelszabaditás Kelet-Európában" [The Abolition of Serfdom in Eastern Europe], *Szazadok* 116 (1982), 562–576; Blum, *Lord and Peasant,* pp. 575–600; Alexander Gerschenkron, "Russia: Agrarian Policies and Industrialization, 1861–1914," in *Economic Backwardness in Historical Perspective* (Cambridge: Belknap Press of Harvard, 1962), pp. 140–248; Nikolai M. Družinin, "Die Agrarreformen der sechziger Jahre des 19. Jahrhunderts und ihr Einfluss auf das russische Dorf," in Rudolf Berthold, ed., *Studien zu den Agrarreformen des 19. Jahrhunderts in Preussen und Russland: Sonderband des Jahrbuchs für Wirtschaftsgeschichte* (Berlin Akademie-Verlag, 1978), pp. 117–288; Nichita Adăniloaie and Dan Berindei, *Reforma agrară din 1864* (Bucharest: Editura Academiei, 1964).

31. For Russia, see Blum, *Lord and Peasant,* pp. 575–600; Gerschenkron, "Russia," in *Economic Backwardness,* pp. 140–248; Ivan D. Koval'čenko, "Das Dorf des Europäischen Russlands vor der Aufhebung der Leibeigenschaft," in *Studien zu den Agrarreformen des 19. Jahrhunderts in Preussen und Russland,* pp. 295–352. For Romania, see Chirot, *Social Change,* pp. 132–145.

32. For questions of the land community, see Maksim M. Kovalevskii, *Le régime économique de la Russie* (Paris: V. Giard et E. Brière, 1898); Vadim A. Aleksandrov, *Sel'skaia obshchina v Rossii, XVII–nachalo XIX v.* (Moscow: Academy of Sciences, 1976); Sergei M. Dubrovski, "K voprosu ob obshchine v Rossii v nachale XX v.," *Ezhegodnik po agrarnoi istorii Vostochnoi Evropy* (1962); Andrei M. Anfimov and Pavel N. Zyrianov, "Nekotorye cherty evoliutsii russkoi krest'ianskoi obshciny v poreformennyi period, 1861–1914 gg.," *Istoria SSSR,* no. 4 (1980), 26–41. For the position of the Romanian peasantry, see D. B. Ionescu, *Die Agrarverfassung Rumäniens, ihre Geschichte und ihre Reform* (Leipzig, 1909);

George D. Creangă, *Grundbesitzverteilung und Bauernfrage in Rumänien* (Leipzig: Duncker and Humblot, 1907); Stahl, *Traditional Roumanian Village Communities,* pp. 217–221.

33. For Hungarian agricultural development in the second half of the nineteenth century, see Péter Gunst and László Gaál, *Animal Husbandry in Hungary in the 19th–20th Centuries* (Budapest: Akadémiai Kiadó, 1977), pp. 11–60; Laszlo Gaal and Péter Gunst, "Livestock Husbandry in Hungary from 1848 to World War I," *Agrártörténeti Szemle* Supplementum (1972), 7–48; Gunst, "Die Entwicklungstendenzen der Hektarerträge in der ungarischen Landwirtschaft zwischen 1869 und 1969; mit internationalem Vergleich," *Jahrbuch für Wirtschaftsgeschichte,* no. 3 (1974), 127–139.

34. See Péter Gunst, "The Comparative Impact of Industrialization on Western and Eastern European Agriculture in the 19th and Early 20th Centuries," *Agrártörténeti Szemle* Supplementum (1976), 15–36. For Romania's agrarian reform of 1908, see George D. Creangă, *Grundbesitzverteilung und Bauernfrage in Rumänien: Die von der Regierung im Jahr 1908 durchgeführten Agrarreformen* (Leipzig: Duncker and Humblot, 1909).

# III

## Einige Probleme der wirtschaftlichen und sozialen Entwicklung Osteuropas

Wenn wir die historische Literatur durchblättern, mögen es umfassende Arbeiten oder kleinere Studien sein, oder das Geschichtsbewußtsein unserer Zeitgenossen kennenlernen, erhalten wir ein ziemlich schematisches Bild der wirtschaftlichen und sozialen Entwicklung Osteuropas. Überall stellen wir fest, daß die wirtschaftliche und soziale Entwicklung Osteuropas im Vergleich zu Westeuropa — oder vom 19. Jahrhundert ab im Vergleich zu Nordamerika — zeitlich später einsetzte und wesentlich langsamer war. Das heißt also, diese Entwicklung war zwar zeitlich zurückgeblieben, verlief aber, was das Wesen anbetrifft, auf demselben Wege, wenn auch mit Niveauunterschieden und Strukturabweichungen. Nehmen wir diesen Standpunkt genauer in Augenschein, erhellt sogleich, daß das westeuropäische Schema nicht nur als Modell für die weitere Entwicklung angesehen wird, sondern daß man auch den zurückgelegten Weg im wesentlichen als gleich betrachtet. Dabei können wir bei weitem nicht sicher sein, daß dies eindeutig so ist. Im letzten Jahrhundert hat sich die historische Perspektive ausgeweitet. Der Horizont der Forschungen ist größer geworden, und neben den Völkern Europas sind auch die Einwohner der anderen Kontinente Gegenstand der Geschichtswissenschaft geworden, wurde auch ihnen Platz in den historischen Arbeiten gewidmet. Und nicht nur, als würde es sich dabei um Statisten handeln. Wenn wir die Dinge jetzt aus dieser Perspektive betrachten, dann bedarf unsere gesamte frühere europa-, ja westeuropazentrische Geschichtsauffassung der Revision. Wenn wir die Welt als ein Ganzes betrachten, so ist darin gerade die Entwicklung Westeuropas die eigenartige, besondere. Dem ist auch dann so, wenn wir anerkennen, daß diese westeuropäische Entwicklung in der Entwicklung der Völker der anderen Erdteile die — häufig aus Blut und Eisen bestehende — Rolle des Sauerteiges gespielt hat. Und aus dieser Perspektive betrachtet zeigt die Entwicklung Osteuropas ein weiteres Charakteristikum: Es ist der Teil der Welt, der Westeuropa als erster und am schnellsten gefolgt ist, seine technisch-wirtschaftlich-gesellschaftlichen Errungenschaften am schnellsten übernommen hat. Es lohnt sich also, wenn wir uns, zumindest skizzenhaft, mit der Entwicklung Osteuropas befassen, vor allem mit jenen spezifischen Phänomenen, die der Prozeß vor uns ausbreitet.

Es gibt mehrere Gründe dafür, daß gerade jene Faktoren im Dunkeln liegen, die die Spezifika der wirtschaftlichen und sozialen Entwicklung Osteuropas darstellen. Den Hauptgrund sehen wir darin, daß Westeuropa, das westeuropäische Modell, früher der Entwicklung der Welt derart seinen Stempel aufgedrückt hat, daß sich die Geschichtsschreibung eines jeden europäischen Volkes gezwungen sah, zu beweisen, daß seine Entwicklung auf dem gleichen Weg wie die westeuropäische verläuft oder verlaufen war. Das gilt besonders für die osteuropäischen Völker. Die Geschichtsschreibung dieser kleinen Völker war noch um die Wende vom 18. zum 19. Jahrhundert bestrebt zu beweisen, die Entwicklung dieser Völker entspreche vollkommen jener der führenden westeuropäischen Völker.

Für den folgenden Abschnitt, der die Geschichtsschreibung dieser Länder in den Jahrzehnten der Bauernbefreiung bestimmte, war bezeichnend, daß die Geschichtsschreibung der osteuropäischen Völker bereits auch die Niveau- und Zeitunterschiede erkannte. Dann erklärten sie, daß die Entwicklung der osteuropäischen Völker auf dem gleichen Wege wie jene der westeuropäischen Völker verlaufen sei, nur zeitlich später, verspätet. Das Zurückbleiben wurde gewöhnlich mit der langen Herrschaft der fremden, gewöhnlich nomadischen Eroberer erklärt — in Rußland mit den Mongolen, in Ungarn und auf dem Balkan mit den Türken. Schließlich kam die Geschichtsschreibung dieser Länder darauf, daß es sich nicht nur, ja, vielleicht nicht einmal in erster Linie darum handelte, sondern um wesentliche an der Basis der wirtschaftlichen und sozialen Entwicklung liegende Ursachen, die von vornherein den geschichtlichen Weg der Völker Osteuropas determinieren.

Auch heute können wir noch nicht sagen, daß die Geschichtsschreibung aller osteuropäischen Völker bis zu dieser Erkenntnis vorgedrungen wäre, daß sie gerade in der Aufdeckung dieser qualitativen Unterschiede ihre Aufgabe erblicken würde. Dazu haben oft auch aus dem Nationalstolz resultierende falsche Schlußfolgerungen beigetragen, daß es nämlich eine irgendwie nachteilige Unterscheidung für die Völker sein würde, wenn sich herausstellte, daß ihre historische Entwicklung nicht auf dem als klassisch geltenden westeuropäischen Weg verlaufen sei. Ähnliche Auswirkungen zeigte auch die starre und dogmatische Auslegung der marxistischen Geschichtsauffassung in den 1950er Jahren. Als Folge dieser Auffassung stellte die Geschichtsauffassung dieser Völker einseitig nur die allgemeinen Entwicklungslinien heraus, statt die spezifischen Kennzeichen aufzudecken, und zwang der Entwicklung dieser Völker ein einheitliches Schema auf, obwohl sie dies mit dem Anspruch, die Spezifika aufzudecken, in der Praxis aber dogmatisch tat. So war das z. B. mit der sehr frühen Entstehung des Feudalismus in einzelnen Balkanländern oder in den russischen Fürstentümern oder mit dem krampfhaften Erkennen der Erscheinung der „zweiten Leibeigenschaft" auch in jenen Ländern, wo es diese Erscheinung überhaupt nicht oder aus ganz anderen Gründen oder in anderer Form gegeben hatte. Wenn wir die konkreten Aussagen der Geschichtsschreibung verallgemeinern, so können wir sagen, daß sie auch heute nur dahin gelangt, festzustellen, daß Westeuropa durch seine Wirtschafts- und Außenhandelsbeziehungen wesentlich auf Osteuropa eingewirkt und dessen Entwicklung in vieler Hinsicht beeinflußt hat [1].

Wie aber sollen wir uns diesen Problemen annähern? Vielleicht ist es der einfachste Weg, kurz zu skizzieren, aus welchen Gründen sich Osteuropas Wirtschaft und Gesellschaft so anders entwickelt haben als die Westeuropas. Vielleicht wäre eine andere Formulierung exakter: Was war der Grund dafür, daß sich Westeuropas Entwicklung *im Vergleich zu den anderen Teilen der Welt* „beschleunigte", auf einen besonderen, gesonderten Weg überging, und welche Konsequenzen hatte das für Osteuropa? Diese letzte Fragestellung scheint uns am richtigsten. Um, was wir sagen wollen, nur an einem einfachen Beispiel zu demonstrieren: Die aus dem 11. bis 12. Jahrhundert stammenden Kirchenfresken in Nowgorod unterscheiden sich weder in der Technik noch in der künstlerischen Sehweise von den gleichzeitigen norditalieni-

[1] In Europa — geographisch gesehen — finden wir neben dem westlichen und dem östlichen Entwicklungstyp noch einen dritten: den des mediterranen Gebietes. Wir halten es jedoch von unserem Thema her nicht für erforderlich, dessen Besonderheiten in der vorliegenden Arbeit zu analysieren.

schen Fresken. Vergleichen wir aber die Renaissancemalerei des 16. Jahrhunderts mit der gleichzeitigen russischen Malerei, so ist der Unterschied zwischen beiden bereits riesengroß. In Rußland scheinen sich weder die Technik noch die Sehweise der Malerei weiterentwickelt zu haben, während die westeuropäische Malerei inzwischen ganze Epochen hinter sich gelassen hat. Dieses Beispiel, das sich — natürlich ohne schematische Unmittelbarkeit — auch auf den Kreis sozialer und wirtschaftlicher Erscheinungen bezieht, gibt zugleich auch eine Erklärung dafür, warum das historische Bewußtsein in erster Linie zeitliche Unterschiede fixiert. Wenn wir nur diesen zeitlichen Unterschied untersuchen, dann stellt sich die Frage derart, daß sich eigentlich die westeuropäische Entwicklung in diesen Jahrhunderten b e s c h l e u n i g t e und daß diese Beschleunigung ihr den riesigen Vorteil verschafft hat, der seitdem bezeichnend ist.

Aber auch wenn wir die Frage so stellen, ergibt sich eine weitere Frage: Wodurch war die Beschleunigung der Entwicklung Westeuropas möglich? Woraus folgte sie? Und schon sind wir beim Grundproblem: Was endlich führte zu der einmaligen Erscheinung der westeuropäischen Entwicklung? Das müssen wir zuerst beantworten, wenn wir die Spezifika der historischen Entwicklung Osteuropas darstellen wollen.

Einer der ersten Faktoren, auf den wir verweisen müssen, ist die Beziehung zwischen dem Boden und der darauf lebenden Bevölkerung. In Westeuropa war die Bevölkerung bereits zu Beginn des Mittelalters bedeutend dichter als in Osteuropa. Als Folge dessen trieb die immer dichter werdende Bevölkerung Westeuropas, die weder Seuchen noch Auswanderung für längere Zeit verringern konnten, vor allem von dem Zeitpunkt ab, da auch in Osteuropa festere staatliche Rahmen entstanden waren, mit ständig wirkender Kraft die intensiveren Formen und Methoden der Entwicklung voran, in der Landwirtschaft — anfangs vor allem dort —, aber auch in den übrigen Sektoren der Wirtschaft, und später vor allem hier. Während in Osteuropa kultivierbares Land unbeschränkt zur Verfügung stand, auch bei der Zunahme der Bevölkerung keine Schwierigkeiten bestanden, den Bevölkerungsüberschuß auf neuen Landgebieten anzusiedeln, wodurch es hier jahrhundertelang nur zur Reproduktion der alten Produktionsstruktur, nicht aber zur Reproduktion auf der erweiterten Stufenleiter zur intensiven Weiterentwicklung kam, waren die Bauern Westeuropas gezwungen, dafür zu sorgen, daß auf demselben Boden mehr Menschen ernährt werden konnten. Dieser

Z w a n g zur Intensivierung beschleunigte die Entwicklung in Westeuropa.

Bei weitem aber nicht so leicht ist zu verstehen, wodurch es möglich wurde, daß Westeuropas Völker diesen Weg der Entwicklung beschreiten konnten. Das können wir in wenigen Worten zusammenfassen als V e r s c h m e l z u n g der technisch-wirtschaftlich-sozialen (rechtlichen) Errungenschaften der antiken Welt mit den technischen, wirtschaftlichen und sozialen (rechtlichen) Errungenschaften der germanischen und keltischen Völker. Natürlich handelt es sich nicht um eine einfache Legierung, sondern darum, daß die antiken wirtschaftlich-sozialen (rechtlichen) Errungenschaften und in zweiter Linie die technischen Errungenschaften in Westeuropa, vor allem in dessen zentralen Gebieten, in Norditalien, im heutigen Frankreich, Westdeutschland, im Gebiet von Belgien, Holland, Dänemark und zum Teil in England im wesentlichen das auf dem gemeinsamen Bodeneigentum basierende System der germanisch-keltischen Welt überwanden [2].

Es ist nicht unsere Aufgabe, an dieser Stelle zu zeigen, wie beim Zusammenbruch der antiken Formen durch Wiederaufleben der Naturalwirtschaft, der Selbstversorgung im Römischen Reich die Einrichtung des Kolonats entstand und wie im Westen des Reiches aus den coloni, den Sklaven und aus den wenigen freien Bauern im Verlaufe weniger Jahrhunderte die feudale Leibeigenschaft hervorging. Es genügt zu erwähnen, daß die Triebkräfte der Entwicklung die aus den römischen Villen gebildeten feudalen Gutswirtschaften waren; sie verbreiteten die neue Produktionstechnik — z. B. den schweren Pflug — ebenso wie die neue Wirtschaftsordnung der Gesellschaft — Hufensystem, Leibeigenschaft. Vom 6. Jahrhundert ab entwickeln sich Leibeigenschaft und Hufensy-

---

[2] In anderen Gebieten Westeuropas, wohin die römische Eroberung nicht reichte, blieb selbstverständlich das System der Dorfgemeinschaft so lange bestehen, bis es von den militärischen Eroberungen hinweggefegt wurde. Auch in England, wo es römische Elemente gab, verbreitete die normannische Eroberung das westeuropäische System und machte es vorherrschend. In Irland, Schottland, Wales und auch in Norwegen blieb die auf der Dorfgemeinschaft basierende Gesellschaft bestehen, bis sie von den englischen oder dänischen feudalen Heeren gestürzt wurde. Das System der Dorfgemeinschaft wurde in Irland von der englischen Eroberung beseitigt, die die Gemeinschaftsfelder in das Eigentum des englischen Staates überführte. In Schottland, wo die Veränderung aus historischen Gründen nicht so drastisch war, blieb sie in den Dörfern des nördlichen Hochlandes bis zum Beginn des 19. Jahrhunderts zurück. Auch in Norwegen brach erst die Eroberung durch die Dänen diesem System das Rückgrat.

stem immer mehr, im 8. bis 10. Jahrhundert war das Bauerndorf mit seiner neuen Siedlungs-, Wirtschafts- und Gesellschaftsordnung in Westeuropa bereits vorherrschend geworden. Das alles basierte bereits auf den von der christlichen Kirche unterstützten siegreichen Prinzipien vom Privateigentum. Dieser im Verlaufe einer mehrhundertjährigen Entwicklung errungene Sieg des Prinzips vom Privateigentum machte es überall im Westen Europas möglich, daß es, als die Bevölkerungszunahme den Punkt erreicht hatte, daß die Menschen auf dem vorhandenen Boden nur durch intensive Produktion ernährt werden konnten, diese freie Bahn erhielt.

Die Produzenten wurden nämlich durch die Geltendmachung des Privateigentums auch einzeln an der Ausweitung der Produktion interessiert. Das aus der Ausweitung der Produktion resultierende Mehrprodukt — oder zumindest ein großer Teil — blieb in ihrem Besitz. In der Landwirtschaft hatte das ursprüngliche System der Dorfgemeinschaft bereits einer Form Platz gemacht, in der das Bewirtschaftungssystem durch den Flurzwang noch zahlreiche Gemeinschaftszüge an sich trug, die Früchte des Bodens bereits in das Eigentum der einzelnen Familien gelangten und auch das Dienstleistungssystem auf dem einzelnen Produzenten und nicht auf der Gemeinschaft als Steuereinheit beruhte. Das war eine riesige Kraft bei der Ausweitung der Produktion, und sie machte die zunehmende Nutzung der antiken und germanischen Errungenschaften der Technik und Produktion, dann der darauf aufbauenden technischen Neuerungen möglich. Der christliche Glaube bzw. dessen römische Form sowie die Durchsetzung der Praktizierung des römischen Rechts garantierten das Privateigentum auch in der Gesellschaft und in deren Rechtssystem.

Dieses Prinzip und System des Privateigentums aber herrschte nicht in anderen Teilen der Welt, so auch nicht in Osteuropa. Selbst innerhalb des Römischen Reiches kam es nur in der Westhälfte zur Geltung, in den griechischen Stadtstaaten, in Italien, in Gallien usw. In den asiatischen Gebieten, ja selbst auf dem Balkan setzte es sich dagegen nicht überall durch. Bezeichnend ist, daß die griechischen Kolonialstädte, die mit dem griechischen Bevölkerungsüberschuß zusammen auch die griechische Gesellschaftsordnung exportierten, diese Gesellschaftsordnung nur dort durchsetzen und erhalten konnten, wo die Zahl der Ureinwohner nicht wesentlich größer war als die der Siedler. Im Osten Nordafrikas, in Kleinasien oder woanders, wo sich die griechischen Kolonien als einsame Inseln aus dem riesigen Meer der örtlichen Bevölkerung erhoben, gelang das nirgends, und während in den Kolonialstädten selbst die griechischen Gesellschaftsformen lebten, blieb in den Dörfern die frühere Form des Bodeneigentums und die darauf aufbauende Gesellschaft unverändert. Die Kolonialstädte waren unfähig, ihre Umgebung umzuformen; im Gegenteil, in den hellenistischen Reichen und später in den asiatischen und afrikanischen Gebieten des Römischen Reiches formten sie sich selbst um. So blieb überall auch weiterhin die örtliche Form des Bodeneigentums erhalten, das die römischen Eroberer achteten.

Die Spaltung der christlichen Kirche zeigt eigentlich die Trennlinie an. Die orthodoxe Kirche verbreitete sich überall in den Gebieten, wo die östliche Form des Bodeneigentums herrschte. Dafür kann es nicht nur ausschließlich geographische Gründe geben oder aber die Tatsache, daß die griechische Kirche in den entsprechenden Gebieten Osteuropas das Christentum verbreitete. Die Rolle der Kirche in der politisch-gesellschaftlichen Struktur dieser Länder wich ebenfalls wesentlich von jener der Kirche in Westeuropa ab. Die östliche christliche Kirche spielte überall gegenüber dem Staat und den ihn vertretenden Herrschern eine untergeordnete Rolle (und zwar ähnlich den Religionen des alten Orients, wenn auch nicht völlig gleich), eine Rolle bei der Erhaltung der despotischen Macht. Nie hat sie sich eine Stellung erkämpft wie die westliche Kirche. Es würde sich lohnen, die sich in den Kirchenlehren zeigenden Gründe eingehender zu untersuchen, wie es ein ähnlich spannendes Thema wäre, aufzudecken, ob und — wenn ja — welche Rolle die Kirchenspaltung, die Verselbständigung der westlichen Kirche und ihre zum Teil von den östlichen abweichenden Lehren bei der Entstehung der Spezifika der westeuropäischen Entwicklung gespielt haben [3].

Es handelt sich um sehr wesentliche Unterschiede, die es lohnt, eingehender zu untersuchen. Die früheren Zivilisationen in Asien und Nordafrika und die Gesellschaft der indogermanischen Völker in Asien und in Europa von Indien bis Irland beruhten alle auf dem Gemeineigentum am Boden. Die konkrete Erscheinungsform dieser Eigentumsformen war, daß die über den kleinen Dorfgemeinschaften stehenden, zusammenfassenden Einheiten, d. h. die Staatsmacht, die einzelnen Herrscher als al-

---

[3] Auffallend ist auch, daß auf dem Gebiet der orthodoxen Kirche überall der Protestantismus, die Reformationen fehlen, was auf eine andere gesellschaftliche Rolle der Kirche in diesen Gebieten hindeutet.

leiniger Eigentümer des Bodens erschienen. Alles Land gehörte dem Herrscher; die den Boden nutzenden Bauern besaßen ihn nicht als einzelne, sondern als Dorfgemeinschaft. Grob ausgedrückt, bildete das lokkere Konglomerat der Dorfgemeinschaften den Staat. Die Dorfgemeinschaft als kleinste Steuer- und Verwaltungseinheit garantierte dem Staat die Steuer, der seine Funktionen aus den eingehenden Steuern versah, die für die Produktion unumgänglich notwendigen Einrichtungen (Bewässerungsanlagen usw.), das Heer, den Beamten- und den kirchlichen Apparat unterhielt. Neben dem als Bodeneigentumsrecht des Herrschers erscheinenden gemeinschaftlichen Bodeneigentum ist die charakteristische Eigenschaft des Systems, daß hier eigentlich die Dorfgemeinschaft dem Staat gegenüberstand, der produzierende Mensch war uninteressant. Für die in den autarken Dorfgemeinschaften produzierenden Menschen existierte die Außenwelt nur insofern, als sie auf diese Gemeinschaft, in der sie lebten, einwirkte. Die völlige Isolierung dieser Dorfgemeinschaften — Industrie- und Handelszentren gab es nicht, die größeren Siedlungen waren lediglich Verwaltungs- und Militärzentren — war die Grundlage des despotischen Systems. Das erklärt zum großen Teil auch die außergewöhnlich lockere Fügung dieser Reiche, denn die Dorfgemeinschaft ist, wenn sie ihre Steuern bezahlt und die staatliche Verwaltung dafür die öffentlichen Einrichtungen unterhält, politischen Veränderungen im Staate gegenüber vollkommen gleichgültig. Dasselbe aber garantierte auch den sehr dauerhaften Bestand der Dorfgemeinschaften. Sie wurden von den entscheidenden Veränderungen im politischen Leben, als deren Folge Reiche untergingen oder neue entstanden, kaum berührt. Gemessen an den Gebieten, wo nicht diese Gesellschafts- und Produktionsordnung herrschte, waren die Gegenden, in denen diese Struktur dominierte, unverhältnismäßig groß: vom Mittelmeerbecken, von der Balkanhalbinsel bis nach Indien, China und Japan, im ganzen eurasischen Kontinent und in Afrika [4]. Die griechische Zivilisation hatte

---

[4] Den Fragen der Dorfgemeinschaft und des darauf basierenden Despotismus ist eine umfangreiche Literatur gewidmet. Hier zählen wir bloß die Arbeiten auf, die für uns außer den alten, schon als klassisch geltenden Werken von Haxthausen, Kovalewski, Maine usw. am nützlichsten waren: K. Polanyi: Primitive, Archaic and Modern Economics. Garden City, N. Y. 1968; K. Polanyi: Dahomey and the Slave Trade. An Analysis of an Archaic Economy. Seattle 1966; K. Polanyi: The Greet Transformation, Boston 1968; E. R. Wolf: Peasants. Englewood Cliffs, Prentice Hall 1969 — Foundations of Modern Anthropology Series —; M. Godelier: Sur les sociétés precapitalistes. Paris 1970; H. Mendras:

zwar einen Teil des Gebiets — durch die Feldzüge Alexanders d. Großen — unterworfen, aber denken wir nicht, daß dadurch die Struktur dieser Gesellschaften verändert worden wäre. In den Ostprovinzen des Römischen Reiches war dieses System ebenso bestehen geblieben, wie es auch früher in den Reichen der Perser und Meder oder Hethiter bestanden hatte.

Die griechische Gesellschaft, die als erste das Privateigentum am Boden eingeführt hat, dann die römische und die westeuropäischen Gesellschaften nach der Völkerwanderung, unterschieden sich grundlegend von dieser allgemein als orientalisch bezeichneten Gesellschaftsstruktur [5]. Die in der Westhälfte des Römischen Reiches auf dem Privateigentum am Boden basierende Gesellschaftsstruktur konnten die Germanen, bei denen ebenfalls das Gemeineigentum am Boden herrschte, nicht verändern, sie übernahmen es zumindest für die Ackerfelder. Für die Weiden und den Wald behielten sie ihr eigenes gemeinschaftliches Eigentum bei. Was hier aus der Wechselwirkung dieser Strukturen entstand, das feudale Westeuropa, bedeutete überall die vollkommene Aufhebung des asiatischen Systems der Dorfgemeinschaft. Hier besaß der Bauer, wenn auch ohne Zweifel die Ordnung der gemeinsamen Flurnutzung gegeben war, das Land als einzelner und stand seinem Herrn als einzelner gegenüber, trug die Leistungen oder einen großen Teil derselben als einzelner ab und daraus folgte, daß auch seine Wirtschäftsführung ihm selbst zugute kam [6]. Der Umstand, daß er der Eigen-

---

Sociétés Paysannes. Paris 1976; A. V. TSCHAJANOW: Die Lehre von der bäuerlichen Wirtschaft. Berlin 1923; Peasants and Peasant Societies. Hrsg. von T. SHANIN. 1971; Peasant Society. A Reader. Hrsg. von J. M. POTTER, M. N. DIAZ, G. M. FOSTER. Boston 1967; K. A. WITTFOGEL: Oriental Despotism. New Haven 1965; U. A. KRASNOW: Rannee zemledelie i zhivotnovodstvo v lesnoi polose vostochnoi Evropi (Früher Ackerbau und Viehzucht in der Waldzone Osteuropas). Moskau 1971; R. E. F. SMITH: The Origins of Farming in Russia. Paris 1959; E. BALAZS: La propriété foncière en Chine. Band II. der Atti del Primo Convegno Internazionale di Diritto Agrario, Mailand 1955; J. L. BUCK: Land Utilization in China. 1—3. Chicago 1937; B. H. BADEN-POWELL: The Indian Village Community. London 1896; B. H. BADEN-POWELL: The Land Systems of British India. 1—3. Oxford 1896.

[5] F. TÖKEI: Az ázsiai termelési mód kérdéséhez (Zur Frage der asiatischen Produktionsweise). Budapest 1975; F. TÖKEI: A társadalmi formák elméletéhez (Zur Theorie der Gesellschaftsformen). Budapest 1968; F. TÖKEI: Antikvitás és feudalizmus (Antiquität und Feudalismus). Budapest 1969.

[6] Eine gute Beschreibung der Dorfgemeinschaft westeuropäischen Typs: K. S. BADER: Rechtsformen und Schichten der Liegenschaftsnutzung im mittelalterlichen Dorf. Wien 1973.

tümer des größten Teils der Ergebnisse der Produktionsausweitung blieb, spornte ihn zu immer neuen Kraftanstrengungen an, was letztenendes der Motor der westeuropäischen Entwicklung wurde. Einer der Hauptunterschiede der beiden Systeme besteht darin, daß die westeuropäischen Gesellschaften d y n a m i s c h waren.

Das östliche System der Dorfgemeinschaften aber, auch ihre slawische Variante und der ganze Aufbau der darauf basierenden Gesellschaft, hatten die S t a t i k der Wirtschaft und Gesellschaft zur Folge, waren für eine intensive Entwicklung der Produktion nicht günstig. Der Eigentümer des Bodens war hier in Gestalt des despotischen Herrschers eigentlich der Staat, die einzelnen Dorfgemeinschaften waren die steuerzahlenden Einheiten, die die Steuern der sie bildenden Bauern — bei kollektiver Verantwortung — dem Staat garantierten. In diesem System zog derjenige den kürzeren, der mehr produzierte, und das ist vor allem die Erklärung dafür, warum überall in diesen Kulturen, von Ägypten bis China, von Vorderasien bis Osteuropa, im Verlaufe der Jahrtausende nur das jeweilige Niveau der Produktion gehalten, die Produktion aber nicht wesentlich ausgeweitet, nicht intensiviert wurde. Denn auch hier, in den größten Teilen Osteuropas, bestand dieses System des Bodeneigentums. Wenn wir die russische Chronik lesen, erhalten wir ein charakteristisches Bild vom Verhältnis zwischen den die Staatsmacht verkörpernden Fürsten und den einzelnen Dorfgemeinschaften, die von den Fürsten auf die primitivste Weise durch die Steuereintreiber ausgebeutet wurden.

Das ist auch die Erklärung dafür, warum sich die Struktur der Feudalgesellschaft in Osteuropa anders entwickelt hat als in Westeuropa. In Westeuropa ermöglichte die Überhandnahme der Praktizierung des Römischen Rechts, der relativ frühe Zerfall des Systems des Bodenbesitzes der Dorfgemeinschaft, daß die ganze Gesellschaft vom Lehenswesen durchzogen wurde, während in Osteuropa überall die außergewöhnlich starke Zentralmacht erhalten blieb — unter den osteuropäischen Staaten war selbst in Ungarn die Staatsorganisation viel einheitlicher als in Westeuropa —, von der der gesamte Adel unmittelbar abhing und die sich deshalb stets als stärker erwies als jener. Die Gliederung der Gesellschaft konnte deshalb nicht so tief, ihre rechtlichen Verhältnisse konnten nicht so kompliziert sein wie in Westeuropa. In den riesigen Gebieten Osteuropas war der Feudaladel fast bis zum Schluß eine Art Beamten-Militär-Adel, der seine Güter vielerorts auch Jahrhunderte hindurch nicht erblich machen konnte und deshalb dem Herrscher sehr entschieden untergeordnet blieb.

Natürlich können wir nicht sagen, daß das System der Dorfgemeinschaften in Osteuropa in der gleichen Form aufgebaut war wie überall in Asien. Wir haben hier keine Möglichkeit, eingehender auf die Unterschiede einzugehen, aber das ist auch gar nicht nötig. Das System der auf den Dorfgemeinschaften basierenden Gesellschaften war bei weitem nicht überall gleich in Europa. Es ist ein außergewöhnlich spannendes Thema und eigentlich bis zum heutigen Tage noch nicht überzeugend aufgedeckt, woraus sich erklärt, daß dieses System bei dem einen Volk in einer despotischen, beim anderen in einer demokratischen Herrschaftsform auftritt. Klar ist, daß dort, wo bedeutende Zivilisationen entstanden waren (Ägypten, Mesopotamien, China, Indien usw.), die Unterhaltung des die Existenzgrundlage bildenden Bewässerungssystems eine zentralisierte Staatsmacht erforderte, die nur in der Form der Despotie wirksam sein konnte. Anders war die Lage bei den germanischen, keltischen oder slawischen Völkern, wo auf das System der Dorfgemeinschaft sowohl das despotische wie auch das demokratische System aufbauen konnten. An einigen Stellen lebten die Dorfgemeinschaften unabhängig voneinander, völlig abgeschlossen voneinander. Auch die einzelnen Familien produzierten mehr oder weniger abgesondert, was nicht ausschließt, daß nicht gewisse Arbeiten für den Bedarf der Gemeinschaft oder als Reserve erforderlich waren; oder sie konnten die Arbeiten auch gemeinsam durchführen, wobei auch die Einrichtung der Vorgesetzten der Gemeinschaft demokratischen oder patriarchalisch-despotischen Charakter haben konnte. Die völlige Isolierung der einzelnen Dorfgemeinschaften ist die natürliche Grundlage des despotischen, in der Form der orientalischen Willkür auftretenden Herrschaftssystems. Bei den slawischen Stämmen erschien dieses despotische System — zu Beginn der Geschichte der patriarchalische Charakter der Vorstandschaft der Dorfgemeinschaft, später der Despotismus des Herrschers —, bei den Kelten oder Germanen und einzelnen nomadischen Hirtenvölkern dagegen die demokratische Form. Aber die konkreten Gründe der Unterschiede zwischen den Herrschaftssystemen sind auch heute noch nicht aufgedeckt.

Wichtig vom Gesichtspunkt unseres Themas her ist, daß in Osteuropa die östliche Form des Bodeneigentums, die auf der kollektiven Verantwortung der Dorfgemeinschaften aufgebaute despotische Herrschaftsform, das wirtschaftliche und rechtliche System der darauf aufbauenden gesamten Gesellschaft von Anfang an — wir können sagen — der Gegensatz der Entwicklung des westeuropäischen Typs war, eine sie auf jeden Fall ausschließende Form. Klar ist auch, daß in einem Herrschaftssystem, in dem die Entwicklung des wirtschaftlich-gesellschaftlichen Gefüges außergewöhnlich langsam war, jede Modifizierung desselben, zumindest aber bis zu Zerschlagung des die Grundlage bildenden Systems der Dorfgemeinschaften, nur durch den Staatsapparat, d. h., durch Reformen von oben geschehen konnte [7]. Das war überall dort gesetzmäßig, wo die auf den Dorfgemeinschaften aufbauenden Staatseinheiten im Verlaufe der Geschichte dazu gezwungen waren. So geschah das auch in Osteuropa. Der Zwang der Übernahme, das oft gerade mit entgegengesetzten Bestrebungen vermischte Endergebnis, führte dazu, daß wir ganze historische Epochen hindurch auf Äußerlichkeiten der Übernahme stoßen, daß sie nicht die ganze Gesellschaft erfassen. Diese Staaten übernahmen von Zeit zu Zeit vom Westen einzelne Termini des Rechts, verstanden aber im täglichen Leben etwas anderes darunter. Sie übernahmen auch einzelne technische Begriffe, diese spielten in der Wirtschaft aber eine andere Rolle. Mit einem Wort, die wirtschaftlich-gesellschaftliche Entwicklung beruhte auf anderen Grundlagen, und das konnte nur außergewöhnlich schwer und im Verlaufe langer Zeiträume geändert werden. Wir möchten jedoch hervorheben: nicht weil hier die asiatische Form des Bodeneigentums herrschte, sondern vor allem deshalb, weil hier diese Form nicht durch die antike Tradition verändert worden war wie in Westeuropa. Das Christentum verbreitete sich auch hier, wenn auch später als in Westeuropa, und auch die Praktizierung des römischen Rechts wurde üblich. Unter anderem auch aus diesem Grunde behauptet die Geschichtsschreibung, daß die Entwicklung Osteuropas verspätet der Westeuropas folgt. Aber die Unterschiede in der Entwicklung dürfen wir nicht oder nicht nur in erster

---

[7] Wir können auch nicht sagen, daß die herrschende Klasse an der Verwirklichung solcher Reformen teilnahm, denn die Mitglieder dieser Klasse waren in ihrer Person auch selbst dem Herrscher ausgeliefert, und der Staatsapparat mußte zur Verwirklichung der Reformen gewöhnlich den konservativen Widerstand ihrer zahlenmäßigen Mehrheit brechen. Es genügt, auf Iwan des Schrecklichen oder Peter des Großen Reformen und auf die Verwirklichung der Bauernbefreiung in Rußland und in Rumänien zu verweisen. Bis zu einem gewissen Punkt blieben auch die Dorfgemeinschaften den Veränderungen gegenüber gleichgültig.

Linie in der zeitlichen Verschiebung suchen. Auf dem riesigen Gebiet Osteuropas gab es auch nicht die geringsten Überreste der antiken Tradition, die Gesellschaft wurde hier von der despotischen Form des Systems der Dorfgemeinschaften gebildet, es war kein so wesentlicher Faktor des Fortlebens und Einflusses erhalten geblieben wie die Bevölkerung, auch nicht der gesellschaftliche Mechanismus, der in Westeuropa diese Traditionen weitergab, selbst in der Völkerwanderungszeit. Deshalb wirkte das Christentum, das römische Rechtssystem im größten Teil Osteuropas lange Zeit nur an der Oberfläche und veränderte das gesellschaftlich-wirtschaftliche System nur formal — oft nicht einmal das —, bildete geradezu eine äußere Hülle, in welcher die auf den Dorfgemeinschaften aufgebaute despotische Herrschaftsstruktur unverändert blieb.

Und wir müssen auch hervorheben: Die Intensivierung der Produktion durch Verschmelzung der antiken Traditionen mit den Errungenschaften der germanischen Welt erfolgte nicht nur in der Landwirtschaft, sondern auf allen Gebieten des wirtschaftlichen Lebens. Und das ist von der Landwirtschaft her gesehen außergewöhnlich wichtig, denn deren Entwicklung hängt von der Entwicklung in anderen Wirtschaftssektoren ab. Es ist leicht einzusehen, daß die Entwicklung der Industrie, die Entstehung und das Anwachsen der Städte, das Ausscheiden eines Teiles der Bevölkerung aus der Landwirtschaft einen immer größeren Markt für landwirtschaftliche Produkte schuf, dessen Entwicklung jetzt, abgesehen von der Bevölkerungszunahme, auch durch den Umstand beschleunigt wurde, daß der Anteil der Produzenten an der Gesamtbevölkerung relativ sank, natürlich nicht in dem Maße wie dann im 19. und 20. Jahrhundert, dennoch aber in immer größerem Tempo. In Westeuropa lösten sich die Städte relativ schnell von der Landwirtschaft und wurden zunächst zu Zentren des Handels, des Warenaustausches und dann der industriellen Produktion. In einzelnen Gegenden brach die industrielle Produktion auch in die Landwirtschaft ein und wurde eine der Existenzformen eines großen Teils der bäuerlichen Bevölkerung.

Der relative Bodenreichtum und das System der Dorfgemeinschaften sowie das völlige Fehlen der antiken Traditionen hatten zusammen zur Folge, daß Osteuropas Entwicklung auf anderen Wegen und viel langsamer voranging als die Westeuropas. Die Produktion auszuweiten, zu intensivieren, bestand weder eine Notwendigkeit noch eine Möglichkeit, denn der unbeschränkt scheinende Bodenreichtum, der vor allem für das

Gebiet des europäischen Rußland bezeichnend war, machte es möglich, daß sich die anwachsende Bevölkerung ihre Existenz ohne Weiterentwicklung der Produktionstechnik und Produktionsorganisation, d. h. in der überlieferten Form, sichern konnte. Sehr bezeichnend ist, daß im europäischen Rußland bis zur Mitte des 19. Jahrhunderts vornehmlich die Zweifelderwirtschaft verbreitet war, nur stellenweise die Dreifelderwirtschaft, dort, wo seit dem Beginn des 19. Jahrhunderts die Bevölkerung stärker zugenommen hatte [8]. Der Bodenreichtum sicherte die Existenz der Bevölkerung auch im Zweifeldersystem. Dementsprechend genügten auch primitive Arbeitsgeräte zur Bewirtschaftung des Bodens, ja, auf den riesigen Bodenflächen konnte auch ohne jedes Düngen geerntet werden, bestand doch die Möglichkeit, nach einigen Jahren neues Land zu umbrechen und die früher bewirtschafteten Felder ruhen zu lassen. Im 18. Jahrhundert ist in Westeuropa schon fast überall die Dreifelderwirtschaft üblich. Vielerorts aber — in England, Holland, Belgien, Nordfrankreich und Norditalien — war auch die Wechselwirtschaft üblich, vor allem in der Umgebung der großen Städte, was die Gewähr schuf, die Produktion zu steigern und Feldfutteranbau als Basis für die Viehzucht zu betreiben. Zu eben dieser Zeit überwog in Rußland, ja in fast ganz Osteuropa noch die Zweifelderwirtschaft, die mancherorts — in sehr weit ausgedehnten Gebieten! — noch von der uralten Praxis des Brachenwechsels unterbrochen wurde. In der zweiten Hälfte des 19. Jahrhunderts dominiert in Westeuropa schon überall die moderne Wechselwirtschaft, sind Kunstdünger, zahlreiche neue Geräte und Maschinen verbreitet. In Osteuropa dagegen finden wir die vielhundertjährige, primitive Produktionspraxis unverändert, die Zwei- oder Dreifelderwirtschaft, die selbstangefertigten Geräte, kaum Meliorationen, das fast völlige Fehlen des Kunstdüngers. In diesen Gebieten sind die jeweils modernen Wirtschaftsmethoden, Geräte, die neuen Pflanzen- und Tierrassen nur in den größten Betrieben verbreitet, die genügend Kapital hatten. Aber selbst in diesen gutsherrlichen Allodien wurden nicht alle im Westen entwickelten technischen Errungenschaften angewandt, so

---

[8] Für die Bodennutzungssysteme in Osteuropa, besonders in Rußland, siehe die bisher erschienenen Bände des Ezhegodnik po agrarnoi istorii Vostocnoi Evropi (Jahrbuch für Agrargeschichte Osteuropas). Der erste Band ist 1959 erschienen. In den seitdem regelmäßig erschienenen Bänden wurden sehr reichhaltige Studien auch über diese Frage veröffentlicht.

bestand z. B. für Erntemaschinen wegen der inzwischen eingetretenen Überbevölkerung auf dem Lande überhaupt kein Bedarf [9].

In Osteuropa verlief nämlich — nicht nur im 18. bis 20. Jahrhundert, noch eher im Mittelalter — die Entwicklung der nichtagrarischen Sektoren außergewöhnlich langsam. Jahrtausende hindurch war die Stadt nichts anderes als eine größere Ansiedlung ohne jede wirtschaftliche und gesellschaftliche Funktion einer Stadt als solcher. Es ist außergewöhnlich wichtig, sich darüber im klaren zu sein, daß die in den historischen Quellen vorkommenden Städte in diesen Jahrhunderten in Osteuropa nicht die gesellschaftlich-wirtschaftliche Rolle spielten wie in Westeuropa. Dort entwickelten sich die Städte, ganz gleich, ob es sich um solche antiker Herkunft handelte, in denen das Leben mehr oder weniger erhalten geblieben war oder aber um neue Gründungen, aus anfänglich königlichen, grundherrlichen oder kirchlichen Verwaltungszentren schnell zu Handelsplätzen, dann zu Industriezentren, die nicht nur Knotenpunkte des Fernhandels waren, sondern auch Mittelpunkte des Produktenaustausches innerhalb der einzelnen Bezirke wurden, später dann zu Siedlungen mit Industriecharakter. Von Stadt sprechen wir im allgemeinen in Westeuropa nur dann, wenn aus den Verwaltungszentren Siedlungen entstanden sind, die bereits diese Aufgabe versehen. Entsprechend der besonderen Rolle innerhalb der Arbeitsteilung bildeten die Einwohner der Städte innerhalb der feudalen Gesellschaft ihren eigenen Stand, das Bürgertum. Die Städte Osteuropas bewahrten noch Jahrhunderte nach ihrer Entstehung ihren ursprünglichen Charakter. Der konnte sehr unterschiedlich sein. Die ersten, zu größeren Städten gewordenen Siedlungen waren die Knotenpunkte des durch den Kontinent führenden Fernhandels. Dieser Charakter veränderte sich eigentlich nicht. Die Größe des kontinentalen Fernhandels veränderte sich auch durch die Entdeckungen nicht — wie z. B. auch der Venedigs oder Genuas nicht. Nach einigen Jahrzehnten erwies sich dieser Handel lediglich, verglichen mit dem an den Küsten des Atlantischen Ozeans entstehenden Handel, als zweitrangig. Der technische Fortschritt, die

[9] Für diese Situation ist der Fall des unter den osteuropäischen am weitesten entwickelten Landes, Ungarn, sehr charakteristisch. Über das damalige Produktionsniveau der ungarischen Landwirtschaft siehe P. Gunst: Die technische Entwicklung der ungarischen Landwirtschaft und die Hindernisse dieser Entwicklung — vom Ende des 18. Jahrhunderts bis 1945. Zeitschrift für Agrargeschichte und Agrarsoziologie 1975.

Entwicklung der Schiffahrt und später die Eisenbahnen verlagerten dann endgültig die Kraftlinien des Welthandels. Bis dahin aber blieb die Rolle dieser Städte als Mittelpunkt des Fernhandels bestehen.

Die Einwohnerschaft dieser Städte aber setzte sich nicht in erster Linie aus der ansässigen Bevölkerung zusammen, sondern aus den Kaufleuten, die Handel trieben. Das waren z. B. in Rußland nicht Russen, sondern Waräger, Araber usw., auf dem Balkan Griechen, Juden, Armenier usw., und sie blieben es auch Jahrhunderte hindurch [10].

Den anderen Typ der osteuropäischen Städte bilden die Militär- oder Verwaltungszentren. Der Herrscher und sein Gefolge, ein größerer Feudalherr und seine Gefolgschaft, ein kirchliches Zentrum oder größere oder kleinere Befestigungen bildeten den Kern dieser Städte, die lange Zeit dadurch gekennzeichnet wurden, daß sie sehr gestaltungsfähig waren. Diese „Städte" bestanden anfangs nicht aus festen Gebäuden, sondern waren lediglich befestigte Zeltlager, nur langsam kristallisierten sich aus ihnen die späteren festen Siedlungen heraus. Sie blieben bis zum 19. Jahrhundert Verwaltungs- oder Militärzentren, dementsprechend war auch die Zusammensetzung ihrer Bewohner. Neben einer gewissen Handels- und Industrietätigkeit — vor allem Dienstleistungsgewerbe — hatte sich im Verlaufe der Jahrhunderte nur soviel verändert, daß die Einwohner, die anfangs vornehmlich aus dem Gefolge und den Haushalten des Fürsten oder der Militärgarnisonen bestanden hatten, mit der Zeit von der modernen Beamtenschicht gebildet wurden [11].

Den dritten Typus in Osteuropa bilden die — eigentlich strittigerweise — als Städte bezeichneten Siedlungen, die lediglich riesig angewachsene Dörfer waren. Es scheint, daß deren Entstehen eng mit der landwirt-

[10] Am charakteristischsten sind die russischen Städte dafür. A. J. NIKITSKI: Istoria ekonomitscheskojo bita Velikogo Nowgoroda (Wirtschaftsgeschichte Großnowgorods). Moskau 1893; K. N. SERBINA: Otscherki iz sozialno-ekonomitscheskoi istorii russkogo goroda (Skizzen aus der Sozial- und Wirtschaftsgeschichte der russischen Stadt). Moskau 1951; M. V. TICHOMIROV: Drevneruskie goroda (Altrussische Städte). Moskau 1956; Zur balkanischen Stadtentwicklung: M. MIRKOVIĆ: Ekonomoska historija Jugoslavije (Wirtschaftsgeschichte Jugoslawiens). Zagreb 1958; La ville balcanique XV$^{e}$—XIX$^{e}$ siècles. Hrsg. von N. TODOROV. Sofia 1970. B. TZVETKOWA: Proutschvania na gradskoto stopanstvo prez XV—XVI vek. (Studien zur Wirtschaft der Städte im 15. bis 16. Jahrhundert). Sofia 1972; Zur ungarischen Stadtentwicklung: E. FÜGEDI: La formation des villes et les odres mediants en Hongrie. Annales ESC 1970; E. FÜGEDI: Középkori mágyar városprivilégiumok (Mittelalterliche Städteprivilegien in Ungarn). In: Tanulmányok Budapest múltjából 1961.

[11] Siehe die in der Anmerkung 10 angegebene Literatur.

schaftlichen Warenproduktion, vor allem mit dem Fernhandel, besonders aber mit der großen Entfaltung der warenproduzierenden Viehzucht zusammenhing. Von den großen Weiden Osteuropas — von Südskandinavien über Polen, die Ukraine und Ungarn bis zur Moldau — begann bereits früh, vom 14. Jahrhundert an, ein breit angelegter Rinderexport, vor allem in die Städte Nord- und Süddeutschlands und nach Norditalien. Zu dieser Zeit entstanden jene „Städte", von denen hier die Rede ist, eigentlich „Marktflecken", deren Einwohner von der Landwirtschaft lebten, vor allem Viehzucht trieben. Hier wechselte das Rind, Hauptwarenartikel der Gebiete, seinen Herrn. Später wurde dann in den Marktflecken auch etwas Industrie getrieben, aber die meisten Handwerker gaben fast bis zur Mitte des 20. Jahrhunderts die landwirtschaftliche Produktion nicht auf, das Handwerk war nur eine Ergänzungsbeschäftigung. In rechtlicher Hinsicht waren die Einwohner fast ausnahmslos überall abhängige Bauern. Ihre Lage unterschied sich von jener der abhängigen Bauern in den Dörfern nur insofern, als sie auf dem Gebiet der Verwaltung eine gewisse Selbständigkeit genossen, aber keinerlei rechtlichen oder gesellschaftlichen Status, wie er für das westeuropäische Bürgertum charakteristisch war. Ihre wirtschaftlich-gesellschaftliche Rolle war anders. Der Marktflecken war keine Stadt und hatte das Niveau einer Stadt nicht aus eigener Initiative, aus eigenem Antrieb erreicht — wenn er es überhaupt erreicht hatte. Die Konjunktur der Exportviehzucht hatte zu ihrer Entstehung geführt, zu ihrer Blüte und erhielt sie, solange ihre Sammel- und Verteilerrolle erforderlich war. Mit dem Rückgang des Viehexports stockte auch ihre Entwicklung. Eine andere Frage ist, ob mit dem Beginn der modernen Wirtschaftsentwicklung, mit dem Erscheinen der modernen Industrie auch in Osteuropa der eine oder andere Marktflecken zum Knotenpunkt dieser neuen Entwicklung werden konnte. Aber selbst dann bewahrte er noch lange Zeit seinen Agrarcharakter [12].

---

[12] Über diesen, für Osteuropa so charakteristischen Siedlungstyp enthält eine Menge von zusammenfassenden Studien: Akademie der Wissenschaften der DDR, Zentralinstitut für Geschichte. Arbeitskreis für Haus- und Siedlungsforschung. Protokoll der 15. Jahrestagung in Weimar vom 16. bis 19. Juni 1974. Berlin 1975. Über die ungarischen Marktflecken siehe: V. Bacskai: Magyar mezővárosok a XV. században (Ungarische Marktflecken im 15. Jahrhundert). Budapest 1965, und P. Gunst: Der ungarische Bauernaufstand von 1514. Historische Zeitschrift 1975, Beiheft 4. Siehe noch A. P. Griczkewitsch: Tschastnovladieltscheskie goroda Belorussii v 16—18. vv. (Grundherrliche Städte in Weißrußland im 16.—18. Jahrhundert). Minsk, 1975.

# III

Diese drei Städtetypen waren in ganz Osteuropa bis zur Mitte des 19. Jahrhunderts charakteristisch. Im westeuropäischen Sinne genommen ist kein einziger eine Stadt, und in keiner einzigen wohnten städtische Bürger, die einen besonderen Stand der Feudalgesellschaft gebildet hätten. Ihre Einwohner lebten zum größten Teil von der Landwirtschaft, zur Stadt wurden sie vor allem durch gewisse Züge ihrer rechtlichen Stellung und den Umstand, daß die dichte Bevölkerung der Siedlungen dem westeuropäischen Betrachter den Eindruck einer Stadt vermittelte, obwohl das äußere Bild auch ihnen die Charakteristika des Dorfes zeigte. Auch in diesen Siedlungen erschien das Handwerk, aber im größten Teil Osteuropas nicht im Rahmen organisierter Zünfte. Natürlich gab es auch Städte im westeuropäischen Sinne, aber sie stellten — einzelne Gebiete abgerechnet — nicht die Haupttypen der städtischen Entwicklung dar. Wir denken an die Städte, deren Einwohner vor allem aus dem Westen eingewanderte, vornehmlich deutsche Bergleute und Kaufleute waren. Die Siedlungsordnung und -struktur, das wirtschaftliche und gesellschaftliche Gefüge und das äußere Bild der vor ihnen gegründeten Städte entsprach jener der damaligen westeuropäischen Städte, und ihre Einwohner besaßen im allgemeinen auch innerhalb der Gesellschaft der osteuropäischen Länder den gesellschaftlichen Status wie damals in Westeuropa. Alle diese Städte waren nicht aus der lokalen Entwicklung hervorgegangen; sie resultierten allenfalls aus dem örtlichen Bedürfnis, die entdeckten Metalle — Edelmetalle, Kupfer — abzubauen. Und da der Bergbau in diesen Ländern unentwickelt war, waren die Herrscher im allgemeinen gezwungen, Bergleute aus dem Westen zu holen. Gerade deshalb fügten sich diese Städte lange Zeit nicht in das örtliche, gesellschaftliche und wirtschaftliche Gefüge ein und blieben daher auch ethnisch lange Zeit Fremdkörper, ähnlich den großen Fernhandelszentren. Als sie sich später eingefügt hatten, läßt sich bei ihnen eine Reagrarisierung beobachten, ihre Entwicklung stockt, mit der Entwicklung der westeuropäischen Städte halten sie nicht mehr Schritt [13].

Dasselbe ist im Grunde genommen auch für die Stadtentwicklung durch

---

[13] Besonders in Ungarn und Polen spielten die deutschen Bergstädte eine bedeutende Rolle. Die große wirtschaftliche Rolle der Bergstädte in Oberungarn im 14. und 15. Jahrhundert und ihr Niedergang im 18. Jahrhundert geben ein gutes Beispiel für diesen Prozeß. Ähnliche Erscheinungen sind auch in Polen im Zusammenhang mit der Verschiebung des Schwergewichts des Wirtschaftslebens zu beobachten.

die Industrialisierung im 19. Jahrhundert bezeichnend. Jetzt verlangten zwar die örtlichen Komponenten der wirtschaftlichen Entwicklung die Entstehung von Städten im modernen wirtschaftlich-gesellschaftlichen Sinne, aber auch sie blieben lange Zeit ethnisch fremd, wurde doch in der ersten Zeit selbst ein großer Teil der Arbeiter aus dem Ausland geholt. Erst die zweite oder dritte Generation verschmolz mit dem Ethnikum dieser Gebiete. Es ist interessant zu verfolgen, wie durch die Verschiebung der einzelnen Abschnitte der wirtschaftlichen Entwicklung in Ungarn und in Polen die deutschen — schwäbischen, österreichischen, mährischen oder böhmischen —, in der Ukraine die polnischen, in Rumänien die ungarischen und in Rußland die polnischen Arbeiter, Ingenieure und andere Fachleute in jeweils anderen Abschnitten erscheinen, mit einem Zeitunterschied von ein bis zwei Jahrzehnten. Entsprechend übernehmen auch die einzelnen Sprachen die verschiedenen Fachausdrücke aus anderen Sprachen; so erscheint der deutsche Fachsprachschatz im Ungarischen oder Polnischen, der ungarische im Rumänischen oder Kroatischen, der polnische im Russischen usw. [14].

Daraus folgt, daß die osteuropäischen Städte des 19. Jahrhunderts vielschichtig sind, daß wir unter der städtischen Bevölkerung bei weitem nicht dasselbe verstehen können wie in Westeuropa. Ein sehr großer Teil der auch in der Statistik als städtisch bezeichneten Bevölkerung hat sich auch im 20. Jahrhundert noch nicht von der Landwirtschaft gelöst. Bezeichnend ist, daß z. B. in Ungarn in der Zwischenkriegszeit der größte Teil der Bevölkerung der „Städte" mit 20 000 bis 40 000 und 40 000 bis 60 000 Einwohnern in der Tiefebene von der Landwirtschaft gelebt hat. So gesehen hängen auch Stadtbild und soziale Zusammensetzung der Bevölkerung sehr eng zusammen. Abgesehen vom Stadtzentrum dieser Städte, das im allgemeinen in der zweiten Hälfte des 19. Jahrhunderts ausgebaut wurde, finden sich kaum mehrstöckige Häuser, die Straßen bestehen auch heute noch aus ebenerdigen Bauernhäusern. Wasserleitung und Kanalisation sowie Asphaltstraßen fehlen — abgesehen vom Zentrum —, wie in den Dörfern. Das ist ein Unterschied, der nicht übersehen werden darf, wenn wir an Westeuropa denken.

---

[14] Die Tischler, Schlosser und andere Facharbeiter, die gar nicht deutsch sprechen können, nennen die Werkzeuge auch heute noch mit ihren deutschen (oder deformierten deutschen) Namen, obwohl die Werkzeuge auch ungarische Bezeichnungen haben. Gleichfalls ist auch heute noch der Name einiger Werkzeuge in der rumänischen Sprache deutsch oder ungarisch.

## III

Aber nicht nur die Stadt und ihr gesellschaftlich-wirtschaftliches Gefüge war anders, auch das des Dorfes. Es genügt, kurz darauf zu verweisen, daß die Bauern in den riesigen Gebieten Osteuropas bis zur Bauernbefreiung mehr oder weniger Sklaven blieben. In Rußland oder auf dem Balkan, besonders in Rumänien und in Ostpolen, erreichten die Bauern bis zur Bauernbefreiung nicht einmal den Status des westeuropäischen abhängigen Bauern — Hörige —, sondern blieben Sklaven, die unabhängig vom Boden gekauft und verkauft werden konnten. Zwischen der Dorfgemeinschaft, dem darauf basierenden despotischen asiatischen Herrschaftssystem und dem Sklavendasein der Mitglieder der Dorfgemeinschaft bestand ein enger und logischer Zusammenhang. Nur in den Gebieten Osteuropas, wo die westliche Kirche das Christentum verbreitete, änderte sich diese Lage. Das aber war nur in der kleineren Westhälfte des Gebietes, im Baltikum, in Polen, Ungarn, Kroatien und Slowenien der Fall. Überall sonst waren die Bauern Mitglieder der Dorfgemeinschaft und Eigentum des Herrschers bzw. der Grundbesitzer: Bojaren usw. Zwar hatte das Christentum auch in Rußland das System der Sklaverei etwas gemildert, aber die Bauern wurden nie im westlichen Sinne Hörige. Die Mitglieder der Dorfgemeinschaft waren füreinander verantwortlich, und dieses primitive Rechtsverhältnis blieb z. B. in Rußland bis in die ersten Jahrzehnte des 20. Jahrhunderts erhalten. Vollkommen unabhängig von der Bezeichnung ihrer gesellschaftlichen Lage hatten die Bauern dem W e s e n nach das gleiche Schicksal. Die Massen der russischen Bauern waren z. B. Sklaven (cholop) und werden in den Quellen zusammen mit dem Vieh erwähnt. Die Quellen kennen auch eine andere Form des Sklaven (Tscheliady) und unterscheiden ihn vom freien Bauern (Smerd). Wie wenig Unterschied aber in der Tat zwischen diesen Schichten bestand, zeigt sich darin, daß das Blutgeld, welches bei ihrer Ermordung gezahlt werden mußte, gleich war. Als sich aber der Prozeß der Vereinigung der verschiedenen bäuerlichen Schichten stärker vollzog, verlief er praktisch auf dem Niveau der Sklaverei [15]. Das ist es, was den größten Teil Osteuropas von dem vorher erwähnten westlichen Streifen absondert, d. h. von Polen, Ungarn, Kroatien, wo

---

[15] Zur gesellschaftlichen Stratifikation des russischen Bauerntums siehe die bis heute grundlegende Arbeit von B. D. Grekov: Krestiane na Russi s drevneischich wremen do XVII veka (Das russische Bauerntum von den ältesten Zeiten bis zum 17. Jahrhundert). Moskau 1945.

diese Vereinigung auf einem etwas freieren Niveau der Hörigkeit erfolgte [16].

Natürlich war hier auch die Lage der Mitglieder der herrschenden „feudalen" Klasse anders als in Westeuropa. In Osteuropa war der Eigentümer des Bodens noch Jahrhunderte hindurch der Herrscher, und der Grundbesitz des Adels vererbte sich lange Zeit nicht automatisch. Im Vergleich zu Westeuropa ist dies ein riesiger Unterschied. Ein Großteil des russischen Adels, der rumänische Adel und der Adel anderer Balkanländer war ein sogenannter Dienstadel, der seine Güter vom Herrscher nur für die Zeit seines Dienstes bekam und sie seinen Nachkommen nicht automatisch vererben konnte. Ein kleiner Teil des Adels war die alte Gentil- oder Stammesaristokratie — z. B. die Bojaren —; sie waren meist unmittelbare Vasallen des Herrschers, was die Gesamtentwicklung der Gesellschaft außergewöhnlich beeinflußte. Im größten Teil Osteuropas hat sich eigentlich das Ständewesen nie herausgebildet, jenes System der adligen „Reichstage", die die westliche Geschichte kennt, die Aufteilung der Macht zwischen Herrscher und Stände war in Rußland oder in den Balkanländern nicht bekannt. Die Duma der Bojaren z. B. war keine Ständeversammlung, sondern ein königlicher Rat, eine überall bekannte Form des Regierungsmechanismus. Die erste große Landesversammlung des Adels lernte die russische Geschichte erst im Jahre 1549 kennen, und sie konnte nie entscheidende Bedeutung erringen. Die ganze Gesellschaft, vor allem die der Bauern und der über und von ihnen lebende Adel war anders organisiert als in Westeuropa. Das Sklavendasein der Bauern war ein riesiger Hemmschuh für die intensive Entwicklung der Wirtschaft. Die Tatsache aber, daß der Grundbesitz des Adels lange Zeit nicht erblich war, führte zu den „asiatischen", „balkanischen" Formen der Ausbeutung. Die Bodeneigentumsform der Dorfgemeinschaft sicherte der zentralen Macht ein Übergewicht, das ähnlich

[16] Wir möchten betonen, daß es unserer Meinung nach gerade durch diese Situation unbegründet ist, daß die Geschichtsschreibung in diesen Gebieten den Ausdruck „zweite Leibeigenschaft" benutzt. Abgesehen davon, daß auch Friedrich Engels diese Bezeichnung nur für einzelne deutsche Gebiete gebraucht hat und bei weitem nicht in dem Sinne, wie es — besonders nach dem Zweiten Weltkrieg — die osteuropäische marxistische Geschichtsschreibung tut. Der Gebrauch dieses Ausdrucks stellt, statt auf die Unterschiede zwischen der Entwicklung in Ost- und in Westeuropa zu verweisen, diese Entwicklung unbewußt auf eine Stufe. Dies ist zumindest für die vorhergehende Epoche — unseres Erachtens — unzulässig.

nur in Asien und in Afrika zu beobachten war, wo die Konservierung des asiatischen Bodeneigentums von den Pharaonen bis zu den türkischen Sultanen und den arabischen Kalifen die despotischen Herrschaftssysteme bewahrte. Dieses Übergewicht der zentralen Macht bedeutete natürlich nicht, daß im Verlaufe der Geschichte entstandene Staatssysteme nicht für längere oder kürzere Zeit auseinandergefallen wären, manchmal sogar in mehrere Teile. Aber diese Aufgliederung hatte einen ganz anderen Charakter als die feudale Staatsorganisation im Westen. Die lokalen kleinen Könige übten in solchen Fällen die gleiche despotische Macht aus wie die Herrscher der größeren Staatseinheiten. Sie wurden zur despotischen Macht, die ebenso stark war wie früher oder später die der größeren Staatsgebilde; und wir dürfen nicht vergessen, daß im Osten, aufgebaut auf den Dorfgemeinschaften, von Anfang an starke despotische Reiche entstanden, im Westen aber die heutigen Länder als Staatsgebilde nicht existierten, Frankreich und Deutschland nur durch Zentralisation entstanden [17], der ungarische Staat aber von Anfang an eine Einheit bildete, in der Partikularkräfte nur sehr kurze Zeit zur Geltung kommen konnten. Es ist also bei weitem kein Vorteil dieser Gesellschaftssysteme, daß — was ihnen jedoch die Geschichtsschreibung der einzelnen Völker zugute hält — die Herrschermacht so stark war wie z. B. in Rußland und sich die sog. feudale Aufgliederung, das Lehenssystem der Gesellschaft und seine Folgen oder die ständische Staatsorganisation überhaupt nicht entwickelten. Das Fehlen des westeuropäischen Bodeneigentums führte dazu, daß sich in Osteuropa die echten feudalen Züge der Gesellschaft nicht herausbildeten.

Ost- und Westeuropa mit seiner unterschiedlichen wirtschaftlich-gesellschaftlichen Struktur lebten ungestört und einander nicht beeinflussend nebeneinander, bis von der zweiten Hälfte des 14. Jahrhunderts an die beschleunigte Wirtschaftsentwicklung Westeuropas Osteuropa berührte und es umzuformen begann. Auch früher hatte es wirtschaftliche, kulturelle, manchmal auch militärische Beziehungen zwischen beiden Strukturen gegeben. Der eine Stadttyp, das Fernhandelszentrum in Osteuropa, ist ja die organische Folge dieser Beziehungen. Aber sie waren

---

[17] Wenn auch eine im 18. und 19. Jahrhundert, aus der Zeit der Entstehung der Nationalstaaten, uns überlieferte Ideologie, vielleicht wegen der leichteren Benutzbarkeit des Materials, die deutsche, französische oder englische Geschichte auch für die vorhergehenden Epochen im allgemeinen in dem später entstandenen staatlichen Rahmen behandelt.

nicht eng, wirkten sich auf Osteuropa direkt überhaupt nicht aus und berührten dessen Wirtschaft und dessen gesellschaftliche Einrichtungen im Grunde genommen nicht. Die aus Asien, Arabien oder vom Nordseegebiet einströmenden Warenartikel, der Fernhandel, veränderten das wirtschaftlich-gesellschaftliche Gesicht Osteuropas nicht. Er war kein organischer Bestandteil des Lebens, da die Bewohner der Handelsstädte ethnisch lange Zeit fremd blieben. Die vielleicht einzige Sphäre des Lebens, wo der Einfluß Westeuropas organisch in das tägliche Leben eingebaut war, war eine Folge der militärischen Konflikte, das aber zeigte sich erst später, vom 10. und 11. Jahrhundert an. Waffen waren eigentlich die einzigen Warenartikel, die ab und an aus Westeuropa nach Osteuropa kamen. Als sich um das 10. Jahrhundert die technische Entwicklung auch in der Bewaffnung zeigte, waren die osteuropäischen Heere — zumindest in den Westeuropa am nächsten gelegenen Randgebieten — mit der Zeit gezwungen, auf die im Westen angewandte Kampfweise überzugehen und Waffen zu importieren, zusammen mit jenen, die sie bedienten, ähnlich wie später bei den Bergleuten. Die ungarischen und die polnischen Heere gingen sehr bald zur Kampfesweise der Ritter über — und natürlich auch zu deren Bewaffnung —, während die Heere der russischen Fürstentümer und der Balkanländer auch weiterhin vor allem aus leichter Reiterei bestanden.

Anders gestaltete sich die Lage vom 14. Jahrhundert an. Die wirtschaftliche Entwicklung Westeuropas, die Ausweitung der westeuropäischen Wirtschaft führte gesetzmäßig zur Einschaltung gewisser Sektoren der osteuropäischen Wirtschaft in diese Entwicklung.

Und gerade aus diesem Umstand resultierte, daß Osteuropa — oder zumindest ein Teil — schon relativ früh gezwungen war, gewisse Elemente des westeuropäischen Entwicklungsmodells zu übernehmen. Vergessen wir nicht, Westeuropa hatte zwar auch früher Verbindungen zum Nahen oder Fernen Osten gehabt, aber diese in ihrem Volumen nicht sehr bedeutenden Beziehungen waren auf dem keine weiteren Auswirkungen gestattenden Niveau des auf einige Warenartikel beschränkten Fernhandels steckengeblieben. So können wir vom wirtschaftlichen Einfluß Westeuropas auf andere Gebiete der Welt nicht sprechen, solange diese Art von Handelsverbindung in einem späteren Abschnitt des wirtschaftlichen Wachstums, vom Zeitalter der Entdeckungen an, nicht zu einer qualitativ anderen Verbindung wurde und sich dann über die ganze Welt erstreckte, auch die in allen Klassengesellschaften bei dem Zusammentreffen entwickelter und unterwickelter wirtschaftlicher und sozialer Strukturen oft hervorgetretene Volksausrottung [18] noch nicht mit sich brachte. Dieser wirtschaftliche Einfluß Westeuropas auf Osteuropa zeigte sich charakteristischerweise von Anfang an auf dem Gebiet der Rohprodukte, ob das landwirtschaftliche Produkte oder Metalle waren. Was letztere anbetrifft, so konnte der Edelmetallbedarf der wachsenden westeuropäischen Wirtschaft vor der Entdeckung der Neuen Welt vor allem aus Osteuropa gedeckt werden. Gerade daraus erklärt sich die schnelle Entwicklung des Edelmetall- und Kupferbergbaus in Ungarn und in anderen osteuropäischen Ländern im 13. und 14. Jahrhundert [19]. Die Edelmetalle wurden entweder im Rohzustand oder in Form von Münzen exportiert und dafür Gebrauchsgegenstände — Waffen, Kleidung, Stoffe — nach Osteuropa importiert. Für die Errungenschaften der westeuropäischen technischen Entwicklung bestand hier bei der herrschenden Klasse lebhafte Nachfrage.

Wir wollen gleich hier an dieser Stelle sagen, wie bezeichnend es ist, daß auf dem Gebiet der Kleidung von da ab Westeuropa die „Mode" diktierte, die aber in Osteuropa nur die herrschenden Schichten übernehmen konnten, denn nur sie hatten die dazu erforderlichen materiellen Mittel. Schon zu Beginn dieser Entwicklung unterschied sich die Kleidung des gemeinen Volkes, der Bauern, von jener der höheren Gesellschaftsschichten. In Westeuropa folgte die bäuerliche und bürgerliche

---

[18] Nehmen wir das Schicksal der Indianer oder anderer sogenannter „Eingeborener" als Beispiel.

[19] Auf den ungarischen Edelmetallbergbau und in Zusammenhang damit auf die Entwicklung der Bergstädte siehe außer den in den Anmerkungen 10 und 13 erwähnten F. Kovats: A magyar arany világtörténeti jelentösége és kereskedelmi összeköttetéseink a nyugattal a középkorban (Die weltgeschichtliche Bedeutung des ungarischen Goldes und die Handelsbeziehungen Ungarns mit dem Westen im Mittelalter). Történelmi Szemle 1922; O. Paulinyi: A magyar aranymonopólium jövedelme a középkorban (Das Einkommen aus dem Goldmonopol im mittelalterlichen Ungarn). In: Domanovszky-Emlékkönyv. Budapest 1937; O. Paulinyi: A középkori magyar réztermelés gazdasági jelentösége (Die wirtschaftliche Bedeutung des ungarischen Kupferbergbaues im Mittelalter). In: Károlyi-Emlékkönyv. Budapest 1934; F. Kovats: Városi adózás a középkorban (Die Steuerung der ungarischen Städte im Mittelalter). Pozsony 1900; J. Szücs: Városok és kézmüvesség a XV. századi Magyarországon (Städte und Handwerk im Ungarn des 15. Jahrhunderts). Budapest 1955; J. Szücs: Das Städtewesen in Ungarn im 15. bis 17. Jahrhundert. In: La Renaissance et la Réformation en Pologne et en Hongrie. Budapest 1963; O. Paulinyi: Tulajdon és társadalom a Garamvidéki bányavárosokban (Eigentum und Gesellschaft in den Bergstädten der Grangegend). Történelmi Szemle 1962.

Kleidung jener der herrschenden Schichten unmittelbar, neue Formen und Materialien breiteten sich relativ schnell aus. In Osteuropa jedoch dauerte dieser Prozeß Jahrhunderte. Und in den einzelnen osteuropäischen Ländern verbreitete sich die neue Mode nicht im gleichen Ausmaß und Tempo. In Ungarn und Polen z. B. trugen nicht nur die Aristokraten, sondern auch die wohlhabenderen oder mittleren Schichten des Adels westliche Kleidung, während sie in Rußland und auf dem Balkan nur von der Aristokratie getragen wurde, die breiten Schichten des Adels aber noch jahrhundertelang bei der „Nationaltracht" blieben.

Ähnlich der Nachfrage nach Edelmetallen zeigt sich seit dem 14. Jahrhundert in Westeuropa eine vielleicht noch größere Nachfrage nach landwirtschaftlichen Produkten. Die Entfaltung der städtischen Entwicklung, die Zunahme der Bevölkerung schuf einen Bedarf an Lebensmitteln, den Westeuropa aus seiner eigenen Produktion nicht mehr befriedigen konnte. Besonders der Fleischbedarf der Stadtbevölkerung konnte aus den unmittelbaren Versorgungsgebieten nicht mehr gedeckt werden; dies war zugleich auch ein Produkt, das leicht zu transportieren war, weil das Vieh den Verbrauchermarkt auf seinen eigenen Beinen erreichte. Nicht zufällig entwickelte sich der Rinderhandel von der zweiten Hälfte des 14. Jahrhunderts an in so schnellem Tempo, wuchs dieser Handel aus Osteuropa — Ungarn, Polen, den rumänischen Fürstentümern — nach Westeuropa. Das ist das erste größere Auftreten der landwirtschaftlichen Warenproduktion in Osteuropa, und das ist zugleich der Wirtschaftsfaktor, der die Entstehung der Marktflecken, dieser weit ausgedehnten Dörfer, mit einer zahlenmäßig beinahe städtischen Bevölkerung in diesen Gebieten ermöglichte. Wir verwiesen bereits darauf, daß ihre Entstehung aller Wahrscheinlichkeit nach eng mit der warenproduzierenden Viehzucht zusammenhängt, und wir können jetzt nur betonen, daß dieser Siedlungstyp nur dort entstand, wo in der Wirtschaft die landwirtschaftliche Warenproduktion, in Osteuropa die Exportviehzucht, der entscheidende Faktor war. Das war auch auf dem amerikanischen Kontinent vor den Eisenbahnen der Fall, z. B. in Nordamerika vom Ende des 18. Jahrhunderts an, oder in Argentinien. Erst nach dem Ausbau des Eisenbahnnetzes spielte die Getreideproduktion für den Export eine Rolle in der Weiterentwicklung dieser Siedlungsform.

Die erste und lange Zeit anhaltende Wirtschaftsverbindung war also der Edelmetallbergbau, dann folgte die Viehzucht. Vom 15. Jahrhundert an kam ein drittes hinzu: das Getreide. Die immer größer gewordenen Städte hatten auch großen Bedarf an Warengetreide. Dieses Getreide lohnte sich aber nur dort zu produzieren, wo auch das Transportproblem gelöst war. Das war im 15. Jahrhundert vor allem in den Bezirken mit Wasserstraßen der Fall. Es ist kein Zufall, daß der Getreideexport aus Osteuropa bis zum Erscheinen der Eisenbahn ausschließlich aus Ostdeutschland, einzelnen Gebieten Polens, aus dem Baltikum, aus Nordeuropa, aus Dänemark und Südschweden erfolgte; diese Gebiete ergänzten Westeuropas Getreidebedarf, aus anderen Gebieten war der Transport des Getreides technisch nicht zu tragbaren Kosten lösbar. Zwar war auch in einigen Teilen Ungarns die Getreideproduktion gestiegen, sie diente aber, die niederösterreichischen Städte und Wien abgerechnet, ausschließlich der Befriedigung des Militärkonsums. In den später so bedeutenden Getreideanbaugebieten, wie z. B. Rumänien, nahm die Produktion erst im zweiten Drittel des 19. Jahrhunderts zu, als mit dem Ausbau des Straßen- und Eisenbahnnetzes die Möglichkeit gegeben war, das Getreide in die Häfen zu transportieren. Aus Rußland und aus der Ukraine begann größerer Getreideexport ebenfalls erst nach dem Ausbau der Eisenbahnlinien.

Auch der Export von Holz und Produkten der Waldwirtschaft und Jagd, der für Westeuropa zunehmende Bedeutung erlangte, war in entscheidendem Maße auf den Wasserweg angewiesen. Neben dem Getreide waren dies die wichtigsten Handelsgüter der Hanse in Osteuropa [20].

Ganz gleich, wie groß das Gebiet war, das in Osteuropa von dieser Entwicklung berührt wurde, der wirtschaftliche Einfluß Westeuropas konnte nicht ohne Folgen für die wirtschaftliche und gesellschaftliche Struktur bleiben. Hauptanziehungskraft hatten das als Gegenleistung für die exportierten Güter nach Osteuropa strömende Geld bzw. die dafür käuflichen Konsumartikel. Die Ansprüche der herrschenden Klasse zwangen sie überall, ihre Geldeinnahmen zu steigern, vor allem infolge der im 16. Jahrhundert in Westeuropa aufgetretenen Inflation, die mit einem schnellen Ansteigen der Preise verbunden war. Der Adel konnte seinen steigenden Geldbedarf nur durch erhöhte Einnahmen decken [21]. Die

[20] Zu diesen wirtschaftlichen Beziehungen zwischen Ost- und Westeuropa siehe M. Malowist: Wschód a zachód Europy w XIII—XIV. wieku (Osten und Westen Europas im 13. bis 14. Jahrhundert). Warschau 1973.

[21] Zur Lage des Adels und deren Folge siehe: J. Topolski: Narodziny kapitalizmu w Europie w XIV—XVII wieku (Die Geburt des Kapitalismus in Europa im 14. bis 17. Jahrhundert). Warschau 1965.

Geldleistungen der Bauern waren nicht wesentlich zu erhöhen, weil das Niveau der osteuropäischen Wirtschaft dazu keine Möglichkeit bot. Die Rückständigkeit der nichtagrarischen Sektoren der Wirtschaft engte die Ware-Geld-Beziehungen derart ein, daß von den Bauern nicht mehr Geld zu fordern war. Deshalb war der Adel gezwungen, sich auch selbst in die Produktion einzuschalten. Das hatte er schon früher getan, denn die meisten exportierten Rinder wurden ja auf grundherrlichen Weiden gehalten. Oder er machte seine Rechte geltend, indem er durch Pachtgelder, Steuern oder Zollgebühren Nutzen aus diesem Handel zog. Beim Getreideanbau oder dem Holzschlag mußte er jedoch eine andere Lösung suchen, denn — im Vergleich zu der extensiven Viehhaltung — bestanden diese aus einer Reihe arbeitsintensiver Arbeitsprozesse, vom Pflügen bzw. Schlägern bis zum Abtransport. Dafür gab es keine andere Methode, als die gutsherrlichen Eigenwirtschaften auszuweiten und auf der vergrößerten Fläche die Produktion durch Nutzung der Fron der abhängigen Bauern zu steigern. So entstand überall da, wo die durch Westeuropa ausgelöste Konjunktur zu spüren war, das System der Gutswirtschaften, die auf der Fron, den kostenlosen Leistungen der abhängigen Bauern, basierte. Der Boden dieser Gutswirtschaften wurde nicht nur mit der Arbeitskraft der abhängigen Bauern, sondern meist auch mit deren Produktionsmitteln bewirtschaftet. Die Bauern transportierten die Ware auch auf den Markt.

Diese — für die ausländischen Märkte erfolgende — Ausweitung der Warenproduktion brachte überall, wo die Gutswirtschaft entstand, große Veränderungen im Leben der Bauern Osteuropas. Die Gutsherren waren hier daran interessiert, möglichst viel Land in ihre eigene Warenproduktion einzubeziehen, was mancherorts und von Zeit zu Zeit auch dazu führte, daß den Bauern das Land weggenommen wurde. Zur gleichen Zeit waren sie aber auch daran interessiert, sich die kostenlose Arbeitskraft der Bauern zu sichern, was zur Erhöhung der Arbeitsrente und ihrer rechtlichen Regelung führte. In einzelnen Gegenden brachte das eine Verschlechterung der Lage der Bauern, so in den Gebieten der deutschen Kolonisation, besonders im heutigen Ostdeutschland und in West-Polen. Dieser Prozeß fiel im größten Teil Osteuropas mit der Vereinheitlichung der rechtlich unterschiedlichen Schichten der Bauern zusammen. Es war das Interesse der Gutsherren, ihre Bauern möglichst an die Scholle zu binden und sich damit ihre Arbeitskraft zu sichern. Die Entwicklung der Gutswirtschaft löste also in Osteuropa eine Welle der An-die-Scholle-Bindung der Bauern aus [22], die von der Wende vom 15. zum 16. Jahrhundert bis zum Ende des 18. Jahrhunderts dauerte, zugleich auch das Tempo anzeigend, in dem sich einzelne Bezirke Osteuropas in die Getreideproduktion für den westeuropäischen Markt einschalteten.

Wir müssen jedoch hervorheben, daß die Bindung der Bauern an die Scholle, die Aufhebung der Freizügigkeit kein einheitlicher Prozeß war. In Ostdeutschland und in einzelnen Teilen Polens, im Baltikum oder in Norddeutschland, wo die Getreidekonjunktur spürbar war, diente sie in der Tat der Entfaltung der gutsherrlichen Eigenwirtschaft. Dort aber, wo noch viel Land umbrochen werden konnte — Walachei, Moldau —, oder wo die Besitzverhältnisse aus irgendeinem Grunde gelockert waren, sollten lediglich die Abhängigkeitsverhältnisse gefestigt werden, d. h. die Interessenunterschiede zwischen den einzelnen Schichten des Adels ausgeglichen werden. Dabei spielte z. B. in Rußland auch eine Rolle, daß als Folge der Besitzumorganisation unter Iwan IV. die Bauernflucht außergewöhnlich zugenommen hatte und es das elementare Interesse einzelner Adelsschichten war, diese zu stoppen [23]. Natürlich müssen wir auch hier mit der Wechselwirkung des Gesetzes der einzelnen Länder rechnen, mit der mechanischen Übernahme einzelner Formulierungen. Das wirkliche Leben aber kam hinter den Gesetzen auf verschiedenste Art zur Geltung.

Der dritte Abschnitt des westeuropäischen Wirtschaftseinflusses gleicht seinem Charakter nach dem vorhergehenden. Seiner Wirkung wegen aber verdient er eine besondere Behandlung. Dieser Abschnitt beginnt eigentlich von der zweiten Hälfte des 18. Jahrhunderts an, als die westeuropäische Industrie von Osteuropa auch immer mehr Wolle beanspruchte. Die Wollkonjunktur führte nicht nur zum Aufschwung und zur Ausweitung der Schafzucht — ebenfalls vornehmlich in den gutsherrlichen Betrieben —, sondern trug durch ihre Fortwirkungen

---

[22] Eine Zusammenfassung dieses Prozesses in Mittel- und Osteuropa gibt: Gy. Székely: Földesúri törekvések a jobbágyság költözési jogának felszámolására Magyarországon — Kelet-európai tipusú társadalmi folyamat az 1514 elötti évtizedekben (Grundherrliche Bestrebungen zur Beseitigung des Wegzugsrechtes der Leibeigenen in Ungarn — Ein gesellschaftlicher Vorgang osteuropäischen Charakters in den Jahrzehnten vor 1514). Agrártörténeti Szemle 1972.

[23] Außer der schon in Anmerkung 15 angegebenen Arbeit Grekovs siehe auch V. I. Korecki: Zakreposchtschenie krestjan i klassovaia borba v Rossii vo vtoroi polovine XVI veka (Die Leibeigenschaft der Bauern und der Klassenkampf in Rußland in der zweiten Hälfte des 16. Jahrhunderts). Moskau 1970.

auch wesentlich zur Modernisierung der landwirtschaftlichen Produktion bei, vor allem in den kontinentalen Teilen Ost-Europas. Die gutsherrlichen Betriebe führten westliche Schafrassen mit feinerer Wolle (Merino) ein und trugen so dazu bei, einen weiteren Pfeiler der Wirtschaftsbeziehungen zu errichten. Die Wolle konnte leichter transportiert werden als das Getreide, und so war der Einfluß der Wollkonjunktur auch in Gebieten spürbar — und darauf beruht ihre epochale Bedeutung —, auf die sie sich bis dahin noch nicht ausgewirkt hatte. Das war v o r d e m E r s c h e i n e n d e r E i s e n b a h n die letzte wirksame wirtschaftliche Auswirkung der westeuropäischen Entwicklung auf Osteuropa [24].

Alle diese Auswirkungen aber, die vor allem den Umstand erklären, daß Osteuropa der Raum der Welt war, der — die übrigen Gebiete überholend — einem dem Westeuropäischen ähnlichen Weg beschreiten, früher als diese viele Errungenschaften der westeuropäischen Entwicklung übernehmen konnte, erstreckten sich nicht auf Gesamteuropa, sondern auf einige Bezirke, bemerkenswert nur auf dessen westliche Randgebiete, auf Ungarn, Polen, das Baltikum und Kroatien. Weiter oben verwiesen wir schon darauf, daß die u n m i t t e l b a r e n wirtschaftlichen Auswirkungen Westeuropas sich wirklich in nennenswertem Maße nur in diesen Gebieten zeigten. Neben vielen Faktoren — z. B. geographische Lage — spielte dabei auch mit, daß die Völker Ungarns, Polens, Kroatiens und des Baltikums das Christentum unmittelbar von der westlichen Kirche übernommen hatten und hier die Elemente des römischen Rechtes — d. h., die des Privateigentumsrechtes — ausschließlicher zur Geltung gekommen waren als weiter östlich. Dabei spielte vor allem eine Rolle, daß diese Gebiete infolge der verhältnismäßig frühen Kolonisation zum größten Teil von westeuropäischen Bauern bevölkert worden waren, sie in diesen Gesellschaften also schon relativ früh größeres Gewicht hatten als weiter östlich. Bei Ungarn müssen wir nicht nur in Betracht ziehen, daß sich bei den landnehmenden Ungarn, einem in seiner gesellschaftlichen Entwicklung bereits fortgeschrittenen nomadischen Hirtenvolk, auch das System der Dorfgemeinschaft anders zeigte als bei

[24] Zur Rolle der Wollkonjunktur in Ungarn um die Wende vom 18. zum 19. Jahrhundert siehe die schon in Anmerkung 9 angegebene Studie von P. Gunst. Bei geringerer Intensität und kleinerem Ergebnis war die Wirkung der Merinoschafhaltung der Gutswirtschaften in Rußland ähnlich.

den meist seßhaften, Ackerbau treibenden osteuropäischen Völkern [25], sondern auch, daß der Westen des Landes, Pannonien, jahrhundertelang an der Entwicklung westeuropäischen Typs beteiligt war, die westlichen Einflüsse also auf den entstehenden ungarischen Staat von Anfang an sehr stark waren. Das wurde auch durch die westslawischen Völker gefördert, die zur Zeit der Landnahme im Westen und Norden des Landes lebten und deren Staaten bereits stark von der westlichen Gesellschaftsorganisation durchdrungen waren. Die landnehmenden Ungarn ließen sich in Transdanubien nicht in entvölkerten oder leeren Gebieten nieder, sondern auf einer Ackerbaugesellschaft, die in jeder Hinsicht großen Einfluß auf die Weiterentwicklung ihrer wirtschaftlichen, gesellschaftlichen und staatlichen Ordnung ausübte. Der Unterschied zwischen dem westlichen Transdanubien und der östlichen Tiefebene, ihre Wechselwirkungen, sind nicht nur ein Beispiel dafür, daß einzelne Staatsgebilde von Beginn an zwei Strukturen haben konnten, sie beweisen auch, welche große Rolle die im Westen des Landes lebenden Slawen und andere Volksgruppen bei der Formung der wirtschaftlich-gesellschaftlichen Rolle des ungarischen Volkes gespielt haben und welchen, noch nach Jahrhunderten vorhandenen Vorteil dies für das Land darstellte [26]. Ähnlich war die Lage auch in Kroatien, mit dem Unterschied, daß im Westen Osteuropas hier der antike Einfluß am stärksten zur Geltung kam, während in Westpolen, im Baltikum und in Polen die deutschen bäuerlichen Siedler und städtischen Bürger Träger der westlichen Entwicklungslinie waren. Leider ist die deutsche Kolonisation im

[25] Auf die nomadischen Einflüsse für die ungarische Entwicklung siehe L. Makkai: Feudalizmus és az eredeti jellegzetességek Európában (Feudalismus und die ursprünglichen Charakteristika in Europa). Történelmi Szemle. 1976. Der Verfasser dieser Studie hebt markant die Bedeutung der nomadischen Elemente für die ungarische gesellschaftliche Entwicklung hervor.

[26] Die ungarische Geschichtsschreibung hat bis zum heutigen Tage den Unterschieden in der historischen Entwicklung des westlichen und östlichen Teiles des Landes wenig Aufmerksamkeit gewidmet, obwohl, angefangen vom Charakter der Siedlungen, dem Wirtschaftssystem, bis zu den gesellschaftlichen Verhältnissen und den Unterschieden in der Folklore zahlreiche Anzeichen auf diese Verschiedenheit hinweisen. Die Regionalforschung fehlt, obwohl zahlreiche Versuche zur Ortsgeschichtsforschung unternommen worden sind. Zwischen der Ortsgeschichte — Geschichte eines Dorfes, einer Stadt, eines kleineren Bezirkes — und den umfassenden Untersuchungen im Landesmaßstab fehlt im allgemeinen eine Stufe, die Untersuchung größerer Gebietseinheiten (Große Ungarische Tiefebene, Transdanubien usw.). Dabei verspricht deren Einfügung in die Untersuchung außergewöhnlich fruchtbar zu sein.

weiteren Verlauf der Geschichte fast überall Teil der nationalen Frage geworden. Dabei haben die Machtbestrebungen der deutschen Kaiser eine Rolle gespielt, denn die Zentralisationspolitik des Deutschen Ritterordens, der Habsburger und der Hohenzollern, die überall in Gegensatz kam zu den feudalen partikularen und ideologisch formulierten Bestrebungen des lokalen Adels und der Aristokratie, später, im Zeitalter des Kapitalismus, zu der die Nationwerdung begleitenden nationalistischen Ideologie. Das ideologische Endergebnis ist auf der einen Seite die Verkündung der deutschen Kultursuprematie, auf der anderen Seite die beinahe völlige Leugnung der Rolle der deutschen Kolonisation in der osteuropäischen wirtschaftlich-gesellschaftlichen Entwicklung. Obwohl es sich hier lediglich darum handelt, daß einigen Völkern Osteuropas die Errungenschaften der westeuropäischen wirtschaftlich-gesellschaftlichen Entwicklung in der Form der Ansiedlung der deutschen Bauern erschienen, am sichtbarsten vielleicht in der Form der Dörfer „mit deutschem Recht" [27].

So entstand also im Randgebiet Osteuropas ein Bezirk mit Übergangscharakter, wozu das Baltikum, Polen, das böhmisch-mährische Becken und Kroatien gezählt werden können. Diese Länder zeigen — Böhmen ausgenommen — die osteuropäischen Charakteristika der Entwicklung, aber mit starker westeuropäischer Einwirkung [28]. Wir halten es für bezeichnend, daß es diese Länder waren, wo überhaupt ein Kontakt zwischen den beiden Strukturen entstand, wo die Entwicklung zwar auf dem osteuropäischen Wege verlief, aber mit so starken westeuropäischen Einwirkungen, daß diese die ursprüngliche Struktur in vieler Hinsicht modifizierten. Dafür einige Beispiele: das System der Gutswirtschaften, das durch die Exportmöglichkeiten nach Westeuropa entstanden war, zeigte sich ausschließlich in diesen Ländern; hier nahm das System der Gutswirtschaften mit Frondienst einen breiten Rahmen ein. Es kam zwar auch in anderen osteuropäischen Ländern vor, daß die Fron rechtlich ausgeweitet wurde — wobei auch eine Rolle spielte, daß in diesen Län-

---

[27] Zur wirtschaftlichen und gesellschaftlichen Rolle der deutschen Kolonisation siehe S. Trawkowski: W sprawie roli kolonizacji niemckiej w przemianach kultury materialnej na ziemiach polskich w XIII wieku. (Zur wahren Rolle der deutschen Kolonisation in der Umwandlung der materiellen Kultur im Polen des 13. Jahrhunderts). Kwartalnik Historii Kultury Materialnej 1960.

[28] Böhmen und Mähren haben sich im Grunde genommen auf dem westlichen Weg entwickelt, allerdings mit starken osteuropäischen Einwirkungen.

dern Produkten- und Arbeitsrente stets die wichtigsten Elemente der Bodenrente waren, daß sie noch nicht von der Geldrente abgelöst worden waren —, aber sie wurde fast nie zur Grundlage der gutsherrlichen Warenproduktion. In Rumänien und in Innerrußland z. B. wurde die Fron der Bauern erst Ende des 18., Anfang des 19. Jahrhunderts erhöht, vielfach auch dann noch nicht. Hier wurden die Geldeinkünfte der Grundherren eher durch verschiedene grundherrliche Rechte, verschiedene Monopole gesichert, z. B. durch Monopole der Schnapsbrennerei, Fleischhauerei usw.[29]. In Ungarn stammte ein großer Teil des grundherrlichen Einkommens aus dem Weinausschank und dem Fleischverkauf, in den rumänischen Fürstentümern oder in Polen noch Anfang des 19. Jahrhunderts vor allem aus dem Monopol der Schnapsbrennerei[30].

---

[29] Über die Rentensysteme in den rumänischen Fürstentümern siehe S. COLUMBEANU: A havasalföldi feudális majorsági földek kérdéséhez a XVIII. században és a XIX. század elsö felében (Zur Frage der Vorwerkfelder in der Walachei im 18. Jahrhundert und zu Beginn des 19. Jahrhunderts). Agrártörténeti Szemle 1971; S. COLUMBEANU: Economia domeniului feudal din Tara Romaneasca in secolul al XVIII—lea (Bewirtschaftung von feudalen Gutswirtschaften in der Walachei im 18. Jahrhundert). Bukarest 1972; V. MIHORDEA: Maîtres du sol et paysans dans les Principautés Roumaines au XVIIIe siècle. Bukarest 1971; D. M. DRAGNEV: Selskoe chozjaistvo feodalnoi Moldavii (konecz XVII-natschalo XIX v.) (Moldauische Landwirtschaft vom Ende des 17. bis zu Beginn des 19. Jahrhunderts). Kischinev 1975; I. CORFUS: Agricultura Tarii Romanesti in prima jumatate a secolului al XIX-lea (Die Landwirtschaft der Walachei in der ersten Hälfte des 19. Jahrhunderts). Bukarest 1969; I. CONSTANTINESCU: Arendarea mosiilor în Moldova pîna la Regulamentul organic (Die Verpachtung der Herrengüter in der Moldau bis zur Periode des Organisationsstatutes). Studii si Materiele de istorie Medie 1973. Über die Dorfgemeinschaften in Rumänien siehe: G. BAKÓ: Despre organisarea obstilor satesti ale epocii feudale timpurii din sud-estul României (Über die Organisation der frühfeudalen Dorfgemeinschaften im Südosten Rumäniens). Studii si Cercetari de Istorie Veche si Archeologie 1975.

[30] Über Ungarn siehe P. Zs. PACH: Az 1514. évi parasztfelkelés és a „második jobbágyság" (Der ungarische Bauernaufstand von 1514 und die „zweite Leibeigenschaft"). Az MTA Filozófiai és Történettudományi Osztályának Közleményei 1972; P. Zs. PACH: A kelet-európai „Gutswirtschaft" problematikájához: robotmunka és bérmunka a földesúri majorságokon a XVI—XVII. századi Magyarországon (Zur Problematik der osteuropäischen „Gutswirtschaft": Fronarbeit und Lohnarbeit auf den ungarischen Herrengütern des 16. und 17. Jahrhunderts). Agrártörténeti Szemle 1971; J. VARGA: Typen und Probleme des bäuerlichen Grundbesitzes in Ungarn, 1767—1849. Budapest 1965; J. VARGA: Jobbágyrendszer Magyarországon a feudalizmus kései századaiban 1556—1767 (Leibeigenensystem in Ungarn im Spätfeudalismus 1566—1767). Budapest 1969. Über Rumänien siehe die in Anmerkung 29 angegebene Literatur. Über Polen: L. ZYTKOWICZ: The Peasant's Farm and the Landlord's Farm in Poland from the 16th to the Middle of the 18th Century. The Journal of Economic History 1972.

Hier zeigt sich charakteristisch der im Grunde genommen westliche Entwicklungsgang des böhmisch-mährischen Beckens. Auch hier finden wir die auf der Fron beruhenden Gutswirtschaften, deren Produktion aber war nicht für den Export bestimmt, sondern zur Befriedigung der Nachfrage durch die städtische Entwicklung in Böhmen-Mähren, dementsprechend war auch die Produktionsstruktur anders. Der führende Zweig der Viehzucht z. B. war lange Zeit die ausgesprochen den örtlichen Markt beliefernde Teichwirtschaft.

Dasselbe können wir auch von den Formen des Bodeneigentums sagen. Die ursprüngliche Rolle der Dorfgemeinschaften war auf dem Balkan oder in Rußland unvergleichlich größer und blieb länger bestehen — ebenso die Dorfgemeinschaft als Steuereinheit, wie auch die gegenseitige Verantwortung der Mitglieder der Dorfgemeinschaft — als in Polen oder Ungarn oder in Kroatien, wo sich das System der Dorfgemeinschaft fast in gar nichts mehr vom westeuropäischen unterschied, wo die Bauern dem Grundherrn, dem Staat als einzelner Steuern zahlten. In diesen Ländern wurde auch die Bauernbefreiung für die einzelnen Bauern durchgeführt, nicht wie in Rußland, wo durch die Bauernbefreiung die Dorfgemeinschaft vielleicht noch besser konserviert wurde — sie aufgrund des Prinzips von der gemeinsamen Verantwortung für die Ablösungszahlungen für den Boden verantwortlich machte —[31]. In Polen und Ungarn blieb zwar der Flurzwang bestehen, da hier das herrschende System der landwirtschaftlichen Produktion die Felderwirtschaft war, und noch einige Elemente der Flurgemeinschaft — Gemeinbesitz an Berg, Wald und Weide; darüber hinaus aber hatte die Dorfgemeinschaft keine solche gesellschaftliche Funktion wie in Rußland, Serbien oder Rumänien. Auch war es nicht in dem Maße wie dort üblich, den Bauern wie einen Sklaven zu behandeln, ihn unabhängig vom Boden zu kaufen oder zu verkau-

[31] M. Kovalevskii: Le régime économique de la Russie. Paris 1898; L. Volin: The Peasant Household under the Mir and the Kholkoz in modern Russian History. New York 1940; V. A. Aleksandrov: Sel' skaia obschtschina v Rossii /XVII-natschalo XIX v. (Dorfgemeinschaft in Rußland vom 17. bis zum Beginn des 19. Jahrhunderts). Moskau 1976; S. Dubrovski: K voprosu ob obschtschine v Rossii v natschale XX.v. (Zur Frage der Dorfgemeinschaft in Rußland am Anfang des 20. Jahrhunderts). In: Ezhegodnik po agrarnoi istorii Vostotschnoi Ecropi 1962.

fen [32]. Auch rechtlich war hier das vom Bauern genutzte Land von dem vom Gutsherrn bewirtschafteten Boden getrennt, und es bestand keine Möglichkeit, die Felder der Bauern zu reduzieren wie in Rußland und Rumänien, wo die Bauernbefreiung mit einer wesentlichen Verkleinerung des bäuerlichen Bodens verbunden war. In diesen Ländern erfolgte eigentlich in der zweiten Hälfte des 18. Jahrhunderts und zu Beginn des 19. Jahrhunderts die Regelung des Frondienstsystems durch den Staat, wie wir es vom Baltikum über Preußen bis zum Österreichischen Kaiserreich überall finden. Im Zarenreich ist das nur in den baltischen Regierungsbezirken verwirklicht worden, während die zaristische Regierung die Regulierung der Fron in den 30er und 40er Jahren des 19. Jahrhunderts nur auf die Bauern der staatlichen Güter ausdehnte [33].

Wir müssen auch darauf verweisen, daß die Städte und die städtischen Bürger in Polen, Ungarn und im Baltikum mehr oder weniger den westeuropäischen Grad der Organisierung zu selbständigen Ständen erreichten, die Städte und die Bürger in Rußland und in den Balkanländern aber nie. Es stimmt, daß im Westen Osteuropas das Bürgertum fast bis zum Schluß auch ethnisch fremd blieb; langsam aber wurde es in das wirtschaftlich-gesellschaftliche Gefüge eingebaut, versah eine selbständige Funktion und assimilierte sich dementsprechend mit der örtlichen Bevölkerung. Dazu kam es in Rußland und auf dem Balkan nie, die Siedlungen mit städtischem Charakter wurden eigentlich nie vom Grundherrn unabhängig, ihre Einwohner hatten den gleichen Rechtsstand wie die Bauern.

Osteuropa war also durch Westeuropas wirtschaftliche — und durch die Einwanderung auch soziale — Entwicklung eigentlich zweigeteilt. Das Baltikum, Polen, Ungarn und Kroatien hatten, stärker erst vom 19. Jahrhundert ab, durch die Auswirkung der Wirtschaftsentwicklung und des Marktanspruchs Westeuropas einen besonderen Weg der Entwicklung beschritten, auf dem ihnen der größte Teil Osteuropas nicht folgte. Hierher drangen Westeuropas Bedürfnisse, als die technischen Möglichkei-

---

[32] Es ist in dieser Hinsicht auch interessant, diese doppelte Struktur in Ungarn zu verfolgen. Der alte Streit, ob in Ungarn Bauern unabhängig von Boden gekauft und verkauft wurden, wird durch die von Zeit zu Zeit auftauchenden Belege jeweils neu belebt. Wenn wir die Angaben auf die Landkarte projizieren, fällt sofort auf, daß sie zum größten Teil aus der östlichen Hälfte des Landes, vor allem aus den Karpaten stammen.

[33] Die Regulierung der Frondienste bei den adeligen Bauern wurde in Rußland bis zur Bauernbefreiung nicht durchgeführt.

ten des Verkehrs den Transport gewährleisteten. Abgesehen von den Gebieten an der See oder an schiffbaren Flüssen war das erst zur Zeit des Eisenbahnbaus der Fall, bis dahin blieb das kontinentale Osteuropa von den westeuropäischen Einwirkungen unberührt (Der Einfluß des Fernhandels kann in dieser Hinsicht übergangen werden, er formte die wirtschaftlich-gesellschaftliche Struktur nicht). Seine Entwicklung verlief in dem langsamen Tempo, das für die auf dem System der Dorfgemeinschaften basierende Gesellschaft vom Altertum bis zum 20. Jahrhundert charakteristisch war.

In einer Hinsicht wurde dieses Bild verändert, in dem die Entwicklung des kontinentalen Osteuropa beschleunigt wurde: durch den militärischen Einfluß Westeuropas bzw. der Westeuropa vermittelnden skandinavischen und mitteleuropäischen Staaten. Die technische Entwicklung, die schwere Reiterei, vor allem aber die Verbreitung der Feuerwaffen zwangen die Ungarn und Polen, die Völker des Baltikums und schließlich die russischen Zaren, mit der Entwicklung Schritt zu halten, wenn sie im Kampf nicht unterliegen wollten. Später dann aber wurde es, weil es sich bei den immer größer werdenden Heeren als billiger erwies, notwendig, die Kriegsindustrie auf ein ähnliches Niveau wie das westeuropäische zu heben. Das war der eigentliche Sinn der Industrieentwicklungspolitik der Zaren vor Peter dem Großen, besonders aber die Industrialisierungsbestrebungen Peters des Großen. Die schnelle Einrichtung von Eisenhütten, Waffen- und Schiffsmanufakturen war in Rußland nur mit staatlichen Mitteln möglich, womit von vornherein der Rahmen dieser industriellen Entwicklung festgelegt war. Das Niveau des industriellen Entwicklungsstandes begründete noch immer keine Manufakturen auf anderen Gebieten des Lebens, und so wurden auch keine oder nur vereinzelte eingerichtet. In den Manufakturen arbeiteten keine Lohnarbeiter, sondern Zwangsarbeiter, vor allem als Sklaven gekaufte Bauern, seltener die eigenen Bauern des Grundherrn. Der oberflächliche Beobachter sieht also im allgemeinen die Entwicklung der Manufaktur — dazu noch in einem in Westeuropa üblichen Rahmen—, obwohl diese Manufakturindustrie einseitig entwickelt war, auf staatlichen Aufträgen basierte und nur die Bedürfnisse der Armee befriedigte und die dort beschäftigten Arbeiter bis zur Bauernbefreiung aus den Reihen der abhängigen Bauern kamen. Die Bedarfsgüterindustrie reichte im größten Teil

Osteuropas bis zum dritten Viertel des 19. Jahrhunderts nicht über den Rahmen des Hausgewerbes hinaus [34].

Überblicken wir jetzt also die Besonderheiten der gesellschaftlich-wirtschaftlichen Struktur Osteuropas in der ersten Hälfte des 19. Jahrhunderts. Noch einmal müssen wir die Zweiteilung des Gebietes betonen, zwei große Sphären, die sich vom Baltikum und Polen bis nach Kroatien erstreckende westliche Hälfte, die von Westeuropas starken wirtschaftlichen, politischen und kulturellen Auswirkungen beeeinflußt wurde, wo vom 15. und 16. Jahrhundert an eine neue Ordnung der gutsherrlichen Warenproduktion in den Allodien entstand, wo auch die große Zahl der westeuropäischen bäuerlichen Siedler und zum Teil städtischen Bürger die Entwicklung beeinflußte — und das kontinentale Osteuropa, Rußland und der Balkan, das eigentlich erst in diesen Jahrzehnten die Auswirkungen der westeuropäischen Wirtschaft erreichte, das sich demzufolge erst jetzt in den Welthandel einzuschalten begann, wo das System der Dorfgemeinschaften unberührt bestehen geblieben, die Rolle der Städte verschwindend gering war, wo vorwiegend nur Hausgewerbe getrieben wurde, wo also durch die langsame Entwicklung die Waren-Verhältnisse auf einem sehr niedrigen Niveau standen und wo natürlich als Folge all dieser Wirkungen das despotische Herrschaftssystem bestehen geblieben war. Die zaristische Politik zog die ungeheuren Unterschiede, die zwischen den westlichen Gebieten des Reiches — Polen, die baltischen Regierungsbezirke — und Innerrußland bestanden, in Betracht. So wurde z. B. die Bauernbefreiung hier und dort ganz anders durchgeführt.

Und hier können wir einen Augenblick innehalten, um die Besonderheiten der Bauernbefreiung in Osteuropa zu überblicken, die — wenn wir sie im einzelnen betrachten — ebenso die strukturellen Unterschiede zwischen beiden Gebieten bezeichnen wie die bisher behandelten historischen Erscheinungen [35].

---

[34] I. Bovikin: Oroszország ipari fejlödésének társadalmi-gazdasági problémai (Soziale und wirtschaftliche Probleme der Industrieentwicklung Rußlands). Történelmi Szemle 1973; Otscherki ekonomitscheskoi istorii Rossii v pervoi polovine XIX v. (Skizzen zur Wirtschaftsgeschichte Rußlands in der ersten Hälfte des 19. Jahrhunderts). Moskau 1959; R. Portal: The Industrialisation of Russia. The Cambridge Economic History of Europe, Band 6. Cambridge 1965.

[35] Über die in den osteuropäischen Ländern durchgeführte Bauernbefreiung E. Niederhauser: A jobbágyfelszabaditás Kelet-Európában (Die Bauernbefreiung in Osteuropa). Budapest 1962.

Natürlich gibt es allgemeine Charakteristika, die Osteuropas Einheit kennzeichnen. Einmal die sehr starke Rolle des Staates bei der Durchführung der Bauernbefreiung, die nicht nur von Bedeutung war, weil sie der Staat selbst durchführte, die Reformen auch gegen den Widerstand der überwiegenden Mehrheit der herrschenden Klasse durchsetzte, sondern auch, weil der wegen der Kapitalarmut des Landes, vor allem aber der Bauern, überall eine wichtige Rolle bei der Sicherung der materiellen Entschädigung des Adels spielte. Zum anderen, daß die Bauernbefreiung überall durch von oben durchgeführte Reformen, im allgemeinen im Verlaufe einiger Jahrzehnte oder eines längeren historischen Prozesses erfolgte. Natürlich gibt es zwischen den einzelnen Ländern viele Abweichungen, die wahren Unterschiede aber lagen, wie wir sehen werden, woanders.

Eines der Hauptmomente war die persönliche Befreiung der Bauern. In dieser Hinsicht gab es gewaltige Unterschiede zwischen Baltikum, Polen, Ungarn, Kroatien und den übrigen Teilen Osteuropas. In der westlichen Zone waren die Bauern in ihrer Person schon früher frei geworden, z. B. im österreichischen Kaiserreich durch die Reformen Josefs II. Der Staat hatte auch den Umfang ihrer Leistungen geregelt. Hier wurde — abgesehen von der Aufhebung der Leistungen — darüber entschieden, ob die Bauern nach der schon früher durchgeführten rechtlichen Trennung des gutsherrlichen und des bäuerlichen Bodens — terra dominicalis, terra rusticalis — auch von der von ihnen genutzten terra dominicalis etwas erhalten sollten oder nicht — in Ungarn nur in bestimmten Fällen, in Russisch-Polen in größerem Umfange. Im Innern des Zarenreiches — Rußland — und in Rumänien jedoch ging der Streit darum, ob

a) die noch immer Sklaven gleichenden Bauern persönlich befreit werden sollten — worüber es im allgemeinen nur geringere Meinungsverschiedenheiten gab — und

b) diese befreiten Sklaven Land erhalten sollten. In diesen Gebieten Osteuropas war nämlich früher das Land nicht in zwei Teile zerfallen, alles Land wurde im Prinzip vom Adel genutzt. Die Bauern benutzten das Land zwar, aber der Gutsherr konnte es ganz nach Belieben wegnehmen, austauschen, verkleinern. Dafür gab es keine rechtlichen Hindernisse — auch nicht gewohnheitsrechtliche —, wie auch dafür nicht, daß die Bauern persönlich käuflich und verkäuflich waren.

Demzufolge wurde sowohl in Rumänien wie auch im eigentlichen Rußland durch die Bauernbefreiung das in der Nutzung der Bauern befindliche Land wesentlich verkleinert. Dabei spielte auch eine Rolle, daß diese Jahrzehnte gerade die Zeit der Getreidekonjunktur waren, durch den Eisenbahnbau die ersten Möglichkeiten zum größeren Getreideexport gegeben waren und daß die Bauern die Möglichkeit erhielten — da sie kein Geld hatten —, den Wert ihrer Dienstleistungen durch Land abzulösen. Daraus folgt, daß unserer Meinung nach die schon früher vorhandenen Unterschiede in der wirtschaftlichen-sozialen Entwicklung der Grund dafür waren, daß die zaristische Regierung die Bauernbefreiung innerhalb des Zarenreiches, in den baltischen Regierungsbezirken und im Königreich Polen jeweils anders durchführte als im eigentlichen Rußland. Damit ziehen wir die Wirkung des polnischen Aufstandes nicht in Zweifel, wie das die Geschichtsschreibung häufig tut. Wir müssen hierbei beachten, daß die Regierung eines auf dem System der Dorfgemeinschaften aufgebauten despotischen Reiches immer außergewöhnlich elastisch ist und die örtlichen Überlieferungen in Betracht zieht, wie das z. B. auch die Türken oder die Mongolen getan haben.

Ein anderer Unterschied zwischen beiden Zonen zeigte sich darin, daß die Bauern in Polen und in Ungarn bei der Bauernbefreiung ihre Felder als persönliches Eigentum erhielten, wofür der Staat die Grundherren entschädigte, in Rußland und in Rumänien die Bauernbefreiung die ehemaligen Sklaven — oder wenn wir so wollen, die Leibeigenen — zwar persönlich befreite und dann lediglich dafür sorgte, daß die gutsherrlichen Felder von denen der Dorfgemeinschaft getrennt wurden. Denn über die den Bauern zugefallenen Felder disponierte auch weiterhin die Dorfgemeinschaft. Die Bauernbefreiung zerschlug in diesen Ländern die Dorfgemeinschaft nicht, sondern stärkte sie in gewissem Sinne, indem sie ihr die Entschädigung des Grundherrn übertrug. In Rußland blieb auch nach der Bauernbefreiung in den Dorfgemeinschaften die nivellierende Bodennutzung bestehen, die den Bauern zugefallenen Felder wurden von Zeit zu Zeit neu verteilt, was ein außergewöhnliches Hindernis für die ungestörte Entwicklung kapitalistischer Verhältnisse war. Die Aufhebung der Dorfgemeinschaften erfolgte in Rußland erst nach dem Bauernaufstand von 1905/06, in Serbien erst nach dem Ersten Weltkrieg, in Rumänien und in Kroatien in den 1880er/90er Jahren. Vom vollrechtlichen Privateigentum der Bauern am Boden können wir also in diesem Gebiet erst nach Auflösung der Dorfgemeinschaft sprechen.

Das geschah — wie schon erwähnt — sehr langsam, weil die Verpflichtungen für die Befreiung auf der Dorfgemeinschaft lasteten; sie übernahm die Bürgschaft für die Geld- und Arbeitsleistungen. Aber auch danach bestanden noch zahlreiche feudale Bindungen. Auch nach der Bauernbefreiung bestellten die Bauern die ehemaligen gutsherrlichen Felder mit Frondienst, womit sie Felder bezahlten, die in ihr Eigentum übergegangen waren. Das System der Fron bzw. der Abarbeitung blieb auch weiterhin bestehen, die Grundherren ließen den Bauern Land zukommen, und diese bezahlten es mit ihrer Arbeit. So entstand in Rußland und in Rumänien das klassische System der Abarbeitung, das für eine ganze historische Epoche charakteristisch wurde. Dieses System zeigte sich in Ungarn und in Polen nur in seinen Elementen und nur für kurze, in Rußland und Rumänien dagegen für längere Zeit. Und das ist ein sehr entscheidender Unterschied, der schließlich in Rußland und auch in Rumänien Ende des 19. und zu Beginn des 20. Jahrhunderts zu heftigen Bauernaufständen geführt hat. Sobald als deren Folge die Dorfgemeinschaften und das die Bauern knebelnde System der Abarbeitung beseitigt wurden, begann die gesellschaftlich-wirtschaftliche Entwicklung im kontinentalen Osteuropa auch in qualitativer Hinsicht an die westliche Zone anzuschließen.

Von der zweiten Hälfte des 19. Jahrhunderts an verlief die Entwicklung in den beiden aufgezeigten Hauptsektoren Osteuropas in derselben Richtung, wenn auch nicht im gleichen Tempo. Der Welthandel, genauer die mit Westeuropa entstehenden Wirtschaftsverbindungen, lenkten die Entwicklung auf dem Balkan eigentlich auf denselben Weg wie in Polen, Ungarn oder Kroatien, wobei natürlich das Fortbestehen des Systems der Dorfgemeinschaften oder sogar dessen Stärkung ganz andere Hindernisse darstellten. So gesehen ist es kein Zufall, daß es Ende des 19. Jahrhunderts und zu Beginn des 20. Jahrhunderts gerade in Rumänien und im zaristischen Rußland zu riesigen Bauernaufständen kam, im Königreich Rumänien 1888 und 1907, in Rußland 1905/06. Sie zeigten die Erschütterungen des Systems an und zwangen die herrschenden Kreise, die Reformen durchzuführen — vor allem die Beseitigung der Dorfgemeinschaften —, die die kapitalistische Entwicklung erleichterten und diese Länder dem polnischen, ungarischen und kroatischen Modell annäherten. Deshalb treten für den heutigen Beobachter allenfalls noch die an statistischen Daten ablesbaren zahlenmäßigen und zeitlichen Unterschiede in den Vordergrund — z. B. daß um die Jahrhundertwende in

Ungarn ungefähr 60% der Bevölkerung von der Landwirtschaft lebte, auf dem Balkan oder in Rußland dagegen 80%, daß von allen Erwerbstätigen der Anteil der in der Landwirtschaft Beschäftigten in Ungarn — um 1930 — 50% betrug, in Jugoslawien noch 1960 an 57%, in Rumänien sogar 70%. Obwohl die hinter den statistischen Angaben verborgenen Unterschiede auch dabei nicht nur quantitative, sondern sehr oft qualitative waren und auf jeden Fall die wesentlichen Unterschiede zeigen, die zwischen den beiden Teilen Osteuropas als Folge der früheren historischen Entwicklung auch dann noch bestanden, als die Wirkung der beide Teile voneinander trennenden Faktoren im kontinentalen Osteuropa bereits aufgehört hatte [36]. Von der Wende vom 19. zum 20. Jahrhundert ab stand die Entwicklung beider Regionen qualitativ auf dem gleichen Niveau, wenn, wie wir aus den wenigen Beispielen gesehen haben, die überkommenen Unterschiede auch weiterbestanden. Durch den Einfluß des Weltmarktes wurde, begleitet von nicht zu unterschätzenden Besonderheiten — feudale Überreste, Kapitalmangel usw. —, die Entwicklung ganz Osteuropas auf den westlichen Weg gelenkt, was natürlich nicht bedeutet, daß der historische Weg Osteuropas im Zeitalter des Kapitalismus qualitativ dem Westeuropas gleich gewesen wäre. Osteuropa aber gelang es, endgültig aus dem für die übrige Welt bezeichnenden Entwicklungsmodell auszubrechen und Westeuropa zu folgen [37].

Die Entwicklung des Kapitalismus zeigt in Osteuropa zahlreiche spezielle Züge. Die Besonderheiten, die sich in der Entwicklung im Verlaufe der früheren Jahrhunderte gezeigt hatten, konnte die Industrialisierung nicht beseitigen — im Gegenteil, nicht zuletzt ihretwegen und auch aus anderen Gründen hat die Entwicklung des Kapitalismus in Osteuropa sehr bezeichnende Besonderheiten. Statt sie im einzelnen zu analysieren — was einer späteren Studie vorbehalten bleiben soll —, wollen wir zur Entwicklung Osteuropas im Zeitalter des Kapitalismus lediglich einige Gedanken aufwerfen, vor allem vom Gesichtspunkt der

---

36 In dieser Auffassung wird die wirtschaftliche und soziale Entwicklung Osteuropas im 19. Jahrhundert geschildert: I. T. Berend-Gy. Ranki: Közép-Kelet-európa gazdasági fejlödése a 19—20. században (Die Wirtschaftsentwicklung Mittel- und Osteuropas im 19. und 20. Jahrhundert). Budapest 1976.

37 Nordamerika hatte das schon früher getan, dort aber hatte mit der Vertreibung und physischen Vernichtung der Indianer eine in vielem von feudalen Überlieferungen freie Form des westeuropäischen Modells von Anfang an gesiegt.

Agrarentwicklung, denn wir glauben, daß die Kenntnis einiger Besonderheiten der neuzeitlichen Entwicklung das Erkennen der weiteren historischen Entwicklung und das Verständnis der späteren Lage der osteuropäischen Länder in vielem erleichtern werden.

### *1. Die Frage von Großbetrieb — Kleinbetrieb*

Bekanntlich gibt es über die Frage, ob der Kleinbetrieb, vor allem der bäuerliche Betrieb, entwicklungsfähig ist, eine umfangreiche Literatur, und bekannt ist auch, daß diese Frage für Osteuropa von ganz besonderer Bedeutung war. Ohne Zweifel haben bei der Beurteilung der Dinge stets auch die aktuellen politischen Probleme mitgespielt. Die Anhänger des sozialen Fortschritts erklärten lange Zeit, daß die wirtschaftliche und soziale Entwicklung in Osteuropa ausschließlich von den auch im Zeitalter des Kapitalismus außergewöhnlich starken feudalen Überresten behindert worden sei, und darunter verstanden sie in erster Linie, oft sogar ausschließlich, die riesigen Latifundien. Darin steckte ohne Zweifel Wahrheit; es wäre aber nicht angebracht, die Frage nur darauf einzuengen. In den westlichen Randgebieten Osteuropas, in Ungarn, Polen, Kroatien und zum Teil in Böhmen hatte die auf dem Frondienst basierende Gutswirtschaft von ihrem Entstehen an gezeigt, daß nur die Großbetriebe große Warenmengen produzieren konnten. Diese Großbetriebe waren gleichzeitig auch in der Lage, die Errungenschaften der modernen Agro- und Zootechnik anzuwenden, die neuen Maschinen und Geräte, den Kunstdünger usw. zu beschaffen, und nicht zuletzt bot auch diese moderne Betriebsorganisation bedeutende Vorteile. Später, als sich das kontinentale Osteuropa in den Weltmarkt eingeschaltet hatte, wurden in Rußland und auch in Rumänien die nach der Bauernbefreiung bestehenden Latifundien zu echten Motoren der landwirtschaftlichen Warenproduktion, sie führten die modernen Produktionsmethoden ein. Nur diese riesigen Großbetriebe hatten das Kapital, das zur Modernisierung der Produktion erforderlich war. Die statistischen Angaben verwischen zwar häufig die Unterschiede zwischen dem Produktionsniveau der Groß- und der Kleinbetriebe, bedenken wir aber, was sich hinter einer solchen Durchschnittsangabe verbirgt. Wenn wir überlegen, wie wenig Kunstdünger in Osteuropa auf eine Gebietseinheit verwendet wurde, dann bedeutet das, daß

a) die Kunstdünger streuenden Großbetriebe ebensoviel verbrauchten wie in Westeuropa, daß aber

b) im größten Teil des Landes überhaupt kein Kunstdünger verwendet wurde.

Es ließen sich mehr ähnliche Beispiele anführen, aber das ist nicht nötig. Schon dieses eine Beispiel beleuchtet das Wesentliche.

Aber auch für die kleinen Betriebe besteht ein Weg der Weiterentwicklung: die zunehmende Nutzung der überzähligen, vom Gesichtspunkt des Betriebes kostenlosen Arbeitskraft der Bauernfamilien. Das zeigte sich vor allem beim Anbau der Pflanzen, die viel Handarbeit erfordern und bei der Entwicklung der arbeitsintensiven Zweige der Viehzucht. Infolgedessen entstand sehr bald die Arbeitsteilung zwischen Groß- und Kleinbetrieben. Entscheidend ist aber, daß die Kleinbetriebe nach wie vor weniger produktiv blieben, und sobald ihre Produktion intensiver wurde, war das fast ausschließlich der starken Ausnutzung der physischen Kraft der Agrarbevölkerung zuzuschreiben.

Es versteht sich von selbst, daß sich alle, die in der Politik gegen den Großgrundbesitz auftraten, über diesen Tatbestand im klaren waren. Daß sie dennoch in diesen, mit moderner Technik produzierenden, die besseren Methoden der Betriebsorganisation anwendenden und daher intensiver produzierenden Großbetrieben das Haupthindernis für die Entwicklung erblickten, hatte noch andere Gründe. Und damit sind wir bei der zweiten Frage.

*2. Die Bodenfrage*

Weil sich in Osteuropa die Industrie langsam entwickelte, weil der größte Teil der Bevölkerung auch um die Mitte des 20. Jahrhunderts in der Landwirtschaft beschäftigt war, hat die Bodenfrage ganz besondere Dimensionen angenommen. Bis in die letzten Jahrzehnte sind die meisten Osteuropäer Bauern geblieben. Als aber vom 18. Jahrhundert an durch die allgemeine Hygiene und andere Errungenschaften die Bevölkerung immer schneller zunahm, ergab sich eine ganz eigenartige Situation: Das Land war zum größten Teil im Besitz der Gutsherren, die anwachsende bäuerliche Bevölkerung mußte also auf der gleichen Bodenfläche existieren. Das führte zu einer bedeutenden Zerstückelung der Parzellen, zur Verarmung vieler Bauern. In Westeuropa wurde diese Frage — zum

Teil aufgrund der germanischen Überlieferung — gelöst, indem nur der älteste Sohn den Bauernhof erbte. Er zahlte die übrigen Geschwister aus, die abwanderten oder Lohnarbeiter wurden, anfangs in der Landwirtschaft, später in der Industrie. Die industrielle Entwicklung in Osteuropa war aber so langsam und so schwach, daß die überschüssige Bevölkerung in der Landwirtschaft steckenblieb. Das Land wurde bei den Bauern proportional vererbt — Realteilung —, so daß durch die gemeinsame Wirkung beider Faktoren die Schicht der landlosen Bauern oder der Zwergbauern unermeßlich vergrößert wurde. In der Hauptsaison der landwirtschaftlichen Arbeiten, beim Abernten und Einfahren, arbeiteten sie auf den großen Gütern oder bei den wohlhabenden Bauern und erhielten dafür ihre Bezahlung in Naturalien, die ihnen das Existenzminimum garantierte, die übrige Zeit des Jahres aber waren sie meist arbeitslos. Sie konnten auch keine Arbeit bekommen, denn durch die außergewöhnlich langsame Entwicklung der nichtagrarischen Sektoren der Wirtschaft bot sich ihnen dort keine Arbeitsmöglichkeit, auch in der Landwirtschaft nicht. Diese immer größer werdende Schicht konnte sich ihr Leben nur innerhalb der überlieferten bäuerlichen Rahmen vorstellen, ihr Traum war ausreichender Landbesitz, die Erfüllung des bäuerlichen Daseins. Ein Teil von ihnen wanderte in der zweiten Hälfte des 19. Jahrhunderts aus, vor allem nach Nordamerika. Damit wurde der offene Ausbruch der gesellschaftlichen Gegensätze teilweise abgebremst. Als aber nach dem Ersten Weltkrieg keine Möglichkeit zum Auswandern mehr bestand, blieb den anwachsenden Millionen nur die Hoffnung, igendwie im eigenen Lande Grundbesitz zu erlangen. Diesen Traum verwirklichten nach dem Ersten Weltkrieg die Bodenreformen in Osteuropa, die vor allem in den Ländern, wo größere Reformen durchgeführt wurden, im Baltikum, zum Teil in Polen und in Rumänien, diesen Wunschtraum um eine Generation verlängerten.

So können wir also ohne weiteres sagen, daß die Bodenfrage in Europa als soziales-politisches Problem eine typisch osteuropäische Erscheinung ist. Sie ergab sich natürlich überall dort, wo die Entwicklung auf dem von der Bodeneigentumsform der Dorfgemeinschaft bestimmten Niveau erfolgte. In Westeuropa stellte sich das bäuerliche Dilemma anders. An der landwirtschaftlichen Produktion war ein immer kleinerer Teil der Bevölkerung beteiligt, die Größe der rentablen Betriebe nahm ständig zu, zur Betriebsführung war immer mehr Kapital erforderlich, der Überschuß der landwirtschaftlichen Bevölkerung erhielt Arbeit in den nichtagrarischen Sektoren der Landwirtschaft, die sich stürmisch entwickelten. Dort stellte sich also die Agrarfrage als Beseitigung der bäuerlichen Existenz, durch die Verminderung der Zahl der Bauern in der Gesamtbevökerung bestimmt. In Osteuropa — und in anderen Teilen der Welt — gab es zur Erhaltung der Existenz der in der Landwirtschaft steckengebliebenen, anwachsenden Millionen keine andere Möglichkeit als die Bodenreform, die möglichst radikale Aufteilung der Großgrundbesitze — so intensiv sie auch produzierten. Diese Massen — und vielleicht auch die ihre Interessen vertretenden Politiker — waren sich nicht immer im klaren darüber, daß dies nur eine vorübergehende Lösung sein konnte.

Unserer Meinung nach war das eigentliche Problem nicht das Vorhandensein der Großgrundbesitze, sondern die sehr langsame Entwicklung der nichtagrarischen Sektoren der Wirtschaft. Gerade in den Ländern, die die osteuropäische Struktur am typischsten vertraten, in Bulgarien und Serbien, wo durch einen Zufall der Gutsherr verschwunden war — die ursprünglich herrschende Klasse hatten die Türken vertrieben, bei der Befreiung von der Türkenherrschaft aber waren die türkischen Grundherren geflohen, und damit hatte auch das grundherrliche System aufgehört zu bestehen —, war die wirtschaftliche Entwicklung am stärksten zurückgeblieben, wurde die Landfrage zu einem derart zentralen Problem, daß z. B. in Bulgarien die Bauern zu Beginn der 1920er Jahre — da es aufteilbares grundherrliches Land nicht gab — untereinander eine Agrarrevolution versuchten und die ärmeren die Felder der wohlhabenderen Bauern aufteilen wollten [38]. Das war natürlich keine Lösung, hätte die Schwierigkeiten allenfalls für eine Generation überbrückt, denn die Grundfrage war ja, daß wegen der fehlenden Industrieentwicklung immer mehr Menschen auf der gleichen Bodenfläche ausschließlich von der Landwirtschaft leben mußten. So ergab sich die eigenartige Situation, daß der bulgarische oder serbische Bauer, der keinen Großgrundbesitz kannte, mit seinem wenige Hektar großen Betrieb auf einem wesentlich niedrigeren Lebensniveau lebte als — sagen wir — der ostdeutsche Agrarproletarier. Die Landfrage war und blieb also nicht an sich, sondern wegen der außergewöhnlich langsamen und schwachen Entwick-

---

[38] Zur Situation in Bulgarien: Z. Petrov: Agrarnite reformi v Bulgaria 1880—1944 (Die Agrarreformen in Bulgarien 1880—1944). Sofia 1975.

lung der nichtagrarischen Sektoren der Wirtschaft das typisch zentrale Problem der osteuropäischen Länder [39].

### 3. *Die Besonderheiten der Industrieentwicklung*

Die Industrieentwicklung begann in Osteuropa nicht nur später und langsamer als in Westeuropa, sie hatte auch innerhalb der Wirtschaft in vieler Hinsicht eine besondere Funktion. Die Entwicklung der Industrie war von Anfang an nicht nur eine wirtschaftliche, sondern auch eine außenpolitische Frage. Es war kein Zufall, daß sich die Industrieentwicklung des Staates vom Ende des 17. Jahrhunderts an in erster Linie auf die kriegswichtigen Industriezweige erstreckte. Alle technisch modernen, auf dem Niveau der Zeit stehenden Industriezweige und Betriebe befanden sich ausnahmslos in diesen Wirtschaftszweigen. Als vom 19. Jahrhundert ab die Entwicklung auch auf anderen Gebieten der Industrie einsetzte, entstand eine ganz eigenartige Lage. Entweder ist die Industriestruktur ungewöhnlich widersprüchlich: neben der modernen Fabrikindustrie existiert das primitive, seine Aufgabe aber gut erfüllende Hausgewerbe — so z. B. auf dem Balkan oder in Rußland, wo — grob ausgedrückt — der Industrieartikelbedarf der bäuerlichen Bevölkerung von letzterem, jener der städtischen Bevölkerung von ersterer befriedigt wird — oder aber — und das ist vor allem für den Westrand Osteuropas bezeichnend —, daß die Industrieentwicklung zwar schneller als allgemein in Osteuropa verläuft und die Wirtschaft tiefer durchdringt und die nichtagrarischen Sektoren eine größere Rolle in der Nationalwirtschaft spielen, diese Industrie aber, und besonders in einzelnen Zweigen eigentlich nicht für den Binnenmarkt, sondern für den Export produziert. Der Binnenmarkt ist eng, was bei der ganzen wirtschaftlichen Entwicklung durchaus verständlich ist. Der größte Teil der Agrarbevölkerung steht fast vollkommen außerhalb, kauft kaum Industrieartikel und

---

[39] Zu den Zusammenhängen zwischen der wirtschaftlichen und sozialen Entwicklung und den Typen der Bauernschaft, zu den Unterschieden zwischen der bäuerlichen Entwicklung in West- und Osteuropa und zu den unterschiedlichen Typen der Bauernschaft in den beiden Regionen siehe P. Gunst: Az agrárfejlödés és a parasztság regionális tipusai Európában (Die Agrarentwicklung und die regionalen Typen der Bauernschaft in Europa). In: Paraszti társadalom és müveltség a 18—20. században. I. Faluk. (Bäuerliche Gesellschaft und Bildung im 18.—20. Jahrhundert. I. Dörfer). Szolnok 1974. (Konferenz zur Ungarischen Ethnographischen Gesellschaft im Jahre 1974 in Szolnok).

produziert auch kaum Waren, die Industrie war also vor allem für Außenhandelszwecke entstanden. Auch für Ungarn wie für Polen war bezeichnend, daß sich vor allem die Industriezweige schnell entwickelten, die nicht den unmittelbaren Konsum der lokalen Bevölkerung befriedigten — einzelne Zweige der Schwerindustrie, die Maschinenindustrie usw. — und nicht für den Inlandbedarf, sondern, in die internationale Arbeitsteilung [40] eingeschaltet, vor allem für die unmittelbar benachbarten westeuropäischen Länder produzierten, während die Befriedigung des Bedarfs der Bevölkerung auch weiterhin dem primitiven Klein- oder Hausgewerbe vorbehalten blieb. Die Schwer- und die Leichtindustrie dieser osteuropäischen Länder produzierte vor allem für den Export, wie in der Landwirtschaft die warenproduzierenden Großbetriebe, demzufolge war die Industrieentwicklung zum Teil einseitig und spielte im Leben der Bevölkerung keine solche Rolle, wie sich im Nationaleinkommen oder in der Nationalwirtschaft staatlich nachweisen läßt. Zwischen Industrie und Binnenmarkt bestand und besteht auch heute noch nicht dieselbe Beziehung wie in Westeuropa. Die Industrie Osteuropas, vor allem die des westlichen Randgebietes, befand sich also in einer ganz besonderen Situation, insofern sie viel stärker vom Export abhing als die der industriell entwickelten westeuropäischen Länder, wo alle Zweige der Industrie bedeutenden Export abwickelten, ihre Produktion aber im Grunde genommen auf dem Verbrauch im Inland basierte, vor allem in den ersten Abschnitten der Entwicklung. In Osteuropa war das umgekehrt: Die Industrie verdankte ihre Entstehung dem Export und baute sich erst langsam auch auf dem Binnenhandel auf.

Gerade unter diesem Gesichtspunkt waren die Bodenreformen von ungeheurer Bedeutung, die den Bauern, diesem riesigen, außerhalb des Binnenmarktes stehenden Bevölkerungsteil die Möglichkeit schuf, sich in ihn einzuschalten. Durch die Bodenreformen wurden die Bauern, wenn auch in geringem Umfange, unmittelbare Konsumenten der Industrieartikel, und so müssen wir sagen, daß die Lösung der Bodenfrage die Voraussetzung dafür war, daß in Osteuropa die Industrie im Wirtschaftsgefüge die Aufgabe erfüllen konnte wie in Westeuropa.

---

[40] Vor dem Ersten Weltkrieg — unter Ausnutzung der damaligen staatlichen Rahmen — in die Arbeitsteilung der Österreich-Ungarischen Monarchie oder im Falle Polens als Partner der deutschen Industrieentwicklung, und die Vorteile dieser Entwicklung nutzend, in die Arbeitsteilung Deutschlands.

*4. Die Rolle des Staates*

In Osteuropa fiel dem Staat in der wirtschaftlichen Entwicklung eine ganz besondere Rolle zu. Die Entwicklung der Industrie, die Sicherstellung der infrastrukturellen Investitionen für den Transport der landwirtschaftlichen Produkte auf den Markt — Eisenbahnen, Straßenbau, Flußregulierung usw. — erforderten so riesiges Kapital, das hier nicht wie in Westeuropa in der Gesellschaft akkumuliert wurde. Deshalb sorgte hier der Staat für das notwendige Kapital, zum Teil durch ausländische Kredite — unter der Garantie ihrer Rückzahlung —, zum Teil durch unmittelbare Investitionen. Der Staat schaltete sich von Anfang an viel stärker als in Westeuropa in die industrielle Entwicklung ein und viel direkter. Vom 17. Jahrhundert an üben zwar auch die westeuropäischen Staaten einen zunehmenden Einfluß auf die Wirtschaft aus, aber, abgesehen von den Jahrzehnten nach der großen Weltwirtschaftskrise (1929 bis 1933), nur indirekt, vor allem durch die den Außenhandel regelnden Mittel. Der ökonomische Liberalismus westeuropäischer Prägung, als Folge der gut balancierten wirtschaftlichen Entwicklung Westeuropas, drängte den Staat sehr bald aus den wirtschaftlichen Unternehmungen heraus. In Osteuropa aber können wir von Peter dem Großen an Zeugen der direkten und sehr aktiven Wirtschaftstätigkeit des Staates sehen. Diese unmittelbare Einschaltung des Staates in die Wirtschaft ist deshalb bis zum Schluß eines der Charakteristika der osteuropäischen Wirtschaftsentwicklung.

# IV

# Dilemma of the Eastern-European Agrarian Development at the End of the 19th Century

One–two decades ago the historiography of the Eastern-European countries mentioned the peasant movements of the turn, or rather the beginning of the 20th century as the proof that the capitalistic development had come to a deadlock and only the socialist revolution could make further development possible. The historiography of certain countries has been dealing with these actions a lot, but surprisingly not an attempt has been made so far to make *comparative analysis* of these particular confusions of the Eastern-European agrarian development. Though the claim to make comparison is obvious and it can also be realized. But the historiography of the involved countries has narrowed the outlook down and comparative analysis has only been done in given cases to illustrate concrete themes (though the idea of making comparative analysis has never been given up). Due to the unknown details and the insufficient data the Western-European historiography could only establish generalities which could not result much advance for us. However, the analysis of these action—taking them into the *concrete* problems of the agrarian development at the time—would mark significantly all those features which determine not only the similarities of the economic and social development of a region but it can also give model of different development in certain regions.

At the turn of the 19th and 20th centuries some Eastern-European countries were shocked by peasant movements taking place in Hungary, Roumania and Russia. In Hungary the social unrest, the so-called "agrarian socialist movements" appeared between 1891 and 1907 first in part of Hungary which got its name after these actions (Viharsarok—it is the south-eastern part of the Great Hungarian Plain where the river Maros melts the Tisza) and later in other regions as well. Sometimes they were so violent that the army had to be put into action in order to break them. In 1888 and 1907 there were bloody peasant risings in Roumania and especially the latter was so violent that about 1400 people fell victims to the actions and the vengeance of the military forces. After the frequent local movements of the last two decades of the 19th century in 1905 series of peasant rising broke out in the Russian Empire spreading all over its European part which could only be suppressed by considerable military forces and the promise of reforms during about one and half years.

As it is seen the peasant movements spread nearly all over Eastern-Europe. In this case "nearly" cannot be neglected since besides Hungary and Roumania the Russian Empire contained both the greater part of Poland and Finland. Namely, only the western and southwestern part of Poland, Bohemia and the south slavic countries—Serbia, Bulgaria—remained untouched from these actions in the territory which is not quite exactly specified as Eastern-Europe today.

The researches have come to this point up till now. It is quite obvious that it is an Eastern-European appearance, series of signs which show the contradictions of the Eastern-European agrarian development and evidently mark the deadlock of the agrarian development which was a capitalistic one despite all the withdrawing forces. The historiography of the previous decades considered them a unit and their causes were believed to be similar everywhere.

This is the starting point of a further analysis. Are these features the same all over Eastern-Europe? Are their causes the same everywhere—in Roumania, Hungary and Russia? Did the same part of peasantry take part in these actions? Were the grievances of the peasantry in the involved countries and the motives of the actions and the demands the same? Can their different violence be attributed to a negligible smaller or bigger deviation? There are those questions which can show that they are by no means the same and they have different economic and social causes, occurrences and violence. But what are these differences? What conclusions can be drawn from them?

The fact that the participants of the movements present the whole peasantry in some of the involved countries only refers to a very essential difference in an important sector of the economic and social development. In both risings in Roumania the whole peasantry of the involved regions took part. The situation is somewhat more complicated in the czarian empire. The whole peasantry moved in the greater part of the empire indeed which meant the great masses of peasants. As the historiography always starts from the centre to the periphery and its European part is so large that no attention was paid to the different peasant risings of the western-southern regions not belonging to the black soil region of central Russia, or rather, the studies on analysis of these risings have not dealt with the different character and content of the western or outer ones. But provisionally we can also consider that all classes of peasantry—even the richer ones moved in the czarist empire.

Nevertheless, the situation was different in *Hungary*. Neither the landed peasants nor one part of the agrarian proletarians (day-labourers having dwarf- holdings) took part in these movements. Their participants got out of the harvesters, jobbers first and considerable less of domestics coming from big farms. Hence the participants of Hungarian "agrarian socialistic movements" were mainly agrarian employes. Although we can't say that certain parts of Hungary remained untouched, yet it is typically marked that they were concentrated in the Great Plain not counting the big strike of servants in Transdanubia. So the bigger part of the country of that time was not involved then.[1]

These differences did not come into being by chance. Namely, the structure of the Hungarian agrarian society essentially differed from the Russian or the Roumanian ones, namely the rate of landed peasantry in the whole agrarian population was much smaller here than in Russia or Roumania. The development of commodity production started sooner and went on to a larger extent in Hungary than it happened in the territories on our east. Even at the time of abolition of serfdom more than half of the agrarian population had belonged to cotters in Hungary, who had not enough land to keep himself and his family. And these strata could not live on their own lands before 1848 and a part of them completely lived on work for the others, although there were others who besides their own lands also worked in large estates or big farms of wealthy peasants to a lesser or larger extent.

During about five decades from the abolition of serfdom the number of strata living on work done for hire increased further. Though the industrialization moved forward with giant steps in this half of the century, but it could not absorb completely the poverty-stricken crowds of the increasing population. Despite all its results the Hungarian industrialization was not able to reduce or to hold the rate of agrarian have-nots in the agrarian population. In Western Europe the industrialization advanced so much and transformed the structure of society that consequently there was not only a decrease in the number and rate of agrarian have-nots but by that time a decrease of landed peasants had already started and a kind of estate concentration had begun which could follow the demands required by the technical development. In the population of the Western-European countries not only the rate of the agrarian population decreased in the 70–80s of the 19th century but it also stopped in absolute

1 For the relatively numerous literature see: *Földmunkás és szegényparaszt mozgalmak Magyarországon. 1848–1948* (Movements of navvies and poor peasants in Hungary, 1848–1948). Ed. by F. Pölöskei – K. Szakács. Vol. I. Budapest, 1962. 107 232, 261–314., P. Simon: *A századforduló földmunkás- és szegényparaszt-mozgalmai 1891–1907* (Movements of navvies and poor peasants at the turn of the century, 1891–1907). Budapest, 1953., F. Pölöskei: *Parasztmozgalmak* 1905–1914 között (Peasant movements between 1905–1914). Budapest, 1959., and the Vol. 7. of the series *"A History of Hungary in Ten Volumes"*, Budapest, 1983. 132–137., 183–204.

number then the peasant population started decreasing. While in the former centuries less and less cultivable land was left to each member of the agrarian population in these countries, now the rate of the agrarian population and the cultivable land improved again and the extent of the possessed land also increased.

The Hungarian situation was different. The industrialization did not spread to such an extent that it could have reduced the number of the agrarian population. Despite that the rate of the non-agrarian population increased in the structure of the entire population, and the industrialization was not so fast on the whole as the significant increase of population lasting from the middle of the 19th century to the turn of the century. So the agrarian population increased numerically though its rate in the entire population decreased even in spite of the fact that there was a significant emigration which decreased the whole population but first of all the number of the poverty stricken strata of the agrarian population. Despite all these the agrarian population grew in absolute number, first and foremost just its poverty stricken proletarian elements increased. Moreover, it increased the number of proletarian and half-proletarian elements further in the agrarian population.

The fairly fast development of economy in the 1860s and 70s even claimed the increase of population, mainly the agrarian population for a while. As long as the industrialization had its extensive period the economical development needed mass physical manpower. The development of infrastructure, the road making and railway construction, the regulation of riverways, the works of embanking gave employment to a great number of men without education (unskilled workers). The extensive development of the agricultural production, the extension of tillage and the structural transformation of husbandry—even the spread of stabling—kept considerable manpower in employment in agriculture. Having lost the villein services of serfs the large estates were forced to employ significant number of paid workers either as servants or jobbers mainly in the 6 or 7 months of the year when the agrarian working processes came together. All these absorbed the increase of population for a time, but only for a time.

This lasted as long as the extensive period of the capitalistic economical development and industrialization came to its end. This took place roughly at the same time in the agriculture and infrastructure. By the end of the 1880s the Hungarian railway system developed and new railway lines were not built in such big rates as in the previous decades. In connection with road making the situation was the same, the building of economical roads which had great importance in the agricultural production was finished. This happened roughly in the agricultural production, when in the 70s–80s of the 19th century the new wave of mechanization and consequently the intensive period of the agricultural development started.

The building of railways connected Hungary with world market. This was accompanied with the increase of the grain-growing area. The Hungarian corn played a more and more important part mainly in the southern German market and afterwards in the industrialized western-part of the Austro–Hungarian Monarchy. Transport of great amount of corn to markets was unimaginable without the shortening of the process of getting grain. Even in the 18th century the growing of corn was entwined with the spread of treading out which meant a more intensive way of getting grain in the territories of corn producer. Then, simultaneously with the development of railway construction a more intensive way of getting grain started spreading, namely the mechanization of threshing. Due to the irresistible development of steam-threshing a significant quantity of manpower was set free from the Hungarian agriculture. The duration of threshing decreased and the job which had lasted for several months was done in 3–4 weeks. Besides these the machines themselves saved a significant quantity of manpower for the farms and superseded it in agriculture. Somewhat later, at the turn of the century a new danger accumulated for the workers in the Hungarian agriculture: the mechanical harvester appeared in the cornfields of big farms.

So much manpower set free from the agriculture and infrastructure at the same time that the industrial development itself was unable to absorb it. The decrease of agricultural wages would have been its consequence even if the *corn crisis* of the 1880s, or rather, the price competition of the relatively cheap corn coming from the overseas had not forced the big farm to do so. The quickly decreasing prices of corn reduced the wages particularly of those strata —mainly *jobbers*—who got the major part of their wages in kind, mostly in corn, and who had to offer the corn for sale in order, to fulfil their financial obligations (first to pay taxes). It was the stratum of jobbers which was most closely concerned by corn crisis and the decreasing need of manpower in agriculture. The other stratum, which was also concerned remarkably, was that of the *navvies*. They were forced to go back to work in agriculture from where they had come and from which they had never been entirely independent. The return of navvies to agriculture pressed the agricultural labour market to a larger extent than it grew the labour supply. At the same time the wages of the navvies (or rather the ex-navies), of course, decreased, because the agricultural wages were not so high. Consequently the "agrarian socialist movements" of 1890–1900s broke out under these circumstances.[2]

The movements themselves do not need a detailed analysis here. But it is important to underline that jobbers and navvies formed the main army of the movements. As they performed collective work in the course of their work and they worked in groups it made relatively easy—altogether possible for them to have political organizing. Though the outbreaks were more or less spontaneous, the organizing of jobbers and navvies at their work-places made the political organizing easier and simpler for them, after all not to speak of the fact that among the navvies there were many who had experienced a lot, travelled in the world and who were more educated than the masses of the average peasantry. The traces of these became visible in the "agrarian socialist movements".

Despite the fact that in these movements the claim and idea of land distribution always appeared everywhere—in their programs among their demands—the central question of these movements was not the land distribution but the wages—in my opinion. They broke out as *wage fights*[3] and as soon as the wage demands were fulfilled they ceased notwithstanding that they also demanded land distribution. Taking the pressed prices of corn in the last decade of the 19th century into consideration the rise in wages could not be solvable till the prices of the world market made their way on the markets of the Monarchy. Only the agrarian customs especially the raise of corn duties in 1906 could lay the foundation for wage-raise. Accordingly the system of large estates got to a particular position. The decrease of corn prices of the world market and the simultaneous wage demands of the agrarian socialist movements set it to crossroads; it fights out the raise of agrarian customs or it starts breaking up by parcellisation just like it had happened in most Western European countries within a longer period. Namely the agrarian wages increased so high on the depriving effect of industrialization there that the profitable subsistence of large estates was not unremunerative. With a longlasting effort the Hungarian large estates—or at last but not at least, making the most of the national fights—achieved their aim; when the national movements overthrew the government in 1905 the king as the first sign of the reconciliation with the coalition raised the agrarian customs by decree first. There are no proofs that the owners of corn producing estates of a few hundred or thousand acres—they felt the corn crisis mainly—took part in the national resistance for only that reason, but the fact, mentioned above, the raise of agrarian customs as the first step of the ruler—marks the close connection. After 1867 the election of 1905 was the only case

2 For all of these see the Vol. 7. *of "A History of Hungary in Ten Volumes", and I.* Király: *Az agrárszocialista mozgalmak történeti problémái* (Historical problems of agrarsocialist movements in Hungary) (Manuscript in the Archives of the Academic Library of Hungary, Budapest).

3 The wage-dispute character of these movements will be emphasized in the historical writings on agrarsocialist movements. See I. Király: op. cit.

in the modern history of Hungary when the government was overthrown. It could not have happened without a serious break *inside* the ruling class. And this break was caused by the dilemma of raising or not raising the agrarian customs. Then the unity of the ruling class was reestablished and at the same time the question of large estates was also settled; they managed to insure the survival of the system for another historical period.

*Roumania*, which was standing at the beginning of its modern development, was shocked twice by bloody peasant risings in the decades of the turn of the century in 1888 and 1907. The latter was more sanguinary, so the revolt itself, its bloody suppression, the cruelty of victimization horrified whole Europe. The hate of peasants touched not so much the landowners, the Boyars but the tenants and the usurers, who were killed brutally in the case of being captured. In the course of restoring the order the army executed the active participants of the revolts by hundreds. The whole population of a village took very often part in the revolts including the local magistracy as well. It was typical that in those territories where the centres of the revolts were the whole peasantry—except the richest peasants only—joined the revolts. They demanded the abolition of sharing leases and usurious loans on the basis of the same principle. They burnt the debentures and the lease-contracts, as it was the aim of the movement and brutality was come to only when the usurers resisted.

The whole 19th century period or, at least, the last 40 years of the Roumanian agrarian development must be looked over in order to understand these. If we disregard from the introduction of the former periods in any case it is necessary to get acquainted with the abolition of serfdom in Roumania.[4] The abolition of serfdom which was put through by Cuza's coup in 1864 allocated the 2/3s of the lands to the peasants depending on how much draught power the families got, or rather, if they had any.[5] And in those parts where there was not enough land for each peasant the state lands were taken away and the peasants were resettled there. Considering that the decree on the abolition of serfdom also said that the newly married couple had to get land and in this way great masses of people were involved. So great masses of the Roumanian peasantry could get land which was not a negligible result of the politics particularly then, if we think over that coup had to be introduced because most of the Boyars strictly opposed the land distribution. They would have agreed to the lifting of the personal dependence of the peasants, as in the former century due

4 For the emancipation of the serfs in Roumania E. Niederhauser: *Jobbágyfelszabadítás Kelet-Európában* (Emancipation of the serfs in Eastern-Europe). Budapest, 1962. 248–271.

5 N. Adăniloăie – D. Berindei: *Reforma agrară din 1864*. Bucuresti, 1967., N. Adăniloăie – D. Berindei: *La réforme agraire de 1864 en Roumanie et son application*. Bucarest, 1966.

to Prince Constantin Mavrocordat's reforms they got used to that the state ruled the connection between peasants and landowners, and practically the Boyars' personal disposal over their serfs (or rather, serfs being in personal dependence) was restricted, but they did not accept the land distribution to the peasants. In their eyes the land was the Boyars' exclusive property and in the centuries of the Roumanian agrarian development peasant and land had not been connected together organically, the Boyars bought and sold peasants with or without land. The violence of the Prince was needed during the realization of abolition of serfdom to overcome the Boyars' resistance and to set the serfs free with land.

At the same time the land distribution to peasants put a big burden on the peasants' shoulders. The peasants had to take the 2/3s compensation of the landowners upon themselves (the state took 1/3 upon itself) within 15 years. This could not be a negligible burden in such a country where the money management was undeveloped and which just began to learn all the characteristics of commodity production only in the latter decades. Roumania was very deficient in funds and though the sum of redemption seemed to be very low it was presumable that it would mean a great burden on peasants and the peasant farms would hardly bear it. The decree on abolition of serfdom also dealt with this and wanted to protect the peasants' lands in the way that it declared that the land given to the peasant was unsaleable and could not be pledged for 30 years. Only the community of the village could decide about the possible selling of lands belonging to peasants.[6] The state power wanted to ensure that the peasantry could keep the land and it could not slip from the peasants' hands. The question whether it happened by considering the circumstances of the abolition of serfdom in Russia or the local circumstances has not been settled yet.

In fact the land was not enough to cover the costs of living of the peasantry. If it is true that only 8–10% of the whole peasantry was set free having only a building site or some garden, namely, they belonged to the agrarian proletarians, most of the peasants set free having land which was by no means big enough to ensure the living of the populous peasant families. Most farms having 2 draught animals got 5.72 hectares in Moldavia and 3.90 hectares in Wallachia and those who had no draught animals got 3.58 hectares in Moldavia and 2.31 hectares in Wallachia. But even the richer peasants with 4 draught animals did not get enough land (7.88 hectares in Moldavia, and 5.31 hectares in Wallachia) which marked the expectable difficulties itself.[7] To a large extent the Roumanian order of succession which based on the principle of children's

6 D.B. Ionescu: *Die Agrarverfassung Rumäniens, ihre Geschichte und ihre Reform.* Leipzig, 1909. (Staats- und sozialwissenschaftliche Forschungen. Heft 136.) 37.

7 Ibid.

equal succession contributed to their taking place. It was presumable that within a rather short period the peasant farms would break and the following peasant generation would face serious difficulties without the acceleration of the industrial development which would absorb the superfluous mass of the agrarian population. But there was no hope of it.

The regularities of the undeveloped—to some extent under the circumstances of subsistence farming—Roumanian economy formed a peculiar solution soon to ensure the undisturbed and continual producing of large estates and at the same time the peasants were also given some more land but sometimes at a horrible price. As everywhere, where the money burdens were beyond the limit of toleration solutions of necessity had to come into being. The peasants needed money and the landowners needed manpower. So the solution was obvious; the peasants raised loans from the landowners, or rather, they took a deposit on the peasants' further work in their land. Apparently nothing special happened, namely the peasants offered their manpower to the landowners for sale. But reality was different.

Taxes and part-payment of compensation would have made most of the farms insolvent sooner or later even if poor crop or other elemental calamity had not taken place. But in the year of abolition and in the following years as well, there were serious elementary damages in the Roumanian agriculture which accelerated the process getting on under necessity. The peasants—especially in Moldavia—ran into debt very quickly. Selling crops on foot was an accepted practice in many places which meant the heaviest burden on the farms, as the peasants sold their manpower in advance. They worked certain number of days in large estates in return for amortization and interest payment. A whole system of this sort of payment was formed. They had to cultivate certain regions or to work there on certain days. This kind of running into debts increased so significantly even in the first years after the abolition of serfdom that in 1866 law ruled these connections, and as in Russia—we will see it later —the village communities were collectively made responsible for the systematic and continuous payment of redemption, in Roumania according to the law of 1866 the village community had to undertake all the guarantees for the peasants labour obligations, and the task of punishment of those who did not pay their obligations. The community also had to offer equal manpower if somebody could not honour his commitment for good and all.[8] At the same time the law also said that the peasants had to make agreement with the landowners in

8 For the Roumanian village community see N. Iorga: *Geschichte des rumänischen Volkes im Rahmen seiner Staatsbildungen*. Gotha, 1905. 200–204., H.H. Stahl: *Traditional Roumanian Village Community. The Transition from the Communal to the Capitalist Mode of Production in the Danube Region*. Cambridge, 1980.

writing—obviously to satisfy the guilty conscience—which could contain labour contracts for max. 5 years. So we have to suppose that even in 1864–1866 there were many contracts which contained obligations for more than 5 years taking the most of the peasants' impecuniosity. The law of 1872 referred to the extent of landowners' abuse, namely the village community which undertook the guarantee for the peasants' labour obligation did not have to fulfil the duties of the contract which obviously were beyond the peasants' capacity.[9] This act refers to the fact that in return for the loans the landowners had the peasants work and this work grew to huge dimensions. A particular situation came into being, a new kind of serfdom was formed on the basis of the work done in return for debts which meant heavier burden on peasants than socage before the abolition of serfdom. Socage meant a certain amount of work but this kind of work was unrestricted. We have to accept it because the enforcement of laws belonged to the duties of the local administration and was in close connection with the landowners. The fact, that in many places the local magistrates themselves bought the peasant manpower in advance and sold it further at a premium to landowners or tenants who needed it also marks this. A great number of studies of the time showed masses of cases when the peasants sold their labour for 5 years in advance.[10]

The lack of money among the peasants also called other special forms of exploitation and usury into being. In Moldavia where the publican's licence still remained the monopoly of landowners after the abolition of serfdom those who took the inns on lease—mainly Jewish innkeepers—became usurers. The peasants undertook work for getting spirits or rather, the innkeepers sold the labour of those who had been sold for spirits to large estates where manpower was badly needed. Here there was a kind of *double exploitation,* namely both the innkeeper and the landowner exploited the peasantry.

In other respect the general lack of money in villages brought about an usurious loan system based on very high interests. According to a study in 1900 the rate of state interest was 5%, in towns it was 10–12%[11] (which was high in comparison with the European ones) and in 1451 of the 3000 Roumanian villages the rate of interest was the following:[12]

9 For all these Ionescu: op. cit. 46–49. and G.D. Creanga: *Grundbesitzverteilung und Bauernfrage in Rumänien. Zweiter und dritter Teil. Die von der Regierung im Jahre 1908 durchgeführten Agrarreformen.* Leipzig, 1909. (Staats- und sozialwissenschaftliche Forschungen. Heft 104.) 103.

10 Ionescu: op. cit. 50.

11 Ibid. 117.

12 For the data: Ibid. 98.

| from loans % | the interest of loans a year |
|---|---|
| 18 | – 8% |
| 18 | 8 – 20% |
| 9 | 20 – 24% |
| 22 | 24 – 36% |
| 22 | 36 – 60% |
| 9 | 60 – 120% |
| 1 | to 250% |
| 0.8 | to 350% |
| 0.2 | to 500% |

More than two thirds of the peasantry could get loans only in the case of paying very high interests. And when we speak of unbearable high interests we do not think of interests at a few hundred p.c. Even the interest of 15–20% imposed extraordinary burden on the peasant farms included also the big ones, especially if we consider that the world market price of corn decreased significantly in the last third of the 19th century and in case of Roumania the tariff war with the Monarchy exploded in 1886 also deepened its consequences.

There was another symptom of the same rank, namely, the lack of land which worsened the impecuniousness of the peasantry. We have already mentioned the extent of land which passed into the peasants' hand at the time of abolition of serfdom. At that time this piece of land was hardly enough to keep peasant families considering the comparatively low crop, as well. Peasants would have needed more land even then. The fast increase of population in the second half of the 19th century grew this lack of land considerably. The Roumanian population which was approximately 3.87 mill. in 1860 increased to 6.39 mill. till 1905.[13] Though the number and rate of non-agrarian population increased in the whole, its dominant part increased the village population with overwhelming force. The extent of land per head decreased significantly.

It is easy to understand that land hunger of peasantry increased quickly. The large estates having survived the abolition of serfdom were greatly in need of man-power (and also tools and draught power of peasants mainly in Wallachia where the commodity production of landlords before 1864 was not so developed as in Moldavia and neither the necessary tools nor draught power needed for the independent farming was be found there; moreover fund was also needed to get these) because they suffered from shortage of funds, the

13 Ibid. 59.

solution was found soon, large estates leased pieces of land to the peasants. After the abolition of serfdom share-farming system came into being very soon but it was only formally a share farming one. Seemingly peasants could get leased parcels on good terms. They gave 1/5 of crop to the landowners in general.[14] The farm rent increased later and at the turn of the century the base of the rent was 1/3 of crop in general[15]—which itself marks the increasing demand of land as the increase of crop did not follow the increase of rent and the world market price of wheat in the 1880s–90s was less than in the 1860s–70s. But all these could have meant bearable burden on peasant farms even if we consider that landowners did not plough the leased parcels as others did in many cases, e.g. in Hungary. It did also not mean a real burden that besides the perception paid as rent the peasants had to provide other different rents in kind on the basis of customary deriving from feudal period.[16] Their real burden was that only those could get leased pieces of land who offered their man-power and tools to the landowners in return for land. In the first place the leasing of land ensured man-power to landowners. The perception paid for leased parcels did not play an important part in their income. The essence of this system was labour rent which meant an obligation to cultivate the landowners' land which was at least half of the leased one at the turn of the century.[17] It is easy to imagine what a destroying influence it had. In comparison with the European conditions the Roumanian peasants were reduced to exigence and could be considered vegetarians as they had meat very rarely on their table.[18]

We have already referred to the landtenants besides the landowners. Roumania was deficient in funds and here the landowners were unable to start cultivating in their pieces of land after the abolition of serfdom so leasing of large estates spread widely and extensively.[19] Most of the tenants did not belong to the capitalists, as e.g. in Hungary but they came of local well-provided people with capital (in villages mainly innkeepers etc.). These tenants used to put their money out at an extraordinarily high profit under the Roumanian circumstances, and the leases were only profitable for them if they ensured at least the

14 Ibid. 61.

15 Ibid. 65. For the increase of the land-rents G.D. Creanga: *Grundbesitzverteilung und Bauernfrage in Rumänien.* Leipzig, 1907. 8. (Staats- und sozialwissenschaftliche Forschungen. Heft 129.) and V. Liveanu – C. Lulea – L. Asănăchescu – V. Medeleanu – C. Moţei: Factorii determinanti ai variaţielor tărănesti la inceputul secolului al XX-lea in România. *Studii*, 1971. 307–331.

16 Ionescu: op. cit. 61–62.

17 Ibid. 63–64. The share-crop system served for ensuring enough manpower for the large estates.

18 Ibid. 93.

19 The land lease system is very well described in the two volumes of Creanga's work.

average usurious rate of interest. Of course, besides the exploitation of the leased land it could be done only by the extraordinarily increased exploitation of the given man-power. Due to this the tenants were the greatest money-lenders in villages who demanded work from the peasants for their money. And at the same time they were also those who transmitted the parcels of the leased large estates as subleases to the peasants—as we have seen—for work.[20] As a matter of fact these were in the full glare of publicity and attracted the peasants' elementary wrath. After the peasants rising in 1907 the government authorities forbade the sublease of land which suggested that this system was responsible for the situation. However, reality is more complicated. There is no doubt that the tenants pocketed enormous profit and played an important part in the exploitation of peasants. But responsibility was not only theirs. Even if the great leasing system had not come into being to such an extent the peasants should have had similar burden as it happened in those regions where the large estates were run by their owners. There is no difference between these regions and the districts of the leasing system as far as the burden of peasantry is concerned. The general lack of capital and shortage of land were the basis of the peasantry's exploitation which drove them to the unbearable misery and exploitation. A parasitic class brought about independently from the tenants, which sucked the peasants' blood like a leech. E.g., the inn-keeper who gave usurious loan, the local magistrate who ensured peasant man-power by loans in order to transmit it to the landowner or tenant, but independently from the system there were also other classes who lived on the peasants. Namely, the parasitic character of the whole system was, or rather gradually became unbearable for the peasants. This was the unbearable burden which started the Roumanian peasants' risings, and above all the parasitic character of the system caused the

20 There are some characteristic data of the large lessees about the beginning of the 20th century. There were 3332 persons who had more than 50 hectares land on lease, 2417 persons of them were Rumanian (72.54%), 472 persons were Jewish (14.17%) and 443 persons were "foreign" (13.29%), first of all of Greek birth. 63.34% of the land given to large lease belonged to Rumanian, 18.87% to Jewish and 17.79% to "foreign" lessees. The total land on lease was more than 2.33 million hectares. The ratio of Jewish large lessees among the really large ones was grater than their average proportion (Creanga: op. cit. Vol. I. 144–145.). Among the greates lessees were the Fischer-brothers who took 138424 hectare land in 1903–1904 and 159399 hectare in 1904–1905. The largest lessee was Mochi Fischer, he alone took 237000 hectare land on lease (Ibid. 3. and 150.). The time of the lease was typical, 410 (63.5%) of 641 larger land lease contracts were valid only for one year and 67 (10.4%) were valid for two years. The large estate owners could keep their hands on the lessees and the peasants by this situation and the lessees were forced for the total exploiting of the land and the peasants. 14% of the land taken on lease by the peasants were smaller than 1 hectare, 23.3% of them were between 1–2 hectares and 23.6% between 2–3 hectares (Ibid. 23.).

rather bloody events, the brutal slaughter of inn-keepers, tenants, landowners, officials, town people in general in those regions, where the exploitation had been the hardest, or they had refused to fulfil the peasants' demands. So the rising of 1907 broke down a system based on usurious exploitation.

In *Russia* the abolition of serfdom in 1861 took place under similar circumstances from many points of view on the basis of the principle which said that land belonged to nobility and consequently it could be a subject of free negotiation. It was a significant victory of the peasantry itself that the state admitted that the peasants *should* get land, too. The personal dependence of serfs ceased without any redemption, and redemption was only given to the nobility for the land which had been got into the hands of peasants.

The extensive territory of the czarist empire cannot be considered organic. We cannot speak of the western Polish Lithuanian territories, and the Baltic countries in this context and we can also take no notice of Finland. If we restrict to the historic Russia we recognize separate parts, namely the northern territories, the so-called industrial part, the black-soil region (which itself is so large that contains many subregions having the same characteristic features to some extent) and the Southern-Russian steppe. Even before the abolition of serfdom the position of the peasantry was different in the three territories, the abolition of serfdom reserved the characters of the territories in consequence of which different circumstances took shape for the peasants.

With the exception of the black soil region the rate of land per head in the peasant population was more disadvantageous than in other parts of the country. But here the majority of the peasants was living on industrial work mostly and not farming even before the abolition of serfdom. In this way the abolition of serfdom let the peasantry get little piece of land but soon these cut up the large estates word by word which were not given man-power, or rather, they could not pay for it. Otherwise, some of the peasants had gone to work to the South-Russian steppe from spring to autumn and this possibility of itinerant work got wider and wider after the abolition of serfdom. The industrial development also absorbed a great number of peasants and changed them into industrial workers whose circumstances were made worse by the abolition of serfdom in the way that their personal dependence became hardly bearable by strengthening the position of the community of land. That is why it happened very often that the peasants renounced their land and left the community of land and farming for ever. As a result of the lack of man-power in large estates giving up farming very soon they changed over to pasturing animal keeping and logging which had formed the greater part of their income earlier, as well. The increasing demand for wood in the country and abroad made it possible for them for a longer period.

The situation was quite different in the black-soil region. The majority of peasant population got land here though somewhat less land was got into the hands of the peasants than they had had earlier. At the same time the industry could not absorb the landless masses of peasantry here. So the greater part of the peasantry remained in agriculture that foreshadowed the considerable decrease of land per head in the following decade. The large estates also remained here because they had no capital to buy tools, machines and draught power and to pay hired workers. In this region both the working out system and the leasing one started spreading soon and in most cases the work done in the large estates was the rent.[21]

In the South-Russian steppe agriculture developed at high speed in the second part of the 19th century. There were plenty of land and relatively low population here, so the peasant farms got more land here than in the other parts of the country notwithstanding that the large estates also kept relatively more here than half of the cultivated land. The southern part was on the move and extending, in the second half of the 19th century great masses came here. From the 1850s the developing railway building connected this territory to the world market which had its influence felt soon on the extension of agricultural production and the agrarian prosperity.[22]

The abolition of serfdom in Russia could take place in this form due to only the condition that it coincided with the railway building practically. The increasing export made possible that the peasants could pay the sum of redemption and taxes.[23] The former version of abolition proposed by the officials of Czar Michael I in the 1830s could have been imagined only if the peasants had been freed without paying any redemption to the landowners, which could not be, of course, brought up.

---

21 For the liberation of the serfs in Rumania see Niederhauser:op.cit. 159–210., N.M. Druzhinin: *Russkaia derevnia na perelome 1860–1880. gg*. Moscow, 1978. N.M. Druzhinin: Likvidatsiya feodalnoi sistemy v russkoi pomeshchichei derevne (1862–1882 gg.). *Voprosy istorii*, 1968. Nr. 12. 3–34. P.G. Ryndzyunski: Ekonomicheski stroi krest'yanskogo nadelnogo hozyaistva Rossii v poreformennoe vremja. Voprosy istorii, 1971. Nr. 11. 32–48. and the studies of N.M. Druzhinin and I.D. Kovalchenko, in: *Studien zu den Agrarreformen des 19. Jahrhunderts in Preussen und Russland*. Berlin, 1978. 117–228., 295–352. (Sonderband des Jahrbuchs für Wirtschaftsgeschichte).

22 J. William Leasure – Robert A. Lewis: Internal Migration in Russia in the Late Ninteenth Century. *Slavic Review*, 1968. Nr. 3. 375–394.

23 There was no any unified internal market of agricultural produces in Russia. I.D. Kovalchenko: Agrarnii rynok i kharakter agrarnogo stroya evropeiskoi Rossii v kontse XIX – nachale XX veka. *Istoriya SSSR*, 1973. Nr. 2. 42–74., I.D. Kovalchenko – L.V. Milov: O printsipakh issledovaniya processa rynka (XVIII–XIX.vv.). *Istoriya SSSR*, 1969. Nr. 1. 27–57.

Considering that the base of the whole solution was the landowners' compensation, the insurance of financial guarantees dictated the czarian power the solution to give the land communities (obshchina) and their administrative equivalents, village communities (mir) an important role in paying the sums of redemption. Otherwise, peasants did not get land as private property but for permanent use only and each village community itself decided on its concrete realization. (By the help of the two decrees in 1866 this right was also given to the ex-serfs of the state who had not shared in this due to former measures.) In this way it was not difficult to hold the land communities responsible for their members paying the sums of redemption and taxes correctly. So the communities assumed collective responsibility for each peasant's commitments and on the other hand they got important rights against them. Probably not only the necessity of paying the commitments dictated that certain peasants were practically fixed to the land community and its permission was needed when they left the village for good and all, or they travelled far or for a longer period but also the fear that free peasants would leave the village in large numbers. Let us not forget about the southern and eastern parts of Siberia where there were available lands for those who escaped which had been a constant practice during the centuries. Consequently the possibility of transmigration existed in theory even if its realization seemed by no means an easy task in practice. Not more than yearly about 200000 people could settle over Ural between 1907–1914 when the state itself helped this process intensively. There were years when it reached 600000, but it was so dangerous that at last the process slowed down.[24] But at the time of the abolition of serfdom the fear of transmigration was significant and that's why they fixed the peasants to village community. The village community decided on the redivision of land, controlled the payment of regular commitments, agreed to the peasant's journey or refused it, decided on the distribution of estates, or moreover, it ordered the not wanted persons to leave the village. And as far as the most important feature is concerned the village community decided on the peasant's leaving the community. Of course, it could only take place when the peasant who was about to leave had already fulfilled all his commitments in connection with redemption. The village community was collectively responsible for the regular payment of its each member or at the very worst if a peasant could not pay for one reason or another the community itself had to pay the amount due. The link fixing each peasant to the community was rather strong and long-lasting because peasant had to pay the sums of redemption for 49 years, the yearly 6% of the sum of redemption together with the normal payment till 1910.[25]

24 B. Brutzkus: *Agrarentwicklung und Agrarrevolution in Russland.* Berlin, 1925. 86–87.

This fixing of peasantry to the village community and the maintenance of the whole system limited the capitalistic development of agriculture and mainly the peasant farms in the highest degree. It is true that the freed peasants needed more and more money than earlier though both the poll-tax paid in money and the annuity of redemption grew but the community of land put a strong stop to the unlimited development of production. Practically the collective taking responsibility served those who could avoid paying the obligation on some pretext and burdened those who produced more than the average did. The strengthening of village community in the decades after the abolition of serfdom also strengthened the maintenance of rotation of corps and in this way it hindered the spread of free rotating crops and the rational tilling of arable lands. The rotation of crops would easily have become weaker if at least the well-to-do people had left the village community freely and got their lands commassatedly.

There was another consequence of conserving this system in those regions where the practice of the redistributive land community system still existed. It is impossible to say exactly how large areas were involved in the second half of the 19th century but both in the northern industrial territory and in some parts of the black-soil region this system spread and it was even stronger from Ural towards the east. The redistribution of land taking place not annually but with more or less regularity did not make the land property unsteady so much that it did not occur at every occasion that different piece of land was given to the same family. Anyhow, in this way it made the system really unsteady and hindered the modern cultivation of land, the appropriate dunging etc., because these investments lasted for a longer period and needed more work than the cultivation in rotating crops did (e.g., only dunging itself was the simplest modernization of all taken into consideration). Another consequence of redistribution was even more pernicious, namely, the extent of land to be given depended on the size of the family, and the available man-power and on the one hand it made a contribution to loosening of peasant land-owning, and did not throw obstacles in the way of the increase of population on the other. It is not necessary to underline that under these circumstances the modernization of

25 For the redemption A. Gerschenkron: *A gazdasági elmaradottság – történelmi távlatból* (Economic backwardness in historical perspective). Budapest, 1984. 335. For the village community literature Gy. Kövér: Az orosz obscsina történetéhez (To the history of the Russian "obshchina"). *Történelmi Szemle*, 1978. 338–354., G.A. Alexeenko: Prigovory sel'skikh skhodov kak istochnik po istorii obshchiny v Rossii vtoroi poloviny XIX veka. *Istoriya SSSR*, 1981. Nr. 6. 116–125., A.M. Anfimov – P.N. Ziryanov: Nekotorie cherty evolyutsii russkoi krest'yanskoi obshchiny v poreformennom periode (1861–1914). *Istoriya SSSR*, 1980. Nr. 4. 26–41.

agriculture which needed more man-power could not take place because even if the land belonged to the same family permanently it was doubtful whether one or two pieces of land would not been given to another family at the following redistribution.[26] The consequences of the increase of population were difficult to foresee. Namely, it was the landowners' interest not to let their serfs become very poor and when a community became overpopulated the landowner saw to resettle parts of the population. But it was over then.

During a number of years after the abolition of serfdom those difficulties with which the peasants had to cope later appeared quickly. The increase of financial burden charged on families so much that not only the normal way of eating became impossible for them in practice but any kind of investment which could have increased the tillage. Apart from the regions of the southern steppe the Russian agriculture went on cultivating under the traditional rotating crops and used the old tools and by means of these the land was impoverished permanently and considerably (traditional usage means that a village could not change its land for 20–25 years).[27] The consequences appeared soon and some decades later there was a significant loss of crop and at the turn of the century the damage caused by drought became steady. Together with these massive starvation and the danger of famishment also appeared in the peasants' houses.

Besides the impoverishing of land there appeared still another consequence about which we have not talked yet namely the relative agrarian over-population.[28] In Russia there were large areas available, but if we compare the agrarian population with extent of the areas we cannot speak of overpopulation. But if we compare the agricultural land with the number of population we find a surprising situation with different results, namely, at the turn of the century the density of the agrarian population *exceeded* that of Denmark, or France, and Germany relating to 100 hectares and in larger districts it outdid the Belgian one, as well.[29] But if we think of the average yield in Russia the level of crop, of course, was under theirs. It is easy to understand the situation that among the peasants land hunger increased because the piece of land got at the abolition of serfdom was not enough to keep body and soul together at all. It was necessary in the Russian history for the first time that intensive methods should

26 A.M. Anfimov – P.N. Ziryanov: op. cit. stresses that the redividing system mostly succeeded in the Black Soil Region and in the Volga-Area. In these parts of Russia the consciousness of the private land ownership was not firmly established among the peasants.

27 Gerschenkron: op. cit. 388–389.

28 S.I. Brik – V.N. Kabuzan: Dinamika i etnicheskii sostav naseleniya Rossii v epokhe imperializma (konets XIX v. – 1917 g.). *Istoriya SSSR*, 1980. Nr.3. 74–93.

29 Brutzkus: op. cit.109.

be introduced instead of the increase of land as a response to the increase of population. But the peasantry had no financial possibility for this.

Due to the lack of money and land the peasants were at the mercy of landowners to the highest degree who needed wage-work for replacing the lost socage, though they could not pay in money. The majority of the Russian landowners could not use the sums of redemption for investments. More than half of the redemption sum was paid for mortgage because at the moment of the abolition of serfdom about 70% of the peasants had already been mortgaged. They were not able, or rather, they did not want to invest the other half though the majority of landowners had neither good equipment nor livestock to start an independent tillage. Not only the man-power of the peasants was needed by the landowners but also their tools and draught power.

The solution was the spread of paying off in labour. The landowners let their lands to the peasants in return for work.[30] In this way they were able to preserve the former level of production at least on the piece of land kept in self-production. And the peasants needed land if they wanted to maintain their family. For a few decades this solution became dominant. As a matter the features reminiscent of the old socage and feudal services—e.g., subsistence farming remained, or rather, appeared again under these circumstances.[31]

During the following two decades the peasants' problems (mainly the lasting lack of money and land) coming from the execution of abolition of serfdom accumulated so much that the state had to interfere. In villages due to the lack of money usury and the most primitive and exploiting form of corn trade, the sell of standing crop spread widely.[32] The situation became so unbearable that at last it was the reactionary government who had to interfere. After the murder of Czar Alexander II the government of the new Czar, Alexander III made significant but essential modifications in the reform. In 1881 he decreased the sums of redemption. The permanent and steady increase of back taxes was a warning signal for the financial administration and showed the intolerableness of the situation. The unrest among the ex-serfs of landowners was especially significant in those regions where they lived together with the ex-state-peasants and that is why the contrast was obvious mainly in the industrial districts where the peasant farm started showing the signs of decline. The reduction of redemption sums was significant, there was a decrease of 27% on average of

30 I.D. Kovalchenko: Arenda zemli byvshimi pomeshchichimi krest'yanami v nachale 80-kh godov XIX.v. In: *Iz istorii economicheskoi i obshchestvennoi zhizni Rossii. Sbornik statei k 90-letiu akademika N.M. Druzhinina.* Moscow, 1976. 44–60.

31 T.L. Moiseenko: Metody izucheniya krest'yanskoi arendy v Rossii po dannym zemskoi statistiki kontsa XIX veka. *Istoriya SSSR*, 1979. Nr. 4. 66–82.

32 About the absence of unified corn market I.D. Kovalchenko: op. cit. (Agrarnii rynok...).

39 provinces, and it was between 30–45% in some provinces outside the black-soil region. In *Olavets* province it reached 92%.[33] At the same time the compulsory redemption was declared by decree, so in those territories where it had not been taken place on the basis of free agreement it was decreed compulsorily.[34]

The tax system was modified to make the redemption quicker and easier for the peasants. Between 1883–1885 the system of poll tax was abolished and a new, modern system of land tax was introduced in the expectation of keeping more money in the peasant farms for the acceleration of redemption. But the base of the abolition of serfdom was still maintained namely, the system of village community, or rather, the principle of loyalty in relation to the payment of redemption sums was reserved.

In 1883 the state founded a so-called "peasant-bank" in order to try to supply the peasants' demand on land to some extent. Its task was to help the peasants on buying lands. Fearing that the idea of land distribution might spread among the peasants they did not make independent part of the bank—e.g. broker's deal—possible, and in this way the function of "peasant-bank" was restricted only to loan transactions. It may not have had an independent policy of parcellisation, the local prices of land had to be taken into consideration due to the steady land hunger. The rate of interest was settled in 5.5% to which 1% was also added for different expenses. The load having given to the peasants was prolonged for 24.5–34.5 years so they had to pay 7.5–8.5% yearly as interest and payment by installments. (In 1885 a so-called "bank of nobility" was also founded to defend the large estates and gave loans to noble families with the interest of 5.25% in order to keep the land of nobility from breaking up.) In 1886 a law was enacted which prohibited the distribution of peasant land among the family members. In 1861 the land was taken into use of certain families and the capitalistic development strengthened the tendency of giving the land into private property which the government wanted to stop. At last in 1889 the district council of Zemstvo was brought about to reserve the situation and it had to give permission to the peasants who were about to leave the community of land.

As it can be seen, some of the decrees lightened the peasants' burden, but the others served the purpose to maintain the former system and hindered the freeway of capitalism in agriculture and mainly in peasant farms. By doing so

33 Brutzkus: op. cit. 32–53.

34 For improvement of the situation of state peasants see A.M. Anfimov: Preobrazovanie obrochnoi podati bavshih gosudarstvennykh krest'yan v vykupnye platezki. In: *Iz istorii ekonomicheskoi i obshchestvennoi zhizni Rossii. Sbornik statei k 90-letiju akademika N.M. Druzhinina*. Moscow, 1976. 27–43.

it went a great way to increase those social problems which at last led to the peasants' risings in 1905–1906. Namely the increase of population meant a steady pressure and would have wanted the peasant farms to get rid of those obligations which blocked the progress on one hand (at first leaving the village community should have been made easier) and on the other the resettlement or the transmigration of inner colonization should have been made possible. But they made every effort to stop it. Despite all ease coming from the state the situation became more and more difficult due to the gradual increase of population simply. The exploitation of land went on by keeping the traditional production technique and technology.

Under the circumstances mentioned above starvation appeared at some places necessarily because peasant farms could not keep corn in reserve by hard times so a poor crop always caused difficulties and came together with local starvation. Considering that in the decades of corn crisis the world market price of corn was very low, that is why the Russian peasants were often forced to sell the corn at a sacrifice price as a consequence of their financial troubles.[35] It was one of the reasons why they had no corn left, so the peasants had no reserves. From the 1890s the exploitation of land made starvation occurring after a poor crop regular and it spread in greater districts. The drought of 1890/91 did not remain within local bounds. In 15 provinces of the black soil region there was a drought without example and the inhabitants could only prevent from famishment that the authority bought corn abroad and divided it in the depressed areas. Starvation was not accidental but one of the consequences of very dry years and between 1890 and 1914 there were 12 years when there was poor crop in most parts of the country. In some places death from starvation occurred, and as a matter of fact famishment was very common and people could not keep themselves without having state support. Then this provoked newer and newer reforms.

It seems that the reforms had already been prepared and at most the authorities had to bring forward the realization of certain ideas. But this did not credit to the solving of the problem, it only increased the frequency of ambiguous solutions. At last the government authorities had to realize that they did not have to be afraid of lack of man-power in the black-soil region—30 years after the abolition of serfdom. At the same time there was also a need of man-power to build the Siberian railway lines which were very important from both strategic and economic points of view, and the population living along the ready railway lines had to be also increased. Consequently the authorities made the

35 B.N. Mironov: Dvizhenie khlebnykh tsen v Rossii v 1801–1914 godakh. *Voprosy istorii*, 1975. Nr. 2. 45–57.

transmigration to Siberia possible. So the tendency of transmigration got faster and between 1895 and 1905 100000 people settled in Siberia on an average every year.[36]

Though it was not the most important reform. The most important one was introduced by the government authorities in 1893 which prohibited the land communities from redistributing land for 12 years. At the same time its control became the duty of district council and the communities had to get the permission of the council to redistribution even if the communities had already made a decision on this.[37] Though this prohibition was a great progress but the authorities had to back to the former state or at least they had to stop. Namely, the system of land community was very popular both in conservative—reactionary—e.g., among the Slavophile as it "defended" the peasantry against the dangers of capitalism on one hand and they recognized some old Slavic characters on the other—and democratic or even more progressive circles—as they recognized the realization of certain equalizing ideas in it.[38] Between two fires the authorities were forced to strengthen this system at last. On 14th December 1893 a new decree was issued which maintained the former system, strengthened the permission to leave and beyond that it forbade the sale and mortgage of peasant parcels to non-peasant persons. In this way the spread of capitalistic conditions became more difficult in villages.

The other part of the reforms dealt with the reorganization of the peasant-bank. In 1894 there was a 1% reduction of interest rates and later in 1895 a through-going change came. The date of repaying loans was prolonged for 51.75 years. In 1898 the rate of interest was reduced to 5.25% together with reduced instalment. In 1895 there was an important change from political point of view, as well. While formerly the authorities opposed the formation of various co-operatives in consequence of political reasons at that time an order made the formation of these possible. By doing so they tried to improve the system of production and distribution.

But the basis remained unchanged. On one hand the system of land community, the cultivation and use of land based on families were maintained by the means of which the free development of capitalist economy was hindered in villages and the migration was also limited at last these contributed to the

36 Brutzkus: op.cit. 70.

37 A.M. Anfimov – P.N. Ziryanov: op. cit.

38 For the socialist ideas on a possible connection between the Russian "obshchina" and modern socialism is the exchange of letters of Vera Zasulich and Marx characteristic. See: *Karl Marx és Friedrich Engels* Művei (The Works of Marx and Engels). Vol. 19. Budapest, 1969. 280–281. (Marx's letter). The three drafts of this letter allow to inspect into the difficulties caused by this question: Ibid. 261–279.

further increase of the peasant population. But on the other side the noblemen's estates also remained unchanged, on the contrary, they were strengthened and efforts were made in order to keep them further on.[39] But estates used to belong to noblemen did not become capitalistic large-scale ones but they formed a kind of annuitant institution by reserving the system of lease and working off which meant oppressive burden on peasants who were also suffering from lack of money and land on another respect.[40] The measures of the 1890s meant only symptomatic treatment because of all these, they did not help, or rather, they made the peasants' situation even worse. After this one need not be surprised if we have date of regular social unrest and local movements in the 1890s which in the inner Russian districts were against the system of lease, the feudal services and the limitation of free leave.[41] At the turn of the century the social tension was so intensified in the peasant society that a chance was expected so that it should get publicity.[42] The defeat against the Japanese gave the possibility of this.

The peasant risings of 1905–6 reflected the social background very well. In the so-called inner Russian areas the peasants as a whole (including also the richer ones) set against the parasitic feudal system, set the castles on fire and in the first place they were about to cancel the lease-contracts. The idea of seizure of land and land distribution appeared every day and in some places these could take place, too. The black-soil region and partly the northern industrial districts were involved above all.

In the western and north-western parts of the country there were different conditions and due to them the risings were different. In the north where the landowners had woodfelling and cutting in practice a wave of strikes developed among the peasants and the situation was the same even in the western-white Russian territories. The same happened in the Baltic countries, too. In all these territories the characteristic organization of peasantry, the community of

39 For the distribution of land properties see A.M. Anfimov – I. P. Makarov: Novie dannie o zemlevladenii evropeiskoi Rossii. *Istoriya SSSR*, 1974. Nr.1. 82–97.

40 N.A. Proskuriakova: Razmeshchenie i struktura dvoryanskogo zemlevladeniya evropeiskoi Rossii v kontse XIX – nachale XX veka. *Istoriya SSSR*, 1973. Nr.1. 55–75.

41 A.M. Anfimov: Krest'yanskoe dvizhenie v Rossii vo vtoroi polovine XIX veka. *Voprosy istorii*, 1973. Nr. 3. 15–31. N.M. Druzhinin – V.A. Fedorov: Krest'yanskoe dvizhenie v Rossii v XX. veke. *Istoriya SSSR*, 1977. Nr. 4.

42 The discussion about the bases of Russian social system could give interesting considerations for interpreting the accumulated social tensions. See for example *Voprosy istorii kapitalisticheskoi Rossii. Problema mnogoukladnosti*. Sverdlovsk, 1972. and I.V. Kuznetsov: Ob ukladakh i mnogoukladnosti kapitalisticheskoi Rossii. *Voprosy istorii*, 1974. Nr.7. 20–30., A.M. Anfimov: K voprosu o kharaktere agrarnogo stroia Rossii v nachale XX veka. *Istoricheskie zapiski*, 1974. Nr. 5.

land which played an exclusive role in the inner Russian parts was missing. The white Russian territories occupied intermediate position. While in the eastern territories (Vitebsk and Mogilev provinces) the community of land was wide-spread, in the western parts (Minsk, Smolensk) it hardly took place, or e.g. in Minsk province it did not come into being at all. In these territories the capitalistic development meant a significant differentiation of peasantry or a kind of disintegration, or rather, its beginning. So the majority of landed peasants kept calm and only certain classes of landless agrarian proletarians started moving.

In the large territory, which is known as Eastern Europe today, there were important social and economic differences which appeared in the peasant risings of the turn of the century, as well. In the western areas (the western part of the Ukraine, Belorussia, the Baltic countries, Poland, Lithuania, Hungary, Croatia, Slovenia) the corn crisis of the 1890s—the fall in world market price of corn due to the overseas competition, made the position of agrarian proletarians worse and made the risings of masses unavoidable. The corn crisis had an influence on the whole peasantry in the territory lying to the east of this line and they presented a united front against the community of land and surviving forms of manorial exploitation. In these parts the agrarian proletariat did not play an important part in the society. But the increase of population, and all those feudal or usurious signals which emphasized the parasitic characters of large estates and provoked the disappointed wrath of peasantry and increased the social unrest to the limit of intolerableness meant even greater danger.

The corn crisis increased the tension in all areas where the industrial development was slow and the industrialization could not absorb the population becoming superfluous in agriculture. In the large Eastern-European territories and also in Russia the increase of population was relatively quick but much as quick the industrial development was it could not absorb the superfluous population and it was forced to stay in agriculture. The size of land per head got smaller and smaller and the development of the agricultural production was not so quick that it should follow the fall in prices. (E.g. in Russia the agricultural development of 2% a year would have been enough to guarantee the same income to the agrarian population having an increase of 1.5% every year, but the fall in the world market price was more than 0.5% a year.) The income of peasant farms hardly outnumbered their expenses and the situation was going from bad to worse, and it led to the Russian and Roumanian outbreaks of the peasantry.

It had hardly any influence on Hungary, Poland, the western and Baltic parts of Russia where the agrarian proletariat lived under similar circumstances. It did not take place neither in Bohemia nor in those Polish parts which were ruled by the German at that time. In Bohemia the industrial development and the urbanization took place quicker than in any other countries of Eastern or Central Europe. Otherwise, the agrarian proletarians of the western Polish districts could easily move to Germany for season work.

The Bulgarian situation showed that not only the corn crisis meant the root cause of the peasantry's crisis but the pressure coming from the increase of population. Here neither the redemption of peasant land nor the different taxes was important because the Bulgarian state realized the peasantry's situation, namely the peasantry had hardly been involved in commodity production and after 1879 the tax paid in money was transformed back into tax in kind until 1900. Here the crisis of peasant life broke out after 1919. Its root cause was the increase of population in the consequence of which the peasant land crumbled up (on the basis of the principle of equal inheritance). This led both to the attempt of land distribution by Stamboliski and its failure in 1923.

The Russian peasant rising in 1905 and the Roumanian one in 1907 practically swept away the old social order. In Roumania the legislature turned the development to new ways and swept away those obstacles which hindered the free way of development. The reforms of Stolypin aimed at the same in Russia which made the elimination of land community system, resettlement etc. possible. But either the analysis of these measures, nor the new wave of development based on them can't be our task in this study.[43]

43 There is no place in this paper for studying the situation of the peasantry in Italy and Spain. In Southern Europe the position of corn production was the same as in Eastern Europe and there was an agrarian unrest among the little peasants in Northern Italy who could not pay taxes and among the farm hands in Southern Italy or in Spain. The problem of the share-croppers was the same.

# V

# Aspekte kommunaler Ordnung im mittelalterlichen Ungarn (bis 1848)

Die Verhältnisse in Ungarn waren im Mittelater und in der Neuzeit formal in vieler Hinsicht denen in Deutschland oder Westeurope ähnlich, in der tagtäglichen Praxis aber unterschieden sie sich wesentlich von ihnen, das heißt, unter der ähnliche Hülle verbarg sich in vielenlei Hinsicht ein anderer Inhalt, und wenn wir das nicht gleich zu Beginn klären, verursachen wir Mißverständnisse.

Bei der Ankunft der ungarischen Stämme im Karpatenbecken, bei der sogenannten Landnahme, bestand das ungarische, nomadische Reitervolk aus Stämmen, die den Ackerbau bereits kannten. Diese Kenntnis war die wichtigste Voraussetzung dafür, daß sie im Karpatenbecken überhaupt Fuß fassen konnten und sie half dem Ungarntum auch bei der Ansiedlung und der Entwicklung eines Dorfsystems. Es versteht sich natürlich von selbst, daß der Wandel eines nomadischen Viehzüchertervolkes zu ansässigen Ackerbauern ein Prozeß von Jahrhunderten ist.

Seit dem Ende des 10. Jahrhunderts wurde dieser Prozeß durch den Einfluß des damaligen feudalen Europas gefördert. Vor allem die aus Bayern, Italien und dem wallonischen Gebiet nach Ungarn übersiedelnden kirchlichen Orden und Personen, Geistliche sowie Ritter und Soldaten — um nur auf das mit der Frau Stephans des Heiligen, der bayerischen Gisela, eintreffende Gefolge zu verweisen —, machten Ungarn natürlich mit den deutschen Verhältnissen, dem Aufbau des Staatswesens bekannt, mit anderen Worten: sie verpflanzten einzelne Elemente des deutschen und westeuropäischen Feudalismus nach Ungarn. Sehr gut läßt sich dieser Prozeß an der Organisation der ungarischen Kirche und des Staates im 11.–12. Jahrhundert an der Gesetzgebung und an der Umbildung der Kriegskunst verfolgen (die deutschen Ritter bildeten das zuverlässige Heer des Königs, das die heidnischen Stammesorberhäupter stoppte). Der König schenkte sowohl der Kirche als auch den nach Ungarn übersiedelten Rittern und Soldaten riesige Güter. Die Oberhäupter der ungarischen Geschlechter und Stämme auf der einen Seite und die Feudalherren, die sich hier niedergelassen hatten, auf der anderen bildeten die ungarische herrschende

Feudalklasse. Die Verschmelzung der beiden war im großen und ganzen in der zweiten Hälfte des 12. Jahrhunderts beendet.

Die Unterworfenen, die mit der Zeit zu Ackerbauern geworden waren, kamen ebenfalls aus Schichten mit unterschiedlichen Rechten und unterschiedlicher ethnischer Zugehörigkeit. Neben den zur Zeit der Landnahme hier lebenden Ackerbau treibenden Bauern, die zu Steuerpflichtigen der Oberhäupter der ungarischen Geschlechter und Stämme wurden, stellten die freien Ungarn, die zahlenmäßig größte Schicht dar. Sie wurden mit der Zeit steuerpflichtig. Wir finden auf den Gütern der Grundherren, der Kirche und des Königs aber auch in Kriegsgefangenschaft geratene Sklaven und Dienstleute verschiedenster Art, die ihre Steuern durch landwirtschaftliche oder handwerkliche Arbeit oder durch Militärdienst ableisteten oder Steuern zahlten. Und schließendlich gab es auch die hierher eingewanderten deutschen Bauern (hospes), die aus den verschiedensten Gegenden des Reiches nach Ungarn auf Güter des Königs, der Kirche oder weltlicher Grundherren übergesiedelt waren. Ihre Zahl ist nicht bekannt, aber ihre zunehmende Rolle in der gesellschaftlichen Umgestaltung läßt darauf schließen, daß sie sich von der Mitte des 12. Jahrhunderts an in immer größerer Zahl im ganzen Karpatenbecken niedergelassen haben.

Aus diesen Völkerschaften mit unterschiedlichen Rechten entwickelte sich mit der Zeit der einheitliche Bauernstand. Dieser Prozeß dauerte mindestens drei Jahrhunderte. Im Jahre 1351 legte ein Gesetz die einheitlichen grundherrlichen Lasten der Bauern im ganzen Land fest. (Das war der Neunt, die Nona, der einheitlich an die Kirche zu zahlende Zehnt, nach der Decima der von jedem Produkt an den Grundherrn zu zahlende neunte Zehnt.) Bis zum Ende des 14. Jahrhunderts waren bereits alle wesentlichen Unterschiede verschwunden, und vor uns steht der ungarische Bauer in seiner feudalen gesellschaftlichen Lage.

Für die Vereinheitlichung des rechtlichen Status der verschiedenen Schichten auf der bäuerlichen Ebene haben die aus den verschiedenen Provinzen des Reiches nach Ungarn einwandernden Bauern (hospes) eine sehr große Rolle gespielt. Bei ihrer Ansiedlung ließen sie sich im allgemeinen mit den Rechten nieder, die ihnen in ihrer alten Heimat zugestanden hatten. Die meisten kamen aus Süddeutschland, und sie bewahrten nicht nur ihr grundlegendes Recht der Freizügigkeit, sondern gaben es allmählich an die Unfreien auf den kirchlichen, weltlichen und königlichen Gütern weiter. Das bedeutet, daß die in verschiedener feudaler Abhängigkeit befindlichen Schichten der Knechte und Halbfreien sowie der absinkenden Freien mit der Zeit Anteil an dem gesellschaftlichen Status der einwandernden Bauern aus dem Reich hatten, und auf dieser Ebene verschmolz die Klasse der in Abhängigkeit lebenden Bauern. Das alles erfolgte parallel zur Entwicklung des Hofsystems und mit der Verbreitung der Zwei- und Dreifelderwirtschaft im Karpatenbecken.

Die Einwanderer spielten nicht nur bei der Entwicklung des gesellschaftlichen Status der bäuerlichen Gesellschaft, sondern auch bei der der Städte die bestimmende Rolle. Die sogenannten freien königlichen Städte, deren rechtlicher Status und gesellschaftliche Lage im großen und ganzen denen der westeuropäischen Städte entsprachen, hatten ohne Ausnahme entweder die Rechtsverhältnisse übernommen, unter denen die eingewanderten deutschen Bürger zu Hause gelebt hatten, oder sie hatten sich ihnen angeglichen. Die frühen ungarischen Städte (Esztergom, Pozsony, Veszprém, Székesfehérvár usw.) waren ursprünglich Residenzstädte des Königs oder der Bischöfe. Sie wurden später Städte mit Zunfthandwerk. Die im nordöstlichen Oberungarn oder in Siebenbürgen entstandenen freien königlichen Städte, die von der Mitte des 13. Jahrhunderts bis zur Mitte des 14. Jahrhunderts gegründet worden waren, waren entweder Bergwerksstädte oder Handelszentren. Diese und die wenigen seit der Mitte des 13. Jahrhunderts vom König gegründeten Städte lebten nach Nürnberger Stadtrecht. In den Städten hatten sich also im großen und ganzen die gleichen gesellschaftlichen Verhältnisse herausgebildet wie auf deutschem Boden, nur war das ungarische Städtenetz viel lockerer als das in Süddeutschland, Österreich oder Böhmen, und die wirtschaftliche Kraft dieser Städte auch von gesingerer Bedeutung. Als die Erzgruben Ende des 16. Jahrhunderts erschöpft waren, ging die wirtschaftliche Kraft dieser Städte schnell zurück, ihre Einwohner wandten sich der Landwirtschaft zu, der in die Städte ziehende zahlreiche Adel wurde dort tonangebend. Bis zum 18. Jahrhundert stockte die Entwicklung der Städte, ihre wohlhabenderen Bürger stiegen in den Adelsstand auf.

Die freien königlichen Städte lebten in unmittelbarer Abhängigkeit vom König. Ihre jährliche Steuerverpflichtung wurde von der Königlichen Kammer festgesetzt. In ihrer inneren Ordnung genossen sie bedeutende Unabhängigkeit, die Richterwahl fand frei statt, auch die Ratsmitglieder wurden frei gewählt. Es versteht sich von selbst, daß dabei die Patrizierschicht der Stadt tonangebend war, stets wurden der Richter und die Ratsmitglieder aus ihren Reihen gewählt. Mit der Zeit nahm die Rolle des Zunftbürgertums an Bedeutung zu. Für seinen Kampf mit den Patriziern im 15. Jahrhundert sind die Auseinandersetzungen zwischen deutsch- und ungerischstämmigen Bürgern in Buda ein bezeichnendes Beispiel. Diese Konflikte sind zugleich auch ein Beweis dafür, daß in die Reihen des ehemals deutschen Bürgertums zunehmend die umgebende ungarische Bevölkerung eingedrungen war.

Die steuerlichen Zahlungsverpflichtungen der Bürger regelte der Stadtrat. Er bestimmte auch den Rahmen des täglichen Lebens. Über die rechtlichen Angelegenheiten zwischen den Bürgern entschied ein eigenes Stadtgericht. Aus dem königlichen Komitat wurde bis zum 13.–14. Jahrhundert das adlige Komitat, dessen Gerichtsbarkeit an den Grenzen der freien königlichen Städte endete.

In den Prozessen zwischen Komitat und Stadt beziehungsweise zwischen Bürger und Adligem urteilte vor allem in den wichtigen Fällen das königliche Gericht.

Seit den vierziger Jahren des 15. Jahrhunderts erschienen die Städte auf den Reichstagen. Sie wurden durch Delegierte vertreten, während der hohe Adel und der hohe Klerus persönlich erscheinen konnten. Nachdem sich auf dem Reichstag die beiden Tafeln herausgebildet hatten (ab 1608), bekamen die Vertreter der Städte ihren Platz an der Unteren Tafel neben den Vertretern des minderen Adels, während der hohe Adel und der hohe Klerus die Übere Tafel bildeten.

Hervorzuheben ist, daß die Rolle der Schultheißen (scultetus) im Leben der Städte allmächlich in den Hingergrund gedrängt wurde. Die bei der Besiedlung führenden Schultheißen bekamen zwar die richterlichen Kompetenzen üblich zugesprochen (sie wurden auch „comes“ genannt wie die königlichen Leiter der Komitate), aber mit Hilfe des Königs drängte die städtische Bürgerschaft deren Privilegien immer mehr zurück, und langsam gingen die Schultheißen im Patriziat auf. Damit wurde das Amt der Richter wählbar, was selbstverständlich zur „Demokratisierung“ des städtischen Lebens beitrug, zur Entstehung einer neuen Patrizierschicht führte und die anfangs starre städtische Ordnung lockerte. Dieser Prozeß war Mitte des 15. Jahrhunderts mehr oder weniger abgeschlossen.

Stellen wir der Stadt das Dorf gegenüber. In Ungarn und in den östlich angrenzenden Gebieten lebten mehrere Volksgruppen, die weiterhin in königlicher Abhängigkeit blieben, kollektiv adlige Rechte genossen, und zwar zumeist als Gegenleistung für den Militärdienst. Dazu gehörten in Siebenbürgen die Szekler, und seit dem Anfang des 17. Jahrhunderts auch die Haiducken. Zwar erreichten diese Gruppen nicht den Anteil an der Gesamtbevölkerung wie ähnlich privilegierte in Polen, der Ukraine oder Rußland, demnoch waren sie auch zahlenmäßig eine bedeutende Schicht der ungarischen Gesellschaft.

Der rechtliche Rahmen, in dem sie lebten, glich im großen und ganzen den Rechtsverhältnissen der Städte oder der Komitate. An ihrer Spitze stand der Comes, er war der Befehlshaber der von ihnen gebildeten militärischen Einheiten und zugleich auch ihr Oberrichter. In jeder Hinsicht hatten sie Selbstverwaltung. Sie setzten ihre Steuerverpflichtungen und das Ausmaß ihres Militärdienstes selbst fest, ihre Rechtsangelegenheiten brachten sie vor ihre eigenen Richter, nur bei Kapitalverbrechen urteilte letztendlich das königliche Gericht (ausgenommen, wenn der Täter auf frischer Tat ergriffen wurde, dann blieb die Angelegenheit vor ihrem eigenen Gericht). Ihr tägliches Leben, die Größe des Landes der einzelnen Szekler- oder Haidukenfamilien legten sie selbst fest, und auch alles andere regelten sie selbst. Im allgemeinen bildeten sie eine geschlossene Gemeinschaft und wachten eifersüchtig über ihre Privilegien. Zuweilen konnten durch Heirat fremde Elemente in ihre Reihen kommen, aber das war sehr selten.

Die bäuerliche Bevölkerung war bis zur Mitte des 14. Jahrhunderts auf der gesellschaftlichen Stufe der aus dem Deutschen Reich einwandernden Bauern vereinheitlicht. Sie genoß im allgemeinen Freizügigkeit, wenn sie alle Verpflichtungen dem Grundherrn gegenüber erfüllt hatte. Stellenweise waren noch verschiedene Dienstleute zu finden, solche die persönlich abhängig waren, ihre Zahl nahm aber sehr schnell ab, so daß wir über ihre gesellschaftliche Rolle hinweggehen können.

Die Bauern lebten in Dörfern. Daß wir uns mit ihren Siedlungsverhältnissen gesondert beschäftigen müssen, erklärt sich aus den besonderen Siedlungsformen und den damit zusammenhängenden gesellschaftlichen Verhältnissen. Traditionelle Bauerndörfer auf königlichem, grundherrlichem oder kirchlichem Grund überwogen. Die sich in die europäische Arbeitsteilung einschaltende ungarische Gesellschaft änderte aber die Rechtsverhältnisse gewisser Dörfer. Die in der zweiten Hälfte des 13. Jahrhunderts beginnende großangelegte Viehausfuhr aus Ungarn, vor allem der Export von Rindern und Pferden, bildete eine, seinen Erfordernissen entsprechende neue Siedlungsform heraus. Es entwickelten sich regelmäßige Routen für den Viehexport mit bestimmten Knotenpunkten, an denen man das Vieh rasten ließ und wo die Händler erschienen, um das Vieh aufzukaufen. Hier nahm die Bevölkerungszahl zu, die verschiedensten Handwerker ließen sich nieder, in erster Linie solche aus den Dienstleistungsgewerben (Schneider, Stellmacher, Stiefelmacher, Schmiede, Böttcher, Schuster). Sie dienten der landwirtschaftlichen Produktion oder befriedigten die Bedürfnisse der Bauernschaft der Umgebung. Diese Siedlungen wurden sehr bald zu Handelsplätzen, wo sich im Jahr mehmals, in den größeren Niederlassungen jedoch in jeder Woche Händler und Käufer versammelten.

Als diese Marktorte eine gewisse Größe erreicht hatten, erhielten ihre Einwohner, die auch weiterhin in Abhängigkeit vom Grundherrn lebten, gewisse Privilegien. Im allgemeinen zahlten nicht die einzelnen Familien gesondert Steuern, sondern die Siedlung als Ganze. Daneben wurden von den Grundherren Naturalabgeben eingenommen, Frondienste hingegen waren nicht mehr gebräuchlich. In der Mehrheit wählten die Bauern dieser Siedlungen ihre Richter selbst und trafen in inneren Angelegenheiten selbst die Entscheidung. Bei Berufungen in Prozessen, die sie untereinander führten, mußten sie sich an den „Herrenstuhl" wenden, da die Einwohner der Siedlungen auch weiterhin in der Abhängigkeit ihrer Grundherren blieben. Ihr Leben aber war viel freier als das der Bewohner der gewöhnlichen Bauerndörfer. Mit der Zeit wurden solche Siedlungen als „Marktflecken" bezeichnet.

Der Marktflecken bot dem Grundherrn viele Vorteile: höhere Geldabgaben, verschiedene Abgaben aufgrund des Handwerks usw. Bedeutende Vorteile gewährte er auch den Bauern. Kein Wunder, daß ihre Einwohnerzahl rasch stieg. Aus diesen sich schnell entwickelnden Marktflecken entstanden bis zum 19. Jahrhundert bisweilen Dörfer mit mehreren tausend Einwohnern. Ihre Entwicklung konnte in den späteren Jahrhunderten in verschiedene Richtungen gehen. Sie konnten das Recht einer freien königlichen Stadt erhalten (z.B. Debrecen), was allerdings in der Regel nur bei Marktflecken auf königlichem Grund und Boden vorkam. Bezeichnend ist, daß Eger, das zu den kirchlichen Marktflecken gehörte, dieses Recht nur kurze Zeit genießen konnte, der Bischof von Eger ließ es aus der Reihe der freien königlichen Städte streichen.

Die meisten Marktflecken verblieben in diesem Rahmen, solange sie den Interessen der landwirtschaftlichen Warenproduktion dienten. Einzelne Marktflecken verloren ihre Rechte und wurden wieder zu gewöhnlichen Dörfern. Andere wieder bewahrten ihre Rechte bis zur Mitte des 19. Jahrhunderts. In den unter türkischer Herrschaft stehenden Gebieten, aus denen die Grundherren geflohen waren, hatte sich die Bevölkerung der Marktflecken auf Kosten der Bewohner der umliegenden Dörfer bereichert. Größere Marktflecken verwandelten sich in Siedlungen, die mit einer Mauer umgeben, manchmal auch befestigt waren (z. B. Kecskemét, Cegléd, Nagykőrös) und die nach Vertreibung der Türken auch in der Lage waren, dem zurückkehrenden Grundherrn gegenüber ihre Selbständigkeit zu bewahren — gegen Zahlung einer nominellen Steuer.

Das Netz der Marktflecken wurde durch das Eisenbahnnetz, dessen Bau in der zweiten Hälfte des 19. Jahrhunderts einsetzte, radikal umgebildet. Viele Marktflecken entvölkerten sich, andere wurden schnell zu Industrie- und Verkehrszentren (z.B. Miskolc, Szolnok usw.). Die Industrialisierung in der zweiten Hälfte des 19. Jahrhunderts führte ohnehin zu einer vollkommenen Umgestaltung des ungarischen Siedlungssystems.

All das zeigt, daß das Prinzip und die Praxis der Selbstverwaltung in den mittelalterlichen und frühneuzeitlichen ungarischen Städten und bei den Siedlungen der Szekler und Haiduken Geltung hatte. Die Bevölkerung der letzteren führte zumeist ein bäuerliches Leben, nur einzelne wohlhabendere Schichten waren in der Tat als adlig anzusehen. Die Szekler, Haiduken usw., mit einem Wort die privilegierten Schichten, machten nur einige Prozent der Gesamtbevölkerung aus, der bedeutend größere Teil waren Bauern auf grundherrlichem, königlichem oder kirchlichem Grund un Boden.

Aus diesen Gruppen mit unterschiedlichen Rechten formte sich bis zum 14. Jahrhundert eine einheitliche Bauernschaft in feudaler Hörigkeit, die größtenteils in Dörfern, zum keineren Teil in Marktflecken lebte. Ihre Rechte und Möglichkeiten hingen davon ab, wo sie geboren waren, wobei sie in ihren grundlegenden Rechten natürlich übereinstimmten. Ihnen stand das Recht des Freizugs zu, die Sicherheit, die die letzte Garantie gegenüber den Forderungen des Grundherrn darstellte. Auf allen anderen Gebieten aber bestimmte die Siedlungsform ihre Möglichkeiten. Die Bauern der Dörfer unterstanden der grundherrlichen Gerichtsbarkeit. Für sie sprach das Gericht das Grundherrn, der Herrenstuhl (sedes curialis), Recht. An der Spitze der Dörfer stand zwar ein Richter und neben ihm einige Geschworene, deren Zahl von der Größe des Dorfes, von der Zahl der Einwohner abhing. Bei kleineren Prozessen war der Dorfrichter erste Instanz, danach konnte beim Herrenstuhl Berufung eingelegt werden. Der Herrenstuhl verschaffte sich aber mit der Zeit eine solche Macht, daß die Rechtsprechung des Dorfrichters — besonders auf den großen Gütern — in den Hintergrund gedrängt wurde.

Die Entwicklung des Herrenstuhls nahm beinahe solange Zeit in Anspruch wie die Entwicklung der einheitlichen Bauernschaft. Auf grundherrlichem und kirchlichem Besitz erscheint er um die Mitte des 12. Jahrhunderts und während er sich anfangs nur auf das vom Grundherrn abhängige Volk, auf die von ihm persönlich Abhängigen bezog, wurde er mit der Zeit territorial organisiert, bezog sich auf die auf dem Besitz des Grundherrn lebenden Bauern, solange, bis sie nicht wegzogen. Die auf dem kirchlichen Grundbesitz beginnende Entwicklung der grundherrlichen Gerichtsbarkeit, die Rechtsprechung des Grundherrn dehnte sich bald auch auf den weltlichen Großgrundbesitz aus. Sehr bald zeigte sich ein neuer Abschnitt: die grundherrliche Rechtsprechung ging auch auf die bisher in die Zuständigkeit der königlichen Gerichte gehörende Urteilsfällung bei Kapitalverbrechen über. Den größten Großgrundbesitzern wurde auch das Blutgericht (ius gladii) zuerkannt. Damit siegte auf den Großgrundbesitzen das Prinzip der territorialen Rechtsprechung: die grundherrliche Gerichtsbarkeit erstreckte sich nicht nur auf die vom Grundherrn abhängigen Bauern, sondern bei einem auf seinem Grund und Boden begangenen Verbrechen auch auf die Bauern anderer Grundherrn, ja, außer auf die auf seinem Besitz lebenden und in seinen Diensten stehenden niederen Adligen, auch auf solche Adlige, die auf dem Gebiet des Grundbesitzes irgendein Verbrechen begangen hatten.

Im 14.–18. Jahrhundert regelten diese rechtlichen Rahmen das Leben des Bauern, ganz gleich, ob sie das Recht hatten, ihren Wohnort frei zu wählen oder ob es sich um einen Leibeigenen handelte. Bei den Bauern in den Dörfern fällte der Dorfrichter als erstes Forum das Urteil, von da konnte man es beim Herrenstuhl anfechten. Zwischen Grundherrn und Bauern urteilte — dem Prinzip nach — der Herrenstuhl, doch das kam selten vor, vom 16. Jahrhundert an so gut wie überhaupt nicht. Bei Grundherrschaften, denen das Recht des Blutgerichts zustand, war die nächste Instanz für den Einspruch nach dem Herrenstuhl das königliche Gericht und in sonstigen Fällen, auf dem Besitz kleinerer Grundherren, das Komitat. Die Todesstrafe konnte nur das königliche Gericht fällen, ausgenommen wenn der Täter auf friescher Tat ertappt worden war.

Im Prinzip galt dasselbe auch für die Marktflecken. Über deren Einwohner, besonders bei Siedlungen mit größerer Bevölkerung, urteilte das eigene Gericht. An größeren Orten finden wir neben dem Richter oder den Richtern (unter ihnen dem Oberrichter) auch Geschworene. Vor diesem Gericht prozessierten die Bauern und Handwerker, auch bei Ruhestörung und Handlungen gegen die öffentliche Ordung bildete dieses Gericht die erste Instanz. Von hier konnte beim Herrenstuhl Einspruch eingelegt werden.

Etwas anders war die Lage in Marktflecken mit großer Einwohnerzahl. In den 150 Jahren türkischer Besatzung haben sich diese großen Siedlungen praktisch die Stellung freier königlicher Städte erkämpft, ja sogar völlige innere Selbständigkeit und Selbstverwaltung. Nach der türkischen Besetzung kehrten die Grundherren zurück, aber sie waren nicht mehr stark genug, um die Selbstverwaltung der Siedlungen zu beschneiden. Deshalb einigten sie sich früher oder später mit ihnen, die reicheren Siedlungen kauften sich los, und damit wurden sie frei. In diesen Siedlungen blieb die Selbstverwaltung praktisch unangetastet bis zum Jahre 1848, als die Bauern des Landes von der Grundherrschaft befreit wurden.

Über das innere Leben der bäuerlichen Gemeinden wissen wir relativ wenig. In den grundherrlichen Dörfern (und das gilt auch für den kirchlichen und den königlichen Grundbesitz) ist der Richter die einzige Person, über dessen Tätigkeit wir etwas wissen. Im allgemeinen bestimmte ihn der Grundherr mit der Möglichkeit der Verlängerung, gewöhnlich für ein Jahr. Den Vorschlag des Grundherrn nahmen die Bauern selbstversändlich an. Der Richter war der Vertrauensmann des Grundherrn (beziehungsweise des Amtmanns), zu seinen Aufgaben gehörte es, dafür zu sorgen, daß die Bauern ihrer Steuerpflicht nachkamen. Neben dem Richter finden wir, abhängig von der Größe des Dorfes, Geschworene (die nicht nur bei der Rechtssprechung mitwirkten), Feldwächter, Flurhüter, die auf die Weinernte achtgaben usw. Das Vieh der Gemeinde wurde von den Gemeindehirten auf die Weide getrieben.

Der Richter und die Geschworenen kamen meist aus den Reihen der wohlhabenderen Bauern, und das Richteramt wirkte auch auf die Vermögensbildung ein, denn der Richter bezahlte während seiner Amtszeit keine Steuern an den Grundherrn.

Der Richter und die Geschworenen wurden auf der Versammlung der Dorfgemeinde gewählt, aber bei voller Kontrolle durch den Grundherrn. Der Richter wurde vom Vertreter des Grundherrn bestimmt und so wurde er gewählt, bei den kleineren Amtsträgern waren die Wahlmöglichkeiten der Gemeinschaft größer. Auch das tägliche Leben des Dorfes wurde vom Grundherrn oder seinem Vertreter, von den Beamten der Gutsverwaltung oder von den Bewaffneten des Grundherrn nachhaltig kontrolliert. Und vom 18. Jahrhundert an übte der Vertreter des Komitats, der Stuhlrichter, die Macht über das Dorf aus.

In die alltäglichen Angelegenheiten des Dorfes mischten sich der Grundherr und seine Vertreter kaum ein, in diesen Dingen kam die bäuerliche Selbstverwaltung zur Geltung. Anfangs hatte das Dorf keine Gemeindekasse, die Entlohnung für die einzelnen Gemeindebediensteten sammelte der Richter von den einzelnen Familien ein. Mit der Zeit entstand, vor allem in größeren Dörfern, eine Gemeindekasse, über die der Grundherr und neben ihm auch die Bauern die Kontrolle ausübten. Die für die Zwecke des Dorfes bestimmten Geld- und Naturalabgaben existierten seit dem 18. Jahrhunder. Die Komitate verpflichteten die Dörfer zur Instandhaltung der Straßen. Diese Arbeiten wurden von der Gemeinschaft durchgeführt, nach Anweisung des Richters. Allgemein üblich wurde eine derartige Belastung der Bauern des Dorfes im bürgerlichen Zeitalter nach 1848.

Das Dorf erließ Vorschriften zur Gemeindeordnung (so würde man heute die „articuli" nennen), vor allem Benutzungsregelung der gemeinsam genutzten Felder, der Weiden, Wälder und der Weinberge, dann und wann auch Verhaltensregeln, zum Beispiel bei der Weinernte. Diese Vorschriften wurden von der grundherrlichen Verwaltung geprüft und gebilligt. Da sie sehr häufig übereinstimmen, ist anzunehmen, daß ein Teil von vornherein von der grundherrlichen Verwaltung abgefäßt worden war. Zu politischen Angelegenheiten hat das Dorf niemals Stellung genommen — natürlich vor 1848. (Wie ein Stand wurden die Bauern nie in den Landtag aufgenommen.)

Mitglied der Dorfgemeinde war jeder Bauer mit einem Hof oder Anteilhof und die aus solchen Familien stammenden verarmten Familienmitglieder. Wenn die Bauernfamilie ausstarb, setzte der Grundherr einen neuen Bauern auf den Hof. Damit wurde der Neuankömmling automatisch Mitglied der Gemeinde. Auf diesem Gebiet gab es keinen Unterschied zwischen Leibeigenen und freizügigen Bauern. Jeder war vollberechtigtes Mitglied der Gemeinde, der Besitz des Bauern war also nicht ausschlaggebend. Auch der landlose Bauer und die Häusler mit nur wenig Land waren vollberechtigt, allerdings mit der Einschränkung, daß sie kein Amt übernehmen konnten, denn die Dorfgemeinde wählte den Richter stets aus den Reihen der reichsten Bauernfamilien. Dies war auch später die Regel, der Besitz des Hofes oder des Wohnhauses machte den Fremden zum Mitglied der Dorfgemeinde.

Es ist nicht leicht, die Frage zu beantworten, wer diese Ordnung regulierte. Ursprünglich bildeten die auf dem Boden des Grundherrn lebenden Bauern die Dorfgemeinde. Dem widerspricht auch die Einwanderung nicht, denn sie erfolgte im allgemeinen im geschlossenen Rahmen, mit der Gründung neuer

Dörfer. Die Zunahme der wüstliegenden Hufen bot die Möglichkeit, die gewohnte Ordnung zu durchbrechen, damals kamen Fremde in die Dorfgemeinde. Der Grundherr war an der Ansiedlung interessiert, vermutlich entstand die Praxis auf Druck des Grundherrn. Die Dorfgemeinde selbst konnte niemanden zurückweisen, der vom Grundherrn einen Hof oder einen Anteilhof erhalten hatte.

Die Verwaltung des Dorfes war sehr einfach. Der Richter als der gewählte Führer, der zugleich der Vertrauensmann des Grundherrn war, vertrat in seiner Person die Ordnung des Dorfes. Er achtete auf die Einhaltung der verschiedenen Vorschriften, er bestimmte diejenigen, die an der Fronarbeit teilnehmen mußten, er sorgte für die Eintreibung der Natural- und Geldabgaben. Er urteilte bei kleineren Problemen zwischen den Bauern, verurteilte die Schuldigen bei Vergehen und Untaten, aber der schwerwiegendere Diebstahl gehörte bereits vor den Herrenstuhl. Er achtete also auf die Ordnung im Dorfe. Die Dorfgemeinde hatte kaum die Möglichkeit, ihn abzusetzen, er schuldete ihr auch kaum Rechenschaft. Wenn die Dorfgemeinschaft etwas gegen ihn vorzubringen hatte, dann konnte sie ihn beim Herrenstuhl verklagen. So war er eindeutig nur dem Grundherrn verantwortlich. Die anderen Amtsträger des Dorfes hingegen legten in erster Instanz dem Richter Rechenschaft ab.

Der Richter wurde im allgemeinen aus den Reihen der wohlabenderen Bauern bestimmt, beziehungsweise gewählt. In den Dörfern entstand ein Kreis von Familien, die die richterliche Würde innehatten, selten kamen Richter aus anderen Familien. Das bedeutet, daß sich die wirtschaftliche Kraft — nach einiger Zeit — mit Erfahrungen paarte, der enge Kreis der mit dem Richteramt Betrauten seine Aufgaben ausgezeichnet kannte. Meist schützte der Richter die Interessen des Dorfes, zum Beispiel indem er die Höhe der Produktion oder die Zunahme des Viehbestandes verschleierte. Diese Praxis kann in manchen Fällen über Jahrhunderte nachgewiesen werden und ist uns nur durch einen Zufall zur Kenntnis gekommen.

Selbst in den größeren Dürfern gab es keinen bezahlten Richter. Der Richter war eben ein Bauer wie die übrigen, solange er im Amt war, blieb er allerdings von der grundherrlichen Steuer befreit. Das war seine Bezahlung. Er erledigte seine Aufgaben je nach Notwendigkeit, also in „Teilarbeitszeit". Wenn eine Familie längere Zeit das Amt des Richters bekleidet hatte, war dadurch ihr gesellschaftsliches Prestige gestiegen, allerdings nur bei den Bauern. Die Beamten des Grundherrn achteten hie und da auch auf die Meinung eines angeseheneren Richters, aber das kam nur gelegentlich vor.

Den Frieden des Dorfes ließ der Richter mit den Mitgliedern der Dorfgemeinde und auch den fremden Elementen aufrechthalten. Hilfreich waren ihm die Bewaffneten des Grundherrn, die die Ordnung garantierten. In diesem

Zusammenhang war der Richter also eindeutig der Mann des Grundherrn. In kleineren Angelegenheiten (Lärm, Trunkenheit usw.) war er der Vertreter der Gemeinschaft, nicht nur, indem er für die Einhaltung der Vorschriften sorgte, sondern indem er auch die Übertretungen selbst bestrafte. Für solche Vergehen gab es darüber hinaus eine grundherrliche Vorschrift, die für den Richter auch dann bindend war, wenn die Dorfgemeinschaft nicht geurteilt hätte. Die größeren Vergehen (Ehebruch, Notzucht, Unzucht usw.) kamen vor den Herrenstuhl.

Bei der Rechtssprechung durch den Richter war die Anwesenheit der Organe des Grundherrn nicht erforderlich. Die Entscheidung des Richters, und wo es sie gab, der Geschworenen, war gültig, mit der Einschränkung, daß beim Herrenstuhl Berufung eingelegt werden konnte.

Dies alles bezieht sich auf die Hofgemeinden. Teilweise anders war die Lage in den Marktflecken. In den Marktflecken, die sich mit der Zeit von der grundherrlichen Abhängigkeit befreit hatten, herrschte vollkommene Autonomie. Sie hatten die Gemeinde im allgemeinen in kleinere Einheiten aufgeteilt, die Versammlung der gesamten Gemeinde des Marktfleckens wurde selten einberufen. Die kleineren Bezirke (manchmal Hundertschaften usw.) wählten ihre eigenen Kandidaten, die Mitglieder des Gemeindevorstandes (in größeren Marktflecken die Senatoren!) an ihrer Spitze mit dem Richter und die Körperschaft der Richter wählte den Oberrichter. Auch die Kontrolle der Einnahmen und Ausgaben der Marktflecken war in Händen des Vorstandes. Diese Marktflecken erhoben Steuern und verlangten von ihren Einwohnern öffentliche Arbeiten. Selbständig entwickelten sie die Vorschriften und Bestimmungen, die ihr tägliches Leben regelten.

Mitglied der Gemeinde solcher selbständigen Marktflecken konnte werden, wer ein Haus und dazugehöriges Land erwarb. Diese Käufe wurden meist dem Gemeinderat zur Billigung vorgelegt.

Diese Marktflecken lebten gewöhnlich außerhalb der grundherrlichen Abhängigkeit, manchmal schon seit Jahrhunderten. Natürlich konnten sie in Kapitalverbrechen kein Todesurteil fällen, es sei denn, der Täter wurde bei der Tat ertappt, in solchen Fällen waren die türkischen Behörden oder das königliche Gericht das höchste Forum.

Der Oberrichter, die Richter und Ratsmitglieder waren im allgemeinen bezahlte Angestellte, aber auch sie betrieben Landwirtschaft oder übten ein Handwerk aus, sie versahen ihre Aufgaben also gewissermaßen nebenberuflich. Auch in diesen Siedlungen kam der Richter aus den wohlhabendsten Familien. Doch wurden hier auch zahlreiche Personen in der Verwaltung der Gemeinde (des Marktfleckens) beschäftigt, deren Aufgaben die ganze Arbeitszeit ausfüllten. Richter und Oberrichter aber waren eindeutig gewählte Vertreter der Gemeinschaft. Hier entstand auch eine Hierarchie der Ämter.

In diesen Siedlungen war die Aufrechterhaltung des inneren Friedens und der Sicherheit Aufgabe des Oberrichters und der ihm Unterstellten. Sie verfügten auch über Bewaffnete, eine Mischung aus Soldaten und Polizei, die sowohl auf die innere Sicherheit wie auf den Schutz der Marktflecken achteten. Die Bestimmungen wurden eindeutig von der Gemeinde selbst aufgestellt, aber dabei spielten die Gemeindebediensteten der Marktflecken eine große Rolle. Die Gerichtsbarkeit in den Marktflecken war von außeren unabhängig. An den Gerichten erledigten rechtskundige Personen die Aufgaben der Anklage und der Verteidigung. Diese Marktflecken unterhielten auch Gefängnisse. Das alles zeigt, daß ihre Abhängigkeit von der grundherrlichen Macht und vom adligen Komitat ziemlich gering war.

In den kleineren, in grundherrlicher Abhängigkeit verbliebenen Marktflecken (und das war der überwiegende Teil) hatte sich keine eindeutige Lage herausgebildet. Die Rolle der Gemeinde bei der Bestimmung ihres eigenen inneren Lebens war weit größer als in den Dörfern, aber nicht so stark wie in den großen Marktflecken. Den Richter wählten sie gewöhnlich selbst, aber der Grundherr mußte ihn bestätigen. Bei inneren Angelegenheiten gingen der Richter und die Geschworenen vor, sie urteilten auch, aber es bestand die Möglichkeit der Berufung beim Herrenstuhl. Bei Kapitalverbrechen konnten diese Marktflecken niemals vorgehen. Für die Ordnung im Innern sorgten sie selbst gewisser Unterstützung durch den Grundherrn. In politische Dinge konnten sie sich niemals einmischen.

Die Zugehörigkeit zur Gemeinde des Dorfes oder des Marktfleckens hing davon ab, ob die Zustimmung zum Kauf des Hofes erteilt wurde. Hier aber waren die Interessen des Grundherrn stärker als wir es bisher gesehen haben. Zeitweilig trachteten die Grundherrn danach, daß der eine oder andere Marktflecken nicht zu sehr anschwoll, denn die Bauern aus der Umgebung strebten hierher. Um dem vorzubeugen, erhöhten sie die Zahl der Höfe nicht, oft untersagten sie die Übergabe eines leeren Hofes an einen Zuwanderer. Sie wollten die Bauern in ihren Dörfern nicht verlieren, und sie wollten auch nicht, daß die Einwohnerzahl der Marktflecken zu sehr anschwoll und damit diese Siedlungen ihnen aus den Händen glitten. An der Wende vom 15. zum 16. Jahrhundert setzte ein allgemeiner Sturm der Grundherrn auf die Privilegien der Marktflecken ein, und deren Widerstand war einer der Hauptgründe für den Ausbruch des Bauernkriegs vom Jahre 1514.

Auch in anderer Hinsicht standen diese Marktflecken zwischen den großen Marktflecken und den Dörfern. In lokalen Dingen besaßen sie so gut wie volle Selbständigkeit, aber bei Gültigkeit der grundherrlichen Autorität. Die Gemeinschaft spielt eine größere Rolle, der Richter ist hier in erster Linie ein Mann der Gemeinschaft, natürlich kommt auch er aus den wohlhabenden Familien, der

Apparat der Gemeindebediensteten ist vielschichtiger als in den Dörfern. Auch hier erledigt der Richter seine Aufgaben als Nebenarbeit, er zahlt keine Steuern und erhält stellenweise auch Bezahlung. Die innere Ordnung wird vom Gemeindevorstand aufrechterhalten, mit eigenem Apparat, den der Grundherr durch seine Bewaffneten von außen unterstützt. In kleineren Angelegenheiten urteilt das Gericht selbständig, bei größeren aber sind die Amtleute des Grundherrn auch im Gericht vertreten. Berufung kann beim Herrenstuhl eingelegt werden.

Die Aufrechterhaltung der öffentlichen Ordnung ging im großen und ganzen wie in den Dörfern vor sich, aber mit größerer Zuständigkeit des Richters und der Gemeindebediensteten. „Letztes Argument" stellten die Bewaffneten des Grundherrn dar, wärend die Marktflecken selbst die Regeln für die öffentliche Ordnung festlegten, stellenweise bei Mitsprache des Grundherrn. In kleineren Angelegenheiten war das Gericht der Marktflecken selbständig tätig, bei wichtigeren Prozessen oder Straftaten nahmen einige Mitglieder des grundherrlichen Gerichts an den Verhandlungen teil. Forum für die Berufung war der Herrenstuhl.

Der Absolutismus des 18. Jahrhunderts versuchte die Gerichtsverhandlung der Bauern vor dem Herrenstuhl zu lockern, zumindest in der Hinsicht, daß das tatsächliche Berufungsrecht der Bauern gesichert sein sollte. Von 1729 ab konnte vom Herrenstuhl beim Komitat Berufung eingelegt werden. Das war keine große Veränderung, denn die Verwaltung des Komitats lag in den Händen des Adels, in Prinzip aber wurde die bäuerliche Abhängigkeit doch gelockert. Von 1765 ab wurde dieses Berufungsrecht weiter ausgedehnt. Neuere königliche Verordnungen führten zu einer weiteren Lockerung der bäuerlichen Abhängigkeit: auch in Urbarialangelegenheiten konnten die Bauern Berufung einlegen. 1786 und 1791 brachten weitere Erleichterungen: auch bei bäuerlichen Strafprozessen wurde die Möglichkeit der Berufung gegeben, bei der Todesstrafe bis zum höchsten königlichen Gericht.

Inwieweit können wir also von kommunalen Strukturen im mittelalterlichen und frühneuzeitlichen Ungarn sprechen? Allein bei den freien königlichen Städten und bei den mit kollektiven Adelsrechten ausgestatteten Volksgruppen ist die Lage klar: sie hatten in der Tat in jeder Hinsicht Selbstverwaltung, konnten in ihren eigenen Angelegenheiten frei entscheiden, von der letztwilligen Verfügung bis zur Wahl der Gemeindebediensteten. Weit komplizierter ist die Situation bei den Bauern und den Handwerkern in den grundherrlicher Gerichtsbarkeit unterstehenden Dörfern und Marktflecken. Die Selbstverwaltung der Bauern in den Dörfern war sehr beschnitten. Aber auch sie waren bewußte und selbstbewußte Menschen, was sich daran zeigt, daß größere bäuerliche Bewegungen (zum Beispiel der siebenbürgische Bauernaufstand von 1437) die

Aufnahme der Bauern als einen selbständigen Stand in den Landtag forderten. Die Bauernschaft in den Dörfern war in jeder Hinsicht sehr eingeengt, selbst in Privatangelegenheiten (nur ein schriftliches Testament wurde akzeptiert, aber bei Aussterben der Familie fiel die Hälfte des beweglichen Gutes sowieso an den Grundherrn).

Etwas anders war die Lage in den Marktflecken. Wie wir gesehen haben, hatten sich die größten Siedlungen praktisch städtische Rechte und Stellung erkämpft. Aber auch der gewöhnliche Marktflecken befand sich in günstigerer Lage als das Dorf. Seine Selbstverwaltung war beinahe vollkommen, die Kontrolle lag allerdings in der Hand des Grundherrn. Trotzdem konnten diese Siedlungen Schritt für Schritt ihre Abhängigkeit lockern. Ein völliger Kommunalismus jedoch konnte sich auch in ihren Kreisen nicht entwickeln. Das war nur im Rahmen der bürgerlichen Umgestaltung nach 1848 möglich — aber das ist bereits ein anderes Thema.

# VI

## DER UNGARISCHE BAUERNAUFSTAND VON 1514*

VON den europäischen Bauernaufständen des 14.–16. Jh.s war der ungarische der östlichste. Nicht nur im geographischen, auch im gesellschaftlichen Sinne. Die ungarische Gesellschaft entwickelte sich nämlich von Anfang an anders als die westeuropäische; auch wenn die Unterschiede vielleicht auf den ersten Blick nicht ins Auge fallen, waren sie doch so wesentlich, daß wir die Problematik des Bauernaufstandes von 1514 ohne eine zumindest oberflächliche Analyse nicht verstehen können.

Das westeuropäische wirtschaftlich-gesellschaftliche Entwicklungsmodell ist heute bereits so bekannt, daß wir hier auf seine Einzelheiten nicht einzugehen brauchen. Es genügt lediglich hervorzuheben, daß bei der Entstehung des westeuropäischen Feudalismus das antike Erbe eine wesentliche Rolle gespielt hat. Im klassischen westeuropäischen Entwicklungsgebiet (Norditalien, das heutige Frankreich, Schweiz, Süd- und Westdeutschland, Niederlande) haben die Wellen der Völkerwanderung die dort lebende Bevölkerung nicht vernichtet, auch viele Städte blieben bestehen. Hier entstand der Feudalismus aus einer Art Verschmelzung der antiken Überlieferungen und der keltisch-germanischen wirtschaftlich-gesellschaftlichen Errungenschaften, wobei die entstehende neue Ordnung der Gesellschaft entscheidend von den antiken Formen des Privateigentums, von der starken Bevölkerungsdichte, von den relativ engen Beziehungen zwischen Dorf und Stadt, von der Ideologie der römisch-katholischen Kirche usw. beeinflußt wurde. In historisch relativ kurzer Zeit entstand aus den verschiedenen Bauernschichten – Sklaven, Freie usw. – die Form der Grundhörigkeit, in der der grundholde Bauer

*) Die Schilderung der Unterschiede zwischen der west- und osteuropäischen wirtschaftlichen und sozialen Entwicklung basiert auf eigenen Forschungen; darüber hinaus faßt das Referat die neuen Ergebnisse zusammen, die von der ungarischen Geschichtsschreibung in den letzten Jahren erzielt worden sind.

persönlich langsam frei wurde, nach Zahlung der Feudalrente die Früchte seiner Arbeit frei genießen konnte. Daher war die westeuropäische Gesellschaft dynamisch; es konnten sich unter dem Druck der Bevölkerungszunahme die Produktivkräfte weiter entfalten. Trotz der in mehreren Wellen erfolgenden Auswanderung der Bauern war im Grunde genommen die Entwicklung der Produktivkräfte charakteristisch für die westeuropäischen Dörfer. Das führte dann sehr früh zum Aufblühen der zum Teil in der Antike wurzelnden, zum Teil neu entstandenen Städte, die aus Verwaltungszentren zu Zentren des Handels und des Gewerbes wurden. Die immer enger werdenden Beziehungen zwischen Dorf und Stadt beschleunigten diesen Vorgang weiter. Ohne näher auf die Einzelheiten einzugehen, erblicken wir hierin das Wesen der westeuropäischen Entwicklung.

Von Grund auf anders war die Situation in Osteuropa, wo die antiken Überlieferungen fehlten. Nicht das Fehlen der Städte ist in erster Linie entscheidend, wenn auch wichtig, sondern das Fehlen der im westlichen Teil des römischen Reiches entstandenen Formen des Bodeneigentums.

Hier ist von so bedeutenden Unterschieden die Rede, daß es lohnt, sie eingehender zu untersuchen. Die früheren Zivilisationen, die in Asien und Nordafrika entstanden waren, oder die Gesellschaften der indogermanischen Völker in Asien und Europa, von Indien bis Irland, basierten auf dem Gemeineigentum des Bodens.

Konkret bedeutete diese Erscheinungsform des Eigentums, daß die über den kleinen Dorfgemeinschaften stehende, zusammenfassende Einheit, die Staatsmacht, der Herrscher der einzige Eigentümer des Bodens war. Die Bauern nutzten den Boden nicht als Einzelpersonen, sondern in der Gemeinschaft des ganzen Dorfes. Grob ausgedrückt: das lockere Konglomerat der Dorfgemeinschaften bildete den Staat. Als kleinste Steuereinheit und Verwaltungseinheit garantierte die Dorfgemeinschaft die Steuer für den Staatsapparat, der aus den einlaufenden Steuern seine Funktionen versah. Neben dem Gemeineigentum des Bodens war die charakteristischste Eigenschaft des Systems, daß für den in der Dorfgemeinschaft lebenden Menschen die Außenwelt nur in soweit existierte, als sie sich auf die Gemeinschaft, in der er lebte, auswirkte. Die vollständige Isolierung der einzelnen Dorfgemeinschaften war die Grundlage dieses despotischen Systems. Vom Mittelmeer, vom Balkan bis Indien, China und Japan, in ganz Eurasien und in Afrika herrschte diese Gesellschaftsstruktur.

Die griechische Gesellschaft, die als erste das Privateigentum am

Boden geschaffen hatte, dann die römische und die westeuropäischen Gesellschaften nach der Völkerwanderung unterschieden sich grundlegend von dieser Gesellschaftsstruktur. Das feudale Westeuropa war gleichsam die Aufhebung des *asiatischen* Systems der Dorfgemeinschaft.

Einer der Hauptunterschiede zwischen den beiden Systemen bestand darin, daß die westeuropäischen Gesellschaften *dynamisch* waren. Das östliche System der Dorfgemeinschaften hingegen, auch die slawische Variante, und der Aufbau der darauf basierenden Gesellschaft waren *statisch*, begünstigten die intensive Entwicklung der Produktion nicht. Die einzelnen Dorfgemeinschaften garantierten dem Staat die Steuern in Form der *kollektiven Verantwortung*. In diesem System schnitt im Grunde der schlecht ab, der mehr produzierte. Das ist vor allem die Erklärung dafür, warum im Verlaufe der Jahrtausende überall in diesen Kulturen, von Ägypten bis China, von Vorderasien bis Osteuropa, lediglich das einmal gegebene Niveau der Produktion gehalten wurde, warum es nicht zur Ausweitung, zur Steigerung der Produktivität kam.

Das ist auch der Grund für die unterschiedlichen Strukturen der „feudalen" Gesellschaften Osteuropas und Westeuropas. In Westeuropa hatte das Lehenswesen die ganze Gesellschaft durchdrungen, während in Osteuropa überall die starke zentrale Gewalt erhalten geblieben war, von der der gesamte Adel unmittelbar abhing und die sich deshalb stärker als dieser erwies. Die Gliederung der Gesellschaft konnte hier nicht so tief sein, wie in Westeuropa. In den riesigen Gebieten Osteuropas war der Adel fast bis zum Schluß eine Art Dienst- und Militäradel, der vielerorts seinen Besitz nicht vererbbar machen konnte und deshalb dem Herrscher in sehr großem Maße untertan war.

Natürlich können wir nicht sagen, daß das System der Dorfgemeinschaft in Osteuropa in der gleichen Form aufgebaut war wie überall in Asien. Das System der auf den Dorfgemeinschaften basierenden Gesellschaften war nicht überall in Eurasien gleich. Eigentlich ist bis zum heutigen Tage noch nicht in allen Einzelheiten aufgedeckt, warum sich dieses System bei dem einen Volk in despotischen, bei dem anderen in demokratischeren Herrschaftsformen zeigte. Bei den slawischen Stämmen erschien das despotische System – zu Beginn der Geschichte der patriarchalische Charakter der Einrichtung des Starostas der Dorfgemeinschaft, später aber der Despotismus des Herrschers – bei den Kelten und Germanen und bei einigen Hirtenvölkern dagegen eher die demokratische Form. Wichtig vom Gesichtspunkt unseres Themas ist hier die Tatsache, daß in Osteuropa die östliche Form des Bodeneigentums, die auf den zur kollektiven Verantwortung verpflichteten Dorfgemeinschaften aufgebaute despotische Herrschaftsform, das hierauf basierende wirtschaftliche und rechtliche System der ganzen Gesellschaft von Anfang an – wir können sagen – das Gegenteil der Entwicklung westeuropäischen Typs war.

Der relative Reichtum an Boden und das System der Dorfgemeinschaften sowie das völlige Fehlen antiker Überlieferungen führten *zusammen* dazu, daß die Entwicklung Osteuropas auf anderen Wegen und viel langsamer erfolgte als die Westeuropas. Die Produktion zu intensivieren bestand weder die Notwendigkeit noch die Möglichkeit, denn der unbegrenzt scheinende Bodenreichtum, der besonders für das Gebiet des europäischen Rußland bezeichnend war, machte es möglich, daß die zunehmende Bevölkerung ohne Weiterentwicklung der Produktionstechnik und der Produktionsorganisation, das heißt in der überlieferten Form ihr Auskommen fand.

In Osteuropa entwickelten sich nämlich die nichtlandwirtschaftlichen Sektoren der Wirtschaft außergewöhnlich langsam. Jahrhunderte hindurch war die Stadt nichts anderes als eine Ansiedlung mit großer Einwohnerzahl, so gut wie ohne jede wirtschaftliche und gesellschaftliche Funktion im Vergleich zu einer richtigen Stadt westlichen Typs. Die in den historischen Quellen genannten Städte spielten in Osteuropa in diesen Jahrhunderten nicht die gesellschaftlich-wirtschaftliche Rolle wie in Westeuropa. Dort hatten sich die Städte – ob es sich um solche antiken Ursprungs handelte, in denen das Leben mehr oder weniger weitergegangen war oder um neuentstandene Städte – aus anfänglich königlichen, grundherrlichen oder kirchlichen Verwaltungszentren sehr bald zu Handels-, dann zu Industriezentren entwickelt, die nicht nur Mittelpunkt des Fernhandels, sondern auch des Warenaustauschs *innerhalb* der einzelnen Gebiete und später zu Industrieansiedlungen wurden. Innerhalb der Feudalgesellschaft bildeten die Bewohner solcher Städte einen gesonderten Stand, den Stand der Bürger. Die „Städte" Osteuropas können wir in zwei Gruppen teilen. Die ersteren, zu größeren Städten angewachsenen Siedlungen, waren die Knotenpunkte des durch den Kontinent führenden Fernhandels, mit Einwohnern, die sich ethnisch von der Umgebung unterschieden. Den anderen Typus der Städte bildeten militärisch-administrative Zentren. Der Herrscher und seine Gefolgschaft, ein mächtiger Feudalherr mit seiner Gefolgschaft, kirchliche Zentren, kleinere oder größere Befestigungen bildeten den Kern dieser Städte.

Diese beiden Stadttypen waren in Osteuropa bis hin zur Mitte des 19. Jh.s charakteristisch. Die Einwohner lebten zum größten Teil von der Landwirtschaft. Als Stadt erschien ein Ort vor allem durch den einen oder anderen Zug seiner rechtlichen Stellung und dadurch, daß er wegen seiner zahlreichen Einwohner auf den westeuropäischen Betrachter den Eindruck einer Stadt machte. Obwohl das äußere Bild dieser Städte auch für ihn stets die Kennzeichen des Dorfes trug. Auch in diesen Siedlungen gab es Handwerk, aber in den meisten Teilen Osteuropas nicht im Rahmen organisierter Zünfte. Zwar gab es auch Städte im westeuropäischen Sinne, aber sie stellten nicht den Haupttypus der städtischen Entwicklung dar. (Wir denken an die Städte, deren Einwohner vornehmlich die aus dem Westen einwandernden, vor allem deutschen Bergleute oder Kaufleute bildeten.)

Wie sich die Städte West- und Osteuropas in ihrer gesellschaftlich-wirtschaftlichen Struktur unterschieden, so auch die Dörfer. In den riesigen Gebieten Osteuropas blieben die Bauern eigentlich bis zur Bauernbefreiung im 19. Jh. mehr oder weniger Leibeigene oder Sklaven. In Rußland oder auf dem Balkan – besonders in Rumänien – und in Ostpolen konnten die Bauern ge- und verkauft werden. Zwischen der Dorfgemeinschaft, dem darauf aufbauenden asiatischen despotischen Herrschaftssystem und der Leibeigenschaft besteht ein enger und logischer Zusammenhang. Nur in den Gebieten Osteuropas, wo die westliche Kirche das Christentum verbreitete, änderte sich die Lage. Das aber gilt nur für die kleinere, westliche Hälfte des Gebietes, für das Baltikum, für Polen, Ungarn und Kroatien. Auch in Rußland hatte sich durch den Einfluß des Christentums die Sklaverei etwas gemildert, aber die Bauern wurden niemals im westeuropäischen Sinne genommen Hörige. Die Mitglieder der Dorfgemeinschaften waren füreinander verantwortlich. Dieses primitive Rechtsverhältnis ist zum Beispiel in Rußland bis in das erste Jahrzehnt des 20. Jh.s erhalten geblieben. Völlig unabhängig von ihrer gesellschaftlichen Stellung, trugen die Bauern, was das Wesentliche anbetrifft, das gleiche Schicksal. Als aber der Prozeß der Vereinheitlichung der verschiedenen bäuerlichen Schichten stärker wurde, erfolgte das praktisch auf dem Niveau der Leibeigenschaft.

Die Leibeigenschaft der Bauern war ein riesiger Hemmschuh für die intensive Entwicklung der Wirtschaft. Daß aber der Besitz in den

Händen des Adels lange Zeit nicht vererbbar war, führte zu den „asiatischen", „balkanischen" Formen der Ausbeutung, also nicht zur sorgsamen Behandlung, sondern zur Aussaugung. Zur gleichen Zeit sicherte die Bodeneigentumsform der Dorfgemeinschaft der zentralen Macht ein so großes Übergewicht, wie es ähnlich nur auf dem asiatischen Kontinent und in Afrika zu beobachten war.

Wir haben schon mehrfach darauf hingewiesen, daß die Situation auf einem schmalen Weststreifen Osteuropas etwas anders war. Die Entwicklung des ursprünglich osteuropäischen Typus wurde auf dem Streifen vom Baltikum über Polen und Ungarn bis Slowenien und Kroatien durch zahlreiche Faktoren beeinflußt. In einzelnen Gebieten – Pannonien, Slowenien, Kroatien – müssen die starken antiken Überlieferungen ebenso in Betracht gezogen werden wie die im Verhältnis zur örtlichen Bevölkerung relativ große Zahl einwandernder Bauern, die das westeuropäische Gesellschafts- und Wirtschaftssystem vermittelt – in Ungarn, vor allem aber in Polen und im Baltikum usw. – und in mehreren Wellen an der Kolonisation des Gebietes teilgenommen haben. Daneben spielten der Sieg der römischen Kirche und andere historische Faktoren eine Rolle. Dadurch wurden in diesem westlichen Streifen Osteuropas – Böhmen und Mähren gehören unserer Ansicht nach nicht hierzu, sondern zum Typus der westlichen Entwicklung! – die sich im europäischen Rußland oder auf dem Balkan – Serbien, Rumänien usw. – zeigenden Besonderheiten der osteuropäischen Entwicklung stark verändert. Es ist auf die Einrichtungen der feudalen Gesellschaft zurückzuführen, daß sich die verschiedenen Schichten der Bauern um die Wende vom 13. zum 14. Jh. in Polen oder in Ungarn nicht auf dem Niveau der Leibeigenen, sondern auf dem gesellschaftlichen Status des westeuropäischen grundholden Bauerntums vereinigten. – Eine große Rolle spielten dabei die vielen angesiedelten deutschen Bauern, die sich in Polen „iure teutonico", in Ungarn nach dem Recht der „Gäste" (hospes) vereinigten. – Es bildeten sich aber auch Städte auf höherem Niveau als dem osteuropäischen. Die Nachfrage nach Silber, Gold und dann Kupfer erhöhte die Metallförderung in vielen Gegenden Osteuropas. Die sich aus Westeuropa, vor allem aus dem Deutschen Reich ansiedelnden Bergleutegemeinden gründeten sehr bald Bergwerksstädte; auch mehrere Handelsstädte entstanden. Dafür bietet Ungarn schöne Beispiele. Es stimmt, daß diese Städte ethnisch von der örtlichen Bevölkerung lange isoliert waren, wirtschaftlich aber fügten sie sich in diese Zonen ein, und das wirkte sich nach einiger Zeit auch auf die

Städtebildung der ansässigen Bevölkerung aus. Es muß jedoch betont werden, daß das Niveau des Städtewesens, das in Ungarn dadurch entstand, weit hinter dem westeuropäischen zurückblieb, wenn es auch höher als das osteuropäische war. Es genügt ein Blick auf die Landkarte Ungarns, um zu sehen, daß riesige Gebiete des Landes, vor allem das von den Karpaten umsäumte Flachland, fast vollkommen ohne Städte westeuropäischen Charakters geblieben sind.

Aber es ist nicht diese bescheidene Stadtentwicklung, die unsere Aufmerksamkeit in erster Linie fesselt. In den zwei Jahrhunderten von der Wende vom 13. zum 14. bis zur Wende vom 15. zum 16. Jh. ist in Ungarn eine schnelle Entwicklung der landwirtschaftlichen Produktion festzustellen. Die Bevölkerungszahl hat sich in dieser Zeit etwa verdoppelt, zu Beginn des 16. Jh.s lag sie bei über 3,5 Millionen Einwohnern. Mehr als 90% der Einwohner waren Bauern und lebten von der landwirtschaftlichen Produktion. Die Bevölkerungszunahme stellte an die landwirtschaftliche Produktion ernste Anforderungen. Dafür boten sich zwei Möglichkeiten: a) Neue Felder wurden durch Rodung in die Produktion einbezogen. Im Land standen riesige Bodenreserven zur Verfügung, sie konnten entweder durch Waldrodungen oder durch Umpflügen von bisher brachliegendem Land genutzt werden. b) Auch die Produktionstechnik wurde verbessert. Im Verlaufe des 14. Jh.s beginnt von Westen nach Osten fortschreitend in den Gärten die Düngung, auch der schwere Scharpflug verbreitet sich, als Folge die Zwei- bzw. die Dreifelderwirtschaft, auf den Wiesen erscheint statt der Sichel die produktivere Sense. Auch die Transporttechnik entwickelt sich schnell – vierrädrige, eisenbeschlagene Wagen usw. Durch all dies stieg die landwirtschaftliche Produktion. In einzelnen Bauernwirtschaften bildete sich sogar ein den eigenen Verbrauch übersteigender Produktionsüberschuß. Dieser Überschuß kam zunehmend auf die im Verlaufe des 14.–15. Jh.s größer werdenden Märkte für landwirtschaftliche Produkte. Dazu zwang die Bauern über die Befriedigung ihres eigenen Bedarfs hinaus auch das Bestreben der Grundherren, ihre Geldeinkünfte schnell zu vergrößern. Die aus dem Westen einströmenden Konsumartikel – Stoffe, Schmuck – und Waffen usw. zu beschaffen, gab es keine andere Möglichkeit. Die traditionellen Arbeitsleistungen und Naturalabgaben der Bauern waren dazu nicht geeignet. Deshalb waren die Grundherren bestrebt, vor allem die Geldrente zu erhöhen. Auch dieses Bestreben lenkte den Produktionsüberschuß der Bauern in Richtung Markt.

Als Ware kam im Prinzip jedes Produkt in Frage, in Ungarn jedoch fehlte es an örtlichen Märkten. Es gab wenig wirkliche Städte und diese konzentrierten sich in den Gebirgsgegenden. Getreide kam wegen der Transportschwierigkeiten weniger und nur aus einem bestimmten Kreis in Frage. Für die entfernter liegenden Märkte boten sich zwei Produkte an: das sie auf den eigenen Beinen erreichende Rind – unter Umständen auch Schaf und Schwein – und der sich auch beim Transport auf größere Entfernungen auszahlende Qualitätswein. Der Handel mit diesen beiden Produkten bildete sich im Lande relativ schnell und in größerem Umfang heraus. Die ungarische landwirtschaftliche Warenproduktion war also von Anfang an auf *Fern*handel aufgebaut, wenn dieser auch vorerst *innerhalb der Landesgrenzen* ablief.

Dieser Fernhandel wurde dann vom 14. Jh. an durch die immer stärker zunehmende Nachfrage der westeuropäischen Städte nach landwirtschaftlichen Produkten gesteigert. Die Auswirkungen der Nachfrage nach Getreide und Fleisch waren sehr bald auch in Osteuropa spürbar, vor allem in dem bereits erwähnten westlichen Gebietsstreifen. Wo die Transportmöglichkeiten günstig waren, stieg der Getreideexport schnell – vor allem in der Weichselgegend –, für das übrige Gebiet wurde der Rinderexport außergewöhnlich wichtig. Das zeigte sich auch in Ungarn, das sich nicht in den Getreideexport einschalten konnte. Der im Fernhandel ohnehin wichtige Rinderhandel übernimmt vom 14. Jh. ab die führende Stelle im Außenhandel Ungarns. In der Rindfleischversorgung der süddeutschen und norditalienischen Städte spielte Ungarn eine immer größere Rolle.

Die Flachlandgebiete in der Mitte des Landes, die sich von der Donau nach Osten und Süden erstreckenden Steppengebiete, die Pußta, aber auch die sich von der Donau nach Westen hinziehenden Hügelgebiete waren – wegen ihrer weit niedrigeren Bevölkerungsdichte als in Westeuropa – sehr gut zur extensiven Rinderzucht geeignet. Der vom 14. Jh. an aufblühende Rinderhandel konnte also sehr schnell zur zentralen Form der landwirtschaftlichen Warenproduktion werden. Die Viehhaltung und der Handel mit den in jedem Jahr in größerer Zahl auf die westeuropäischen Märkte getriebenen Rindern machten sehr schnell ihren Einfluß auf die wirtschaftlichen und gesellschaftlichen Verhältnisse des Landes spürbar.

In der Folge der sich schnell entfaltenden landwirtschaftlichen Warenproduktion entstand eine neue Siedlungsform: der Marktflekken (oppidum). Seine Entstehung ist ohne die schnell zunehmende landwirtschaftliche Warenproduktion unvorstellbar, eine mindestens so große Rolle spielte dabei jedoch auch das Fehlen der Städte im westeuropäischen Sinne. Diese eigentlich mächtig angeschwollenen Dörfer wurden zu Zentren des landwirtschaftlichen Handels – vor allem des Rinder- und Weinhandels. Sein Erscheinen ist überall dort zu beobachten, wo in Osteuropa die landwirtschaftliche Produktion angestiegen war, vor allem im westlichen Grenzstreifen, in Polen, in der Ukraine, in Ungarn, Kroatien usw. Dieser Siedlungstypus wurde der charakteristische Knotenpunkt des landwirtschaftlichen Fernhandels. – Im wesentlichen ähnliche Umstände hatten auch andernorts ähnliche Konsequenzen. Der Marktflecken wurde zum Beispiel im 19. Jh. in den nord- und südamerikanischen Rinderzucht- und Getreideanbaugebieten zur charakteristischen Siedlung. Die gleiche Situation herrschte um die Mitte des 19. Jahrhunderts in Südrußland und auch in einzelnen Gegenden Sibiriens.

Die Marktflecken erreichten in Ungarn im Verlaufe des 14.–15. Jh.s eine besondere gesellschaftliche und rechtliche Stellung. Ihre Einwohner waren Bauern, die ihrem Grundherrn die gleichen Renten, Grundzinsen, Naturalabgaben und Fronen entrichten mußten wie die Bauern in den Dörfern. Sie beschäftigten sich mit Ackerbau und Viehzucht, und in ihren Händen konzentrierte sich der größte Teil des Rinder- und Weinhandels. Ihre günstigen Möglichkeiten nutzten diese Siedlungen vor allem, um ihre Abgaben und Leistungen in Geld zu verwandeln. Ihr Bestreben war zugleich auch das Interesse ihrer Grundherren, die von ihren weniger an den Markt gebundenen Bauern in den Dörfern kaum zu mehr Geld kommen konnten. So kamen die Marktflecken sehr bald in die günstige Lage, daß anstelle der Naturalabgaben und der Fronarbeit die Geldrente allein herrschend wurde. Die enge Selbstverwaltung der Dörfer weitete sich in diesen Siedlungen aus, und ihre Einwohner wurden in inneren Angelegenheiten bis zum gewissen Grade unabhängig vom Grundherrn. Die Einwohner der Marktflecken konnten ihre Steuern jährlich in einer Pauschalsumme in Geld ablösen, das statt von den Beamten des Grundherrn vom gewählten Richter der Marktflecken nach einem festgesetzten Schlüssel eingesammelt wurde. Das schuf für die Bauern in den Marktflecken eine wesentlich günstigere Lage als für die Dorfbewohner, daher übten die Marktflecken auf die gesamte ungarische Bauernschaft, vor allem auf die wohlhabenderen Schichten, eine große Anziehungskraft aus.

Die Entwicklung der landwirtschaftlichen Warenproduktion, die zunehmende Rolle der Geldrente trugen wesentlich zu der im 14. Jh. einsetzenden Aufsplitterung der ungarischen Bauernschaft bei. Die Warenproduktion lieferte die Bauern den Gesetzen der Marktwirtschaft aus. Der Hufner war nicht selten wirtschaftlich derart geschwächt, daß er sein Land und auch seine anderen Produktionsmittel aufgeben mußte, damit zum Hintersassen (inquilinus) und unter Umständen völlig mittellos wurde. Am Ende des 15. Jh.s machte diese Schicht 25–30% der bäuerlichen Bevölkerung aus. Ein Teil der Hufner konnten zwar im Wettbewerb bestehen, viele aber hatten nur noch eine halbe Hufe, die meisten weniger. Der Anteil der Bauern, die Ende des 15. Jahrhunderts noch eine ganze oder sogar mehrere Hufen besaßen, dürfte lediglich 4–6% betragen haben. Viele der aus verschiedenen Gründen – oft durch reale Erbteilung – verarmten Bauern nahmen Arbeit bei anderen Bauern an, die Habenichtse aber fanden im Rinderhandel Arbeit: sie wurden Rindertreiber (Heiducken). Die reicheren Bauern pachteten vom Grundherrn die leerstehenden Hufen, manchmal auch Bodenflächen des Adels – allodiale Böden – und trieben, die Arbeitskraft der verarmten Bauern nutzend, Warenproduktion, in erster Linie Viehzucht. Andere wieder wurden Viehhändler.

In den Marktflecken zeigten sich alle Konsequenzen der Warenproduktion und des Übergangs zur Geldrente in konzentrierter Form. Hier war die Verarmung am stärksten, hier lebten die meisten Hintersassen, aber auch die reichsten Bauern. Auf dem zu den Marktflecken gehörenden Land finden wir die meisten verlassenen Hufen – deserta sessio –, aber hier wurden auch die meisten verlassenen Hufen von Bauern gepachtet. Auf den ausgedehnten Weiden der Marktflecken wurde ein bedeutender Teil des ungarischen Rinderbestandes gehalten, in ihren Weingärten wurde ein großer Teil des auf den Markt gebrachten Weines produziert. Hier konzentrierte sich der Rinder- und Weinhandel und zum Teil – in der Nähe wirklicher Städte – auch der Getreidehandel. In diesen Siedlungen entstand auch Handwerk, vor allem Dienstleistungsgewerbe. Die meisten Handwerker lösten sich nicht von der Landwirtschaft, betrieben ihr Handwerk und versorgten die Umgebung mit Kleidung, Schuhwerk und mit zur landwirtschaftlichen Produktion, zum Transport erforderlichen Geräten. Aus all diesen Gründen übte der Marktflecken eine große Anziehungskraft auf die Dorfbauern aus, vor allem auf die wohlhabenden und die ärmsten, die den Umstand, daß sich die Freizügigkeit im 14. Jh. so gut wie auf die gesamte Bauernschaft erstreckte, nutzten und in immer größeren Mengen in die Marktflekken zogen. Ende des 15. Jh.s finden wir in mehr als 800 Marktflekken 20% der Gesamtbevölkerung des Landes, insgesamt eine dreiviertel Million Menschen.

Die Entwicklung der landwirtschaftlichen Warenproduktion, die schnell zunehmende Bedeutung der Geldrente, die Entwicklung der Marktflecken und ihr Erstarken – dies alles zusammen begann die Ordnung der feudalen Gesellschaft umzugestalten. Die Bodenpacht ist in dieser Hinsicht vielleicht am wichtigsten. Für die gepachtete Hufe gab der Pachtbauer dem Adligen nicht die üblichen Grundzinsen und Abgaben, sondern lediglich eine Pachtsumme. Ein Teil der Bauern kam zu Feldern, die dem Adel gehörten und früher von Adligen bewirtschaftet worden waren, und in gewisser Hinsicht entwickelte sich über die Felder ein Eigentumsrecht. Über die gerodeten oder gekauften Felder verfügte der Bauer – aufgrund eines schnell entstandenen Gewohnheitsrechts – frei. Das Eigentumsrecht des Bauern an diesen Feldern anerkannten die die Vererbung regelnden Gewohnheiten und auch die Gesetze. Zur gleichen Zeit bot sich für den Bauern auch die Möglichkeit, aus seinem bäuerlichen Stand emporzusteigen. Der Umzug in den Marktflecken bedeutete zwar nicht, daß sie städtische Bürger wurden, erhöhte aber die gesellschaftlichen Möglichkeiten der Bauern. Wegen der schwachen Städteentwicklung war für die wohlhabenderen nicht die Stadt das Ziel, sondern der Adel. Zwischen Adligen und Bauern zog sich damals eine relativ dünne Trennlinie, die reicheren Bauern konnten relativ leicht Adlige werden. Entweder heirateten sie in eine adlige Familie ein oder pachteten oder kauften Adelsland und wurden von der Umgebung bald selbst als Adeliger angesehen und nach einer gewissen Zeit sogar vom Adel als Adeliger anerkannt. Das war natürlich nur für die oberen, reichsten Schichten der Bauern erreichbar. Die Bedeutung aber war sehr groß: die Gegensätze zwischen Adel und Bauern wurden abgestumpft, und gerade jene wurden aus den Reihen der Bauern entfernt, die die bewußtesten und gebildetesten Kämpfer für den gesellschaftlichen Fortschritt hätten sein können. Außerdem brachte diese Richtung der gesellschaftlichen Mobilität auch zum Ausdruck, daß die Möglichkeit, Bürger zu werden, wegen der schwachen Stadtentwicklung beschränkt war.

Das alles verschärfte die Gegensätze zwischen dem Kleinadel und der Aristokratie. Die Adligen, zu deren Besitz keine Marktflekken gehörten, verloren durch die Freizügigkeit gerade ihre besten

Steuerzahler. Diese Gegensätze führten eine Zeit lang nicht zur Explosion, als aber zu Beginn des 16. Jh.s in Westeuropa die Inflation begann, hatte dies ernste Folgen.

Die Inflation zwang den Adel Osteuropas zur erhöhten Ausbeutung der Bauernschaft. In den inneren, kontinentalen Gebieten Osteuropas gab es dazu keine andere Möglichkeit, als die verschiedenen grundherrlichen Geldeinkünfte zu steigern. In Rußland, in Rumänien usw. bot sich dazu der Ausbau der verschiedenen grundherrlichen Monopole an – Schnapsbrennerei usw. –. Im westlichen Streifen bestanden günstige Möglichkeiten für den Getreideexport, deshalb begann sich das System der Gutswirtschaft zu entwickeln, mit allen seinen Konsequenzen – Gutsherrschaft, zweite Leibeigenschaft.

In Ungarn konnte sich das System der Gutswirtschaft bis zum Ende des 18. Jh.s nicht durchsetzen. Die geographische Lage des Landes schloß einen größeren Getreideexport aus. Der Adel war gezwungen, seine Geldeinkünfte auf anderem Wege zu steigern. Zum Teil durch Abschöpfung des Überschusses der bäuerlichen Warenproduktion und durch unmittelbare Einschaltung in den Handel mit landwirtschaftlichen Produkten. In Anbetracht der Tatsache, daß dies bei der zunehmenden Unzufriedenheit der Bauern eine entscheidende Rolle gespielt hat, müssen wir uns näher damit beschäftigen.

Die ersten Wirren in der sich bis zur zweiten Hälfte des 15. Jh.s ungestört entwickelnden landwirtschaftlichen Warenproduktion rief die Staatsmacht hervor. Matthias' Hunyadis nach westlichem Vorbild entstehende zentralisierte Staatsmacht – vor allem die Unterhaltung eines ständigen Söldnerheeres – bedeutete für die Bauern eine riesige Belastung. Die Städte waren unentwickelt, die städtische Bürgerschaft nur eine dünne Schicht, so daß der größte Teil der Lasten auf den Bauern ruhte. Wie Berechnungen ergeben haben, verfünffachte die Staatsmacht mit der regelmäßigen Erhebung des sog. subsidium die staatliche steuerliche Belastung der Bauern. Das hatte eine doppelte Auswirkung. Es zwang die Bauern zu verstärkter Warenproduktion und trug gleichzeitig zur Verarmung breiter bäuerlicher Massen bei. Um diese Zeit tritt der Wüstungsprozeß in Ungarn in größerem Umfang in Erscheinung, in erster Linie deshalb, weil die ärmeren Bauern, um sich dem oft sogar ihre Existenz in Frage stellenden Druck der staatlichen Lasten zu entziehen, von ihren Hufen flohen, manchmal sogar mit Hilfe des Grundherrn – sie wurden zu Häuslern (Hintersassen) oder aber als solche eingestuft.

Nach Matthias' Tod wurden die Ergebnisse der Zentralisation

zunichte, der Adel nutzte die Schwächung der Staatsmacht, um seine Geldeinnahmen zu steigern. Zum Teil durch Beschneidung der „zentralen Renten“, der königlichen Einnahmen, denn ein sehr großer Teil der staatlichen Einkünfte floß nicht in die Schatzkammer, sondern wanderte in die Taschen der Aristokratie. Aber sie erhöhten auch die Geldlasten der Bauern, durch Heraufsetzung der Zinsen, vor allem aber durch stärkere Ausnutzung der taxa extraordinaria, durch Erhöhung der Ablösesummen für verschiedene Naturalleistungen (Feiertagsgeschenke), und durch Steigerung besonderer Einkünfte – Waldpacht, Wiesengelder usw. Sie nutzten die Schwächung der Staatsmacht auch dazu, die Zahl der Zollstellen im Lande zu vergrößern, was den landwirtschaftlichen Handel schwer traf. So ging vor allem die Aristokratie vor, die dadurch den Nutzen der bäuerlichen Warenproduktion von außen abschöpfen wollte.

Auch die Kleinadligen traten nach 1490 gegen die Bauern auf. Sie verletzten vor allem die bessere Lage der Marktflecken, ihre Anziehungskraft auf die Bauern. Schließlich erreichten sie, daß der Landtag auch für die Marktflecken wieder die Naturalrente – die sog. nona – zur *Pflicht* erklärte. Damit wurden die Möglichkeiten der bäuerlichen Warenproduktion eingeschränkt, und für die größeren Grundherren, die Aristokratie, bot sich die Möglichkeit, sich in den landwirtschaftlichen Handel einzuschalten. Das alles – zusammen mit der neuerlichen Bekräftigung der Zollfreiheit des Adels – bedeutete für die Marktflecken, daß der auch außerhalb der Landwirtschaft Zwangsmittel anwendende *grundherrliche Warenhandel als Konkurrent* erschien.

Zu den Bestrebungen des Adels, die bäuerliche Warenproduktion abzuschöpfen und zurückzudrängen, kamen auch Bestrebungen auf gesellschaftlicher Ebene. Vor allem der Kleinadel versuchte, die Freizügigkeit der Bauern einzuschränken. Das Ziel war die völlige Aufhebung der Freizügigkeit, was natürlich nicht im Interesse der Aristokratie war. Deshalb kam der Kleinadel nur langsam zum Ziel. Im Verlaufe einiger Jahre erreichte er durch mehrere Gesetze, daß die mit dem Wegzug zusammenhängenden Beschwerden der Bauern an das Komitatsgericht, also an das Gericht des Kleinadels verwiesen wurden. Von Zeit zu Zeit wurde der Wegzug in einzelnen Teilen des Landes, manchmal sogar im ganzen Land für eine bestimmte Zeit untersagt.

Jetzt war das Bestreben des Adels bereits darauf gerichtet, sich gegen die Bauern abzuschließen, starre Trennwände zwischen Adel und Bauern zu errichten. Die gegenüber der Aristokratie das Prinzip „alle Adligen sind gleich“ betonenden Kleinadligen mußten, um ihr Ziel zu erreichen, ihre Reihen zu den Bauern hin schließen. Um so mehr als der Weg des Emporsteigens sogar auch ihnen nicht mehr offen stand. Die weitere Vermischung mit den Bauern malte das Gespenst des gesellschaftlichen Niedergangs an die Wand.

Die Auswirkungen, die Folgen der gleichzeitig aus mehreren Richtungen auf die Bauernschaft einsetzenden Angriffe, waren sehr kompliziert. Sicher ist, daß ein großer Teil der wirtschaftlichen Beschränkungen – z. B. die verpflichtende Eintreibung der Naturalleistungen in den Marktflecken – in einem großen Teil des Landes nicht durchgeführt wurde. Darum wurden die entsprechenden Gesetze mehrfach erneuert. Auch die Maßnahmen gegen die Freizügigkeit dürften nicht erfolgreich gewesen sein, denn die Komitatsbehörden konnten – in einer Zeit, da die zentrale Macht auseinandergefallen war – die kleineren Adligen nicht gegen die Willkür der Magnaten schützen. Ungeheuer war die Wirkung jedoch dadurch, daß alle diese Maßnahmen zur gleichen Zeit erfolgten. Die Einwohner der Marktflecken, vor allem die wohlhabenderen, konnten mit Recht das Gefühl haben, daß ihre grundlegende wirtschaftliche Tätigkeit und zur gleichen Zeit auch die ihre Lage garantierenden wirtschaftlich-gesellschaftlichen Vorteile in Gefahr geraten waren. Wodurch die gesellschaftlichen Spannungen in nicht zu unterschätzender Weise vergrößert wurden.

Das war insofern von besonderer Bedeutung, weil es mit einem anderen Prozeß zusammenfiel: die Erschütterung der Existenzgrundlage der ärmeren Bauern durch die Übertreibung zunächst der staatlichen, dann der grundherrlichen Forderungen. Das geschah praktisch zur gleichen Zeit wie das Auftreten gegen die Marktflecken und führte dazu, daß in der bäuerlichen Gesellschaft trotz der früheren Differenzierung das Gefühl des Zusammenhalts die Oberhand gewann. Beide Prozesse wirkten stärkend aufeinander, das Abschließen des Adels, der auf gesellschaftlicher Ebene begonnene Angriff auf die Bauern, besonders auf die Marktflecken, konnte deshalb zu einer ernsthaften Gefahr werden. Die reicheren Schichten der Marktflekken wurden natürlich zur Seele der Unzufriedenheit, nicht nur, weil sie sich in günstigerer Lage befanden als die Dorfbewohner, sondern auch, weil es für eine ganze historische Epoche fraglich geworden war, ob sie in ihrer einmal erreichten gesellschaftlichen Lage verbleiben konnten oder auf das Niveau der Bauern auf dem Dorfe zurücksanken. Das dürfte, neben der Besonderheit ihrer Lage, auch der Grund dafür sein, daß die Marktflecken im Bauernaufstand, bei der Entstehung der Ideologie des Aufstandes in Ungarn eine so große Rolle gespielt haben.

Was die Ideologie anbetrifft, wollen wir schon an dieser Stelle darauf hinweisen, daß die in den Marktflecken entstandene Intelligenz dabei eine führende Rolle gespielt hat; und *zwar nicht* nur die Priester aus den Marktflecken und Dörfern, die die Sorgen ihrer Gemeinden kannten oder die in den Marktflecken wirkenden Orden, vor allem der nach strengeren Regeln lebende, reformierte observante Zweig der Franziskaner, dessen zahlreiche Vertreter in den Dörfern oder Marktflecken geboren waren und dort auch wirkten. Diese inmitten des Volkes lebenden Observanten begründeten die ungarischsprachige Klosterliteratur. Aus ihrem Kreis ging Perbált Temesvári hervor, der schon zu Zeiten Matthias' Corvinus die gesellschaftlichen Mißstände kritisiert hatte oder Osvát Laskai, der Ende des 15. Jh.s in seinen Predigten über die Habgier der Herren gesprochen und geschrieben hatte, daß die Armen das Recht hätten, sich zu wehren. Ihre Bedeutung ist, gerade weil sie von vielen gehört wurden, nicht zu leugnen, dennoch wäre es falsch, keine Kenntnis zu nehmen von einer sich in der Tiefe hinziehenden Schicht der Intelligenz. Es handelt sich um die in den Marktflecken im Verlaufe des 15. Jh.s größer werdende Schicht von *Literaten,* um jene, die irgendeine Schule besucht hatten. Ihre Zahl unter den Einwohnern der Marktflecken ist relativ hoch, selbst in der zweiten Hälfte des 15. Jh.s stammt ein Viertel der an der Universität von Wien und in Krakau studierenden Ungarn aus den Marktflecken. Diese verhältnismäßig große Zahl Intellektueller wurde nur zum Teil Lehrer, Schreiber oder Wirtschaftsverwalter, die meisten blieben vermutlich in den Marktflecken, trieben Landwirtschaft oder Handel, und manchmal wurden sie hier Richter oder Beamte. Sie dürften viel dazu beigetragen haben, die Unzufriedenheit der Bauern zu formulieren, sie ihnen zu Bewußtsein zu bringen.

An der Wende vom 15. zum 16. Jh. hatten also die gesellschaftlichen Spannungen wesentlich zugenommen, hatte sich in der bäuerlichen Gesellschaft gefährlicher Sprengstoff angesammelt. Das bäuerliche Bewußtsein hatte jedoch noch nicht die ideellen Formen des Auftretens gegen die herrschende Klasse gefunden. Daraus erklärt sich, daß im Auftreten der Bauern die religiösen Thesen eine so große Rolle spielten. Das erklärt aber auch, daß es ohne die Verkündung des Kreuzzuges im Jahre 1514 nicht zum Bauernaufstand gekommen wäre. Deshalb hatte wahrscheinlich auch die herrschende Klasse, als der Kreuzzug gegen die Türken verkündet wurde, die angestaute Unzufriedenheit der Bauern außer acht gelassen und die Versammlung der Bauern erlaubt.

Versuchen wir jetzt, in wenigen Sätzen den Ablauf des Bauernkrieges zusammenzufassen. Wesentlich ist, daß Papst Leo X. nach seiner Wahl im Jahre 1513 seinen größten Gegner, den Kardinal-Erzbischof von Esztergom, Tamás Bakócz, mit der Verkündung des Kreuzzuges gegen die Türken und mit einem päpstlichen Legat versöhnen (und damit aus Rom entfernen) wollte. Die Verkündung des Kreuzzuges traf den ungarischen Königshof nicht im günstigsten Augenblick. Ihm war am Frieden mit den Türken gelegen, denn er war mit dem Kleinadel und dem mit dessen Unterstützung nach dem königlichen Thron strebenden János Szapolyai in einen schwierigen innenpolitischen Kampf verwickelt. Dennoch stimmte der königliche Rat schließlich dem Kreuzzug zu und erlaubte dessen Verkündung (23. März 1514). Die bestehenden Gegensätze jedoch führten dazu, daß nicht einer der Magnaten an die Spitze des bei Pest versammelten Hauptheeres gestellt wurde, sondern ein unbekannter Szekler Soldat (György Székely), der sich um diese Zeit in einem der kleineren Geplänkel mit den Türken ausgezeichnet hatte (24. 4.).

Nach der feierlichen Verkündung des Kreuzzuges am 9. April strömten die Bauern in Massen nach Pest und in andere Lager (Várad, Eger, Kassa usw.). Das bei Pest versammelte Hauptheer brach am 10. Mai nach Süden auf. Die ersten kleineren Zusammenstöße mit den sich dem Kreuzzug widersetzenden Kleinadeligen hatten bereits stattgefunden – aber vom Bauernaufstand war noch keine Rede –, als das Hauptheer in Békés am 18. Mai die Nachricht erreichte, der königliche Rat habe am 15. Mai jede weitere Anwerbung untersagt. Zu diesem Zeitpunkt machte sich György Székely selbständig und wechselte die Marschrichtung, wollte aber noch immer gegen die Türken kämpfen. Am 23.–24. Mai trat die endgültige Wende ein: bei Nagylak stießen die Bauerntruppen mit einer größeren Einheit des Adels zusammen und schlugen sie. Mehrere Aristokraten und höhere Geistliche wurden hingerichtet. Zu dieser Zeit, am 24. Mai, aber unabhängig von diesen Ereignissen, stellte der König auf Druck des Adels den Kreuzzug ein und rief die Bauern auf, nach Hause zurückzukehren. Damit wurde der Kreuzzug „offiziell“ zum Bauernaufstand „erklärt“.

Inzwischen waren die in der Großen Ungarischen Tiefebene und in den Randgebieten versammelten Bauerntruppen ebenfalls mit dem Adel in Kämpfe verwickelt worden. Die erste eigentliche Schlacht des Bauernkrieges war das Treffen bei Várad, wo die Bauern die Truppen des Adels in offener Schlacht schlugen (22. Mai). Nach dem ersten Auftreten des Hauptheeres bildeten sich mehrere kleinere Gruppen. Gestützt auf die kleineren Truppeneinheiten zog das Hauptheer an beiden Ufern des Maros nach Osten. Am 6. Juni wurde Lippa eingenommen, am 9. Juni die Burg Sólymos, dann zog das Heer in Richtung Temesvár. Die Belagerung der Stadt und der Burg begann am 13. Juni.

Inzwischen war der Woiwode von Siebenbürgen, János Szapolyai von einem kleineren Zug gegen die Türken nach Siebenbürgen zurückgekehrt und mobilisierte seine Truppen gegen die Bauern. Bei seinem Zaudern spielte die Tatsache eine Rolle, daß die Bauern bis dahin vor allem die Besitzungen seines Hauptgegners, Georg von Brandenburg, heimgesucht hatten. Ende Juni brach er dann trotzdem gegen das Temesvár belagernde Hauptheer auf. Zur Entscheidungsschlacht kam es am 15. Juli. Sie endete für die Bauern mit einer blutigen Niederlage. Am 20. Juli wurde György Dózsa Székely mit seinen Gefährten hingerichtet.

In anderen Gegenden des Landes war der Aufstand um diese Zeit noch im Gange. Die letzten Zusammenstöße, die ausnahmslos mit einer Niederlage der Bauern endeten, fanden Ende Juli statt. Im August herrschte im Lande wieder Ruhe.

Die bäuerliche Unzufriedenheit hatte also in Ungarn zu Beginn des 16. Jh.s noch nicht die Voraussetzungen für einen spontanen Aufstand geschaffen. Als aber 1514 der Kreuzzug gegen die Türken verkündet wurde und die Bauern in großen Massen versammelt waren, war die plötzliche Aufhebung des Kreuzzuges, das Verbot der weiteren Anwerbung und dann die Auflösung des Kreuzheeres wie ein Funke, der die Glut wieder zu hellen Flammen schürte. Um so mehr als das Bauernheer durch die päpstliche Bulle, die sie zu den Waffen gerufen hatte, davon überzeugt war, daß das „heilige Heer und die gesegnete Versammlung" eine heilige Aufgabe erfülle und jeder, der es behindere, im Bunde mit dem Teufel stehe.

Zur Wahrheit gehört, daß die Aufstellung des Kreuzheeres das Land unvorbereitet traf. Die Versorgung von ungefähr 40 000 Kreuzfahrern war nicht gesichert, die dafür vorgesehenen Summen waren sehr gering. Schon als das bei Pest lagernde Hauptheer nach

Süden zog, waren Gewalttätigkeiten zu beobachten, vor allem – aber nicht ausschließlich – gegen das Eigentum des Adels. Etwa zu dieser Zeit beginnt auch der Widerstand des Kleinadels gegen den Kreuzzug. 40 000 Kreuzfahrer waren nicht viel, etwa 5–6% der arbeitsfähigen männlichen Einwohner des Landes, da aber die Bevölkerung Siebenbürgens, des Temesköz-Gebiets, im Oberland und in Transdanubien nicht mobilisierte, konnte es sich in den betroffenen Gebieten auch um 12–13% gehandelt haben. Das konnte für den Kleinadel dieser Gebiete den völligen Verlust der Arbeitskräfte bedeuten. Deshalb also begannen die Komitatsorgane – des Kleinadels also – ihre Manöver zur Einstellung der Anwerbungen. Sie gingen sogar mit Waffengewalt gegen die sich versammelnden Bauern vor und vermochten schließlich den König und den Kardinal-Erzbischof von Esztergom, Thomas Bakócz, zu bewegen, die Anwerbungen zu untersagen, den Kreuzzug zu verbieten. Damit aber gaben sie den Bauern eine starke Waffe in die Hand: den Glauben, daß im Sinne der päpstlichen Bulle das Recht auf ihrer Seite sei. Was also die Bauern in Ungarn von selbst nicht hatten zuwege bringen können, das bot ihnen die schlechte Politik der Regierung, des Kardinal-Erzbischofs und des Adels geradezu fertig dar: die entsprechende Ideologie.

Daß die Bauernschaft unvorbereitet war, ersehen wir daraus, daß nur die Bauern des Tieflandes und seiner Randgebiete an den Kämpfen teilnahmen, in anderen Gebieten versammelten sich die Bauern auch später nicht. Dort, wo sie an den Kämpfen teilnahmen, waren die Dörfer und Marktflecken gleicherweise beteiligt, in relativ größerer Zahl jedoch die Marktflecken und vor allem die Armen aus den Marktflecken. 1512/13 zeigte sich in Westeuropa ein wirtschaftlicher Rückfall, deshalb waren im Frühjahr 1514 zahlreiche Rinderhirten und Rindertreiber (Heiducken) arbeitslos, daher ihre große Zahl unter den Kreuzfahrern. Zu ihren Lasten geht ein großer Teil der Ausschreitungen, aber als waffenkundige Männer waren sie auch wesentlich an den militärischen Erfolgen beteiligt, an der siegreichen Beendigung von vier offenen Feldschlachten.

Die Führer des Bauernaufstandes gingen aus zwei Schichten hervor. In geringerer Zahl schlossen sich den Bauern Kleinadlige an. So der Anführer selbst, Georg (Dózsa) Székely und sein Bruder Gregor, die die kollektiven Adelsrechte der Szekler Militär-Bauern genossen. Allerdings galten sie außerhalb des Szeklerlandes nicht als Adlige. Aber es schlossen sich den Bauern auch wirkliche Kleinadlige an, die eigentlich wie Bauern lebten. Die zahlenmäßig weit bedeutendere

Schicht der Führer des Aufstands kam aus dem Priesterstand. Dabei handelte es sich gleicherweise um Priester aus den Marktflecken und aus den Dörfern. Viele Franziskaner waren unter ihnen. Die Franziskaner wurden von Kardinal Bakócz beauftragt, die Kreuzbulle zu verkünden und die Bauern anzuwerben. Viele Dörfer oder Marktflecken kamen unter Führung ihrer gewählten Körperschaft, des Richters und der Priester im Lager an und nahmen in diesem Verband bis zum Ende an den Kämpfen teil. Nicht nur in solchen Fällen wurden die Anführer gewählt, den Hauptführer des Kreuzheeres bestimmte der königliche Rat, alle anderen wurden von den Bauern selbst gewählt.

Unter den Bauernführern waren also die Priester aus den Marktflecken in der Überzahl. Und das ist nicht erstaunlich. Wenn auch die Marktflecken unter den Teilnehmern am Aufstand nicht in der absoluten Überzahl waren, so war ihre Teilnahme doch außergewöhnlich wichtig, und außerdem fand der Aufstand im Hauptgebiet der ungarischen Marktflecken, in der Großen Ungarischen Tiefebene statt. Wenn wir das mit der Herkunft der Bauernführer in Verbindung bringen, können wir sicher sein, daß der Bauernaufstand dort der stürmischste war, wo die Wiege der Warenproduktion der Marktflecken stand. Wenn also der Aufstand auch die Unzufriedenheit aller ungarischen Bauern mit ihrer Lage und den ungünstigen Veränderungen der letzten Jahrzehnte zum Ausdruck brachte, so war er doch *in erster Linie* mit den wohlhabenderen, emporstrebenden Elementen der Bauern verbunden und dabei spielten die *Marktflecken* die Hauptrolle.

Der Aufstand traf selbst die Bauern überraschend. Es ist also kein Wunder, daß ihre Ideologie nicht das gewohnte Niveau der europäischen Bauernaufstände erreichte. Die Kreuzzugsideologie dominierte. Es ist der besondere Zug des ungarischen Bauernaufstandes, daß der kirchliche Auftrag zum Kreuzzug in den Augen der Bauern auch ihre Taten rechtfertigte, die Worte der Bulle, die sich gegen die Widerstand Leistenden richteten, stärkten das Bewußtsein des Auserwähltseins der Aufständischen, bestätigte ihnen die *Berechtigung* ihres Kampfes gegen die, den Kreuzzug gegen die Türken verratenden Adligen.

Das war die ideologische Grundlage des Kampfes, die Klammer, die alle daran teilnehmenden Schichten zusammenhielt. Alles andere, was wir wissen, ist eher negativ: die Verweigerung der Steuerzahlung, das Auftreten gegen die Zölle, die massenweise Verbrennung der die Dienstleistungen fixierenden, als Symbol der feudalen Rechtsordnung betrachteten Urkunden, das Vorgehen gegen adliges Eigentum – manchmal aber auch gegen das der Bauern oder der Marktflecken –, stellenweise das Bestreben der physischen Vernichtung der herrschenden Klasse – obwohl wir von zahlreichen entgegengesetzten Fällen wissen, wo die Bauern Adlige in ihre Reihen aufnahmen. Das ist alles nicht viel, und da es in erster Linie negativ ist, zeigt es, wie unvorbereitet der Aufstand die Bauernschaft traf. Positive Züge hatte die bäuerliche Ideologie so gut wie gar nicht. Aus der zufälligen Bestimmung des Anführers ergab sich, daß er den Versuch unternahm, unter den Kreuzfahrern die Szekler kollektive adlige Freiheit als Ziel zu verbreiten. Ob sich das nur auf die Bauern oder auf die ganze Gesellschaft bezog, das wissen wir nicht. Wir wissen auch nicht, ob das Bestreben, den Adel physisch zu vernichten, dahin gedeutet werden muß, daß sich die Bauern die Beseitigung des Feudalismus zum Ziel gesetzt hatten. Das war natürlich in der Tiefe ihres Bewußtseins verborgen, aber selbst in den Reifsten hatte das noch keine Formulierung gefunden.

Im ersten Augenblick mag es überraschend sein, daß wir von dem ungarischen Bauernaufstand sagen, daß ihn eine unvorbereitete, instinktiv handelnde Klasse bis zum Ende gekämpft habe. Dabei ist das gar nicht so überraschend. Die in der ungarischen Bauernschaft entstandene reichere – also gebildetere – Schicht hatte sich jahrzehntelang selbst zum Adel hin gewandt und war so nicht geeignet, ein über ihren Instinkt hinausweisendes Selbstbewußtsein zu entwikkeln. Deshalb sind auch solche Tatsachen nicht erstaunlich wie die, daß das Bauernheer nur schwer zusammengehalten werden konnte, daß auf den Aufruf des Adels hin viele nach Hause gingen, flohen. So mußte Dózsa schließlich sogar Soldaten von der Bauernbevölkerung ausheben. Und erstaunlich ist es auch nicht, daß auch in den adligen Truppen ausgehobene Bauern kämpften.

Was also im Hinblick auf das Ziel und die Ideologie des Bauernaufstandes auszumachen ist, ist nichts anderes als die Beschwerden der Marktflecken – Steuer und Zoll sind typische Beschwerden der Marktflecken – und die religiöse Ideologie: das Bewußtsein der Auserwähltheit, das aus dem Heiligen Krieg gegen die Türken resultierte; die Kritik der Observanten am Franziskanerorden gerade in den Marktflecken. Diese Ordensbrüder identifizierten sich fast ausschließlich mit den Aufständischen und beeinflußten so auch deren Ideologie.

Diese stark religiös erfüllte Ideologie, die sich nur auf das zu Vernichtende konzentrierte und was die Zukunft anbetraf, vollkommen stumm blieb, zeigt in ihrer Beschränktheit, daß das Zentrum des ungarischen Bauernaufstandes die Marktflecken waren. Nicht der für die Dorfbauern wichtige Zehnt oder das Patrimonialgericht, sondern die Besteuerung und die Zölle waren die Zielscheibe. Auch geographisch gesehen spielte sich der Aufstand hier ab: Der Aufstand fand weder in den echten Städten noch bei den Bauern der anderen Gebiete des Landes Verbündete.

Welche Rolle spielte der Bauernaufstand in der weiteren Geschichte Ungarns? Sehen wir zuerst die unmittelbaren Folgen. Nach der Niederschlagung des Aufstandes berief der König einen Landtag ein, der das Decretum des Jahres 1514, das sog. „Vergeltungsgesetz" erließ. Das Gesetz bestimmte vor allem die Ausrottung der Anführer des Bauernaufstandes, der Aufwiegler und der Mörder und setzte den alten Wunsch des Adels in die Tat um, die erbliche Leibeigenschaft der Bauern, den Verlust der Freizügigkeit, also die Bindung an die Scholle. Es verbot den Bauern auch das Tragen von Waffen. Es sorgte für die Wiedergutmachung der Schäden. Setzte die Dienstleistungen der Bauern einheitlich fest – unter anderem wöchentlich einen Tag Fronen, was ebenfalls den Interessen des Kleinadels diente. Zusammen mit Werböczys Tripartitum (Dreigeteiltes Buch des Gewohnheitsrechts Ungarns) machte das Gesetz einen wesentlichen Schritt auf das Bodenmonopol des Adels zu, als es das Verfügungsrecht der Bauern über den Boden leugnete. Die ewige und erbliche Leibeigenschaft, die Aufhebung der Freizügigkeit, das adelige Bodenmonopol – das alles diente dem Zweck, die Trennwand zwischen Adel und Bauern zu versteifen. Das Gesetz sorgte auch dafür, daß in Zukunft niemand, der bäuerlicher Herkunft war, eine hohe kirchliche Würde erhalten sollte. Was vor allem aus dem Haß gegen den aus einer Bauernfamilie stammenden Kardinal Bakócz resultierte. Die andere Seite dieses Bestrebens, die Erklärung: „Alle Adligen sind gleich" hatte bei weitem nicht solchen Erfolg.

Aus alledem könnte man zu der Schlußfolgerung kommen, daß das Erscheinen der „zweiten Leibeigenschaft", der Gutsherrschaft in Ungarn eigentlich auf den Bauernaufstand zurückzuführen ist. Aber davon kann keine Rede sein. Die Freizügigkeit der Bauern wurde im Jahre 1530 wiederhergestellt. Das Waffentragen der Bauern war auch weiterhin üblich. Der Angriff des Kleinadels hatte zwar 1514 das Zünglein an der Waage ausschlagen lassen, aber sie kam sehr bald wieder zur Ruhe. Wir können eigentlich nur mit fernen Auswirkungen des Gesetzes von 1514 und des Tripartitums rechnen. Damit nämlich, daß es gelang, die bäuerliche Warenproduktion im allgemeinen später – z. B., am Ende des 16. Jh.s und dann Ende des 18. Jh.s endgültig – einzuschränken. Im eigentlichen Sinne des Wortes spielten diese Bestimmungen keine Rolle, auch der Aufstand nicht. Mit Auswirkungen der Gesetze müssen wir dennoch rechnen. Dadurch nämlich, daß die Vergeltungsgesetze von vornherein all das in ein geschlossenes Rechtssystem faßten, was zum späteren Sieg der Warenproduktion des Adels erforderlich war; daß sie durch ihre Existenz zum späteren Sieg der Gutsherrschaft beitrugen.

Wir verwiesen bereits darauf, daß der Ausbruch des Aufstandes einem Zufall zuzuschreiben ist; das zeigt sich auch an seinem Ablauf, an seinen Zielen und an der nachfolgenden Vergeltung. Wenige Jahre nach 1514 war die alte Ordnung wiederhergestellt. Das bedeutete für die Bauernschaft und vor allem für die Marktflecken eine etwas ungünstigere rechtliche und gesellschaftliche Stellung als früher. Der Kampf zwischen der bäuerlichen und der adligen Warenproduktion aber war noch nicht entschieden und welche Richtung er nehmen würde, dabei spielte weder der Ausbruch des Bauernkrieges noch sein Ausgang eine bestimmende Rolle. Mächtigere Kräfte der Geschichte bestimmten den Weg, auf dem die Entwicklung der ungarischen Gesellschaft verlief.

# VII

# Europa — Ost-Elbien — Ungarn. Besonderheiten der ungarischen Agrarentwicklung im 16.–18. Jahrhundert

Die Überschrift läßt einen breiten perspektivischen Überblick vermuten, dazu aber bietet der uns zur Verfügung stehende wenige Raum kaum Möglichkeit. Wir müssen uns damit begnügen, einige besondere Züge der ungarischen Agrarentwicklung aufzuzeiten und wir können lediglich als Ausblick einige Bemerkungen über die breiteren europäischen Zusammenhänge machen.

Die Besonderheiten der ungarischen Agrarentwicklung müssen wir — zumindest in groben Zügen — schon in den vorangegangenen Jahrhunderten betrachten, wenn wir ein reales Bild von der Agrarentwicklung des 16.–19. Jahrhunderts zeichnen wollen. Auf jeden Fall müssen wir darauf hinweisen, daß die ungarischen Stämme, die Ende des 9. Jahrhunderts, mit der letzten Welle der Völkerwanderung eintreffend, das Karpatenbecken in Besitz nahmen, in den letzten Jahrhunderten ihrer Entwicklung, möglicherweise schon früher, den Ackerbau kannten. Nicht nur in der Weise, daß die unterworfenen Völker ihr Land bebauten und von ihren Erträgen an die Ungarn abführten, sondern daß auch die ungarischen Stämme aktive Ackerbauern waren — zumindest in einem Teil des Jahres, an ihren Winterquartieren. Darauf deutet eine Schicht des Wortschatzes der ungarischen Sprache, die in dieser Zeit von Turkvölkern übernommen worden ist (der Grundwortschatz des Getreideanbaus). Es ist auch nicht uninteressant, daß sie ständige Sommer- und Winterquartiere hatten, ihr Leben als Nomaden also von einer inneren Entwicklung auf den Weg zum Ackerbauern geführt wurde.

Im Karpatenbecken wurde das Ungarntum durch die ständige Ansiedlung, durch die relativ große Zahl der hier lebenden verschiedenen ackerbautreibenden Völker weiter auf dem Weg zur aktiven Landwirtschaft vorangetrieben. Als die Ungarn unter Führung der Arpaden zum Christentum übertraten und damit zugleich die heidnischen Sitten verfolgt wurden, wurden Siedlung und die Herstellung eines festgefügten Dorfsystems zur grundlegenden Frage. Deren Förderung, gepaart mit den Aufgaben des Kirchenaufbaus steht im Mittelpunkt der

Gesetze Stephans des Heiligen. Zehn Dörfer mußten eine gemeinsame Kirche errichten und unterhalten, die Einführung des Zehnten für die Kirche schuf die materielle Grundlage der Kirchenorganization.

In dem Kämpfen Ende des 10. und in den ersten Jahrzehnten des 11. Jahrhunderts wurden die Grundlagen für die Organe, das System der Institutionen des entstehenden feudalen ungarischen Staates gelegt, beeinflußt von westlichen, in erster Linie bayerischen Vorbildern, natürlich spielten dabei auch die von der Stammesgesellschaft durch die innere Entwicklung zur Klassengesellschaft führenden ungarischen Besonderheiten eine Rolle. Die aus dem Westen ins Land strömmenden Kleriker, Soldaten, bayerische Vornehme, Italiener und Franzosen, die sehr bald Mitglieder der entstehenden feudalen Aristokratie in Ungarn wurden, verschmolzen mit dem Teil der Stammesaristokratie, die treu zur Politik der Arpaden stand. Sie erhielten riesige Schenkungen, auch ihr Gefolge bekam die entsprechende Versorgung. Durch sie erschien auch in Ungarn der Grundbesitz nach westlichem Muster. In der ungarischen feudalen Entwicklung ist also von Anfang an der Grundbesitz des Stammes und der der Sippen vertreten sowie neben den Dienstgütern die in Privatbesitz überführten Schenkungsgüter.

Mit dem bäerlichen Grundbesitz war es nicht so. In der Arpadenzeit hatte das Dorfvolk noch starke Züge der Feldgemeinschaft bewahrt. Die Dörfer entrichteten zumeist die Steuern als Ganzes, das heißt, die Dorfgemeinschaft bildte eine Steuereinheit und sorgte zugleich für die öffentliche Sicherheit. Das Immunitätsrecht auf den Gütern und damit die Entstehung der Patrimonialgerichte mit dem Recht über Leben und Tod, dem Blutbann, können wir auf den Beginn des 13. Jahrhunderts ansetzen. Die Rolle der Dorfgemeinschaft war sehr groß, sie war praktisch wie ein Keil zwischen das produzierende Individuum und den Grundherrn getrieben.

Das änderte in größerem Umfange erst die zu Beginn des 13. Jahrhunderts Ungarn erreichende deutsche Kolonisation. Besonders die nach dem Tatarensturm (1241) in großer Zahl nach Ungarn kommenden deutschen Bauern, die zum Teil vom Herrscher, zum Teil von den Grundherren systematisch angesiedelt wurden, ließen sich zusammen mit ihren Gesellschaftsverhältnissen (und nicht zuletzt mit ihren Produktionsverhältnissen) im Karpatenbecken nieder. In den ungarischen historischen Quellen kommt der Ausdruck „iure teutonico" zwar nur vereinzelt vor, trotzdem hegen wir keinen Zweifel daran, daß die Ansiedlung der deutschen Bauern den Beginn einer neuen Epoche in der ungarischen Agrarentwicklung darstellte. Bei den gleichzeitig verlaufenden städtischen Ansiedlungen ist die Entwicklung viel eher greifbar, aber auch so geschah es in den Dörfern: die mit Arbeitskräftemangel kämpfenden ungarischen Grundherrn nach dem Vorbild der deutschen Bauern gezwungen waren, auch die Rechtstellung des ungarischen Bauern zu ändern, ihm die gleiche Rechtsstellung zu geben, die für die Verhältnisse der Ansiedler bezeichnend war.

Hier müssen wir uns — wenn auch sehr kurz, zusammenfassend — mit der Lage der westeuropäischen Agrarentwicklung befassen. Das westeuropäische wirtschaftliche–gesellschaftliche Entwicklungsmodell ist heute bereits so bekannt, daß wir hier auf Einzelheiten nicht einzugehen brauchen. Ich halte es für das wichtigste auf die Einzigartigkeit dieser Entwicklung hinzuweisen. Nirgendwo in der Geschichte kam es vor, nur bei der westeuropäischen Entwicklung, daß die Bauern ihren Herren, der Kirche und dem Staat persönlich steuerten, und daß ihre Steuern prozentual festgelegt wurden, d.h. daß sie an die Erträge der Mehrproduktion einen persönlichen Teil und dadurch ein persönliches Interesse haben konnten. Diese Situation ist die Folge eines sehr komplizierten Entwicklungsprozesses. Es handelt sich darum, daß die Wellen der Völkerwanderung die Bevölkerung des klassischen westeuropäischen Gebiets nicht vernichtete. Dadurch entstand hier der Feudelismus aus einer Art Verschmelzung der antiken Überlieferungen und der germanischen–keltischen wirtschaftlichen–gesellschaftlichen Errungenschaften, wobei die entstehende neue Ordnung der Gesellschaft entscheidend von den antiken Formen des Privateigentums und der Ideologie der römischen Kirche beeinflußt wurde. In historisch relativ kurzer Zeit entstand aus den verschiedenen Bauernschichten — Sklaven, Freien, usw. — die Form der Grundhörigkeit, in der der grundholde Bauer persönlich langsam frei wurde und nach Zahlung der Rente die Früchte seiner Arbeit frei genießen konnte. Frei von den Herren und frei von der Dorfgemeinschaft. Diese einzigartige Lage der Bauern gab der westeuropäischen Gesellschaften eine solche Dynamität, die nur hier festzustellen ist.

Von Grund auf anders war die Situation in Osteuropa, wo die Bauern den Boden nicht als Einzelpersonen nutzten, sondern in der Gemeinschaft des ganzen Dorfes. Hier waren die Dorfgemeinschaften die kleinsten Steuereinheiten, die für den Staatsapparat die Steuer garantierten. Die einzelnen Dorfgemeinschaften garantierten dem Staat die Steuer in Form einer kollektiven Verantwortung. In diesem System schnitt im Grunde der schlecht ab, der mehr produzierte. Das ist vor allem die Erklärung dafür, warum im Verlaufe der Jahrtausende überall lediglich das einmal gegebene Niveau der Produktion gehalten wurde, warum es gar nicht, oder nur sehr langsam zur Ausweitung, zur Steigerung der Produktivität kam.

Das ist auch der Grund für die unterschiedlichen Strukturen der „feudalen" Gesellschaften West- und Osteuropas. Im Westeuropa hatte das Lehenswesen die ganze Gesellschaft durchdrungen, während in Osteuropa überall die starke zentrale Macht erhalten geblieben war, von der der gesammte Adel unmittelbar abhing, und die sich deshalb stärker als dieser erwies. Die Gliederung der

Gesellschaft konnte hier nicht so tief sein, wie in Westeuropa. In Osteuropa war der Adel fast bis zum Schluß eine Art Dienst- und Militäradel, der z.B. in Rußland seinen Besitz bis zu den Reformen von Peter dem Großen nicht vererbbar machen konnte.

Nur in den schmalen Grenzgebieten Osteuropas, wo die westliche Kirche das Christentum verbreitete, änderte sich diese Lage. Das aber gilt nur für die kleinere, westliche Hälfte des Gebietes, für das Baltikum, für Polen, Böhmen, Mähren, Ungarn, Kroatien und Slowenien. Die Entwicklung des ursprünglich osteuropäischen Typus wurde auf diesem schmalen Streifen durch zahlreicher Faktoren beeinflußt. In einzelnen Gebieten — Pannonien, Slowenien, Kroatien — müssen die antiken Überlieferungen in Betracht gezogen werden. Die im Verhältnis zur örtlichen Bevölkerung relativ große Zahl der einwandernder Bauern, die das westeuropäische Gesellschaft- und Wirtschaftssystem vermittelten in Ungarn, vor allem aber in Polen und im Baltikum und in mehreren Wellen der Kolonisation des Gebietes teilgenommen haben, spielte eine sehr große Rolle in diesem Prozeß. Der determinierende Faktor war aber die westliche Kirche, die auch hier eine große Rolle an der Herausbildung der gesellschaftlichen Pruralität spielte. Dadurch wurden in diesen Ländern die sich in europäischen Rußland oder auf dem Balkan zeigenden Besonderheiten der osteuropäischen Entwicklung stark verändert. Die verschiedenen Schichten der Bauern um die Wende vom 13. zum 14. Jahrhundert in Polen, Böhmen, oder in Ungarn sich nicht auf dem Niveau der Leibeigenen, sondern im großen und ganzen auf dem sozialen Status des westeuropäischen grundholden Bauerntums vereinigten. Eine große Rolle spielten dabei die vielen angesiedelten deutschen Bauern, die sich in Polen „Iure teutonico“, in Ungarn nach dem Recht der „Gäste“ (hospes) angesiedelten.

Wie früher gesagt: die ungarische Grundherrn gezwungen waren, die Rechtstellung der ungarischen Bauern zu ändern, ihnen die gleiche Rechtsstellung zu geben, die die deutschen Bauern hatten. Zumindest damit gleichwertige Veränderungen fanden auch in der Produktion statt. Zu den höheren gesellschaftlichen Verhältnissen der deutschen Bauern gehörte auch eine höherstehende Technik (in den Gärten die Düngung, der asymmetrische, schollenwendende schwere Pflug, der Flurzwang) und die damit verbundene Technologie (Hufensystem, das damit zusammenhängende System der Flurnutzung), d.h. die Zwei- bzw. Dreifelderwirtschaft. Das alles ergab sich als Folge der deutschen Kolonisation, nachweisbar seit der Mitte des 13. Jahrhunderts im Südwesten des Landes, und breitete sich von hier aus weiter nach Osten und Nordosten aus. Das Ergebnis der Entwicklung war nennenswert, selbst wenn lange Zeit noch der alte leichte und der neue schwere Pflug nebeneinander in Gebrauch waren und wenn neben den im Rahmen eines festen Hufensytems produzierenden, die

Bewirtschaftung mit Flurzwang einführenden Dörfern auch ältere, andere Siedlungsformen erhalten geblieben waren.

Als Folge der Kolonisation hatte sich bis zur Mitte des 14. Jahrhunderts die neue Lage, die gesellschaftliche Stellung der Bauern herausgebildet. Bezeichnend dafür war die persönliche Freiheit, die Möglichkeit des Freizugs und die Besteuerung nach Familien, d.h. den Bauernwirtschaften. Der Wirkungsbereich der Dorfgemeinschaft war — in großen Zügen gesehen — auf die Regelung der Flurnutzung zurückgedrängt worden, die Bauern hatten das zu ihrer Hufe gehörende Land endgültig in Besitz, die neuverteilende Feldgemeinschaft hatte überall aufgehört. Durch die relativ schnelle Entwicklung der Ware–Geld–Verhältnisse war es auch dem Bauern möglich geworden, Land zu pachten und durch das gepachtete Land das Einkommen zu steigern. Wesentlich trug dazu der von der Mitte des 14. Jahrhunderts ab beginnende Warenexport nach Mittel- und Westeuropa bei. Für die entfernter liegenden Märkte boten sich zwei Produkte an: das sie auf den eigenen Beinen erreichende Rind — unter Umständen auch Schaf und Schwein — und der sich auch beim Transport auf größere Entfernungen auszahlende Qualitätswein. Der Handel mit diesen beiden Produkten bildete sich im Lande relativ schnell und in größerem Umfang heraus. Die ungarische landwirtschaftliche Warenproduktion war also von Anfang an auf Fernhandel aufgebaut. Dieser Fernhandel wurde dann vom 14. Jahrhundert an durch die immer stärker zunehmende Nachfrage der westeuropäischen Städte nach landwirtschaftlichen Produkten gesteigert. Der im Fernhandel ohnehin wichtige Rinderhandel übernimmt vom 14. Jahrhundert an die führende Stelle im Außenhandel Ungarns. In der Rindfleischversorgung der süddeutschen und norditalienischen Städte spielte Ungarn eine immer grössere Rolle.

In der Folge der sich schnell entfaltenden landwirtschaftlichen Warenproduktion entstand eine neue Siedlungsform: der Marktflecken (oder Agrarstadt, lateinisch Oppidum). Seine Entstehung ist ohne die schnell zunehmende landwirtschaftliche Warenproduktion unvorstellbar, eine mindestens so große Rolle spielte dabei jedoch das Fehlen der Städte im westeuropäischen Sinne. Diese eigentlich mächtig angeschwollenen Dörfer wurden zu Zentren des landwirtschaftlichen Handels — vor allem des Rinder- und Weinhandels. Sein erscheinen ist überall dort zu beobachten, wo in Osteuropa die landwirtschaftliche Produktion angestiegen war, vor allem in den westlichen Grenzstreifen, in Polen, in der Ukraine, in Ungarn. Dieser Siedlungstypus wurde der charakteristische Knotenpunkt des landwirtschaftes Fernhandels. — Im wesentlichen ähnliche Umstände hatten auch anderswo ähnliche Konsequenzen. Der Marktflecken wurde z.B. im 19. Jahrhundert in den nord- und südamerikanischen Rinderzucht- und Getreideanbaugebieten zur charakteristischen Siedlung.

Diese Marktplätze, die eigentlich Dörfer waren, erreichten in Ungarn im Verlaufe des 14–15. Jahrhunderts eine besondere gesellschaftliche und rechtliche Stellung. Ihre Einwohner waren Bauer, die ihrem Grundherrn die gleichen Renten, Geldzinsen, Naturalabgaben und Fronen entrichten mußten wie die Bauern in den Dörfern. Ihre günstigen Möglichkeiten nutzten diese Siedlungen vor allem, um ihre Abgaben und Leistungen in Geld zu verwandeln. Die Marktflecken kamen bald in die günstige Lage, daß anstelle der Naturalabgaben und der Fronarbeit die Geldrente allein herrschend wurde. In diesen Siedlungen lebten die Bauern freier, die Selbstverwaltung der Bauern weitete sich aus, sie wählten ihre Richter selbst (in den Dörfern bestimmte der Grundherr den Richter), und wurden in inneren Angelegenheiten bis zum gewissen Grade unabhängig vom Grundherrn. Die Marktflecken konnten ihre Steuern jährlich in einer Pauschalsumme in Geld ablösen, das von von ihnen gewählten Richtern nach einem festgesetzten Schlüssel eingesammelt wurde. Das schuf für die Bauern in den Marktflecken eine wesentlich günstigere Lage als für die Dorfbewohner.

Auf den ausgedehnten Weiden der Marktflecken wurde ein bedeutender Teil des ungarischen Rinderbestandes gehalten, in ihren Weingärten wurde ein großer Teil des auf den Markt gebrachten Weines produziert. Hier konzentrierte sich der Rinder- und Weinhandel und zum Teil — in der Nähe wirklicher Städte — auch der Getreidehandel. In diesen Siedlungen entstand auch Handwerk, vor allem Dienstleistungsgewerbe. Die meisten Handwerker lösten sich nicht von der Landwirtschaft, betrieben ihr Handwerk und versorgten die Umgebung mit Kleidung, Schuhwerk und mit zur landwirtschaftlichen Produktion, zum Transport erforderlichen Geräten. Aus all diesen Gründen übte der Marktflecken eine große Anziehungskraft auf die Dorfbauern aus, vor allem auf die wohlhabenderen, die den Umstand, daß sich die Freizügigkeit im 14. Jahrhundert so gut wie auf die gesamte Bauernschaft erstreckte, nutzten und in immer grösseren Mengen in die Marktflecken zogen. Ende des 15. Jahrhunderts finden wir in mehr als 800 Marktflecken 20% der Gesamtbevölkerung des Landes, insgesamt eine dreiviertel Million Menschen.

Von der Mitte des 14. Jahrhunderts ab wurde also das Verhältnis Grundherr–Bauern im wesentlichen von den Umständen der „Grundherrschaft" bestimmt, mit der Sicherung des persönlichen Freizugs der Bauern und den von ihnen für die Nutzung des Bodens erbrachten verschiedenen Leistungen. Diese Leistungen waren in Art, Form und Umfang sehr unterschiedlich. Allgemein läßt sich nur sagen, daß die Bauern dem Grundherrn für die Nutzung des Bodens Geld-, Natural- und Arbeitsleistungen entrichteten. Dies alles war die Folge der Kolonisation, die Rechtsordnung der deutschen Bauern wurde zur Grundlage der ungarischen Verhältnisse. Nur im Ostteil des Landes, in den von rumänischen

Schäfern und Bauern bewohnten Gegenden Siebenbürgens finden wir noch Überreste der persönlichen Unfreiheit der Bauern.

Auch die Formen des adligen Landbesitzes veränderten sich. Innerhalb des ungarischen Adels hatte sich zwar sehr bald eine Gliederung auf Vermögensgrundlage herausgebildet, aber ein reines Verhältnis Senior–Vasall war nicht entstanden. Die Großgrundbesitzer, nicht nur die Magnaten (Barones), sondern auch die gut begüteten Adeligen bezogen zwar einen großen Teil der kleinen Adeligen in ihre „Familien" ein, das aber zeigte bei weitem keine solche Gesellschaftsschichtung wie in Westeuropa. Auch das Lehnsgut vom Typ des Feudums entstand nicht.

Der adlige Grundbesitz zerfiel in zwei Teile: in den Besitz des Geschlechts, der nicht frei vererbbar war und den erworbenen Besitz (königliches Schenkungsgut, Kauf, Pfand), der frei vererbt und veräußert werden konnte. Mit der Zeit verwischte der Unterschied zwischen beiden, obwohl die Unterschiede bis 1848 im Prinzip fortbestanden. Obwohl die Großgrundbesitzer schon früh versuchten, Privilegien zu erhalten, war der Adel rechtlich gesehen einheitlich. Die Zuordnung zu den „barones regni" bedeutete noch nicht die Entstehung einer gesonderten aristokratischen Schicht. Rechtlich war der ungarische Adel einheitlich, jeder Adlige war dem König unmittelbar unterstellt.

Die Praxis wich natürlich von den Prinzipien ab. Die Magnaten versuchten Vorrechte zu erringen, strebten danach, daß ihre Güter abgeschlossen, d.h. gebietsmäßig konzentriert waren. Wo dies gelang, da gerieten die zwischen ihr Land gezwängten kleineren Adligen in eine untergeordnete, von ihnen abhängige Lage. Die zusammenhängenden Grundbesitzkörper der Magnaten trugen stellenweise Keime territorialer Selbständigkeit in sich, doch war die königliche Gewalt bis zum Ende stark genug, eine deratige Entwicklung zu verhindern.

In die Reihen des Adels aufgenommen zu werden, war nicht übermäßig schwierig. Zwischen Adeligen und Bauern zog sich damals eine relativ dünne Trennlinie, die reicheren Bauern konnten relativ leicht Adelige werden. Die Bodenpacht war in dieser Hinsicht die erste Stufe für die Bauern. Ein Teil der Bauern kam zu Feldern, die dem Adel gehörten und früher von Adeligen bewirtschaftet worden waren und in gewisser Hinsicht entwickelte sich über die Felder ein Eigentumsrecht. Über die gerodeten oder gepachteten, manchmal gekauften Felder verfügte der Bauer — aufgrund eines sehr schnell entstandenen Gewohnheitsrechts — frei. Das Eigentumsrecht des Bauern an diesen Feldern anerkannten die die Vererbung regelenden Gewohnheiten. Die nächste Stufe war, daß die reicheren Bauern in eine adlige Familie einheirateten. Diese Bauern wurden bald von der Umgebung selbst als Adeliger anerkannt. Erleichtert wurde es durch die Tatsache, daß zeitweise, selbst in späteren Jahrhunderten noch, einzelne Militärdienst leistende Schichten kollektiv in den Adelsstand erhoben wurden (anfangs die Szekler, dann die Ansiedlungen der Haiducken, früher von Kumanen, dann der Militärdienst leistenden Bauern im Grenzgebiet). Demzufolge dürfte die Zahl der ungarischen Adligen in Europa nach den polnischen Adligen am höchsten gewesen sein (4–7% der Gesamtbevölkerung). Die große Zahl von ihnen lebte natürlich wie die Bauern und wirtschaftete auch wie sie. Neben den kleinen Adligen, die nur wenig Land, hin und wider ein Stückchen Dorf besaßen, finden wir eine relativ wohlhabende Schicht des Mitteladels (seine Mitglieder bildeten im 14. Jahrhundert die Reiterschaft), während die Magnatenfamilien riesige Ländereien besaßen. Der eine oder andere Magnat hatte zeitweilig einen Landbesitz, dessen Größe der des königlichen Besitzes nahekam. Trotzdem waren nach dem Recht alle Mitglieder des Adels gleich. Das zeigt sich darin, daß jedes Mitglied des Adels am Landtag teilnehmen konnte (obwohl vom 14. Jahrhundert ab wahrscheinlich der Kleinadel aus den Komitaten durch Vertreter, die Magnaten [Barone, barones regni] aber persönlich daran teilnahmen).

An der Wende vom 15. zum 16. Jahrhundert trat in der Entwicklung der Agrarstruktur Europas ein bedeutender Wandel ein: vermutlich durch die gemeinsame Wirkung mehrerer Faktoren veränderte sich im Westen wie im Osten das Verhältnis Grundherr–Bauer. Die Preisrevolution im 16–17. Jahrhundert zwang den Adel in ganz Europa zur Steigerung seiner Geldeinkünfte. Im Westen durchdrangen Warenproduktion und Geldwirtschaft immer stärker die Wirtschaft, die Dichte des Stadtnetzes machte es auch dem Bauern möglich, sein Land zu verlassen oder zumindest nach einer anderen Beschäftigung zu sehen. Das wurde offensichtlich, zumindest teilweise auch durch das System des Anerbenrechts, oder geschlossenen Erbschaft gefördert, denn die Bauern waren seit Generationen an den Gedanken gewöhnt, daß sie den väterlichen Wirtschaftshof verlassen mußten. Die Geldwirtschaft hatte die ganze Gesellschaft viel stärker durchdrungen als in Osteuropa und dabei spielte das System der geschlossenen Erbschaft eine wichtige Rolle (die Geschwister wurden gewöhnlich durch Geld entschädigt). Die Bauern waren hier also viel mehr an den Wechsel der Umstände gewöhnt, auch daran, andere Arbeit anzunehmen.

Die Bauern wurden überall zu Pächtern des Bodens und die Pacht entrichteten sie meist mit Geld. Die Lohnarbeit war teuer geworden, die Grundherren waren also immer mehr gezwungen, die Eigenbewirtschaftung ihrer Güter aufzugeben, die Bauern wurden mehr zu Pächtern. Rechtlich ging dieser Prozeß oft schleppender voran und stellenweise blieben dem Grundherrn zahlreiche feudale Vorrechte, das aber änderte nichts an der Grundformel: die Bauernschaft hatte den Weg zur Unabhängigkeit beschritten. Wo der Grundherr selbst wirtschaftete, so geschah das vornehmlich mit Lohnarbeitern. Der ganze Prozeß war ein wichtiger Schritt in die Richtung auf die Kapitalisierung.

Anders paßte sich der Adel an die neuen Gegebenheiten, vor allem an die Preisrevolution in Ost-Europa an. Östlich der Elbe versuchte der Adel seine Einnahmen zu steigern, aber es boten sich ihm keine Möglichkeiten, die denen in Westeuropa ähnlich waren. Natürlich stiegen die Preise für die Exportprodukte, aber die Preise für die importierten Luxusartikel stiegen noch mehr. Die Geldleistungen der Bauern war durch verschiedene Gesetze früher festgelegt worden und das konnte nicht geändert werden. Auf den in die Ostsee mündenden größeren Flüssen wie Elbe und Moldau (aus dem Vorfeld der Sudeten), Weichsel und Bug (aus dem Vorfeld der Karpaten) und auf der Memel boten sich jedoch günstige Möglichkeiten für den Getreidetransport, was den dortigen Adel bewog, seine warenproduzierende Tätigkeit zu steigern. Für die Erhöhung der Arbeitsleistung gab es kein gesetzliches Hindernis, so daß die Grundherren ihr selbst bewirtschaftetes Land ausdehnten (selbst mit Gewalt), was dann die Bauern mit Fronarbeit, mit ihren Gerätschaften und ihren Zugtieren bearbeiteten. Mit der erhöhten Produktionsmenge vergrößerten sie ihre Einnahmen.

Die Steigerung der Fronarbeit löste den Widerstand der Bauernschaft aus. Um ihn zu brechen mußte ein ganzes System von Maßnahmen ausgearbeitet werden, angefangen von der Bindung des Bauern an die Scholle bis zur Neuregelung des Verhältnisses Grundherr–Bauer. Im Rahmen dieses Prozesses nahm dabei in der Region östlich der Elbe die persönliche Abhängigkeit des Bauern vom Grundherrn zu, in den einzelnen Gebieten in unterschiedlichem Maße, aber mit der gleichen Tendenz. Der Kern dieses Prozesses war die völlige Unterordnung des Bauern unter den Grundherrn. Die Fronlasten stiegen stellenweise bis an die Grenze des Erträglichen, auch wirtschaftlich wurde der Bauer vom Grundherrn abhängig, denn er konnte jederzeit gezwungen werden, seine Hofstelle zu verlassen (Bauernlegen). Zu der auch früher schon bestehenden starken Beschneidung der persönlichen Freiheit (Heiratszwang, grundherrliche Erbrechte usw.) kamen das Verbot des Wegzugs und die verstärkte Patrimonialgerichtsbarkeit.

Dies alles war in vieler Hinsicht in ganz Osteuropa so, dennoch müssen wir die osteuropäische Entwicklung von der in Mittelosteuropa unterscheiden. Östlich der Elbe, bis hin zur Memel herrschte das System, das man zusammenfassend Gutswirtschaft und Gutscherrschaft nennt. Dieses System war in den preußischen und polnischen Gebieten, zum Teil in Böhmen und Mähren und in Niederösterreich anzutreffen. Noch weiter östlich, in dem riesiegen osteuropäischen Steppenggebiet, wo es keine billige Transportmöglichkeit mehr gab, da konnten auf den Grundherrschaften (ob es sich um großen oder kleineren Besitzstand handelte), die Bedingungen der Gutswirtschaft nicht mehr zur Geltung kommen. Das produzierte Getreide konnte nämlich nicht auf den Markt gebracht werden, — das war der Grund dafür, daß der Grundherr in den ausgedehnten Gebieten Osteuropas andere Methoden des Geldgewinns anwenden mußte.

Das Mittel dazu war die Durchsetzung verschiedener grundherrlicher Monopole beziehungsweise die Ausdehnung von deren Wirkungsbereich. In Ostpolen, in den baltischen Ländern und vor allem in Rußland und in der Walachei war dieses Mittel das grundherrliche Recht der Schnapsbrennerei und des Ausschanks. Die Geldverpflichtungen der Bauern konnten nicht mehr erhöht werden, eine größere Erweiterung der Arbeits- und Naturalleistungen lohnte sich nicht, durch die Schnapsbrennerei und den Ausschank aber konnten die Grundherren ihre Einnahmen wesentlich steigern. Wo sich das Schnapsmonopol nicht von allein durchsetzen ließ, da wurden die Bauern zum Kauf einer bestimmten Menge Schnaps verpflichtet, nach dem vom Grundherrn festgelegten Preis. Dieses System vertiefte die Wurzeln des Alkoholismus in Osteuropa. Aber dieses System garantierte dem Adel die für seinen Konsum erforderlichen Geldeinkünfte.

Natürlich finden wir in dieser mittel- und osteuropäischen Entwicklung zahlreiche *regional* auftretende Besonderheiten. Sowohl bei den Verpflichtungen der Bauern wie bei der grundherrlichen Wirtschaft. Wo wird es nicht erstaunen, wenn wir darauf aufmerksam machen, daß die ungarische Entwicklung — in diesen Rahmen — in vieler Hinsicht eigene Wege beschritten hat.

Bestimmend für die Besonderheiten der ungarischen Agrarentwicklung ist die geographische Lage des Landes. Hauptfluß des Karpatenbeckens ist die Donau, die aber ins Schwarze Meer mündet. Der ungarische Abschnitt des Flusses war im großen und ganzen zwischen Wien und Győr schon vom 16. Jahrhundert ab, zwischen Győr und Pest, später bis Baja vom Ende des 17. Jahrhunderts ab schiffbar, das Schleppen gegen die Strömung war allerdings sehr kostspielig. Selbst wenn die Türken nach 1541 nicht einen großen Teil des Landes besetzt hätten, hätte sich der Getreidetransport auf der Donau nicht ausgezahlt. Die Besetzung der Mitte des Landes und eines Teiles von Ostungarn brachte natürlich auch die Einführung des türkischen Wirtschaftssystems mit sich, was schon an sich die Massenproduktion von Getreide verhinderte. Die adelige Herrschaft wurde aufgelöst, das türkische Spahi-System aufgestellt, wobei ein Spahi (ein türkischer Kavallerist) nur ein- bis drei Jahre in einem besetzten Land blieb. Die Spahis waren eher an eine völlige Abschöpfung, Ausbeutung der ihnen untergeordneten Bauern interessiert, als an eine eigene Bewirtschaftung des Landes. Das türkische Wirtschaftssystem begünstigte eher die Viehzucht, die in halbnomadischer Form betrieben wurde.

Ende des 15. Jahrhunderts war auch die Tiefebene und das als „Pußta" bezeichnete Steppenland mit Hunderten von kleinen Dörfern bedeckt. Die

Bevölkerung lebte vornehmlich von der Viehzucht, was einen gewissen Getreideanbau zur Selbstversorgung nicht ausschließt. Die Bevölkerungsdichte war gering, die halbnomade Weide–Viehwirtschaft brauchte riesige Flächen. Diese kleinen Dörfer traf die türkische Besetzung nach 1541 besonders hart. Den türkischen Soldaten auf Gedeih und Verderb ausgeliefert, kamen die kleinen Dörfer an den Rand des Ruins. Die Bauern entlassen diese Dörfer, und zogen sich in die größeren, befestigten Ortschaften, in die Marktflecken oder Marktstädte ein. Diese größeren Ortschaften standen meist unter unmittelbarer Oberhoheit des Sultans, lebten unter relativ geordneten Verhältnissen, was bestimmte jährliche Steuer und Selbstverwaltung bedeutete, und waren vor den Soldaten gesichert. Die Einwohner der naheliegenden Dörfer flohen in diese Oppida und diese schlugen die Weiden der entvölkerten Dörfer zu den ihren. So entwickelten sich weiter die größeren Landstädte wie z.B. Kecskemét, Debrecen, Nagykőrös, Cegléd, usw., die über mehrere Zehntausende Hektar, ja manchmal 100tausende Hektar Land verfügten. Diese Situation begünstigte aber die halbnomade Viehsucht.

Trotzdem meldete sich ein gewisser Bedarf an Getreide, und gerade als Folge der Türkenkriege des 16.–17. Jahrhunderts. An den Grenzen der von den Türken besetzten Gebiete entstand ein Netz von Grenzfestungen, die Präsenz des im großen und ganzen stehenden Heeres stellte auch in Friedenszeiten einen Aufnahmemarkt dar. In der Umgebung der Grenzfestungen (aus einer Entfernung von etwa 30–40 km lohnte es sich noch, das Getreide mit dem Wagen zu transportieren) entstand die grundherrliche Warenproduktion, eine Art Gutswirtschaft, wenn auch nicht in der strengen Form wie in Mittel- oder Ostdeutschland. Solange die durch das Heer geschaffene Konjunktur bestand, solange war die Produktion der gutsherrlichen Wirtschaften rentabel (besonders deshalb, weil sie kostenlose Fronarbeit benutzten). In Westungarn, entlang der österreichischen Grenze, erschien um diese Zeit bereits auch die Wirkung der österreichischen städtischen Märkte, neben Wien, Wienerneustadt und Graz bildeten die österreichischen Kleinstädte einen langsam größer werdenden Markt für das Getreide der ungarischen Gutswirtschaften.

Abgesehen von der Konjunktur an der Grenze und von der Anwesenheit des Heeres war die Getreideproduktion nicht bedeutend und auf den gutsherrlichen Wirtschaften nahm sie auch nicht zu. Den Binnemarkt bildeten neben dem Gesagten einige größere Städte, die technischen Möglichkeiten des Exports aber waren beschränkt. Das ungarische Straßennetz war ziemlich zurückgeblieben, der Bau der Heeresstraßen, die ein leichteres Vorankommen ermöglichten, wurde erst gegen Ende das 16. Jahrhunderts begonnen, von Wien nach Győr (Raab) und von Pozsony (Bratislawa, Preßburg) nach Kassa (Kosice, Kaschau). Aber bis zum Ende des 17. Jahrhunderts waren nur die Anfangsschritte beim

Straßenbau unternommen worden. Auf den vorhandenen Straßen konnte das Getreide nur sehr langsam und in kleine Entfernungen transportiert werden, sonst hätte das Zugvieh die Ladung selbst aufgefressen.

So war auch weiterhin das Rind der Hauptexportartikel des Landes, im allgemeinen Lebendvieh, das die Märkte auf seinen eigenen Beinen erreichte. Dieser Export war schon seit der Mitte des 14. Jahrhunderts überliefert, um diese Zeit kauften die süddeutschen und norditalienischen Städte bereits in großer Zahl ungarische Rinder (über geringfügigen Pferdeexport besitzen wir aus früherer Zeit Angaben). Bis zum 16. Jahrhundert erreichte der Rinderexport im Jahre 100–150000 Stück und im großen und ganzen wurde diese Menge ganz bis zum 18. Jahrhundert aus Ungarn ausgeführt. (Der Schweineexport war im 18. Jahrhundert im Ansteigen).

Der andere wichtige Exportartikel neben dem Vieh war der Qualitätswein. Aufnahmemarkt für den westungarischen Wein bildeten die österreichischen Erblande, während die berühmten Weinsorten aus der Tokajer Weingegend vor allem nach Polen, in kleineren Mengen aber an die Fürstenhöfe und den Adel ganz Europas geliefert wurde. Der Transport über die Karpaten lohnte sich nur bei den wertvollsten Weinen, während nach den östereichischen Erblanden größere Weinmengen geliefert wurden.

Der Vieh- und Weinexport bestimmte die Umstände, unter denen sich der Adel in den Handel einschaltete. Die Adligen konnten zollfrei exportieren, das machte die Ausfuhr für sie vorteilhaft. Die Produktion, das heißt, die Herstellung der Waren blieb in bäuerlicher Hand, denn weder die Rinderzucht noch der Weinanbau konnten durch Fronarbeit ausgeführt werden. Vom Ende des 15. Jahrhunderts ab versuchten also die Adligen den Rinder- und Weinhandel zu monopolisieren. Nach 1490 zerbrachen sie erfolgreich die Privilegien der Marktflecken und setzten eine stärkere grundherrliche Kontrolle durch. Schließlich erreichten sie, daß der Landtag auch für die Marktflecken wieder die Naturalrente — die sogenannte nona — zur Pflicht erklärte. Damit wurden die Möglichkeiten der bäuerlichen Warenproduktion eingeschränkt und für die größeren Grundherren, für die Aristokratie bat sich die Möglichkeit, sich an den landwirtschaftlichen Handel einzuschalten. Zu den Bestrebungen des Adels, die bäuerliche Warenproduktion abzuschöpfen und zurückzudrängen, kamen auch Bestrebungen auf gesellschaftlicher Ebene. Der Kleinadel versuchte, die Freizügigkeit der Bauern einzuschränken. Das Ziel war die völlige Aufhebung der Freizügigkeit, was aber nicht im Interesse der Aristokratie war. Das Bestreben des Adels war darauf gerichtet, sich gegen die Bauern abzuschließen, starre Trennwände zwischen Adel und Bauern zu errichten. Die gegenüber der Aristokratie das Prinzip „alle Adeligen sind gleich“ betonenden Kleinadeligen mußten, um ihr Ziel zu erreichen, ihre Reihen zu den Bauern hin schließen. Die

Auswirkungen, die Folgen der gleichzeitig aus mehreren Richtungen auf die Bauernschaft einsetzenden Angriffe waren sehr kompliziert. Der Widerstand der Marktflecken führte schließlich zu dem großen Bauernaufstand vom Jahre 1514. Der Aufstand wurde niedergeschlagen und die Hauptstrafe der Vergeltung war die „ewige“ Bindung der Bauern an die Scholle, das heißt, die Aufhebung der Freizügigkeit. Rechtlich hatte diese Bindung an die Scholle nur bis zum Jahre 1556 Geltung, die Gesetze dieses Jahres stellten die Freizügigkeit wieder her, aber mit einschränkenden Bedingungen.

Das 16. Jahrhundert war ohne Zweifel das Jahrhundert des Adels. Es gab zwar Jahrzehnte, in denen Frieden herrschte, dann ging die Getreidekonjunktur zurück, auch der Fall einer Grenzfestung veränderte die Marktlage, im großen und ganzen bildeten dennoch die Bedürfnisse des Heeres einen ständigen Binnenmarkt und das schuf in bestimmten Gegenden, in erster Linie im westlichen Oberungarn den ständigen Markt, der die Grundlage für die adelige Eigenwirtschaft bildete. Auch die Erhöhung der Fronlasten erfolgte überall, wo das erforderlich wurde. In den Gegenden, wo die Grundherren eine größere Arbeitsdienst von den Bauern brauchten, wurden die Robotleistungen der Bauern in sehr abwechslungsvoller Form erhöht. In einigen Gütern waren die verschiedenen Arbeiten aufgezählt, die die Bauern zu leisten hatten, bei anderen Fällen waren die Zahl der Robottage befestigt, woanders waren von den Arbeiten der Bauern nur erwähnt, daß sie „nach Notwendigkeit“, oder „ohne Limitierung“ arbeiten sollen, daß die Robotleistung unbegränzt ist. Im allgemeinen sind aber diese Ausnahmeerscheinungen, die gutsherrlichen Ackerländer blieben verhältnismäßig klein, und diese Robotleistungen berührten nur die Bauern, die zum selben Dorf gehörten, wo diese Ländereien lagen.

Doch dürfen wir nochmals betonen, daß das 16. Jahrhundert das des Adels war, der seine Bestrebungen durchsetzen konnte. Den Höhepunkt des Prozesses bildete die charakteristische bürger- und bauernfeindliche Gesetzgebung des Landtages vom Jahre 1608. Der Landtag läßt u.a. das Gesetz verbriefen, daß der König ohne Einwilligung der Stände keine Stadtprivilegien erteilen und Marktflecken (oppida) nicht mehr in den Stand der königlichen Freistädten und Bergstädten erheben könne; er erklärt, daß die sich in den königlichen Freistädten und Bergstädten niederlassenden Adeligen Kommunalwürden bekleiden und Stadthäuser käuflich erwerben können; bestätigt zugleich das Übergewicht des Adelsstandes an der „Untertafel“ (im Unterhaus) gegenüber der Vertretung der Städte. Einige Jahre später, 1638 wurden vom Landtag mehrere Landstädte (Marktflecken) jenseits der Theiß in den „einfachen Bauernstand“ zurückgedrängt.

Vor allem triumphierten aber restlos die feudalen adeligen Interessen über das Bauerntum. Die Tendenz setzte sich mit gesteigerter Schärfe durch, die

Bauern in einen Stand zurückzudrängen, der ähnlich zur Bindung an die Scholle war. Im Sinne eines anderen Gesetzes des Landtages vom Jahre 1608 wurde die Regelung des Umzugs der Bauern vollauf in den Amtsbereich der Komitate verwiesen, d.h. in den Amtsbereich der kleineren und mittleren Adeligen. Es ist vielleicht kein Zufall, daß um diese Zeit auch die Absonderung der Aristokratie endgültig wurde, die Magnaten (Barone, Grafen) schlossen sich zu einer selbstständigen Tafel im Landtag zusammen, zur Magnatentafel, und konnten persönlich anwesend sein, während in der Tafel der Komitatsgesandten, d.h. der einfachen Adeligen jeweils zwei Gesandte die Komitate vertraten.

Das 17. Jahrhundert aber brachte eine bedeutsame Wende. Der Türkenkrieg war schon eine ganze Zeitlang vorbei, der beständige Frieden, der nur von kürzeren kleineren Grenzenkriegen unterbrochen wurde, beendete die Getreidekonjunktur. Für das königliche Ungarn und Siebenbürgen insgesamt war die Getreidekonjunktur ohnehin nicht bestimmend gewesen, bildete lieber eine Ausnahme. Die absolute Mehrheit der Grundherren mußte sich also im 16.–17. Jahrhundert nach einer anderen Geldquelle umsehen. Neben dem Vieh- und Weinhandel blieb ihnen dafür nur eine einzige Möglichkeit: die Ausweitung der Gültigkeit der verschiedenen grundherrlichen Rechte.

Das ungarische Rechtssystem sicherte dem Adel die ausschließliche Nutzung der Schenke, der Schlächterei und der Mühle, die sogenannten niederen königlichen Nutznießerungen (Monopole) zumindest die Hälfte des Jahres. Diese Rechte mußte der Adel nutzen beziehungsweise mißbrauchen, um seine Einkünfte zu steigern. Im ganzen Land wurden die Bauern verpflichtet, mindestens von St. Georgi (29. April) bis St. Michaelis (29. Sept.) wo sie kein Weinland hatten, von Weihnachten bis St. Michaelis die Schenke der Herren besuchen, wo nur der Wein des Grundherrn verkauft werden konnte. Den Wein beschaften die Grundherren von den Naturalleistungen der Bauern. Sie waren bemüht, die früher gegebenen Vergünstigungen aufzuheben, die Geldleistungen nach dem Weinland der Bauern in Naturalleistungen zu rekommentieren. Die herrschaftlichen Weineinkünfte wurden vielerorts durch die Pacht des kirchlichen Weinzehents vergrößert. Darüber hinaus zwangen sie die Bauern, ihnen auf den für den Handel bestimmten Wein, das Vorkaufrecht zuzugestehen. Es war also ein Zwangsverkauf. So kamen sie zu den Weinmengen, die an die Bauern verkauft wurden. Mühlen und Fleischbankregal sowie Mautrecht wurde das ganze Jahr nach grundherrlichem Recht betrieben. Dieses Betriebsrecht für die Schenke, die Mühle und die Schlächterei verpachteten die Grundherren. Die Schnapsbrennerei hatte in Ungarn nicht die gleiche Bedeutung wie weiter nach Osten Europas, hier war so gut wie in jeder Baurnwirtschaft auch Weinanbau anzutreffen.

Der größte Teil der grundherrlichen Einkünfte bestand im 16.–17. Jahrhundert aus den Geld- und Naturalleistungen der Bauern (die, wenn möglich, verkauft wurden) und aus den Einnahmen aus den grundherrlichen Monopolen. Im Prinzip war die Fronlast stellenweise bedeutend, gleichsam als Kennziffer dafür, daß einmal stärkerer grundherrlicher Getreideanbau betrieben worden war, in der Praxis aber wurde sie nicht in Anspruch genommen. Wo die Möglichkeit bestand, ließen die Grundherren dieselbe von den Bauern durch Geld ablösen. Aber das kam selten vor.

Die bäuerlichen Leistungen waren sehr vielfältig. Sie waren mit dem Gewohnheitsrecht entstanden, wenn im allgemeinen auch als Prinzip galt, daß die Leistungen nach der Hufe erbracht wurden. Die Größe der Hufe war jedoch regional verschieden, Umfang und Art der danach erbrachten Leistungen ebenfalls. Im allgemeinen war die Geldleistung gleich, für eine ganze Hufe galt 1 Forint, gleich war auch der Umfang der Naturalleistung (vom Ertrag jedes bäuerlichen Produkts ein Zehntel und vom Schwein und Schaf ein Zwanzigstel). Die Arbeitsleistung und die Gültigmachung der grundherrlichen Monopole aber zeigen viele lokale Besonderheiten.

Die Grundherren steigerten ihre Einkünfte auch, indem sie, wo es möglich war, die gesamten bäuerlichen Leistungen in Geld konvertierten. Solche Bauern wurden „taxás“, „árendás“ usw. genannt. Das waren im Grunde genommen erste Schritte zur westeuropäischen Entwicklung hin. Überall im Lande gab es solche Bauern, aber nur in geringer Zahl.

Grundlegend veränderte sich die Lage vom Anfang des 18. Jahrhunderts an. Nach der Vertreibung der Türken lagen riesige Gebiete leer, auf ihnen begann die Kolonisation, zum kleineren Teil von den überbevölkerten Teilen Oberungarns, zum größeren Teil aber aus dem Ausland. Aus dem Süden des deutschen Reiches wanderten im Verlaufe eines Jahrhunderts Hunderttausende ein, zum Teil im Rahmen der kaiserlichen Ansiedlung, zum Teil auf Initiative der Grundherren. Die Bevölkerung nahm schnell zu, in den früher entvölkerten Gebieten der großen ung. Tiefebene wurden Dörfer gegründet. Im allgemeinen wurde der Raum für die auf dem Weidegang beruhende halbnomadische Viehzucht enger und es wuchs die unter den Pflug genommene Bodenfläche.

Die Verkehrsverhältnisse besserten sich. Der Warentransport auf der Donau weitete sich zwischen Baja und Wien aus. Die in der Nähe der Grenze liegenden österreichischen Städte bildeten auch weiterhin einen wichtigen Getreidemarkt. Im Nordwesten des Landes hatte die Länge der Heeresstraßen zugenommen, der Getreidetransport über die Karpaten nach Böhmen–Mähren konnte beginnen. Das alles führte jetzt bereits tatsächlich zur Entwicklung der grundherrlichen Eigenwirtschaft und zum Erscheinen der Gutswirtschaft, vor allem im Gebiet zwischen der Westgrenze des Landes und dem Balaton sowie zwischen Westkarpaten und Donau. Diese grundherrlichen Wirtschaften lagen relativ nahe an der Donau, was den Transport des Getreides nach Österreich ermöglichte.

In diesen Gegenden Transdanubiens kamen in der zweiten Hälfte des 18. Jahrhunderts die wirklichen Gutswirtschaften zustande. Einige Magnaten-Familien, die hier tatsächlich große Besitze hatten, wie z.B. die Fürsten und Grafen Esterházys, die Grafen Széchényis, Batthyánys oder Festetichs formten von den ihnen zur Verfügung stehenden allodialen Ländereien Eigenwirtschaften von einigen Tausend Hektar Land, bauten Knechte- und Gesindehäuser, siedelten einen Teil ihres Gesindes an und betrieben Viehhaltung oder Ackerbau. Dies waren die sogenannten „Pußten" in Transdanubien, kein Steppartiges Land also, sondern das Zentrum eines Gutsbetriebes, der Siedlungsplatz mit den Wirtschaftsgebäuden, die Wohnungen für die Knechten und das Gesinde, die Häuser des Gutsinspektors und der Verwaltungsbediensteten, manchmal auch mit einem herrschaftlichen Gutshaus. Diese „Pußten" waren eigentlich in den von den Türken besetzten Gebieten Transdanubiens an den Stellen zu finden, wo zu Beginn das 16. Jahrhunderts noch blühende Dörfer gestanden hatten. Die Türkenkriege, vor allem der Befreiungskrieg Ende des 17. Jahrhunderts haben hier außergewöhnliche Blutopfer gefordert und ganze Komitate entvölkert. Die ehemaligen und neuen Grundherren begannen auf ihrem wiedererhaltenen oder neuerworbenen, entvölkerten Grundbesitz im 18. Jahrhundert ebenfalls mit extensiver Weide-Viehwirtschaft und deren Zentren entstanden auf diesen „Pußten". Von der Mitte des 18. Jahrhunderts an schuf die Nähe der österreichischen Märkte günstige Möglichkeiten auch für den auf dem Frondienst der Bauern basierenden Getreideanbau.

Die Frontleistungen nahmen zu, besonders in den westlichen Komitaten des Landes. Für eine ganze Hufe betrugen sie bis zum Jahre 1760 in einzelnen Gegenden bereits 3–4 Tage pro Woche. Im Zwischenstromland und in der Tiefebene blieb aber zugleich das alte grundherrliche Wirtschaftssystem weiter bestehen. Hier gab es keinen Markt für das Getreide, die Bevölkerung in den Städten und in den Marktflecken deckte seinen Eigenbedarf selbst. Langsam entstanden allerdings auch in diesen Gebieten auf der Fronarbeit beruhende grundherrliche Großbetriebe, wenn ein entsprechender Markt gegeben war (das waren vorerst nur die Garnisonen), aber der Prozeß war hier augenmerklich viel langsamer als in Transdanubien. Folge der Bevölkerungszunahme war, daß die Zahl der Rinder, die exportiert werden konnten, stark zurückging. Der Rückgang war so stark, daß Anfang des 19. Jahrhunderts zeitweilig sogar Wiens Fleischversorgung gefährdet war.

Die Zunahme des Frondienstes führe in den 1760er Jahren in mehreren westlichen Komitaten zu Bauernbewegungen. Die Bauern verweigerten den Gehorsam, wollten den Robotverpflichtungen nicht mehr nachkommen. Es handelte sich also nicht um eine verborgene Resistenz der Bauern, die sich in Form der Vernachlässigung der Robotarbeiten sehen ließ, worüber wir für das

16., 17. und 18. Jahrhundert genügende Informationen haben, und zwar von den Briefwechseln von Gutsverwaltern und Gutsherren. Zur verborgene Resistenz gehörte auch, daß manchmal statt der arbeitsfähigen Männer Kinder zum Frondienst geschickt wurden. Was aber am meisten verbreitet war, war die Vergrößerung der Bauernfamilien. Die Bauern wurden nach Familien (d.h. nach Haushalten) zur Robotleistung verpflichtet. Es hat zur Folge, daß erwachsene Bauernsöhne (mit eigener Familie) im väterlichen Haushalt verblieben, oder daß Bauerngeschwister „vom gleichen Brot" (d.h. in einem Haus, unter einem Dach, aus einer Hufe) lebten. Hier handelte es sich aber um einen offenen Widerstand. Zu dem Bauernaufruhr hatte hie und da die Schmälerung oder der Raub bäuerlichen Landes, also das Bauernlegen beigetragen. Die Nachricht von der Unzufriedenheit der Bauern erreichte auch den Wiener Hof, so daß am Ende Marie Theresia beschloß, nach dem Vorbild der Erblande auch in Ungarn ein Urbarialpatent einzuführen. Damals waren schon in einzelnen österreichischen Ländern, noch früher in Böhmen–Mähren, die Verpflichtungen der Bauern durch Patente geregelt worden, das Vorbild war also gegeben. Auf dem Landtag vom Jahre 1764–65 gelang es der Herrscherin nicht, die Zustimmung des Adels zu der Regelung zu erhalten, deshalb führte sie 1767 das Urbarialpatent auf dem Verordnungswege ein. Das Verfahren nahm lange Jahre in Anspruch. Da die Bauernbefreiung von 1848 das Urbarialpatent zur Grundlage nahm, bestimmte dieses die wirtschaftlichen Möglichkeiten der Bauernschaft geradezu bis zum Jahre 1945.

Das Urbarialpatent war die erste, breiteste und die meisten Details erfassende Maßnahme der Staatsgewalt, die zum Schutze des Bauernlandes, der Steuergrundlage unter den juristischen Kategorien der Bauern (Erbuntertanen) und unter den verschiedenen Formen der Grundbesitzverhältnisse irgendeine Ordnung anstrebte. Auf Grund der üblichen Praxis umriß das Urbarium den Begriff des urbarialen, d.h. einer Hofstelle zugehörigen Landes, der sog. Außenhufe, verfügte die Einfassung dieser Grundstücke nach Gemeinden und erklärte, daß der Nießbrauch des gesamten Bauerntums an diesem Boden ein unbestreitbares Recht sei, so daß die Gutsherren von diesen im Kataster erfaßten Grundstücken nunmehr nichts ihren in Eigenbewirtschaftung behaltenen Ländereien einverbleiben dürften. So wurde also der Mindestumfang des urbarialen bäuerlichen Landes festgelegt. Zugleich setzte das Urbarium die nach Komitat und Gemeinde unterschiedliche Größe einer Vollhufe bzw. des zur Hufe gehörigen Acker- und Wiesenlandes fest und limitierte das Maximum der Arbeits-, Naturalien- und Geldleistungen, die von den Gutsherren nach den Voll- oder Teilhufen gefordert werden konnten. Schließlich unterschied die Verordnung deutlich zwischen den bis dahin vielerorten verwischten, in landweitem Belang nicht einheitlich gebrauchten Begriffen des Hübners (Hufenbauers, Grundsaßen) bzw.

des Häuslers (Kätners, Söldners, Kleinhäuslers). Die Fronbauer, die Acker- und Wiesenland von mehr als einer Achtelhufe besaßen, wurden zur Kategorie der Hübner, Bauern mit geringerem Grundbesitz zu jener der Häusler gezählt. Das im Urbarium ausgewiesene und der Größe nach angeführte Land war das eigentliche Urbar (die Urbarialität), mochte es nun auf den Namen der einzelnen Bauern oder aber als Besitz der Gemeinde verzeichnet sein.

Das Urbarium war jedoch auch durch zwei Negativa gekennzeichnet. Das Patent zog es eine endgültige juristische Mauer zwischen urbarialem und allodialem Land. Dagegen verfügte es über den bäuerlichen Grundbesitz, der nach den erwähnten Merkmalen nicht eindeutig oder überhaupt nicht Anteil der Bauernhufe war, teils gar nichts, teils aber zu Ungunsten der Bauer. Hinzu kam noch, daß die Urbarialregelung zum gegebenen Zeitpunkt nur theoretisch, formell ausgeführt wurde. Die Mehrheit der fertiggestellten Urbarien bei weitem nicht die wirklichen Verhältnisse widerspiegelte.

Im ganzen Land wurden also die landwirtschaftlichen Nutzflächen erfaßt und es wurde rechtlich geklärt, welches Land von den Bauern und welches von den Grundherren genutzt werden konnte. Danach wurde das bäuerliche Land in einzelne Hufen aufgeteilt und an die Bauern ausgegeben. Von jetzt ab konnten die Grundherren das von den Bauern genutzte Land nicht mehr in Allodien umwandeln. Auch die Dienstleistungen wurden erfaßt und zu den neuen Hufen wurden neue, einheitliche Leistungen vorgeschrieben. Damit war das Verhältnis Grundherr–Bauer einfacher, übersichtlicher geworden. Ohne Zweifel aber hatten sich die Verhältnisse der Bauern im Osten verschlechtert. Die Regulation nahm die Verpflichtungen der westlichen Teile zur Grundlage, schwächte sie ab, besonders was die Fron anbetraf. Die so einheitlich vorgeschriebene Pflicht zur Fron (ein Tag Spanndienst oder 2 Tage Handdienst pro Woche für einen Vollhof) hatte einen Umfang, der im großen Teil des Landes unbekannt gewesen war. Deshalb erfüllten die Bauern vielerorts diese Verpflichtungen nur dem Namen nach.

Wohl oder übel berührte des Patent das Bauern–Herren-Verhältnis auch in einem anderen Zusammenhang. Die Bauern hatten die Möglichkeit, über ihre Hufen hinaus weitere Böden benützen. Diese Grundstücke waren also rechtlich nicht urbariale sondern allodiale Länder, waren aber in Nutzung der Bauern. Diese Grundstücke konnten von den Grundherren zumindest prinzipiell ihren untertänigen Bauern entzogen und nach Belieben verwertet werden, wenn nur die Herrschaften den bestimmten Bedingungen dem bestehenden Recht entsprechend nachkamen. Das heißt, die Herren konnten nur dann über diese Felder verfügen, nachdem sie den Entgelt für den Fleiß, der in diesem bäuerlichen Besitz steckte, auch beglichen hatten. Damit sollte prinzipiell der Gegenwert der Arbeit erstattet werden, die die Bauern dazu aufgewendet hatten, um diese ursprünglich unbrauchbaren Flurstücke urbar zu machen. Zwei Typen dieser Felder waren allgemein bekannt: das Rodungsland und der Weinberg. Was die Weinberge betrifft, verfügte das Urbarialpatent über das Weinland von den Rodungen gesondert. Es war nämlich untersagt, den Bauern nach der Regulation den Besitz von Weinland kurzweg zu entziehen. Die Ackerländer wurden aber den Bauern in den kommenden Jahrzehnten Stufenweise entzogen.

Dieser so große Eingriff des Staates drängte die ungarische Agrarentwicklung in neue Bahnen. Josefs II. Leibeigenenverordnung von Jahre 1785 verbesserte die persönliche Freiheit des Bauern weiter, obwohl in Ungarn der Freizug im allgemeinen gesichert war, selbst bei den „ewigen Leibeigenen" (auf Grund von Komitatsverordnungen). Durch die freie Berufswahl der Bauern und andere Verordnungen wurde die feudale Abhängigkeit weiter gelockert. Den nächsten großen Eingriff in die Verhältnisse der Bauern bildeten die Gesetze von 1836, die die Abschaffung des Zehnten von der Brache erklärten und allgemein das bäuerliche Wirtschaften erleichterten.

Nach diesem großen staatlichen Eingriff ist es nicht verwunderlich, daß die große Konjunktur des 18.–19. Jahrhunderts keine wesentliche Verschiebung zugunsten der grundherrlichen Wirtschaft bringen konnte. Die napoleonischen Kriege brachten eine große Konjunktur der Getreidewirtschaft, so daß jetzt auch im Osten des Landes die Tendenzen der grundherrlichen Eigenbewirtschaftung stärker wurden, aber das konnte allenfalls bedeuten, daß es den Grundherren auch möglich war, die von der Urbarialregelung gesteckten Grenzen wirklich mit Fronarbeit ausfüllen zu können. Wesentliche Veränderungen traten also nicht ein, auch nicht durch die Wollkonjunktur der 1820–1840-er Jahren, die die grundherrliche Wirtschaft selbst auf Gebieten stärkte, die die Auswirkungen der Getreidekonjunktur nicht erreicht hatten. In diesen Gegenden vergrößerten die Grundherren die Zahl ihrer auf der Gemeinweide gehaltenen Tiere (Schafe), was nach der Befreiung von 1848 Folgen hatte, sonst aber geschah nichts.

Wichtige Veränderungen traten aber in anderer Hinsicht ein. Das Erscheinen der modernen Schafzucht, die Verbreitung der neuen, westlichen Schafrassen in den grundherrlichen Wirtschaften leiteten in diesen Betrieben die Anwendung neuer Verfahren ein, den Anbau von Futterpflanzen, das Erscheinen neuer Geräte und Maschinen. Da diese neuen Techniken und Technologien den Bauern fremd waren, waren die Gutsherren daran gezwungen, die Futterbauproduktion neuerer Pflanzen, durchgeführt mit neueren Geräten und Maschinen, in Eigenbetrieb zu nehmen, und auf den für diesen Zweck herausgebildeten Ackerfeldern Lohnarbeiter anzustellen. Damit begann die höhere Agrotechnik und Viehzuchtpraxis der Großbetriebe. Die Fachleute aus den am weitesten entwickelten Gutswirtschaften lernten die Technik und Technologien der besten westeuropäischen Wirtschaften kennen. Es setzte der Prozeß ein, als dessen Folge sich in der zweiten Hälfte des 19. Jahrhunderts grundherrliche (großbetriebliche) und bäuerliche Wirtschaft voneinander trennten, die bis zum Beginn des 19. Jahrhunderts die gleiche Technik und die gleichen Produktionsverfahren angewandt hatten.

Wie wir schon erwähnten, nahm die Baurerbefreiung von 1848 die Urbarialregelung zur Grundlage. Das damals allodiale Land bekamen im Verlaufe der Verfahren der folgenden Jahrzehnte die Adligen, das von den Bauern genutzte sogennante Urbarialland aber die Bauern. So erbte die das kapitalistische Zeitalter ansteuernde Bauernschaft das alte System. Fast die Hälfte der ungarischen Bauernschaft wurde ohne jedes Land frei, der größte Teil der anderen Hälfte hatte nicht einmal das zum Erhalt der Familie erforderliche Minimum. Nur eine dünne Schicht von Bauern hatte Betriebe, die die Bedürfnisse der Familie befriedigen konnten und sehr dünn war die Schicht der wohlhabenden Bauern.

Die Zahl der landlosen Bauern wurde noch durch den Umstand erhöht, daß alle Bauern, die sich früher (z.B. während der Kolonisation) auf allodialem Land niedergelassen, hier Dörfer gegründet hatten, jetzt den größten Teil ihres Bodens verloren, denn dieser war, in rechtlicher Hinsicht, grundherrliches Land. Im ganzen gesehen aber war die Bauernbefreiung für die Bauern nicht ohne Vorteil, denn ihre Wirtschaften waren nicht mit persönlichen Zahlungsverpflichtungen belastet, die Entschädigung der Grundherren übernahm der Staat. Das alles aber führt uns schon hinüber in die Problematik der Agrarentwicklung im Kapitalismus.

***

Die ungarische Agrarentwicklung vom 16. bis zum 19. Jahrhundert trägt also auch mehrere Entwicklungseigenheiten der ostelbischen Regionen an sich. Der Adel konnte seine Geldeinkünfte in der ersten Hälfte der Epoche nicht durch den Ausbau der Gutswirtschaften steigern, deshalb benutzte er zu diesem Zweck, genau wie in Rußland, seine Monopole. Als sich aber dafür die wirtschaftliche Möglichkeit bot, da griff der Staat bremsend ein. Zur Veranschaulichung der Rolle des Staates müssen wir hervorheben, daß die Agrarpolitik des Wiener Hofes im allgemeinen von den entwickelteren österreichischen und böhmisch–mährischen Verhältnissen bestimmt wurde, und das war für Ungarn günstig. Die städtische Entwicklung war in den Erblanden viel stärker, die Dichte des Stadtnetzes bot gute Möglichkeiten für die Mobilität der Bauern. Die auch in Ungarn zur Geltung kommende Agrarpolitik des Reiches vermittelte diese entwickelteren Verhältnisse nach Ungarn. So zeigte die Agrarentwicklung des Landes eher die österreichisch–böhmisch–mährischen (zum Teil bayerischen) Tendenzen, allerdings mit stärkerer Geltung der östlichen Elemente. Wir verstehen darunter in erster Linie den zunehmenden Druck der Grundherren auf die bäuerliche Wirtschaft, was sich — bei allem staatlichen Schutz der Bauern — bis 1848 durchsetzen konnte. Die Bürokratie des Komitats war in den Händen des örtlichen Adels, und das lieferte die Bauern in vieler Hinsicht den adligen Bestrebungen aus.

# VIII

# Hungarian Towns in the 18th and 19th Centuries (1687–1848)

As the history of Hungary and, of course, the special characteristics of the development of Hungarian towns are not so well known in Europe, I would like to tell you something about the earlier stages of urban development in Hungary, as a short introduction.*

When—at the turn of the 10th and the 11th century—the feudal Hungarian statehood was established, we had no towns in the sense that was used for municipalities at that age in Western Europe. It was the seat of the king and that of the archbishop and bishops and the significant feudal power centers that had the potential of later becoming towns. Though we are aware of the fact that towns were usually trade centers and later, in Western Europe, also the centers of industrial development, still, in this early stage of the history of Hungary, towns were rather administrational–military–clerical centers and only later and very slowly did they become economic centers.

As far as the legal system and the special social development is concerned, the history of Hungarian urban development is not different from the development in Central Europe. We can speak about a town (about an independent royal town, which is *liberae regiae civitatis* in Latin), after the municipality gets under the direct authority of the king and so becomes independent of feudal lords or of the church. After this step the municipality will get its own privileges. (I would like to remark that the first independent royal towns were the domains of the king.) It was a part of the urban life that the towns directly dependent on the king served as the administrational and jurisdictional bodies in the first degree, they could themselves elect their judge and administrational officials. The town, as a whole, had the same privileges as noblemen did, town dwellers were exempt from paying duty and stallage just like the noblemen. The town had its lands as a proprietor. They were entitled for some royal usufructs like the right to run pubs, butcheries or mills, the town itself could own estates the way, the noblemen did (though the individuals could have pieces of land only inside the town), but later they had to recognize the rule of the county authority. Towns had to participate in wars the same as noblemen did,

* Paper held on the 10th April 1993 in Giessen (Germany)

to protect themselves in the first place. Usually they built a stone wall around their settlement. Some towns had staple rights and in most cases they were allowed to hold markets. Except the tax for the king, the tax for the military and later the obligation to accommodate soldiers, no other national burden was placed on them. From the time when the system was based on the estates, towns formed the fourth estate. In the parliament they were represented by delegates.

In the 11th–13th century there were only a few independent royal towns. Some county seats and the seats of bishops were to become towns later on. Only from the middle of the 13th century can we speak about an intelligent town development policy of the king. Béla IV., after the Mongol invasion of Hungary (1241), raised a number of settlements to the level of independent royal towns, because after the experience of the Mongol invasion he wanted Hungary as many settlement surrounded by stone walls as possible. The starting struggle between the king and the aristocracy also played a role in forming the king's town development policy, as towns could provide him with massive material support. They became more and more important.

This urged the kings to support the immigration of foreigners, who came mainly from German territories. Kings helped these hospites (guests)—as they were called—to settle down in an organized way. Most of these people became town dwellers. The legal system the immigrants had in the towns which they had come from became the basis of laws in Hungarian towns as well. At earlier times it was the Magdeburg legal system that had the greatest influence on the laws of Hungarian towns, but from the 14th century on the legal system of Nürnberg became more and more dominant, but, of course, they were adapted with regard to the Hungarian special characteristics. After some time in Hungary we had our own legal systems, for example Buda, Selmecbánya, Nagyszeben, Szepes and Zágráb influenced the legal system of a number of towns, but the original basis was Magdeburg and Nürnberg.

In spite of all this development the network of towns in Hungary was not satisfactory. Towns were situated far from one another, and the number of these settlements was small compared to the inhabitants of Hungary. The situation did not change much, in spite of the fact that from the middle of the 14th century the development of towns was boosted by another factor, which was mineral resources (gold, silver and copper). The huge demand for these materials created a new type of towns: towns based on mining. As in other parts of Eastern Europe, it was the German miners who made it possible to exploit these minerals. The inhabitants of the towns settled with the help of the king were Germans, and the mining laws were of German origin as well. The towns based on mining in Northern Hungary and in Transylvania were exclusively settled by German miners. In the 14th–15th century Hungarian gold, silver and copper played an important role in Europe's economic life. This fact boosted the development of towns in Hungary—at least until the mines were completely exploited (and this was to be seen from the middle of the 16th century).

From the things mentioned above, it can be seen that the network of independent royal towns was very dense in the Middle Ages, those few were mainly situated in the Carpathian mountains. In the more central parts of the country there are hardly any towns. This situation will explain, that from the middle of the 14th century we can speak about a new phenomenon: villages under the authority of a nobleman became the places of trade and this is the starting point of their becoming a town. The economic basis for this phenomenon was the agricultural production, or rather, the perceptible growth of the agricultural export, from the middle of the 14th century. The most important goods for the agricultural export were live-stock and wine. The Hungarian cattle, raised on the huge pastures of the Great Hungarian Plain, became more and more demanded on the markets of the South-German and North-Italian towns. Traders had vast herds driven through the country, on different routes. The buying-up and collection of the cattle, as well as their shipping, postulated organized trade, together with stores and places for fodder, etc. The other important article for export was wine (mainly from the South, but from other regions, too, such as Western Hungary.) The transportation of both articles needed smaller trade-centres, where later other industrial services came to life (tubbers, smiths, tailors, shoe-makers, rope-makers, etc.) Some villages under nobleman authority were more suitable than others because of their geographical situation or for some other reasons, so in these places a new type of settlements started to develop, which was the peasant town. The name of these settlements refers to the fact that the inhabitants of the peasant towns remained serfs from the point of view. Peasant towns (or agrarian towns) were primarily the centers of long distance trade and industrial services. Landlords supported their development, because the inhabitants of these peasant towns paid their duties and services to their landlord at one time and in cash. These landlord "towns" had the right to have markets, and later on the landlord allowed them to elect their judge and administrational officials, which means they had self-government to a certain extent. They were entitled to distil brandy, to brew beer and to sell wine. Győr had staple right as well, but this was really exceptional, and I have to add, that between 1271–1273 Győr was an independent royal city. These town's dependency on the landlord certainly did remain.

Hungarian historians are still debating, whether the formation of these agricultural peasant towns contributed to the development of towns in general or, on the opposite, it hindered it. This question becomes really important if we take into consideration that by the end of the 15th century we know about 800 peasant towns, so their number is much higher than the number of independent royal towns, it is about ten times as much, and their economic strength was very significant, too. As some of these peasant towns under nobleman authority were on the way to gain the privilege of being an independent royal city from the king, in my opinion the development of peasant towns increased the number of settlements that had the potential to achieve the status of "real" towns and this could contribute to make the network of towns in the central and Southern parts more dense.

But in the 15th century the development of the peasant towns was blocked by the nobility and mainly by the wealthiest aristocrats. Because of the price revolution the economic situation of the noblemen became very unstable. Their income was devaluated, so they were forced to find new sources of income. From Hungary it was not possible to export wheat and corn like they did from the region East of the Elbe (it was not easy for ships to go upstream on the Danube), so they had to find other sources of income. Noblemen became more and more involved in the trade of livestock and wine (they sold the wine they got from the peasant as tithes), so they became strong competitors for peasant towns. From that time on, they began to restrict the trade activity of these towns and tried to set back their development. After the lobbying of the noblemen the parliament also accepted the idea of restrictions. It was not by chance that the leaders of a great peasant revolt in 1514 were the peasant towns. As a consequence of that after the downfall of the revolt the privileges of peasant towns were further restricted. In the 16th century the pressure from the nobility became so overwhelming that the king had to accept their proposal not to raise any more peasant towns into the status of independent royal township.

It was the Turkish occupation of Hungary that periodically prevented that peasant towns should get into an unbearable situation. Between 1541 and 1699 the central region of Hungary was a part of the Turkish empire. The Turkish rule helped the development of peasant towns. These settlements were placed under the direct rule of the sultan, so they had about the same privileged situation as the independent royal towns in Hungary. The sultan's rule contributed to their development. Most villages got under the authority of Turkish soldiers and got their revenues from the village dwellers. The landlord's authority ceased to exist. If there was a peasant town in the neighbourhood, most people from these villages preferred to seek rescue in the town. The lands of the villages increased the town's territory for pasture. Many agrarian towns were even surrounded by walls to protect the inhabitants from the raids of Turkish troops. And the landlords, who had been chased away by the Turks, were just too happy if the peasants visited them and gave them some symbolic gifts showing that they still recognize them as their landlords. From far away they could not restrict the rights and privileges of peasant towns any longer, what is more: they supported their development.

At the same time, the economic development of most of the independent royal towns stopped. The precious metal mines were exploited, and the output of the copper mines decreased, too. Beside the burgesses of the mining towns, in the 17th century, the number of the noblemen moving into towns, also increased. The burgesses also strove for getting the title of nobility. In the Royal Hungary, and partly, in Transylvania, too, some kind of a reagrarisation i.e. the process of becoming more agrarian once again could be observed. The wealthy burgesses bought the title of nobility, then they invested their money into lands, practically, they became noblemen. The wealthiest circles of towns became noblemen, and thus, they ceased to promote the development of their town. By the end of the 17th century, the earlier rate of the progress of Hungarian towns broke, and the economic role and importance of towns in the country's economic life gradually decreased. The nobility tried to take advantage of the opportunity, fearing that the monarch, during the country's liberation from under the Turkish oppression, could give the peasant towns the rights of an independent royal town, in the Parliament, in 1687, declared again: the monarch cannot increase the number of the independent royal towns.

In many respects, a new situation came to life after the expulsion of the Turks. The Habsburg monarchs accomplished an again well-perceivable town-policy. Their aim with the improvement of towns and the extending of the rights of an independent royal town to new settlements was not only to increase the revenues of the court, but also to influence the backward, one-sided social progress of the country properly. They hoped to restrict the power of the nobility with the help of a strong bourgeoisie. On the territories reconquered from the Turks, they immediately began to organize the administration of the considerable settlements. Earlier, there was also a conflict between the nobility and the monarch in the question of town-improvement, because, after the royal territories had run out, authorizing a settlement with the rights of an independent royal town meant, that that settlement fell out of the nobiliary ownership. On the other hand, the noblemen were not ready to disclaim their income from the peasant towns.

By the turn of the 17th and the 18th centuries, the power relations had changed. The nobility became weak, and though the struggle for independence (1703–1711), lead by Ferenc Rákóczi, confirmed the privileges of the Hungarian nobility, it broke their earlier power that surpassed that of the central government. In the battles between the nobility and the court, usually the latter was victorious. The situation was not quite the same in the case of the Church.

It was not a coincidence, that those cases, when a settlement was hindered to be established as an independent royal city, and to get the rights of a city, or, by chance, these rights were withdrawn from a particular settlement, happened mainly in the case of peasant towns owned by the Church. Eger, which got the rights of an independent royal city in 1697, and lost them already in 1699, was an episcopal seat, and also, for a long time, the bishop of Pécs hindered that the town could get the rights of an independent royal city.

Still, at the turn of the 17th and the 18th centuries, a new town-establishing movement could be witnessed. The towns got free from under the Turkish oppression, successfully renewed their rights as an independent royal city (Buda, Pest, Székesfehérvár in 1703, Szeged in 1719, etc.) during the decades after the liberation, and beside them, new settlements gained the rights of an independent royal city. Debrecen in 1693, Győr, Komárom, Zombor, Újvidék in 1751, Szabadka, Temesvár, Versec, Károlyváros in 1791. By the end of the 18th century, there were more than 60 independent royal cities in Hungary. Some settlements became independent royal towns but the parliament did not ratify this decision, like Pécs, Arad and Eszék. But these towns could practically make use of all the privileges that were usually provided for towns.

So in spite of all the efforts made by the noblemen to make development difficult for towns, some of the peasant towns became independent royal cities. So everything seemed to be all right, but the reality did not look so rosy at all. By the 18th century the development of Hungarian towns turned into a serious crisis, and the way out of this economic and social crisis proved to be the development of peasant towns.

The reason for this crisis was that Hungary's situation in the European economy had changed. The main characteristic of this was that the structure of the imported goods changed. While earlier, until the turn of the 16th and the 17th century, it was more valuable goods or luxury articles (valuable weapons, cloth, pieces of art, etc.) that were dominant in Hungary's imports, from the last third of the 16th century the importation of mass products increased to a large extent. These were goods that not only the more wealthier noblemen but also ordinary people could afford to buy. Especially after the end of the Turkish wars, which means during the 18th century the importation of these goods from Austrian, Czech and Southern-German territories increased in large proportions. These goods, which were of every day use, became competitors and very often insurmountable competitors for the Hungarian industrial production.

The Hungarian industrial production was several stages underdeveloped compared to the production in Central and Western Europe at the same time. During the 18th century in Western Europe besides guilds there were more and more manufactures, from the system where different parts of the production were carried out in different places, from the so-called Verlag-system through the different stages up to the formation of concentrated manufactures, the so-called 'fabrika-s'. The new organizational system resulted in the production of new types of goods, things that had been produced earlier under different circumstances, in different forms and in different quality. The leader of this technical development was the textile and clothing industry (the invention of cotton fabric was revolutionary in itself), but also some branches of the iron industry changed significantly. Besides these, in almost every industry the rapid technical–technological development took place.

In the 18th century and in the first half of the 19th century in Hungary, there was no manufactural development compared to Western Europe. The guild system was almost absolutely dominant in the 18th century and it was a very slow process that they lost their importance by the middle of the 19th century. Guilds were dominant not only in independent royal towns but from the 16th–17th centuries on also in peasant towns, what's more: also in some villages. So the guilds of tailors, shoe makers, boot makers, butchers, candle makers, etc. were almost exclusively dominant in the whole country. On the other hand domestic industry in villages was deeply underdeveloped by European standards, actually they were trying to provide goods for the family's own basic needs, at least in most parts of the country. There were some regions, though, where the shortage of lands or the lands of bad quality or the poor harvest forced the peasants to develop domestic industry in order to add to their revenues. So from the middle of the 18th century some regions became typical of producing certain goods, like regions where pottery, weaving or wool processing was more dominant. Still in the whole of the country the regions did not play a major economic role. It is typical that while in Central and Western Europe domestic industry could provide the textile industry with materials, in Hungary, when larger manufactures producing textile were started, it turned out that they did not have enough thread because the domestic industry in villages was just unable to produce the necessary quantities of this material.

In independent royal towns and also in peasant towns the social development was blocked or it was not on the right track. While earlier all the burgesses—or at least most of them—were allowed to participate in the town's self-government (primarily in the general assemblies), by the end of the 17th century this relatively democratic characteristic of the town's social political life became—step by step—rigid, and disappeared. In the course of the 18th century the general assemblies in towns lost the importance they had had before, and the administration of the towns practically got into the hands of the wealthiest families. The positions of the judge and the counsellors became life-long and later hereditary positions. A small, oligarchical elite ruled. The members of the so-called inner council and outer council (the first one was the bigger and the second one was the smaller in numbers) were elected for their lives, and very often these councils co-opted additional members from the wealthiest families.

It was not so much the less democratic government of towns or the oligarchical ruling that had harmful effects on the development of towns, but what accompanied this: the wealthiest families in the town became noblemen (by the end of the 17th century this was the case practically everywhere), their way of life, their life-strategies became similar to the nobility. So it was not so important any more that in the 17th–18th century noblemen moved to the towns in massive numbers any way. The fact that the ruling elite in a town gained nobility was enough in itself to block further development. Well-off burghers—after gaining the nobility—bought up pieces of land and they gave up their trade or industrial activities, which resulted in the aristocratic administrational ruling of towns. The elite became uninterested in further economic development.

Very similar phenomena can be seen in the economic and social life of those peasant towns, that—up to this point—had been the leaders of agrarian town development, and who had been getting closer and closer to a real urban—maybe not so from a legal point of view, but in reality. Primarily I am referring to the peasant towns in the Great Hungarian Plain with huge territories. These towns became relatively independent in the Turkish times, and they did not lose this independence after the occupation, either. But in these towns, too, the elites turned into an oligarchy small in number, and—at the same time the wealthiest families became noblemen. The outcome was very similar to that in independent royal towns: these settlements also became indifferent to the needs of further economic development.

The result has already been mentioned: the industrial development of Hungary was blocked at the level of the guild system. But there was something else that followed this process: the consuming goods flowing in from Central Europe gradually gained control of the Hungarian markets so the domestic industrial production had to find new markets, which was the East. Wallachia, Moldavia and the Balkan became the markets for Hungarian products, besides those in the Hungarian domestic market who were no so keen on the quality of goods.

Besides the fact that Hungarian industrial production gradually turned to Eastern markets, there is another important development that took place at that time: the focus of the economic life moved from Western parts of the country to the Great Hungarian Plain. Sopron and Pozsony ceased to be the most important trade centers. After the liberation of the whole country from the Turkish occupation, it was quite natural that Pest became an important trading center once again. But as the population was growing and immigrants were coming constantly from Germany, in territories that people had abandoned because of the Turkish occupation, the growth of the population grew rapidly in 3–4 decades. This in itself resulted in moving the focus of the economic life—at least to a certain extent. The exportation of goods to Eastern markets also contributed to the process. As a result of that Kolozsvár became an important trade center and—in general—industrial population and the number of towns increased rapidly in the central and Eastern parts of the country. However, this growth—as I have mentioned already—did not mean the modernisation of industrial development in Hungary.

Under these circumstances, when there was no group among the burgesses or the wealthier peasants of the peasant towns, or among craftsmen and merchants, which could have been the leader force of the industrial development in Hungary, the only initiative, in the 18th century, came from the court. On the court's initiative, new manufactures came to being in the centre of some crown-estates, or in favourable places as far as natural conditions were concerned. But these early manufactures after some years' or decades' existence ceased to work during the first half of the 18th century. Those, that were established in the second half of the 18th century proved to be more long-lasting, but by that time not only the treasury but also some members of the aristocracy had established manufactures on the territory of their large estates. They usually used the socage service for unskilled work, while for jobs where some skills were necessary they employed wage-labourers from abroad or even from other parts of Hungary. They employed personnel for the manufactures mainly from abroad. These manufactures established by the treasury and landowners formed some kind of an industrial basis but not in the towns, rather in the centre of large estates owned by noblemen. These manufactures established in the second half of the 18th century were much more long-lasting than their forerunners. Some of them could survive until 1848 and even during the period of the modern industrial development in Hungary. But their importance was not considerable, their role during the industrial development could not become significant.

From all this we can see clearly the crisis of the Hungarian town-development in the 18th century: on the one hand, the development of the traditional and the royal independent towns came to a standstill, their character faded, and on the other hand, the number of inhabitants in peasant towns rapidly increased, though without giving a chance for some kind of a qualitative change. In peasant towns service industry became dominant working in the framework of the traditional guild-system. The manufactural development, from which the modern industry could have developed later, could not be realized. Neither the treasury manufactures, nor the ones belonging to the wealthiest landowners could help the industrial development, mainly because they could not find a suitable partner in the venturesome social layers in the towns and the peasant towns. These venturesome social layers themselves were missing in the 18th century because the wealthier circles of towns and peasant towns getting the title of nobility abandoned business life. That is why there was a necessary division within the industrial development as well: when the conditions of the modern industrial development took shape industry was established not by towns or peasant towns, the population of which was rapidly growing in the 18th century, but by new social elements which had no or hardly any rights, and were on the periphery of the traditional feudal society.

The village and countryside could not be the basis for modern industrial development, either. To use a British term, the so-called "Rural Industry" could not start developing because it was contradicted by the traditions in the domestic industry and by the fact that hardly any of its products got into the money–goods circulation, which means their products were not taken to the market, they were restricted to the families' own consumption. This happened in almost every cases, only very few products here and there could get to the market. There were some other factors, which hindered the development, even to a greater extent than the one mentioned above: this is the perpetual serfdom that had its serious effects on almost every aspect of Hungary's life. We use the term "perpetual serfdom" despite the fact that—at least theoretically—most peasants were allowed to leave their landlord after they paid all the taxes and duties they were obliged to. The reforms of Joseph II. (1780–1790) on serfdom loosened the system up so much that the rights to move freely to another place and to choose one's profession were granted for the peasants. So in theory they all had these rights, but it seldom worked in reality, especially if someone wanted to move to a town. (To move from one landlord to another was more possible.)

The question of perpetual serfdom was interesting not so much from the peasants' point of view, but for those who started or could have started modern industrial production. In towns the situation became worse for them, as the leadership of these settlements supported the guilds. But they could not move to the villages, either, because the fact that those who were not noblemen could not own pieces of land made it practically impossible. Those who were not noblemen were not allowed to buy a piece of land to start a manufacture or so other industrial activity. They could of course get hold of lands that were used by serfs, but this was not ownership. Besides heavy burdens like socage, taxes for the landlord and for the king were attributed to these lands. But even more embarrassing was the fact these land were under the jurisdiction of manor courts, so there was no way to solve their legal disputes in a normal way. All these factors resulted in the situation that buying pieces of land used by peasants proved to be no solution to their problem.

Still from the last decades of the 18th century there were individuals who, realizing the growing social needs, would have been willing to start industrial enterprises. In the countryside—as we have seen this—practically there was no way to this, because of the pressure of guilds and the system of perpetual serfdom. To a certain extent their situation was easier in towns, primarily in those settlements that really had the privileges of a town, because privileges provided by the king could give the exemption against the guilds, and from the 1830s the legal conditions improved, too. In 1840 there was a law guaranteeing the right to set up a "factory". So in the first half of the 19th century enterprises could practically count on the political support of the central government. The result of this support was that though the traditional society of town-dwellers did not show much interest in starting modern industrial activity, but the leadership of these towns at least did not prevent starting the enterprises of those, who were more inclined for this. Especially from the 1830s there were more and more professionals from abroad (Swiss, Austrian, Czech and Bavarian entrepreneurs) who were willing to help at the birth of modern trade in Hungary. Besides there were many Jewish people with deep roots in the Hungarian society who accumulated their wealth here as craftsmen or merchants. These were the two factors that took part in the formation of the industrial production in Hungary.

Their chances in the countryside were rather limited. On the lands of some aristocrats they could start such activities but as I have just said, their chances were limited. There were only the outskirts for them. These were the real basis for the modern Hungarian industry. They could establish their workshops in the outskirts of Pest, Óbuda, Miskolc, Pozsony, Kassa and other independent royal cities. City councils gave them the appropriate permissions, so such industrial activities were not restricted by them. In the first half of the 19th century these elements formed the core, from which the modern Hungarian industrial development could take shape, after the start of the industrial revolution in the second half of the century.

And that was all. The proportion of town-inhabitants within the whole population practically did not change between the census in 1784/87 and 1870, and the percentage of the industrial population was insignificant. There were 124 manufactures in 1785 with 9395 workers. In 1840 there were 545 manufactures (and fabrika's) with 23400 workers. The rate of this number's growth was the same as the growth of the population, maybe just a little bit higher. Some kind of labour-division could be observed: the manufactures that needed a lot of mechanical energy were mainly established on the large estates of the aristocracy (glass works, paper mills, forging mills), while the textile works were established in towns and were the property of the bourgeoisie. (These workshops obtained the necessary raw material from abroad or they themselves established spinning workshops outside Hungary.)

This was only the beginning in the first half of the 19th century. The lack of town-development in Hungary meant that until the 1870s the number of town-habitants hardly changed (except for Pest) and the traditional structure of towns did not change either. The conditions, under which the network of Hungarian towns could change, developed in the last third of the 19th century. But it postulated the development of the railway-system, a new transportation-system, and the integration into the whole European economy through the railway. Only when these conditions were in place, could the town-development in Hungary change entirely, and step into a new era as a result of modern industrialization. The realization of the modern network of towns in Hungary is not the issue of this lecture. But I have to note that the turn in the Hungarian town-development began not in the first third of the 19th century, as it was the case in Western and Central Europe, but only in the last third of the century. The census in 1870 still reflected the existence of the traditional network of towns. The rapid transformation was beginning only at that time.

# IX

## HUNGERSNÖTE UND AGRARAUSFUHR IM SPÄTMITTELALTERLICHEN UNGARN (1700–1848)

Im Zuge der Untersuchung der so eigenartigen Erscheinungen der spätmitellalterlichen Hungersnot unterscheidet die Forschung zwischen den Hungersnöten infolge natürlicher und anderer, plötzlich entstandenen Katastrophen (Kriege, Seuchen usw.), und der in den entwickelten westeuropäischen Ländern in der Anfangsphase der Industrierevolution unter der auf einmal angeschwollenen städtischen Bevölkerung wahrnehmbaren, etwa ein Jahrhundert hindurch auftretenden chronischer Unterernährung, die an manchen Stellen genau solche Verheerung anrichtete, wie die Hungersnot nach den natürlichen Katastrophen. Die Auflösung des Gleichgewichts zwischen der Bevölkerung und den Möglichkeiten der Lebensmittelproduktion war meistens die Folge plötzlich entsandener natürlicher Katastrophen (Dürre, Frostschäden usw.), und die verursachte Hungersnot war zumindest dermaßen Folge des Produktionsausfalls, als dessen, daß die Lieferung der Massenlebensmittel (Getreidesorten) auf dem gegebenen technischen Niveau auf kontinentalem Wege nicht gelöst wurde. Das ist der Grund dafür, daß die größeren Hungersnöte immer auf solchen Teilen des europäischen Kontinents aufgetreten sind, die von den Möglichkeiten der Beförderung auf See-, im allgemeinen Wasserwege weit gefallen sind, und so zum Großteil auf ihre eigene Produktion angewiesen waren. In der Lebensmittelversorgung der zu den Meeren nahe liegenden, oder von dort leicht zu erreichenden Gebiete spielte die Beförderung auf Seewege sowieso eine große Bedeutung, so stellte die Hungersnot auf diesen Gebieten im 18. Jahrhundert nicht mehr ein technisches, sondern in erster Linie ein gesellschaftliches Problem dar. In Zeiten nämlich, als infolge der schlechten Ernte die Lebensmittelpreise gestiegen sind, konnten die niedrigsten Schichten nicht einmal die zum Lebensunterhalt notwendigen Lebensmittel kaufen. Auf ähnliche Weise soll die in den Städten mit angeschwollener Bevölkerung zu verzeichnende chronische Unterernährung im Kreise der ärmsten Tagelöhnerschichten als gesellschaftliches Problem behandelt werden, das die Entfaltung der Industrierevolution ganz bis zur Mitte des 19. Jahrhunderts begleitete.

Im Vergleich zu den entwickelten Ländern Europas im 18.—19. Jahrhundert hört man in Ungarn relativ selten über Hungersnöte. Der Grund dafür ist sehr einfach: in diesen Jahrhunderten war in Ungarn die Volksdichte noch sehr niedrig, so konnte nicht einmal eine in einer größeren Region auftretende Hungersnot größere Volksmassen betreffen. Infolge der niedrigen Volksdichte, sowie der unentwickelten wirtschaftlichen und gesellschaftlichen Verhältnisse bleibt auch die städtische Entwicklung stark zurück. In Ungarn war weder die Zahl der Städte, noch die Bevölkerung so groß (auch nicht im Vergleich zur Zahl der Gesamtbevölkerung), wie in Westeuropa. Eine Großstadt gab es im damaligen westeuropäischen Sinne des Wortes gar nicht, und auch der überwiegende Teil der Bevölkerung der vorhandenen Städte war in der Lebensmittelproduktion selbstversorgend, d. h. er stellte die Mehrheit der für sie notwendigen Lebensmittel selbst her. Die Industrierevolution war noch weit weg, so konnten solche Großstädte, deren Bevölkerung von ferneren Gegenden hätte mit Lebensmittel versorgt werden sollen, nicht entstehen. Es wurden also die gesellschaftlichen und Produktionsumstände noch nicht geschaffen, unter denen die Grundlagen der größere Massen betreffenden Hungersnöte hätten entstehen können.

Im Gegenteil, Ungarn lieferte sogar in den Jahrhunderten des Spätfeudalismus Lebensmittel in großer Menge nach Mittel- und Westeuropa. Vor allem soll hier die Rinderausfuhr erwähnt werden. Früher verließen regelmäßig jährlich 70—100 Tausend Rinder das Land und wurden auf die Märkte der Städte Österreichs, Böhmens, Süddeutschlands, Norditaliens oder Elsasses befördert. Ebenfalls bedeutend war die Weinausfuhr, vor allem unmittelbar nach dem benachbarten Österreich, Böhmen und Polen. Getreide wurde um diese Zeit nur noch unmittelbar vom westlichen Grenzgebiet des Landes in die österreichische Städte geliefert, die noch in greifbarer Nähe gelegen sind.

Im Laufe des 18. Jahrhunderts hat sich auf dem Gebiet der Lebensmittelausfuhr eine neue Situation ergeben. Infolge der Beschleunigung des Baus der Landstraßen, im allgemeinen der Verbesserung der Straßenverhältnisse wurde es möglich, daß von gewissen Gebieten Ungarns, die zu den österreichischen und südböhmischen Märkten nahe gelegen sind, der Getreideexport nach diesen Gebieten eingeleitet wird. Es handelt sich praktisch um den Landstreifen zwischen dem Balaton und der Donau, sowie der Donau und den Kleinen Karpaten. Von Mitte des Jahrhunderts an sind auf diesem Gebiet getreideproduzierende Gutswirtschaften entstanden, und dieses Gebiet wurde im allgemeinen die landwirtschaftlich entwickelteste Region des Landes. Von hier aus, sowie im Laufe der Zeiten südlich von diesem Streifen, auf allen Gebieten, von wo die Donau auf dem Fuhrwerk erreicht werden konnte, wurde die Produktion des Warengetreides, vor allem auf Export, nach Österreich und Böhmen begonnen.

Es genügt vielleicht ein Blick auf die wichtigsten Angaben, um die Menge der Ausfuhr ermessen zu können. Nur zwischen 1733—1752 und 1767—1786, und dann 1815—1845 kennen wir die entsprechend bewertbaren Daten der Zölle. Auf Grund dieser Fakten wurden gegen Mitte des 18. Jahrhunderts jährlich regelmäßig etwa 55 000 Rinder und 22 000 Schweine ausgeführt. In den Jahren zwischen 1767—1786 kam es zum Export von durchschnittlich 95 000 Rindern und etwa 70—72 000 Tonnen Getreide (vor allem Gemengkorn und Roggen, sowie Hafer, in kleinerer Menge Weizen und Gerste).[1] Die Tendenz kann darin abgezeichnet werden, daß solange einerseits wegen dem Aufbruch der Weiden, andererseits der Erhöhung des inneren Verbrauchs die Menge der Rinderausfuhr abgenommen, die Ausfuhr der Getreidesorten regelmäßig und kontinuierlich zugenommen hat, aber nicht einmal Mitte des 19. Jahrhunderts den Wert der Rinderausfuhr überstiegen hat. In den 40er Jahren

[1] Die Zolleinnahmendaten bezüglich der Ausfuhr werden zusammenfassend bewertet in: *I. Wellmann:* A magyar mezőgazdaság a XVIII. században (Die ungarische Landwirtschaft im 18. Jahrhundert). Budapest. 1979. S. 81—85.

des 19. Jahrhunderts machte die Getreideausfuhr im Jahresdurchschnitt etwa 100 000 Tonnen aus. Die Möglichkeiten wären viel größer gewesen, denn wir wissen davon, daß sogar auf Gebieten, von wo bereits regelmäßig Getreide ausgeführt wurde, in vielen Gutswirtschaften Reserven für 6—8 Jahre angehäuft wurden, die dann verfaulten.[2]

Natürlich gab es auch in Ungarn Hungersnöte im Laufe des 18.—19. Jahrhunderts. Die Gründe waren ähnlich, wie wir auch im Zuge der westeuropäischen Hungersnöte kennenlernen konnten. Lassen Sie uns diese nacheinander aufzählen.

Es sind vor allem die langen *Kriege*, infolge deren wirklich auf ganzen Landesteilen Hungersnot entstanden ist. Es handelt sich im wesentlichen um die Erscheinung, die auch die europäische Geschichte kennt, und deren eklatantestes Beispiel vielleicht der Feldzug von Napoleon im Jahre 1812 nach Rußland gewesen ist. Im Laufe der Feldzüge soll je eine Region außer der dort seßhaften normalen Bevölkerung regelmäßig, längere Zeit hindurch eine bedeutende Armee versorgen, und es bedeutete — nicht zuletzt wegen den in den Armeen im allgemeinen höheren Verbrauchsnormen, als in der Bevölkerung — für das jeweilige Gebiet unlösbare Aufgabe. In einem solchen Fall hat entweder die Bevölkerung nicht genügend Lebensmittel, oder die Heere sterben Hungers. Infolge der Kräfterverhältnisse liegt die Lösung an der Hand, die durchziehenden Armeen zehren die Lebensmittelreserven des betroffenen Gebietes, oft auch das Saatgut auf, und das Schicksal der Zivilbevölkerung ist unvermeidlich die Hungersnot. Glücklicherweise enthielt die Geschichte Ungarns in der behandelten Periode nicht sehr viele Kriege solchen Ausmaßes, welche ähnliche Folgen gehabt hätten, aber auch von deren Mangel kann keine Rede sein. Wir verweisen auf zwei solche Perioden, als in Ungarn die Hungersnot wegen den Kriegen vorgekommen ist. Zwischen 1683—1699, als die Austreibung der Türken aus dem Gebiet des Landes vor sich gegangen ist, folgten die Zeichen der Hungersnot und Hungerstodes unvermeidlich dem Befreiungskrieg. Besonders in der zweiten Hälfte des Krieges, nach den Feldzügen auf den südlichen Teilen des Landes gab es Hungersnöte, die ganze Komitate, und sogar auf einmal das Gebiet mehrerer Komitate betroffen haben. Eine andere solche Kriegsperiode war der Rákóczi-Aufstand (1703—1711). Wegen der Kriegsführung der beiden Seiten beuteten weniger die Feldheere die einzelnen Gebiete aus, viel eher verursachte Hungersnot die Zerstörung, welche die Kriegspartner der Bevölkerung und den Produktionskräften zugefügt haben.

Die Kriege hatten auch eine andere, indirekte Wirkung zur Folge, die wir ebenfalls berühren sollen, wenn wir die Zusammenhänge des Krieges und der Hungersnot in Ungarn berühren. Es handelt sich um den Fall, als zwar der Krieg nicht unmittelbar auf dem Gebiet des Landes geführt wurde, hier also keine direkten Schäden verursacht hat, die Kriegskonjunktur jedoch auch im Falle einer bereits mittelmäßigen Ernte die Lebensmittelpreise so in die Höhe geschraubt hat, daß auf Gebieten, wo die Bevölkerung ihren Le-

[2] Die Ausfurangaben bezüglich der ersten Hälfte des 19. Jahrhunderts werden zusammengefaßt in: *Gy. Mérei:* A magyar királyság külkereskedelmi piacviszonyai 1790—1848 között (Die außenwirtschaftlichen Marktverhältnisse des ungarischen Königreiches zwischen 1790—1848). Századok. 1961. S. 502.

bensmittelbedarf nicht selbst bedecken konnte, sondern aus anderen Gebieten auf Einfuhr angewiesen war, die ärmsten Schichten in diesen Jahren die notwendigen Lebensmittel nicht kaufen konnten. Zu diesen gehören die Komitate Oberungarns, die das Getreide von der Ungarischen Tiefebene beschaffen haben, sowie ein Teil Kroatiens und Slawoniens. Und wenn es für die ungarischen Verhältnisse gilt, daß die Funktion der Jagd und des Fischfanges wesentlich größer war in der Lebensmittelversorgung, als der europäische Durchschnitt, stimmte es nicht mehr für diese Gebiete. Auf den bewaldeten Gebieten Transdanubiens spielte die Jagd (und das Weiden im Wald), auf der Tiefebene der Fischfang (wir sollen nicht vergessen: es war noch das Land vor der Flußregulierungen und Abzapfung!) so große Rolle, daß die ausgebliebene Getreideproduktion kompensiert werden konnte, auf den bezeichneten Gebieten war es aber bereits unmöglich. Auch in diesen Fällen begegnen wir dem gesellschaftlichen Phänomen der Hungersnot (d. h., eine Schicht der Bevölkerung konnte die hohen Lebensmittelpreise nicht bezahlen). So war es 1757, aber vor allem 1788—89.

Im Laufe des 18.—19. Jahrhunderts meldete sich ab und zu auch die andere Form der Hungersnot, als wegen den *Launen der Natur* serienweise schlechte Jahre in der Landwirtschaft erfolgten. Aber auch diese führten nur in manchen kleineren Regionen des Landes zu wahren Hungersnöten, an solchen Stellen, wo die Zahl der Bevölkerung bereits das Niveau der örtlichen landwirtschaftlichen Produktion übertroffen hat und regelmäßig auf Einfuhr innerhalb des Landes angewiesen war. Wenn in solchen Jahren auch in den Regionen, welche diese Gebiete unmittelbar versorgten, schlechte Ernte vorgekommen ist, konnten diese Gebiete von dort nicht versorgt werden, und umsonst stapelten sich infolge der Unfähigkeit der Beförderung auf anderen, ferneren Gebieten des Landes Reserven in für Jahre ausreichender Menge auf, konnten diese nicht mobilisiert, da ja nicht an Ort und Stelle befördert werden können. So kam es besonders in der nordöstlichen Region des Landes (in den Komitaten Máramaros, Ung, Ugocsa, Bereg) und in den bergigen Gegenden Siebensbürgens regelmäßig zu solchen Situationen. Auf diesen Gebieten ist das Getreide nicht in größerer Menge gewachsen, die Bauern kauften deshalb Getreide von der Tiefebene ein. Als aber die Ernte in der versorgenden Region schlecht gewesen ist, und sich diese schlechte Ernte 2—3 Jahre lang wiederholte, ist die Hungersnot im dritten Jahr unvermeidlich angebrochen. So war es auch z. B. 1786—1789, als die Bevölkerung u. a. die Rinde der Bäume zum Mehl gemahlen hat. In diesen Jahren begegnen wir hier regelmäßig den Fällen des Hungerstodes.

In den Regionen, die zur Selbstversorgung nicht imstande waren, konnte die Hungersnot auch aus anderen Gründen eintreten. 1831 ist es auf den von Cholera betroffenen oberungarischen Gebieten geschehen, die durch die Behörden wegen der Seuche abgesperrt wurden, und dadurch wurde die Einfuhr des notwendigen Getreides in die Gegend verhindert. Die Folge war ein blutiger Aufstand, in dessen Ausbruch die Hungersnot (und der Glaube, daß die Behörden die Bevölkerung zur Hungerstod verurteilt haben) bedeutende Rolle spielte. Im allgemeinen auf den Umstand, wie ungleichmäßig die Versorgung des Landes z. B. vom Getreide gewesen ist, verweist die Tatsache, daß in den Preisen sehr große, manchmal direkt zehnfache Unterschiede zu verzeichnen sind. Die Ungelöstheit der Beförderung führte auch zur eigenartigen Situation, daß während in der nördlichen und östlichen Regionen des

Landes manchmal Hungersnot tobte, ging von den westlichen Gebieten der Export im gleichen Maße vor sich, als in anderen Jahren. Auf den westlichen Gebieten, von wo das Getreide regelmäßig exportiert wurde, waren die Preise wesentlich höher, als auf den Gebieten der Tiefebene, wo das Getreide überhaupt keinen Markt hatte, oder nur den örtlichen Verbrauch deckte, und wo die Preise niedrig waren. Hier knüpften sich jedoch weite Schichten der Bevölkerung der Warenproduktion und Geldwirtschaft noch kaum an, d. h. sie hatten kein Geld, das Getreide zu kaufen, als die Ernten chronisch schlecht gewesen sind. So kam die Hungersnot zustande. Glücklicherweise spielte das Fleisch ünd der Fischfang, die Jagd infolge des wirtschaftlichen Rückstandes des Landes in der Ernährung eine wesentlich größere Rolle, als in Westeuropa, und es bremste die Auswirkungen der Hungersnot, verhinderte die massenweise Verhungerung. Zu solchen großangelegten Hungersnöten, wie sie in den bezeichneten Fällen dargestellt wurden, ist es relativ selten gekommen.

An besonderer Stelle sollen die Verluste erwähnt werden, welche die Viehzucht, vor allem die in der Ernährung grundlegende Rolle spielende Rinderzucht betroffen haben. Hier fügten vor allem die *Tierseuchen* sehr große Schäden zu, die Verluste konnten aber durch die Einfuhr aus dem Osten relativ schnell ersetzt werden (dadurch tauchten übrigens im Lande die Rinderpest und andere Infektionskrankheiten auf). Manchmal beschränkte die Dürre dermaßen die Möglichkeiten des Weidens, daß dies zur Reduzierung des Rinderbestandes führte. All dies hat sich aber — von einigen Ausnahmen abgesehen — im allgemeinen dann gemeldet, als die Getreideproduktion relativ gut war, und zur Entstehung der Hungersnöte nur beigetragen, sie aber nicht hervorgerufen hat.

Die Forschungen der letzten Jahre haben auch ein solches Symptom der Hungersnot erschlossen, auf welches die ungarischen Forscher früher nicht aufmerksam geworden sind. Vor allem im Zuge demographischer Forschungen wurde in die Wirkung der chronischen Unterernährung auf die Fruchtbarkeit, bzw. auf die Zyklizität der Fruchtbarkeit,[3] bzw. auf deren Zusammenhänge mit der beträchtlichen Sterblichkeit infolge der Seuchen Licht geworfen. Bereits am Ende des 18. Jahrhunderts hat das unlängst aufgestellte Korps der Amtsärzte (Physikusse) letzteres deutlich erkannt, worauf auch die zeitgenössischen Akten hinweisen.[4] Es war offensichtlich kein zufälliges Phänomen, daß gleichzeitig mit den Hungersnöten die verschiedenen Seuchen der Zeit, vor allem in den von der Hungersnot heimgesuchten Regionen, viele Opfer genommen haben. Was die Wirkungen der chronischen Unterernährung auf die Fruchtbarkeit anbelangt, diese scheint dann die Analyse der Empfängnisperioden besser erforschen zu können.

Die Untersuchung der spätmittelalterlichen Hungersnöte wird durch den Umstand sehr erschwert, daß es keine solchen Quellen zur Verfügung stehen, die deren Ausmaße, Gründe eindeutig definieren würden. Bis zu den 1780er

[3] In dieser Hinsicht sind die jüngsten Ergebnisse von *Zoltán Kováts* sehr interessant. So zuletzt seine Abhandlung über die Gestaltung der Bevölkerung von Debrecen im Band „Debrecen története 2. 1693—1849" (Die Geschichte Debrecens 2. 1693—1849). Red. von István Rácz Debrecen. 1981. S. 15—69.

[4] Darauf hat bereits Henrik Marczali in seiner Monographie über Ungarn in der Zeit Josephs II. hingewiesen. *H. Marczali:* Magyarország története II. József korában (Die Geschichte Ungarns in der Zeit Josephs des Zweiten). Bd. III. Budapest. 1888. S. 396—399. Marczali zitiert eine Anweisung Josephs II. im Laufe des Kampfes gegen die Hungersnot, woraus es hervorgeht. daß auch der Kaiser darüber im klaren war, daß die Seuche unter den vom Hunger abgeschwächten Menschen bald ausbricht.

Jahren gab es regelmäßig Hinweise auf die Hungersnot, so verfügen wir bezüglich des 17. und. 18. Jahrhunderts über Angaben, daß Hungersnöte 1611 in Westungarn und Siebenbürgen, 1621 in Oberungarn, 1622 in Siebenbürgen und Oberungarn, 1629 in Slawonien, 1652 und 1653, dann 1654 auf verschiedenen Teilen des Landes, 1677 in Oberungarn, 1685 in Siebenbürgen, 1687 in Oberungarn, 1691 in Siebenbürgen, 1697 in Siebenbürgen, 1698 in Oberungarn, 1703 zwischen der Donau und der Theiß, zwischen 1717—1719 in Siebenbürgen, 1726 in Siebenbürgen, 1727 in Oberungarn und Siebenbürgen, 1731 in Siebenbürgen, 1740 in Siebenbürgen, 1757 in ganz Ungarn, 1777 in Südungarn vorgekommen sind, ab und zu und hie und da gab es auch massenweise Verhungerungen. Diese Daten sind aber sporadisch, bewegen sich in Allgemeinheiten, und ermöglichen nicht auch die Ausmaße der Hungersnot kennenzulernen. Ein Teil der Aufzeichnungen ist subjektiven Charakters und enthält an manchen Stellen vielleicht auch Übertreibungen.[5]

Erst von den 1780er Jahren an haben wir die Möglichkeit, die Lage regelmäßig zu ermessen. Der Absolutismus von Joseph II. versuchte nämlich gegen die Hungersnot aufzutreten und der Verhungerung sogar durch die Nutzbarmachung der Getreidereserven der militärischen Magazine vorzubeugen. So können wir die Hungersnot von der Regierungszeit Josephs II. an besser verfolgen. Joseph II. erließ bereits 1770—1771 in Böhmen Maßnahmen für die Verhinderung der Hungersnot und sammelte 1773 auch im Banat ernsthafte Erfahrungen. Vom Beginn seiner Regierungszeit an hat er die Lage beobachtet und angestrebt, rechtzeitig die Initiative ergreifen zu können. So ließ er 1782 ein Ausfuhrverbot in Kraft treten,[6] damit das Getreide im Land bleibt, denn auf der Tiefebene war eine schlechte Ernte zu erwarten. Die erste ernsthaftere Kraftprobe mußte er 1785 bestehen, als wegen der schlechten Ernte sowohl in Nordostungarn wie in Siebenbürgen Hungersnot ausgebrochen ist, die auch dadurch gesteigert wurde, daß die Ernte auch in Galizien schlecht gewesen ist, so konnte in die nordöstlichen ungarischen Komitate auch von dort kein Getreide eingeführt werden. Die Hungersnot war in den Komitaten Máramaros, Ugocsa und Ung am größten. dazu kam auch eine Infektion. die vermutlich durch den Verbrauch des unreifen Maises hervorgerufen wurde. Auch die Eröffnung der militärischen Magazine konnte die massenweise Verhungerung nicht verhindern. zeitgenössische offizielle Meldungen schätzen die Zahl der Verhungerten auf über 14 Tausend Menschen, etwa 8,5% der Bauernbevölkerung der drei Komitate.[7] Auch die Regierung hat erkannt, daß die Hilfe nicht nur an der Eröffnung der Getreidespeicher, sondern auch der schnellen Möglichkeit der Übermittlung gelegen ist. So wurde 1786—87 nur für die Hälfte der zur Unterstützung der Notstandsgegenden zugewandten 687 Tausend Forint Getriede gekauft, 135 Tausend machte das Bedürfnis der Beförderung und Mahlens aus, während die gleiche Summe für Straßenbau ausgegeben wurde.[8] Dennoch gab es auch 1786 und

[5] Zu den Daten s. *A. Rethly:* Idójarasi esemenyek és elemi esapások Magyarorszagon 1701–1800–ig (Meteorologische Ereignisse und elementare Schläge in Ungar von 1701 bis 1800). Budapest, 1970. Auf Grund der sehr sorgfältigen Datensammlung des Meteorologen Rethly können wir ein ziemlich genaues Bild sowohl bezüglich des ganzen Landes als der einzelnen Regionen gewinnen. Hier haben wir nur die Angaben Bezüglich der größeren Gebiete des Landes hervorgehoben.

[6] S. *Marczali* z. Werk.

[7] Ebenda.

[8] Ebenda.

1787 Zeichen für die Hungersnot, vor allem in Siebenbürgen, unter der rumänischen Bevölkerung der öden Berglandschaften. 1787 trat auch im Südland großer Lebensmittelmangel auf, der durch die Eröffnung der militärischen Lagerhäuser gelindert wurde.

Als dann Joseph II. Ende 1787 im russischen Bündnis der Türkei den Krieg erklärt hat, mußten auch die Bedürfnisse der im Südland stationierenden Armee durch diese Gegend befriedigt werden. 1788 und 1789 konnte der Kaiser die begonnenen Hilfsaktionen nicht mehr fortsetzen, denn die Armee beanspruchte sowohl das Geld wie das Getreide. Die außerordentlich schlechte Ernte im Jahre 1789 stellte jedoch den Herrscher vor einen Scheideweg: entweder verzichtet er auf das Feldheer, oder es wird seine finanzielle Lage erschüttert. Diese Lage trug im bedeutenden Maße zum Zusammenbruch des Systems von Joseph II. bei. Die Staatsorgane erwiesen sich in dem Maße als unfähig, daß sie nunmehr die Buchel der Bevölkerung in den nordöstlichen Teilen empfohlen haben. Der Servilismus der zeitgenössischen Wissenschaft läßt sie durch die Tatsachen zeigen, daß die Pester Universität diese Möglichkeit für vorstellbar gehalten hat — der Kaiser hingegen nicht.

Von der schlechten Ernte im Jahre *1789* haben wir im großen und ganzen ein *Landesbild*. Der Herrscher, der sich von der Lage informieren ließ, wies die königlichen Kommissare an, die Erntesituation zumindest in groben Zügen darzustellen. So wissen wir, wenn auch nicht vom ganzen Lande, aber etwa 10 000 Gemeinden, ob die Ernte gut, mittelmäßig oder schlecht gewesen ist. Die Ernte war:

| | gut | mittel | schlecht in | |
|---|---|---|---|---|
| Weizen | 417 | 2968 | 5271 | |
| Roggen | 703 | 4376 | 4731 | |
| Sommerweizen | 54 | 745 | 2234 | |
| Gerste | 685 | 3059 | 4787 | |
| Hafer | 710 | 4043 | 5236 | |
| Mais | 1204 | 2589 | 3432 | |
| Buchweizen, Erbse, Linse usw. | 748 | 2308 | 3846 | |
| Hirse | 196 | 810 | 1597 | |
| Heu | 698 | 3297 | 5669 | Gemeinden.[9] |

Von den wichtigeren Produkten war also in diesem Jahr in allen Fällen in mehr als der Hälfte der Gemeinden die Ernte ausgesprochen schlecht. Nur die aus früheren Jahren reservierten Produkte haben es ermöglicht, daß die Hungersnot sich nur auf die nordostungarischen Komitate beschränkte.

Ende des 18. Jahrhunderts gab es noch 1794 eine das ganze Land berührende Hungersnot. Im ausgehenden 18. Jahrhundert waren die Erträge bereits ausgesprochen gut. So hören wir erst zwischen 1817—1819 über eine weitere Hungersnot,[10] ferner — wie erwähnt — 1831, in Nordostungarn, zur Zeit des Choleraaufstandes. Und schließlich drohte 1847 zum letzten Mal der Alptraum der Hungersnot.[11]

[9] Ebenda.
[10] Magyarország története 1790—1848 (Die Geschichte Ungarns 1790—1848). Chefred. Gyula Mérei. Budapest. 1980. (Magyarország története tíz kötetben — Die Geschichte Ungarns in zehn Bänden). Bd. 5. S. 428., 475.
[11] Ebenda.

In der beträchtlichen Konsolidierung der Lage spielten mehrere Faktoren bei. Vor allem die Verbreitung des Kartoffelbaus in der ersten Hälfte des 19. Jahrhunderts auf den bergigen, unfruchtbaren Gebieten, wo man früher mit Mais versuchte, der sich jedoch als unzuverlässig erwiesen hat. Die Kartoffel brachte wesentlich ausgeglichenere Erträge, so war ihre stabilisierende Rolle sehr groß. Darin erlangte auch die Weiterentwicklung der Verkehrsverhältnisse eine große Bedeutung. Zwischen 1790—1850 erhöhte sich das Straßennetz von 770 auf 1770 km, die Entwicklung war besonders in Nordostungarn, sowie bei der Begegnung der *Berglandschaft und der Tiefebene*, von wo das Getreide der Tiefebene nach Nordosten strömte, beträchtlich.[12] Seit Joseph II. war der Zusammenhang zwischen dem Verkehr und der Hungersnot allgemein bekannt, so ist es nicht überraschend, daß mit dem Ausbau des Eisenbahnnetzes in den 1850—1880er Jahren die Hungersnot in Ungarn endgültig aufgehoben wurde. (Die letzten zwei Hungersnöte in der zweiten Hälfte des 19. Jahrhunderts waren anderen Charakters.)

[12] Ebenda. S. 237.

# X

## Development of agriculture in Hungary from 1848 to the First World War

The literature on European economic history from the 15th–16th centuries usually mentions Hungary as one of the main meat suppliers of an enormous cattle reserve of Central and Western Europe. The more than a hundred thousand cattle regularly driven out of Hungary every year supplied the markets of Venice, Vienna, of the South and Central German towns, and sometimes even of more distant West-European towns over centuries. As generally known today, Hungary was only a part of the semicircular zone stretching from Southern Scandinavia through the German seaside and Polish steppes down to Moldavia which produced an ever increasing amount of meat required for the developing Western and Central European towns.

On the other hand, 19th century Hungary, was described in works on economic history as one of the vast granaries of Europe. From the middle of the 19th century, Hungary was for years one of the largest grain exporters of Europe; and only if we consider that the European grain markets received from Hungary the amount left behind by the western part of the Hapsburg Empire, Austria and Bohemia, that is less than half of the grain surplus produced in Hungary, can we wholly assess the great change that took place in the production structure of Hungarian agriculture at that time.

The fact, that in the middle of the 19th century it was no longer the Hungarian meat but the Hungarian cereals that played the more important role on the markets of Europe, was not only due to developments in agriculture in Hungary. The western part of the Hapsburg Empire purchased an increasing amount of meat and so animals were exported from Hungary beyond the customs frontiers of the Empire in a reduced amount. But, of course, these are not the only reasons.

The traditional structure of Hungarian agriculture characterized by cereal production based on the shift of crop, and by nomadic or semi-nomadic livestock rearing (first of all cattle raising, then sheep and pig breeding), at the turn of the 18th century and later began to undergo a transformation. Up to that time cereal production had been controlled by the limited possibilities of transportation. Land transport over greater distances was not profitable, and water transport on a larger scale along the Danube toward Vienna only started in the second half of the 18th century. It was the realization of this transport possibility as well as a demand raised in Lower Austria (Graz) that caused the extension of cereal production in the West-Transdanubian estates in the second half of the 18th century. Where this transport possibility was not available the extension of cereal production was determined by the capacity of the local market. The peasantry grew crops primarily for self-consumption; town markets only played a role in small districts. Considering, however, that the majority of Hungarian towns had not yet broken away from agriculture at that time, and a considerable part of their population grew crops and kept animals themselves, the town markets grew but very slowly and were restricted to some industrialized towns in Hungary. Only one larger consumer presented itself until the end of the 18th century, the army, which created a constant and regular demand for agricultural produce. The grain surplus beyond satisfying the demand of the army rotted in storehouses. This applies in the first place to large estates which produced grain crops by utilizing serf labour but – excluding the manors in the western part of the country – having small markets, were often compelled to store their produces for years. Manorial farming based on serf labour was thus limited by the lack of transport facilities in Hungary unlike e.g. Poland or Germany where the rivers (e.g. Vistula) flowing into the sea ensured relatively early an excellent water-way for the export of cereals and timber.

Hence, up to the end of the 18th century animals rather than cereals were the most important agricultural commodities of Hungary. Namely, cattle could be driven to such markets where grains could not be transported. That is why the grey Hungarian cattle raised on the excellent Hungarian (mainly lowland) pastures and covering considerable distances without any difficulties predominated over centuries in the exports of the country. Cattle rearing was the leading branch of agriculture; pigs and sheep were raised by the serfs mainly for own consumption (food, clothes), and horses for carting. There was, naturally, another form of utilizing cattle: as a draught animal, where it played an important role. The management of large estates was on the whole characterized by similar conditions.

All this began to change in the second half of the 18th century, and mainly at the turn of the 18th century, following the Napoleonic wars. The first wave of an increased European interest in wool reached Hungary in the seventies and eighties of the 18th century. As a result of the economic policy of Maria Theresa's enlightened despotism, improved sheep breeds, first of all of Spanish origin, were introduced in Hungary, and following a rise in the price of wool, sheep breeding gradually came into prominence on the large estates too. This was backed by a temporary upswing during the war at the turn of the century which, however, affected cereal production as well. The rise in number of the army, the accumulation of reserves, etc. caused a boom in grain production which was felt all over the country, in accordance with the structure of agriculture first of all – naturally – in the seigniorial farms, since the production cost of grain crops grown on the tax-free seigniorial lands by serf labour, i.e. with unpaid labour and draught power, and delivered to the market by means of serfs was minimal, and the cash requirements hardly worth mentioning. The price advance of commodity grain crops only raised the seigniorial income, while the structure of peasant production remained unchanged.

The increased interest in grains during the Napoleonic wars accelerated the process of growth of arable areas which began in the second half of the 18th century parallel with drainage works. Fertile meadows were ploughed up and converted to arable ones. Hence the frames of livestock breeding based on grazing began to shrink, and this foretold the future crisis of the traditional method of animal husbandry at the beginning of the 18th century already. Namely, the amount of fodder crops produced to replace the yield of lost pastures was very low. Therefore, the livestock – primarily that of serfs – was hard hit by the boom in grain production.

The first phase of the crisis was a structural transformation in the livestock. From the beginning of the 18th century sheep breeding became the leading branch of livestock farming. From the gradually shrinking grazing lands the cattle was pushed out by the extraordinarily growing stock of sheep. The landlords were the first to sell their herds (and sometimes even their studs) in order to be able to increase the number of their flocks(1). This made its effect felt as early as in the first years of the 19th century in the higher price of beef, and in towns in the shortage of beef(2). The process was completed in the 1820s. Several years after the Napoleonic wars a great drop in grain prices began. Between 1818 and 1824 grain prices fell by 70 per cent. This fall in income was compensated for by a great boom in wool in the twenties caused by the rapid post-war development of the Western European textile industry. Between 1820 and 1826 the price of fine wool rose by 70 per cent in Hungary(3). For several years, until the prosperity of the Central European wool business was arrested by an upswing in the overseas and Russian wool production, this situation rendered sheep breeding the leading branch of livestock farming in Hungary too. The owners of large estates quickly changed over to raising fine-wooled Merino sheep, and their animals occupied the common pastures(4). The effect was by and large the same as in England in the 15th–16th centuries which Thomas Moore described so illustratively.

It must be emphasized that the high profitability of both grain and wool production in the seigniorial farms was possible primarily on account of the unpaid serf labour employed, thereby entailing extremely low production costs. They could not, however, do without certain investments since both the extension of cereal production and the promotion of sheep breeding – as it has already been mentioned – changed the traditional pattern of production. Ploughing up of meadows and pastures made the production of cultivated fodder crops necessary, at least to some extent, and the demand for fine wool called for the introduction of new sheep breeds, or at least the improvement of the traditional Hungarian ones (racka, cigája). It was at this point at the turn of the 18th early century that seigniorial and serf-peasant farming separated from each other in the agriculture of Hungary. Like the other economically undeveloped countries, Hungary was characterized by the following: land was almost the only capital, that is, any capital sufficient for the modernization of production only accumulated in the possession of an owner with land of a certain size(5). While with the modification of production structure and the prosperity of wool there began a modernization of production, transformation of cropping system, introduction of improved breeds of sheep and of more developed western breeding and management methods

X

Hungary before World War I.

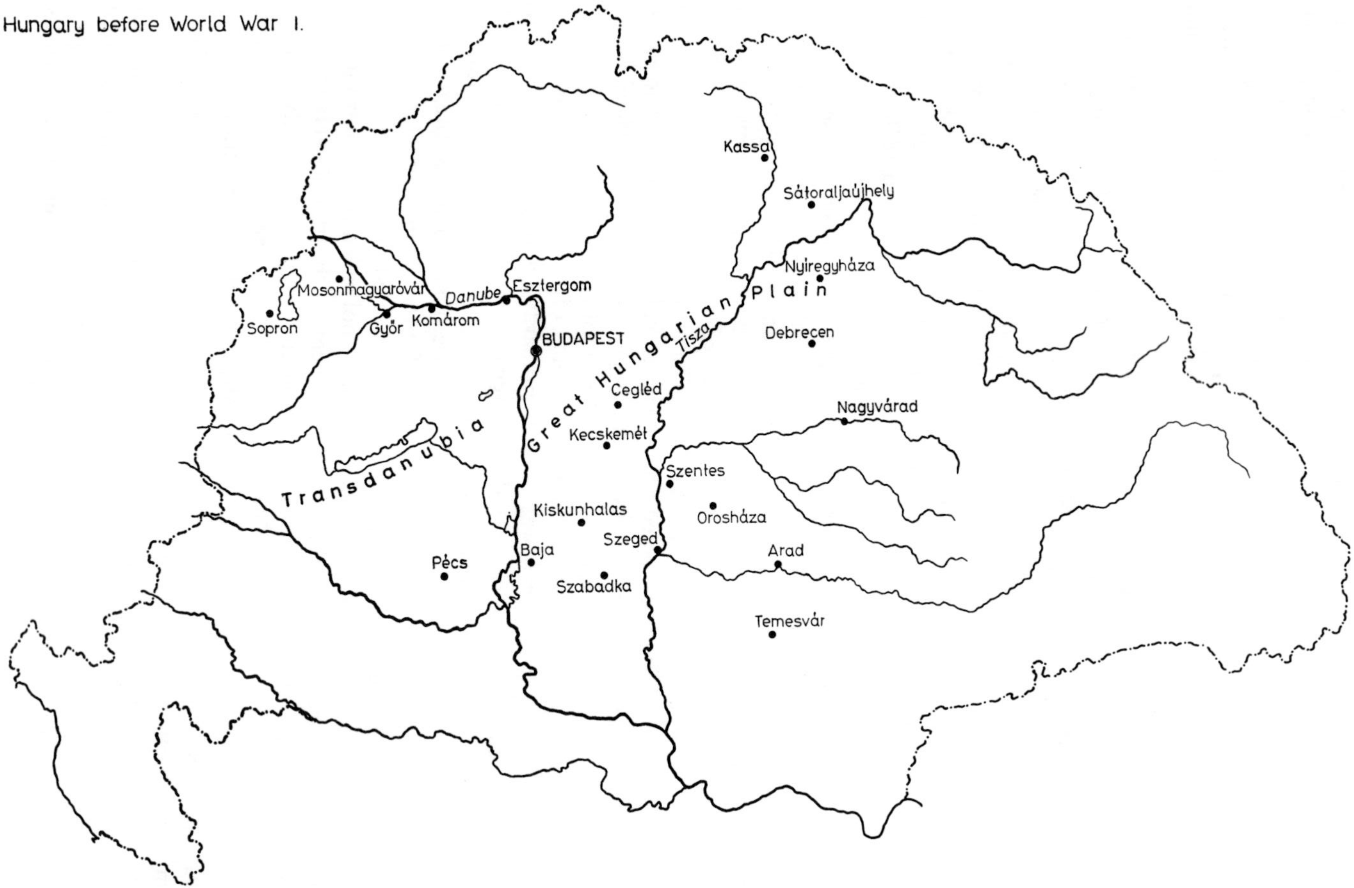

in the seignioral farms, peasant farming was not affected either by prosperity or by structural transformation(6). Serfs could not produce more grains, since they had to reserve their grazing areas for their animals, and the system of common pastures and the strict pattern of crop rotation excluded the possibility of change anyway. As for the prosperity of wool production only its drawbacks were felt since the demand for wool of the traditional breeds of sheep did not grow, and the structure of peasant sheep raising had not changed so far; in the farming of serfs sheep continued to serve the purposes of nutrition (milk, meat) and clothing. On the other hand, the fight for the pastures became more acute, the animals of the serfs were gradually pushed out(7). So up to the end of the 1840s – as long as wool production was a prosperous business – the position of other branches of livestock breeding continued to decline.

The cattle-plague of eastern origin had a considerable part in the decreased importance of cattle rearing during the whole period(8) especially between 1838 and 1842, then between 1848 and 1867. As a further cause the upswing in sheep breeding brought about the same result as in England in the 16th century: the continuous decrease of the cattle stock ousted from the pastures made importing necessary. The import and rapid improvement was followed by the marketing of Moldavian cattle in Hungary too. This import of animals increased, in turn, the damages done by the anyway spreading cattle-plague. Under influence of all these factors the structure of export naturally changed as well. In the first years of the 19th century as many as 150 thousand cattle were exported from Hungary a year. This number fell to about 90 – 100 thousand in the twenties and to 70 thousand in the thirties of the 19th century. The wool export, on the other hand, which at the beginning of the century amounted to some 60–65 thousand quintals was doubled in the thirties, and reached a peak of about 146 thousand quintals in 1846 (most of it was unwashed wool). The export of sheep increased as well, amounting to an annual number of about 217 thousand at the end of the twenties. The export of pigs grew from an average of 148 thousand in 1816–18 to 345 thousand by 1845. In 1845 the share of the major animal products in the total value of Hungarian exports was 46·1 per cent. The value of wool exports was 29 per cent, while that of cattle export only 5·8 and of the export of pigs 5 per cent of the total value of exports. The export of leather amounted to 1·9 per cent. No other animal product (sheep, horse, feather, suet, honey, wax, egg, meat, lard, milk, butter, cheese, etc.) even reached 1 per cent of the total value of exports, and all of them together only amounted to 6·3 per cent. This alone underlines the economic importance of sheep breeding(9).

But what was livestock rearing like in Hungary in the middle of the last century? We can safely say that it was in livestock husbandry of all sectors of agriculture that the difference between large-scale techniques adopting the up-to-date professional knowledge of the age and the backward traditional peasant practice was the most striking. The larger half of the livestock of Hungary was owned by the peasantry. This stock consisted exclusively of animals of traditional breed (grey Hungarian cattle, "racka" or "cigája" sheep, "bakonyi", "szalontai" or other native pigs, Hungarian horses). These breeds fulfilled the requirements of the contemporary peasant farm inasmuch as the Hungarian cattle was an excellent draught animal, the "racka" and "cigája" sheep produced sufficient amounts of milk (and milk products), wool satisfying the demands of Hungarian peasants, fur and leather, and meat as well. The Hungarian horse was of small size, appearing scrubby compared to the contemporary European breeds, but a strong animal fit for the conditions of roads in Hungary, and well-proved in carting. Hungarian pig breeds were used to being fed almost exclusively on mast, occasionally on spoiled grains, pig-wash, etc. in the peasant farms, that is, modern feeding techniques were still unknown in pig breeding. The animals were raised in the open and only kept under lean-to roof overnight (and sometimes in winter). An overwhelming part of the peasant livestock (except the horses) lived thus exclusively on pastures. Hence the usually neglected animals raised in the open suffered disadvantages in every respect. They were insufficiently fed (stronger animals grazed at the expense of the weaker ones) and hardly cared for. Even the most elementary rules of mating were not observed, mating was controlled entirely by nature – of course at the expense of quality again. Pastures were not cared for either; neither their cultivation nor their utilization was satisfactory. As a consequence, yields were low. According to contemporary descriptions e.g. the annual milk production of grey Hungarian cows kept mostly in the open ranged between 425 and 570 litres(10). The animals were, in general, uncared-for, dairy farming e.g., which involved at least partial stabling, was only introduced in certain regions of the country. This totally extensive method of animal raising in peasant farms was in sharp contrast with the more intensive techniques used in developed seignioral large farms. The sheep stock of larger estates e.g. consisted exclusively of merino (electoral-negretti) flocks. Even if their management was still mostly extensive (feeding on pasture played a much more important role than, for example in England), these animals were already fed according to the standards of those times, on field-grown fodders. Their utilization was of course more one-sided than that of peasant sheep, since these animals were not milked and usually not maintained for their meat, but their wool yield was superior both in quality and quantity to the traditional Hungarian breeds. The maintenance of these breeds transformed also the pattern of crop growing in large farms since their feeding had to be provided for. The situation was the same with respect to other animal species too. In cattle farming e.g. western dairy-type cows were introduced in some large farms, especially in West-Transdanubia. The first import of western cows was recorded in 1680, but in the first half of the 19th century western type dairy plants generally began to spread in large-scale farms, which, naturally, involved, the introduction of up-to-date methods of management. Large-scale pig-rearing too underwent transformation. It was in the thirties and forties of the 19th century that the "mangalica", a breed of mostly southern origin, was introduced in large-scale farms and the traditional breeds were completely pushed out. This breed, inclined to fattening, of which the bacon and lard could be exported was, naturally, fed on field-grown fodders in large farms. There were changes in the seignioral horse breeding too. Attempts were made to improve the Hungarian stock of horses by importing western (partly English) and Arabian horses. Even this attempt by the government in the interests of the army was felt in the first place in the horse-stocks of large-scale farms; the heavier cold-blooded horses too began to spread here(11).

Livestock husbandry in Hungary was thus characterized by a rapidly developing duality in the middle of the last century. It bore the marks of traditional, primitive peasant animal raising based mainly on nomadic pasturage on the one hand, and of the modern stabling methods applied in larger, more developed estates, corresponding to the level of the age, on the other. The latter had a great influence on the crop production of the farm, namely in such farms an interaction developed between livestock breeding and crop production.

The traditional system of agricultural production in Hungary was broken up in the middle of the 19th century by the abolition of serfdom. As a result of the revolution in 1848 serfs became emancipated in Hungary too. The abolition of serfdom left the allodial, seignioral lands – i.e. those not used by the serfs before1848 – in the landlords' possession, maintaining thereby for long decades the system of large estates, since nearly half of the territory of the country remained in the former landlords' hands, while the lands earlier used by the serfs (lands held in villeinage with the common pastures, forests, etc. belonging to them) were given – with a promise of compensation by the government – to the serfs as absolute property. This peculiarity of the abolition of serfdom was one of the factors determining agricultural development in Hungary for the subsequent decades.

The abolition of serfdom changed the former structure of agriculture completely. The landlords lost overnight the unpaid labour of the serfs, and in addition in most farms even the working tools of serfs which had been used free of charge. State compensation, on the other hand, protracted over decades, did not supply the cash required to continue farming (employ labour force, purchase working tools). True, the abolition of entailment made it possible to borrow money and obtain capital thereby, but the general deficiency of funds in the country, and the fact that the western part of the Hapsburg Empire was in a similar need of capital import made this available only for the richest aristocrats, the proprietors of the largest estates. The mortgage system – though developing at a rapid rate and getting established by the turn of the century – did not by far make up for the very serious want of capital. Especially in the period between 1850 and 1870 the former landlords were forced to apply the most extensive management methods possible on their farms. Many of the owners of large estates let their lands on lease at that time, mainly to tenants well provided with capital, and those who managed their farms by themselves were compelled to find other solutions to overcome the shortage of capital. They tried to pay labour – at least temporarily – in kind, that is, to satisfy the large numbers of landless and smallholder agrarian proletariat by letting lands on lease on a fifty-fifty or one-third basis, employing them in share harvesting, etc. Harvesting was usually performed by share croppers, while hoeing and other tillage operations by labourers working for half or one-third of the crop. The permanent servants of large estates as well as of larger peasant farms too were paid mainly in kind. They were employed for lodging, care of cows, land use, some grains, timber, clothes, and only a fraction of their salaries was paid them in cash. This system was characteristic of the whole capitalist era of Hungarian agriculture, only the inner proportions changed with time; in the course of development the number of day labourers working for cash payment increased to some extent, and the proportion of cash money in the wages became higher, respectively.

Hence the large estates were forced to carry on extensive farming, since they had insufficient capital; it was, therefore, only too natural that for decades they did not primarily strive for developing the capital-intensive livestock branch, but making use of the new European boom in cereals in the fifties changed over to a large-scale grain production. This was coupled with a second boom in wool in the fifties which opened the way to developing the least capital-intensive livestock branch: sheep breeding.

This was the only possibility of peasant farms, and especially of the poorest peasants set free in 1848 completely landless or with lands of only half to two hectares. Serfs having owned whole or fragmental plots before 1848 were set free with some lands, grounds, arables, pastures, meadows, forests. The overwhelming part of the cottars, however, were given only pieces of the common pasture or forest used in common. After the separation of seignioral and peasant lands peasants tried to plough up the allotted parts of meadow or pasture and convert them to arable ones to be able to produce at least the amount of grain required for the family. Beside the boom in grain crops this represented an additional force in promoting the conversion of pastures and meadows to arables after 1848. As we shall see, all this reduced the possibilities of livestock breeding for decades.

The other factor that influenced the situation and development of Hungarian agriculture – and livestock husbandry within it – in the second half of the 19th and first decades of the 20th century was the peculiar economic relations established between Hungary and the western half of the Hapsburg Empire after the end of the struggle for independence in 1848–49. Before 1848 there was a customs frontier between Hungary and the other parts of the Hapsburg Empire which was abolished on 1st October 1850; from that time on Hungary was a part of the uniform customs area of the Hapsburg Empire, then – after the compromise of 1867 – of the Austro-Hungarian Monarchy up to 1918. Besides the union of customs areas and the common customs frontiers Hungary was connected with the other parts of the Empire by an identical monetary system too. Accordingly, from then on Hungary could transport its agricultural produce to other parts of the Monarchy duty free. The frontiers of the Monarchy served as common customs frontiers for its countries which meant that the Monarchy ensured but partial economic independence for its countries, the economy of each country formed a part of the economy of the Monarchy, that is, the Monarchy was a *united economic community* with the partial economic independence of the two main parts: Austria (and Bohemia) and Hungary. Hence the economic symbiosis between Hungary and

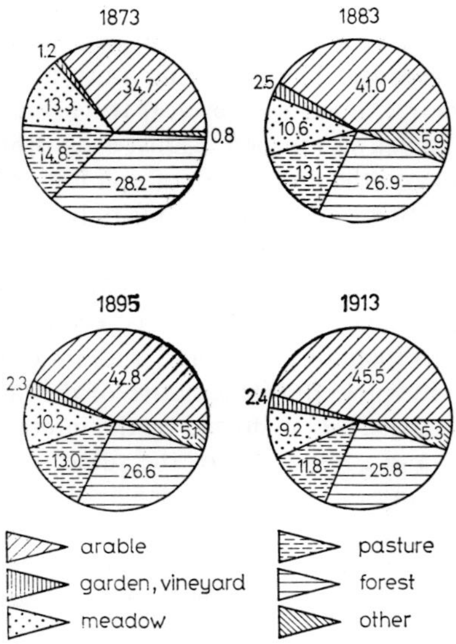


Fig. 1. Distribution of land area, 1873–1913 (in per cent)

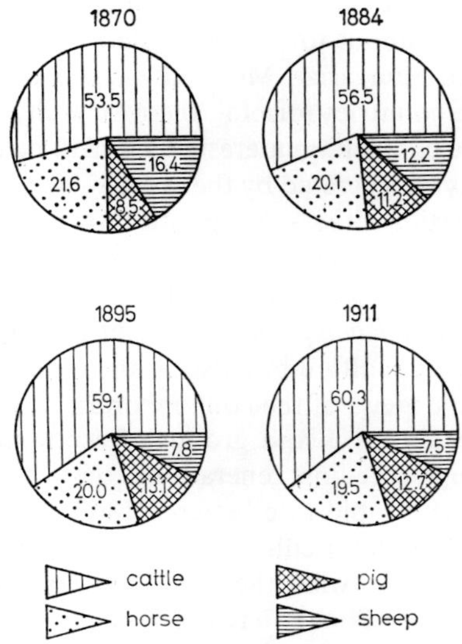


Fig. 2. Distribution of livestock, 1870–1911 (in per cent)

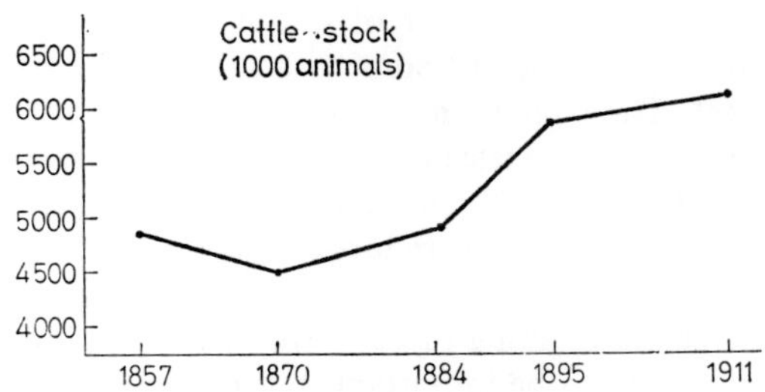


Fig. 3. Trend of the number of cattle stock, 1857–1911

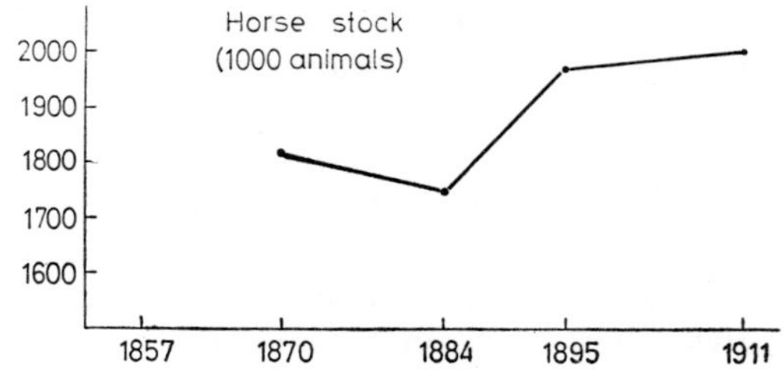


Fig. 4. Trend of the number of horse stock, 1870–1911

the other half of the Monarchy developed at an increasing rate after 1850. The interdependence of Austrian-Bohemian industry and Hungarian agriculture brought about totally new relations in those decades. The economic unity of the Austro-Hungarian Monarchy was a fact to be reckoned with even if the peoples of the countries forming the Monarchy were sometimes turned against each other by the conflicting interests of the ruling classes and the differences of opinion artificially exaggerated by them, and – as a result of this, and of the animosity between the nationalities – the political construction of the Empire rested upon very unstable foundations. We cannot say either that the contemporaries clearly saw that the existence of the Monarchy, the sound functioning of this vast economic unit was *advantageous* to each of its components including Hungary, and not only to the agriculture but also to the industry of Hungary. But irrespective of the fact that the views of the contemporaries were influenced and distorted by the interests of certain areas and groups of economic life, and irrespective of the subjectivity of the succeeding generations, the whole economy of Hungary undeniably developed at a rapid rate between 1849 and 1918, especially in the second half of this period, and agriculture had a part in this rapid progress.

Let us see what the economic development taking place in those decades was like. Those factors have to be pointed out in the first place which determined the development of agriculture as well. If we compare the picture of Hungary before the First World War to that in the 1850s we find enormous changes. The dimensions of industrialization were colossal, though when compared with the progress made by the developed industrial countries the change was not nearly so great. The population of the country increased by some 50 per cent between 1850 and 1910, and the number of the urban population increased very quickly; first the capital swelled, but some other industrial towns too started a sudden development. The change in the occupational distribution of the population was a very characteristic measure of the economic development. In the middle of the 19th century nearly 90 per cent of the population of Hungary worked in agriculture; this proportion was reduced to about 64 per cent around 1914, and also the share of agriculture in the national income was some 62 per cent. When compared with the changes taking place in the developed industrial countries this does not naturally seem to be important, but under East-European conditions this change was enormous. Still greater were the changes in the infrastructure, which were promoted by the government with appropriate investments ensured. The regulation of riverways, the drainage operations and anti-inundation work which considerably increased the agriculturally utilizable areas were surpassed in importance only by the development of railway construction. Before 1848 the agricultural products were transported mainly by carts drawn by oxen or horses, and partly on rivers (regulation of the Danube, Tisza made navigable), which restricted the market possibilities to a great extent. True, the regulation of rivers had not even been completed when the construction of railways began in Hungary, which then changed the transport conditions of agriculture radically. As a completion of the railway lines built on the western, Austrian-Bohemian areas of the Hapsburg

Empire, railway construction in Hungary started first of all with the view to making the transporation of agricultural produce possible. The first 46 km section was opened in Hungary in 1846, and railway connection between Budapest and Vienna was realized in the fifties. This was followed by a more rapid extension of the Hungarian railway system. Pest (Budapest) became the centre of the Hungarian railway system connecting the largest centres of agricultural production to the European railway network. In 1854 Szeged, in 1857 Temesvár and Debrecen, in 1858 Nagyvárad and Arad were joined to the railway network. The Transdanubian railway system connected the agricultural production of Hungary with the markets of Graz on the one hand, and with Trieste, on the other, which from 1860 made way for sea transports from Hungary. The largest districts of grain production and livestock husbandry as well as the sites of industrial raw material occurrence thereby were linked to the transport network. By 1866 a 2,160 km stretch of railway line was ready and in the meantime transportation by water and road increased as well. Between 1851 and 1867 the volume of commodities transported on the Danube increased from 0·5 to 1·2 million tons. The length of public roads grew from 2,030 km in 1848 to more than 21 thousand km by 1866. It was after the Austro-Hungarian compromise of 1867 that railway construction showed a real upswing. By 1873 the length of the railway lines increased threefold, to 6·3 thousand km, in 1900 it was already 17 thousand and in 1913 more than 22 thousand km. The main and side lines functioning then, and the relatively dense network of local railways provided up-to-date transport possibilities for agriculture too(12).

But no matter how rapidly the economy of the country grew, including the non-agricultural sectors, the rapid growth and modernization of agricultural production was not even after 1850 based primarily on the economic development of Hungary, although, naturally, it had some part in it. The increasing urban population, the growing demand for industrial raw materials, which accelerated especially between 1890 and 1914, contributed to the development of agriculture, but was not the main force that determined developments. The general European boom was initially the mechanism of the development of production, gradually being replaced by the rapid economic growth of the developed industrial half of the Austro-Hungarian Monarchy: Austria and Bohemia. The intensive economic growth of the more industrialized countries of the Monarchy, the rising living standard of their populations were the important factors accelerating the development of agricultural production in Hungary. The market of Hungarian agricultural produce was extended in this way becoming the basis for the rapid development of Hungarian agriculture. Around 1910 both in Austria and Bohemia only 38–40 per cent of the population made its living by working in agriculture, the larger part was engaged in industrial, commercial and service activities. The increased population in the Austrian-Bohemian industrial towns, the fact that from the very beginning the population there fell away from agriculture much more intensively than the similar level urban population in Hungary, still closely attached to the land – all make it understandable that it was the developed industrial parts of the Monarchy rather than domestic consumption that primarily provided the market for Hungarian agricultural production. While in the 1850s and 1860s Hungary exported mostly *beyond* the customs frontiers of the Monarchy, by the end of the century agricultural exports were restricted almost *exclusively to the territory of the Monarchy*, however, the Monarchy imported a considerable volume of additional agricultural produce outside the Hungarian exports too.

Of course this did not happen overnight. The enormous cereal boom evolving in the 1850s was not yet based exclusively on the market provided by the industrialized part of the Monarchy, considerable volumes were still exported at that time beyond the frontiers of the Monarchy, in the first place to the German provinces, but also to more distant Western European markets, e.g. to London. Then when the grain prices were depressed by an increased overseas competition, and the Western European markets, first of all in France and Germany, were blocked for the Hungarian exports by the introduction of protective duties, Hungarian agriculture based on the predominance of grain production came to a crisis. It was from this crisis of the 1870–80s that Hungarian agriculture was relieved by the progress of the industrial part of the Monarchy, and the rapid extension of its markets. The progress was so great that even the increased Hungarian production could not satisfy the demands, and at the turn of the century, and especially in the early 1910s, the Monarchy – besides absorbing the almost total agricultural production of Hungary – imported agricultural produce from abroad too. By that time generally 90 per cent of the Hungarian agricultural export, and of certain products almost the total export (e.g. 95 per cent of the cattle exports, 95 per cent of the grain and flour exports, 94 per cent of the wine export) found markets within the Monarchy. Only a few products (sugar, timber, feather, eggs) were exported in larger quantities beyond the frontiers of the Monarchy(13).

In spite of the relative acceleration of industrial development agricultural exports played a highly important role in the economic life of Hungary. The structure of exports before 1848 underwent a gradual transformation. The agricultural produce maintained their dominance especially in the first decades, only the livestock products were substituted by the cereals after 1848. Up to the eighties of the last century only data difficult to control are available. But even in the 1880s about 80 per cent of the Hungarian export was represented by agricultural product, and by the end of the period this proportion only decreased to 70 per cent. As for the years between 1882 and 1913 Table 1 (14) will convince us of the great importance of agricultural exports. Even if only the major items are considered we find the share of agricultural produce in the total exports really significant.

Although we can obtain a realistic picture of the development of agricultural production by examining the agricultural exports from the 1880s on, however, this Table does not give information on the conditions of 1850–70. It is clear, all the same, that the trend of development in Hungarian agriculture – though dependent partly on transportation, partly on the development of processing and preserving technologies – was primarily determined by the demands of the boom. In the years following the abolition of serfdom, grain production and parallel

**Table 1. Shares of major agricultural produce in the total exports of Hungary (%), 1882–1911**

| Year | Cereals | Flour | Sugar | Slaughter and draught animals | Livestock products | Total |
|---|---|---|---|---|---|---|
| 1882–1891 | 21·5 | 11·9 | 1·3 | 16·6 | 3·7 | 55·0 |
| 1892–1901 | 19·2 | 13·4 | 2·8 | 17·1 | 4·5 | 57·0 |
| 1902–1911 | 17·4 | 13·7 | 3·1 | 15·9 | 4·8 | 54·9 |

with it sheep farming showed an upswing in accordance with the second boom in wool. After the separation of seignioral and serf lands – as mentioned before – a considerable part of the meadows and pastures was ploughed up and converted to arable land. In the 1850–60s extensive drainage and canalization work began which again made an area of considerable size fertile, first of all for the purpose of crop production. In the 1850–60s, however, new arable areas were obtained, primarily by ploughing up pastures and meadows. Although there are no precise statistical data available on those years, there are reliable estimates at the beginning of the 18th century according to which the arable area of Hungary was 5·35 million ha, that is 18 per cent of the territory of Hungary, while at the end of the 1860s it was around 10 million ha, about one third of the total area(15). This growth – as we have mentioned – was mostly the result of meadows and pastures having been converted to arable land.

This excessive growth of the arable area is the only explanation of how cereal production in Hungary could increase to such an extent as it did. The extremely low grain yields of 5–7 q/ha even in the first half of the 1870s did not rise for a while, the upswing in cereal production was exclusively a result of increases in the area of arables (Table 2). As for this upswing of production there are no precise statistical data available, only estimates. We can follow in the first place the grain export of the Monarchy, and even from that essential conclusions can be drawn. In spite of the fact that in the 1850–60s the average per capita cereal consumption grew (by some 20 per cent) both in Hungary and in the western part of the Monarchy, from the middle of the 1850s the Monarchy – which in the early 1850s was still compelled to import cereals – exported a constantly increasing volume of bread and fodder grains. It was characteristic above all of the extension of Hungarian cereal production (since the grain export of the Monarchy originated *exclusively* from Hungary) that imports in the early 1850s were replaced by 1867 by exports of about 9 million q bread grain and flour, and 3 million q fodder grain and maize(16).

All this was – of course – evoked by the sudden advance in grain prices. From the years of the Crimean War between 1850–51 to 1854–55, the price of wheat rose by 130 per cent. The price trends of other grain crops – including maize – were more or less similar to that of wheat. The growth of cereal production in Hungary was accelerated at the very beginning of the fifties by the price advance, which around 1855 overstepped the frontiers of the Monarchy. Although after the Crimean War grain prices fell, at the beginning of the sixties a new wave of

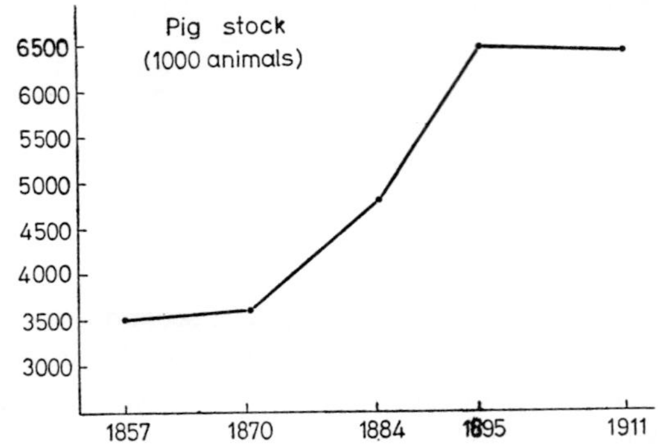


**Fig. 5. Trend of the number of pig stock, 1857–1911**

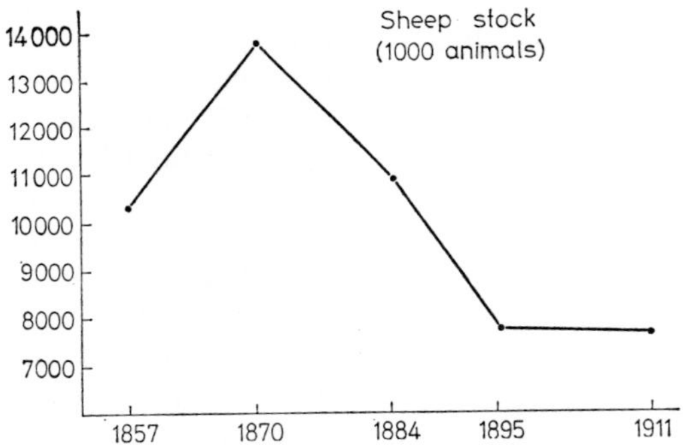


**Fig. 6. Trend of the number of sheep stock, 1857–1911**

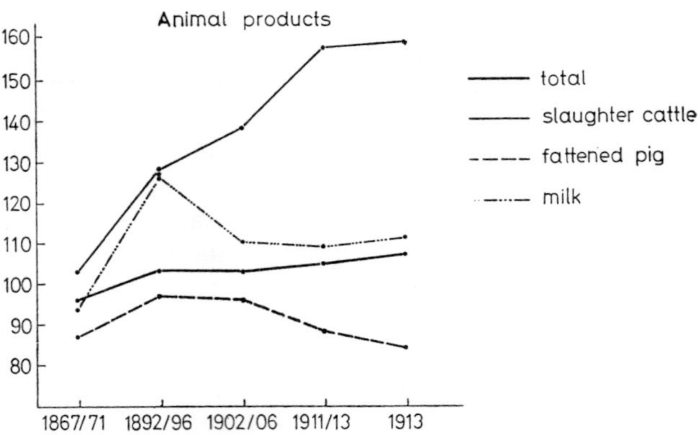


**Fig. 7. Changes in the agricultural prices, 1867–1913**

**Table 2. Distribution of the area by branches of cultivation (in 1000 ha)**

| Year | Total | Arable | | Garden | | Meadow | |
|---|---|---|---|---|---|---|---|
| | | ha | % | ha | % | ha | % |
| 1873 | 27 884·2 | 9 663·3 | 34·7 | ? | ? | 3 704·3 | 13·3 |
| 1883 | 28 280·1 | 11 584·4 | 41·0 | 347·7 | 1·2 | 2 993·6 | 10·6 |
| 1895 | 28 105·6 | 12 030·8 | 42·8 | 376·0 | 1·3 | 2 864·9 | 10·2 |
| 1913 | 28 227·5 | 12 833·7 | 45·5 | 378·8 | 1·3 | 2 610·9 | 9·2 |

price advance started which culminated in 1873. This increase in prices – though not reaching the peak of 1854 – remained always above the prices of the years 1850–51, at least by 70 per cent on the average of the period(17). The above described price trends were already parallel to those of the world market. By extending the railway system and increasing the waterways, Hungary entered the world market with the trade of grain crops. As a result the production of grain crops and maize grew. Compared to the beginning of the 19th century the production of wheat and rye increased twofold, that of barley and oat more than twofold (from a total of 20 million q to more than 40 million q), and maize production at least twelvefold (!), from about 1 to 12 million q(18).

This favourable trend of grain prices pushed all other sectors of agriculture into the background. The decrease in the acreage of pastures and meadows greatly limited the possibilities of livestock breeding, especially those of cattle rearing. The prices of grain (with the necessary inputs taken into consideration) were so favourable compared to the prices of any other agricultural produce, that fodder cultivation on the area converted to arable – which was the only possible way of developing the livestock branch – was out of question. This was coupled by the earlier mentioned general shortage of capital which caused a considerable setback in livestock breeding, first of all on the large-scale farms. Even if reliable data on the distribution of livestock are not available we have ample evidence of the large-scale farms, one after the other, having sold almost all their livestocks (keeping only the draught animals) to change over to one-sided grain production. The earlier described transformation of work organization on large estates following the abolition of serfdom did not at all favour the labour-intensive branches of livestock rearing in those decades. This was the reason why even large-scale farms could not make use of the possibilities already available in those years in the marketing of animals and animal products on the territory of the Monarchy. These were indicated by the trade of animals on the common customs area of the Monarchy, which in the 1850–60s was consistently passive, with an annual number of 14–15 thousand beef-cattle and 200–600 thousand pigs(19). Hence Hungary could have considerably increased the slaughter animal production even if relying only on the markets of the common customs area.

That it still did not happen in those decades was caused – besides the cereal boom – by a temporary decline in the farming of large estates after the abolition of serfdom. This transition took at least two or three decades. Before 1848, on the large-scale farms managed tax-free and with unpaid serf labour, the structure of

| Vineyard | | Pasture | | Forest | | Other | |
|---|---|---|---|---|---|---|---|
| ha | % | ha | % | ha | % | ha | % |
| 339·9 | 1·2 | 4 113·5 | 14·8 | 7 875·5 | 28·2 | 2 187·9 | 7·8 |
| 358·0 | 1·3 | 3 709·6 | 13·1 | 7 598·3 | 26·9 | 1 688·3 | 5·9 |
| 281·5 | 1·0 | 3 660·9 | 13·0 | 7 475·7 | 26·6 | 1 415·8 | 5·1 |
| 303·1 | 1·1 | 3 323·0 | 11·8 | 7 280·2 | 25·8 | 1 497·8 | 5·3 |

production changed, since not even the taxes could have been paid from the very low output of animals maintained on the vast pastures under extensive conditions. So the pastures were ploughed up. The herds and studs grazed on them were mostly sold by the landlords to alleviate the monetary shortage, then from the money thus obtained, the necessary equipment was purchased and the working capital indispensable in farming raised. The possibilities of peasant livestock farming were equally limited for similar reasons, mainly as a result of pastures and meadows having been converted to arables.

In the 1850–60s livestock husbandry came thus to a crisis. The reasons are quite clear, especially when considering that the area of pastures and meadows decreased from about 10·5–12 million ha at the beginning of the 19th century to 7·9 million ha by the sixties. Decrease mostly took place in the fifties. Roughage was only grown on 2 per cent of the arable area. Livestock farming still was based completely on grazing, and the hay yield of pastures must have been maximum 17–19 q/ha. We must emphasize, however, that this was a national average; radical changes occurred in the output of pastures and meadows. The lowland pastures renowned earlier for their thick grass (from which only the horns of the large grey Hungarian cattle stuck out!) became stunted after the drainage work. According to contemporary estimates in the 1850–60s the output of pastures in the Great Hungarian Plain could not be more than 9–12·8 q/ha, that is, one hectare was able to sustain one or two sheep at the most, and the grazing land requirement of one cow ranged between 5 and 10 ha(20). Under such conditions it was obvious that the numerical increase in the extensively managed livestock stopped. In the Great Plain the livestock, especially cattle, decreased in absolute number, while in the western part of the country, in Transdanubia, where the meadows and pastures were better due to more favourable conditions of precipitation, the livestock increased somewhat. It was at that time that the centre of cattle breeding shifted to Transdanubia where the climatic conditions were more favourable for fodder growing too. On the Great Plain the ploughed up pastures were replaced by arables, where mainly wheat and rye were grown. This resulted, in turn, in an increase in the horse-stock of the Great Plain, where on the sandy soils of the detached farmsteads and small holdings of former cottars lighter, iron-bound ploughs were introduced that could be drawn by horses too; so the horse, since it could be used for conveyance too, became for decades the most important animal on the Great Plain, due also to the extension of the system of detached farmsteads taking place in those decades. The other parts of the country, on the other hand, continued to use oxen as draught animals.

At the time of the cereal boom only sheep were worth keeping. From the fifties up to 1873 the price of wool rose again, however, even with the reduced possibilities of grazing the sheep stock remained at the former level and – for a while – did not radically decrease. Although the available statistical data show an increase in the number of sheep between 1857 and 1870 (for only 11·1 million sheep were registered in 1857 and 14·7 million in 1870), according to sources from 1868 the registration figures of 1857 ought to be increased by at least 30–40 per cent, because after the defeat of the war of independence the executive apparatus of the absolutism was unable to cope with such spontaneous forms of national resistance as with failure to register animals, etc. And this could be most easily done with sheep (and pigs). Thus the sheep stock was about the same in the two decades; its number was somewhat less than in the 1840s when it was estimated to be about 17 million in Hungary. The decrease probably occurred in the first half of the fifties and the number did not rise later.

Sheep breeding, on the other hand, changed as a consequence of the abolition of serfdom. Fine wooled, more exacting sheep were reared at a loss in contrast to the coarse wooled breeds which tolerated the extensive method of rearing well. From the fifties the larger estates no longer tried to improve the fineness of wool, they attempted instead to increase its quantity as that was more profitable. Although the price of coarse wool was not as high as that of fine wool, the profitability with the former was much higher (with the cost of production too taken into consideration).

Contributing to this change, moreover, was the fact that at that time the textile industry was already able to produce good fabrics from less fine wool too, and the demand for finer cloth was gradually replaced by one for coarser, worsted fabrics all over the world. Sheep farming in Hungary responded but slowly to these demands of the textile industry, as the lack of capital in large-scale farms did not allow quick changes in breed. As a result of this Hungarian sheep breeding broke away from its earlier basis, the Austrian-Bohemian textile industry. The sheep stock of Hungary was smaller than in the 1840s, still in the fifties and sixties increasing volumes of wool were exported beyond the frontiers of the Monarchy. In the forties only seven thousand tons were exported. At the same time the wool import of the Hapsburg Empire was very low, maximum 2·5–3 thousand tons. In the 1850–60s, on the other hand, the imports of wool increased to 10 thousand tons in the Monarchy, while the exports (almost exclusively from Hungary) exceeded 10 thousand tons(21). It was at that time that the Austrian-Bohemian textile industry and the Hungarian sheep farming separated from one another which sealed the fate of the Hungarian silk-wool breeds within two decades. So the cereal boom prevented an upswing in sheep farming and in the period of an apparent stagnation prepared, in fact, the rapid decline of sheep breeding.

This period of agricultural development in Hungary which was characterized by an extraordinary boom of grain crops and which, at the same time, meant the changing over from the feudal pattern of agriculture to capitalist production, lasted only for two to three decades. At the beginning of the 1870s grain prices

Table 3. **Changes in the price structure of agriculture (1867–1913)**

| Produce | 1867/71 | 1877/81 | 1892/96 | 1902/6 | 1911/13 | 1913 |
|---|---|---|---|---|---|---|
| Wheat | 100·0 | 107·7 | 80·3 | 74·4 | 76·3 | 75·0 |
| Barley | 100·0 | 103·6 | 95·6 | 92·5 | 92·6 | 86·7 |
| Maize | 100·0 | 103·6 | 90·1 | 98·3 | 89·9 | 90·3 |
| Agricultural products | 100·0 | 105·4 | 85·9 | 87·5 | 94·6 | 83·5 |
| Beef-cattle | 100·0 | 103·1 | 128·3 | 138·1 | 158·0 | 159·2 |
| Fattened pig | 100·0 | 86·6 | 96·7 | 96·2 | 88·0 | 83·8 |
| Milk | 100·0 | 94·4 | 126·8 | 109·7 | 109·3 | 111·3 |
| Livestock products | 100·0 | 94·5 | 113·0 | 112·5 | 115·4 | 116·5 |
| Total products | 100·0 | 100·0 | 100·0 | 100·0 | 100·0 | 100·0 |

(firstly the most characteristic one: the price of wheat) were still rising, then from 1873 began to decline (Table 3), even if this decrease was not rapid till 1882. It was then that prices suddenly began to fall and this process lasted for more than ten years, up to 1895. At the turn of the century the price of wheat showed a high fluctuation, then from 1907 began to rise again, accompanied, of course, by an increase in the prices of other grains too(22).

The fall in grain prices was not a phenomenon occurring only in Hungary, it was a general world-wide process. After the American civil war the rapidly growing agricultural areas supplied the market with an enormous volume of grain, and as a result of a fast progress in railway construction in a few years the produces of the United States and Canada reached the European markets. The low production costs of the American continent, then the rapidly decreasing costs of transport by railway, and first of all by ship, produced extremely low prices, so Hungarian grains were gradually pushed out from the world market (practically from the Western European market). This was paralleled by an increase in Russian and Romanian wheat shipments becoming more and more competitive from the end of the 1850s, then after opening of the Suez Canal by the competition of Indian wheat; all this resulted in the Hungarian wheat being finally ousted from the markets of Western Europe. Although the transport costs of Hungarian wheat decreased too – by 1895 it was only 53 per cent of that in 1867–77 on the Trieste–London line –, but during the same time the transport costs on the New York–Liverpool line fell to 33·1 per cent(23). But it was the high production cost in Hungary as compared to Russia, Poland, Romania and the overseas countries rather than anything else that caused the low competitiveness of Hungarian grains. Of course, selling wheat or other grains was no problem at all in that period, the grain crisis at the end of the last century was no crisis of selling, that is, it did not cause an accumulation of unsold products. Grains could be marketed all the same, the crisis only meant lower attainable prices, that is, a decrease in the economic efficiency of production. Thus there was a *price* crisis, in Hungary too.

Hungary did not recognize the phenomenon as one of which the effect would be felt for decades, and which would have an impact on the whole of agricultural production. The large estates engaged mainly in grain production were especially slow in realizing what it meant. First they only thought that the fall in prices was caused by the European record yields and would, therefore, be temporary. It was only in 1882 that they realized that the price of wheat was no longer determined by the yield amounts produced in Hungary, but by the overseas and Russian wheat prices. Namely, yields were good that year in Hungary—while generally poor in Western Europe—, still prices continued to fall. In 1884 when the price of wheat was 19·26 crowns in June and only 15·96 crowns in October, it became obvious that the situation resulted from the increased overseas competition. That the fall in grain price would be of some duration was suggested by the fact that while the grain supplies of America and Russia appeared to be depleted in the 1890s, and the inner consumption of the United States grew rapidly, the world market price of wheat continued to fall, as further overseas areas (Argentine, etc.) entered the competition. The wheat price touched bottom in August 1895 with 12·60 crowns/q(24). This meant the failure of grain production on the large farms.

Another reason why the large farms in Hungary did not initially realize the seriousness of the grain crisis was that inland consumption in the Monarchy continued to grow at a very fast rate even when the grain exports to Western European countries rapidly shrank, consequently Hungarian grains could be sold just as before. As long as the volume of grain exports exceeded the demand of the Monarchy, that is, a considerable proportion of the exports went beyond the customs frontiers, the Monarchy did not follow the more developed Western European countries in introducing customs duties for grains. The demand on grains grew, however, at a very fast rate in the Monarchy, exceeding the grain exports of Hungary as early as at the beginning of the 1880s. Then in 1882 the Monarchy followed the example of France and Germany and introduced import duties on grain (1·19 crowns/q for wheat). In 1887 the tariff was raised (to 3·57 crowns/q), but even this did not help much(25). Prices continued to fall in spite of the fact that any amount of grain produced could be sold on the markets of the Monarchy.

But even in this critical period the cropping area of cereals did not decrease, only its rate of growth became slower, and its share in the total arable area fixed(26). Yet, substantial changes occurred which in a few decades fundamentally transformed the pattern of agricultural production. Namely, the crisis of cereals upset the former price structure of agricultural produce and radically improved the marketing possibilities of livestock farming. Considering that meat and dairy products were more and more sought after by the increasing urban population of Western Europe, and of the Monarchy too, the demand for these products was rapidly rising in those decades and their prices generally increased (the prices of course did not change equally in the different livestock branches). This shift in the price structure in favour of livestock products soon resulted in an upswing of the livestock sector. Even if not overnight, the situation changed. While attention was concentrated earlier exclusively on grain production, from the beginning of the eighties livestock farming became the leading sector of agriculture in Hungary. The pastures and meadows already converted to arables were not, naturally, restored to their former state, but crop production was instead combined with livestock husbandry. The sowing areas of maize and roughage crops grew, and their share in the arable area became larger too. Within grain production higher importance was attached to the production of fodder grains.

All this meant that both the structure and level of livestock husbandry changed. It was, in fact, in that period that stabled rearing became *general* in Hungary, especially in the central regions of the Carpathian Basin, where a higher than average proportion of pastures and meadows had been converted to arables in the previous decades, and where agricultural production was more intensive than elsewhere. These were, at the same time, the industrially more developed regions of the country, where the proportion of the urban population was larger too, involving wider market possibilities. It was there that the capital – actually the only important inland market of the period – was situated, and this contributed to a more rapid development of the central part of Hungary.

Prosperity thus changed the economic conditions of livestock husbandry and transformed its overall pattern. Livestock husbandry based on up-to-date feeding instead of grazing differed even in its objectives from the rearing methods of the previous decades or centuries. The progress of communication, the rapid technical improvement of processing (e.g. introduction of the milk separator), the increasing marketing possibilities together resulted in the transformation of livestock husbandry. For example, cattle rearing had earlier been aimed at providing draught power on the one hand, and producing (exporting) meat providing thereby the possibility of the cattle being driven to the market, on the other; dairy farms based on stabled or yarded rearing and up-to-date feeding techniques were only established on larger West-Transdanubian estates situated close to the market of Vienna. There was no longer any need for animals to be driven to the market, and with the improvement of the network of roads and of the technical level of agriculture – and above all ploughing (iron plough) – the cattle found a rival in the horse becoming widely employed in ploughing from the second half of the 19th century. And even on farms that continued to use oxen for ploughing, cattle breeds as strong as those used earlier were no longer necessary. Hence the aim of livestock husbandry changed; the necessity of providing draught power was subordinated to the aspects of fattening and milking capacity. Cattle bred one-sidedly for centuries in Hungary was gradually replaced by various dual or triple purpose western breeds, and the specific types developed in the Carpathian Basin in the last decades of the 19th century were all spotted breeds. As a result of these changes in rearing methods and breeds the structure of cattle farming was based on crop production, and the further development of agriculture took thus a new direction (at least for some decades). Similar changes in rearing methods and breeds occurred in the pig branch where the "mangalica" breed, much more fertile and easier to fatten than the native breeds, came into prominence. The spread of this lard-type pig brought about a radical change in feeding. The earlier practice of feeding swine on mast was almost completely given up, especially in the central part of the country, and maize and other field-grown fodder crops became the basic foodstuffs of pigs. Pig-wash only had a role in small peasant farms and with the poorer urban strata rearing pig. Horse breeding too became transformed; the importance of large-bodied, cold-blooded breeds more suitable for draught work began to increase. Differences in sheep husbandry between the manorial and peasant farms gradually disappeared. All these changes in feeding, and the replacement of breeds – both separately and jointly – testified that from the early 1880s livestock breeding in Hungary was approaching the West-European level, and – though, of course, it did not reach it either quantitatively, or qualitatively – followed the same line.

Prior to discussing the conditions of livestock husbandry prevailing at the turn of the 19th early 20th century in any detail, we have to be informed about another important change. As we have seen, by the time of the abolition of serfdom the production of large manorial farms had separated from the traditional peasant crop rotation system and livestock husbandry based on grazing. Large-scale farms best provided with capital used an up-to-date system of crop rotation even before 1848, and field crop growing generally was co-ordinated with the fodder requirements of livestock (first of all sheep) farming. Even sheep were reared on improved pastures and given fodder as supplement.

After the abolition of serfdom large farms responded to the cereal boom in the same way as the small farms did. In the first place the cropping area was expanded. The abolition of serfdom and separation of peasant lands from manorial lands did not, however, stop at once the traditional shifting of crops. The want of capital in the peasant farms prevented the owners from consolidating their holdings. Shifting of crops was maintained for further decades. True, the new crops, first of all the row-crops (maize, potato, etc.), as well as from the eighties the extension of the sowing area of rough fodders gradually broke up the old patterns and made consolidation necessary. On the other hand, livestock rearing based on the system of common pastures and on the possibility of grazing the fallow strips of land tended to keep up the system of crop shifting. Mainly those peasant owners of small holdings were against the consolidation of holdings who possessed insufficient land to grow fodder crops on in addition to the grains required for the sustenance of their families. The grain crisis resulted, however, in essential changes in this respect too. The attention of the peasantry turned toward livestock husbandry; the extension of the sowing area of fodder crops, stabled rearing introduced in the peasant farms too, gave an impetus to consolidation, elimination of lay lands, and introduction of a better system of crop rotation. This process can be characterized by the following data: the acreage of lay lands decreased from 2·3 million ha in the early 1870s to 1·1 million ha by the outbreak of the First World War, and was mostly restricted to the border lands. In the decades preceding the First World War there was but a negligible acreage of lay lands in the central part of the country(27).

The upswing of livestock husbandry, its co-ordination with the pattern of field cropping transformed thus the traditional structure of crop production as well. But – as we have seen – even livestock breeding itself was transformed. Differences of this kind existing before 1848 between the large manorial estates and the serfs' farms did not, naturally, cease, but were partly preserved, partly modified. Livestock rearing in small peasant farms made a great progress, large-scale farms continued, however, to hold the first place in livestock husbandry. Large farms mostly endeavoured to raise the qualitative level of livestock breeding. This explains that an overwhelming part of the livestock – except sheep – was found in small farms, further, that for this very reason the livestock structure of large farms was built primarily on livestock breeding and rearing in small holdings. It was characteristic of capitalist Hungary until 1945 that the animals – especially cattle – were reared in small farms, and it was from these peasant farms that large farms purchased draught oxen and young cattle. Large-scale farms took advantage of having begun the change of breeds decades before the small farms, and switched over, therefore, to rearing breeding animals (in all branches of livestock farming), and producing mainly for urban and export markets (in each branch of livestock breeding in a different way). In the cattle branch most large farms operated dairy plants (generally purchased cows from peasants); with respect to breeding, pig production of lard and bacon was the main objective, and in an initial form rearing and processing meat-type pigs; in the horse branch the raising of breeding animals already began. Livestock husbandry in the large-scale farms was built in every respect on the extremely wide system of small peasant livestock farming, numerically exceeding the large-scale farms. Large-scale stocks generally were of better than average quality, yielded more milk, fat, finer wool than those of peasant farms. They were forced to choose this solution because – with livestock husbandry being a highly labour-intensive branch – they were not able to develop all its phases to the same extent. They found it more profitable to maintain a lower number of better quality animals.

It was just in the quality that peasant farms could not keep pace with large-scale farms in livestock rearing. True, livestock density in peasant farms was incomparably higher than in large-scale farms, but this followed mainly from a need of draught power and useful animals in every farm. However, the number of livestock in peasant farms increased greatly. The labour reserves of peasant farms could be very well utilized in livestock breeding the products of which were increasingly sought after in the last decades of the 19th century. The extension of livestock rearing in small holdings meant an increased exploitation of family labour available free of charge. There began a qualitative development of livestock husbandry in these farms too, e.g. the establishment of dairy co-operatives promoted the improvement of the cow stock of peasants in the most developed western regions of the country, nevertheless, it was not this but the higher number of animals maintained which was characteristic of the peasant farm. By the turn of the century, however, the production structure of peasant farms too underwent an essential change in which the leading role was played by the development of livestock breeding.

It must be noted that the main production line of large-scale farms – in spite of what has been told about their qualitative superiority to small farms – was not livestock breeding; they continued to be engaged primarily in crop growing.

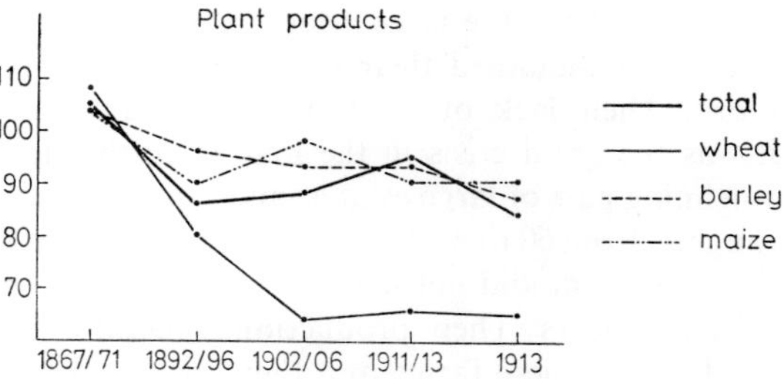


**Fig. 8. Changes in the agricultural prices**

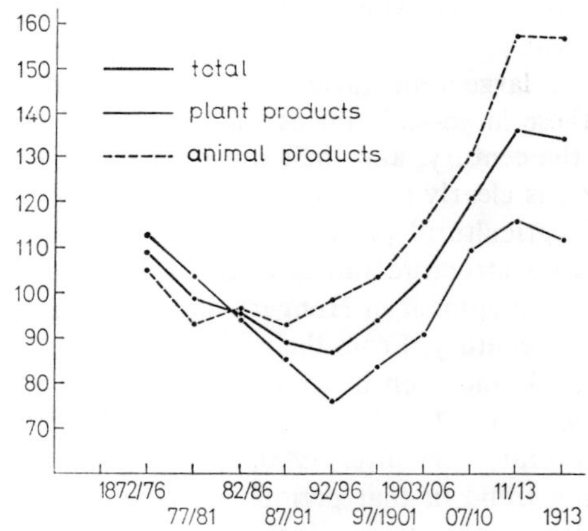


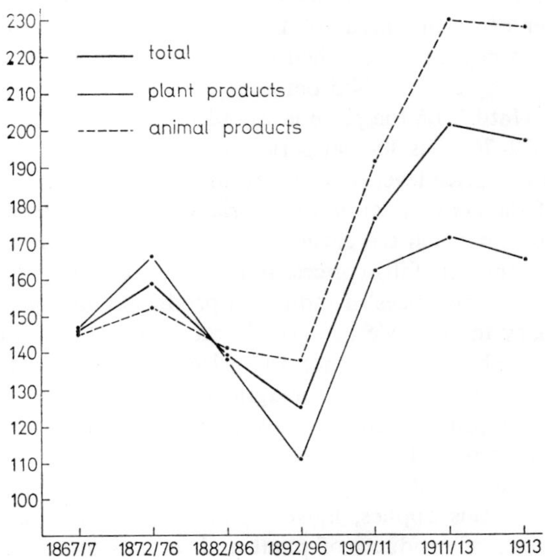


**Figs 9–10. Wholesale price index of agricultural products, 1867–1913**

The majority of the large estates, especially in the central and eastern part of the country, maintained their traditional, partly extensive pattern of growing grain crops. Their lack of funds prevented any essential adjustment of production; it was the grain crisis in the first place that limited their possibilities. The overwhelming part of large estates, and especially medium-sized farms, with an acreage ranging from 60 to 6–700 ha, which were not large enough to manage a model livestock farm, did not have the possibility of changing over to livestock breeding in a few years. Their production structure remained traditional, built on grain production; these farms and their owners, respectively, were interested above all in a rise of grain prices. The small farms which did not produce grains exclusively for the market and where family labour made an increase in the number of livestock possible, generally were affected less seriously by the fall in grain prices than were large-scale farms which commanded a stock of commodity grains. It was these large-scale farms that raised the claim of higher grain prices at the turn of the century, and their owners became leaders of the agrarian movement.

All this is clearly seen from Table 4 showing the trends of the wholesale price level of agricultural produce. With prices in 1848–52 taken as a basis, shifts in the price structure indicate the factors that fundamentally determined agricultural development in Hungary and its characteristic features in the second half of the 19th century. From the middle of the 1870s the price level of crop products rapidly sank and even if it did not fall to the initial level, its declining tendency compared to the top level was strongly felt from the second half of the 1870s up to several years after 1900. No doubt, agricultural prices generally show a decreasing trend in that period. While on the average of the years 1867–71 the wholesale price level of all agricultural produce studied exceeded the price level of 1848–52 by 46·1 per cent and in 1872–76 continued to rise by a further 10·9 per cent compared to the base period, from 1877 to 1906 it showed a declining tendency. Prices touched bottom between 1892 and 1896 when exceeding the basic level by a mere 24·5 per cent.

Until 1906 the price level did not reach either the 1867–71 level or the peak of 1872–76. This 30-year period was thus characterized by a fall in prices, a permanent lower price level of agricultural produce, in spite of the fact that around the turn of the century, after 1897, prices slightly increased again, although this increase did not reach the earlier peak. As a whole, the period was still characterized by a permanent fall in prices, and this referred not only to the prices of agricultural produce. The prices of industrial products and raw materials, and of articles of primary importance in agricultural production fell considerably too, sometimes at a much faster rate than the prices of agricultural produce, and this circumstance ensured a price gap for agriculture throughout the whole period in spite of the fall in prices. Hence the overall position of agriculture did not worsen even at the lowest price level; it was by taxes rather than through an agricultural price gap that a definite proportion of agricultural returns was creamed off.

All this applies, however, to agriculture as a whole only. If we consider the prices of products of plant and animal origin separately, a modification in the

| Year | Plant | Animal | Total | Change compared to previous period |
|---|---|---|---|---|
| | | products | | |
| 1848/52 = 100 | | | | |
| 1867/71 | 147·2 | 145·0 | 146·1 | +46·1 |
| 1872/76 | 165·8 | 152·3 | 159·1 | +10·9 |
| 1882/86 | 137·8 | 140·9 | 139·4 | −12·4 |
| 1892/96 | 110·8 | 138·3 | 124·5 | − 8·9 |
| 1907/10 | 162·2 | 190·5 | 176·4 | +37·6 |
| 1911/13 | 170·8 | 230·3 | 200·7 | +13·8 |
| 1913 | 165·4 | 228·2 | 196·9 | − 1·9 |
| 1867/71 = 100 | | | | |
| 1872/76 | 112·5 | 105·0 | 108·8 | + 8·8 |
| 1877/81 | 104·1 | 93·4 | 98·8 | − 9·9 |
| 1882/86 | 94·3 | 97·3 | 95·8 | − 0·4 |
| 1887/91 | 84·9 | 92·7 | 88·8 | − 7·3 |
| 1892/96 | 75·8 | 98·5 | 87·2 | − 1·8 |
| 1897/1901 | 83·6 | 103·6 | 93·6 | + 7·3 |
| 1902/1906 | 90·6 | 116·1 | 103·6 | +11·1 |
| 1907/1910 | 110·3 | 131·0 | 120·7 | +16·5 |
| 1911/1913 | 116·1 | 158·4 | 137·3 | +13·8 |
| 1913 | 112·5 | 156·9 | 134·7 | − 2·0 |

**Table 4. Wholesale price level of major agricultural products(28)**

price level is revealed, a process that determined the situation of livestock husbandry. Within the overall tendency of a decline in prices, the prices of livestock products showed trends other than those of plant products. The general trend of the agricultural price level was determined in the first place by the prices of products of plant origin, which means that their drop in prices was more intensive than average. The prices of livestock products, on the other hand, did not decrease to the price level of plant products, viz. did not reach the rate of decline of the latter, and with the overall tendency of fall in prices taken into consideration, this in itself meant a relative price advance. Characteristically, at the lowest level between 1892 and 1896 the prices of plant products were 75·8 per cent, while those of livestock products 98·5 per cent of the basic prices of 1867–71; in this context it is also worth mentioning that until 1906 the price level of plant products only rose to 90·6 per cent (compared to the base), while that of livestock products exceeded the base by 3·6 per cent as early as between 1897 and 1901, and between 1901 and 1906 was already 116·1 per cent. In other words, the prices of livestock products had increased to a considerable extent before the customs duties were essentially raised.

This trend of the price level caused a turn in the last third of the 19th century toward livestock breeding in Hungary. Since the prices of livestock products did not decrease with the general fall in prices and with the prices of plant products, respectively, moreover their decrease was much below the average in those decades, the increase in their price level began likewise almost a decade earlier than in the case of plant products – consequently it was livestock husbandry of all sectors of agriculture that made a rather steady progress in Hungary too. This permanent shift of proportions in favour of the livestock husbandry, which characterized the price structure of agriculture over thirty years or so, induced highly important structural changes resulting in the typical pattern of modern livestock husbandry in Hungary.

The transformation of livestock husbandry in Hungary was the result of a long process which could not have taken place without the above described changes in the price structure.

The above modification of the price structure was not, however, enough for the transformation of the pattern of livestock breeding. It only resulted in a *general* increase of interest in livestock husbandry, especially on the part of small farms where the necessary labour force was available. All this may account for the increase in the number of livestock in the period in question, but cannot explain the structural transformation. The changes in the structure of livestock husbandry were decisively determined by the substantial differences in prices that occurred even between individual livestock products.

Within the general trend of price movements the prices of different animals and of their products did not change in the same way. If we only want to outline the major tendencies it is enough to cast a glance at Table 5 (29) to see that the changes in the structure of livestock followed this price trend. Essentially, this consisted of a rather steady increase in cattle prices irrespective of the customs measures. With the prices of 1867–70 taken as a basis, the prices of cattle always exceeded the basic price, and around the turn of the century the rise in prices accelerated without any interference (customs measures). The prices of pig, on the other hand, were characterized by a constant decline touching bottom between 1886 and 1895. The same applies to the price of fat – when related to the same basis –, due mainly to competition by the American fat and bacon. The situation was similar with wool of which prices touched bottom between 1892 and 1896 and never reached the basic price of 1867–71. The extent of fall in prices in wool was

| Year | Cattle | Calf | Pig | Sheep | Wool** |
|---|---|---|---|---|---|
| 1867/70 | 47·49 | 92·36 | 109·37 | 68·40 | 315 |
| 1871/75 | 49·36 | 108·36 | 117·70 | 81·17 | 348 |
| 1876/80 | 48·15 | 92·10 | 96·00 | 77·70 | 319 |
| 1881/85 | 51·64 | 92·58 | 98·37 | 84·23 | 294 |
| 1886/90 | 48·76 | 90·94 | 89·10 | 73·69 | 277 |
| 1891/95 | 53·12 | 96·14 | 93·28 | 69·09 | 239 |
| 1896/1900 | 57·59 | 94·27 | 94·19 | 72·62 | 274 |
| 1901/1905 | 65·44 | 105·01 | 103·50 | 77·64 | 305 |
| 1906/1910 | 75·39 | 117·24 | 124·75 | 94·67 | 328 |

**Table 5. Price trends of animals and wool in 1867–1910* (q/crowns)**

* Prices of the St. Marc Zentralviehmarkt in Vienna. These prices influenced the Hungarian prices. More than 60 per cent of the animals driven to the market originated regularly from Hungarian exports.

** The prices of wool are given with a year's delay. The basic years are 1867/71. From theu on the five-year averages are those of 1872/76, 1877/81, 1882/86, etc. up to 1907/1911.

equal to that in wheat which explained the chronic crisis of sheep farming beside the depression of wheat production. The price of mutton, on the other hand, was above the basic price throughout the whole period, that is why a relatively large proportion of the sheep stock was maintained in Hungary in spite of the radical fall in wool prices. While the volume of raw wool imported to Europe from overseas grew eightfold between 1860 and 1910, resulting in a general decrease of the sheep stock in the European countries, in Hungary this decrease was only 50–75 per cent of that recorded in the developed Western European countries. This phenomenon can be accounted for by the quite high level of mutton prices at that time(30).

All this served as a basis of the development characterizing livestock breeding between 1870 and 1910. Let us see what the figures say.

The numerical development of livestock in the second half of the last century – between 1857 and 1911 – are shown in Table 6.

Considering that our data are but approximately reliable, the absolute numbers of livestock – though not indifferent either – are not as important for us as the *changes* reflected by the columns of figures. Namely, these changes allow measuring the rate and tendency of development and the changes in structure.

The first peculiarity revealed by the columns of figures in Table 6 is the increase in the whole livestock from 1870. With livestock – or at least large animals – converted into standard animals a considerable increase in the livestock can be demonstrated by the turn of the century, or until the 1910s. When using the contemporary key of conversion (1 standard animal-1 cow, or 1 horse, or 5 pigs, or 10 sheep) and disregarding the changes that took place during these forty years partly in the structure, partly in the breeds of the livestock which may have modified e.g. the average weight, we find the livestock to have grown from 8·40 million in 1870 to 10·23 million by 1911 (21·54 per cent). Growth was not uniform at all. Between 1857 and 1870 the livestock only increased by 1 per cent, between 1870 and 1884 by 3·21 per cent, while from 1884 to 1895 the growth was 13·84 per cent (from 8·67 to 9·87 million of standard animal), declining again to 3·44 per cent between 1895 and 1911 (from 9·87 to 10·23 million of standard animal). The highest rate of increase occurred thus in the ten years from the middle of the 1880s to the mid-1890s, i.e. when the grain crisis was at its worst. All this suggests that the situation did not change for the next ten years; further increase in the livestock only began after a considerable rise in the agricultural customs duties. But no matter how it happened, there is no doubt that radical changes occurred in the number of livestock in the last third of the 19th century.

| Year | Cattle | Horse | Pig | Sheep |
|---|---|---|---|---|
| 1857 | 4 775·0 | 1 769·3 | 3 499·0 | 10 261·0 |
| 1870 | 4 496·9 | 1 819·7 | 3 573·3 | 13 760·7 |
| 1884 | 4 879·0 | 1 748·9 | 4 803·6 | 10 852·1 |
| 1895 | 5 829·0 | 1 972·9 | 6 436·6 | 7 813·1 |
| 1911 | 6 184·4 | 2 001·4 | 6 416·4 | 7 697·7 |

**Table 6. Changes in livestock numbers (1000 animals)**(31)

This change seems even more important when taking the transformation of the structure of livestock into consideration. An analysis of the absolute number of livestock makes it clear that it was the case of a double process in which the sheep stock of the country decreased at a relatively fast rate compared to 1870, while the cattle and pig stock—and even the horse stock—increased in number. The changes did not, however, take place simultaneously. The reduction of the sheep stock compared to 1870 was then not only substantial—as sheep decreased to about 55 per cent of the original number—but also continuous. Namely, no matter how unreliable the data of 1870 are, all experts are of the opinion that

| Year | Cattle | Horse | Pig | Sheep |
|---|---|---|---|---|
| 1857 | 57·7 | 21·8 | 8·5 | 12·4 |
| 1870 | 53·5 | 21·6 | 8·5 | 16·4 |
| 1884 | 56·5 | 20·1 | 11·2 | 12·2 |
| 1895 | 59·1 | 20·0 | 13·1 | 7·8 |
| 1911 | 60·3 | 19·5 | 12·7 | 7·5 |

**Table 7. Changes in the composition of livestock** (%)

the figures must have been much higher than that. With the other animal species, on the other hand, a higher rate increase only began after the mid-eighties. As we have seen, increases in livestock number accelerated between 1884 and 1895 and were even more rapid in the case of pigs and cattle; increase in the number of the latter made up an overwhelming part of the total increase, since the horse stock grew but slightly, and the number of sheep decreased. As a result the structure of livestock underwent radical transformation in these thirty years. From the beginning to the middle of the 19th century sheep breeding was the leading branch of livestock farming. From the 1870s this situation changed fundamentally. When studying the changes in standard animal number (Table 7) we find the cattle to have been 53·5 per cent of the total livestock in the 1870s, and 56·5, 59·1 and 60·3 per cent in 1884, 1895 and 1911, respectively. The joint share of cattle and pig in the total number of livestock rose from 62 per cent to above 72 per cent. This circumstance meant the radical transformation of the livestock. Livestock breeding assumed an intensive character since the stabled forms of livestock farming —primarily cattle and pig breeding—became dominant instead of the relatively extensive branch of sheep farming.

Another question must be touched upon. We have hardly any data on small animals complementing the livestock, beside the large animals, e.g. on the poultry stock. There are some data available concerning the size of the poultry stock from 1895 when it comprised more than 29 million fowls. Though this is not a high number but—when added up with the constantly increasing export—indicates that small animals played a considerable role in livestock farming. Beyond this, however, there are indirect data suggesting these components of the livestock to have shown signs of a considerable increase at the end of the 19th century.

This increase in livestock number must be compared, however, to the population number as well. In the last third of the 19th century decisive changes occurred in this field too. At that time, namely, increase in the number of livestock was already unable to keep pace with the increase of population. In 1884, 602 standard animals fell to 1000 people. Between 1884 and 1895 the rapid increase in the livestock still exceeded the increase in the number of inhabitants: in 1895, 616 standard animals fell to 1000 people. From then on, however, animal density relative to the number of inhabitants was not only unable to grow, but even the attained level could not be maintained. By 1911 only 554 standard animals fell to 1000 people in spite of the fact that extensive emigration took place in the meantime, and the increase in population slowed down anyway at the turn of the century. Livestock number relative to the number of inhabitants was decreasing at that time. This relative loss appearing thus in livestock products could only be made up for by increased yields.

The decrease of livestock did not, however, occur in all species. Even the per 1000 head decrease in livestock number expressed in standard animal does not mean the same trend for each species. When examining the absolute numbers of individual species we find the following trends (Table 8).

Increase in the number of stock gave thus different results for each species. Decrease in sheep number – even when related to 1000 head – reduced the size of the livestock to a considerable extent. The per 1000 head number of horses decreased too, though not significantly. The notable increase in the cattle stock between 1884 and 1911 was just able to keep pace with the increase of population; the number of cattle per 1000 head was about the same in 1884 and 1911. Pig was the only species in which increase in numbers exceeded the increase of population. Numerical increase in the pig stock was especially impressive between 1884 and 1895; even a subsequent swine-fever that reduced the stock could not decrease the 1884 ratio of pig number per 1000 head. No doubt, however, that without the losses caused by the swine-fever the number of pigs could have been much higher, and the per 1000 head pig number too would have increased considerably. Anyway, only the pig stock of all animals was able to keep pace with the given rate of population increase.

In spite of all this, numerical increase and structural transformation in the livestock were equally significant in the four decades between 1870 and 1911. But still more important was the qualitative change (we may safely say: improvement) of the individual animal species. To understand this, however, we have to know the peculiar position and development of each branch of livestock breeding separately.

In the first place we have to study the most important branch of livestock husbandry: *cattle farming*. The overall increase in the number of livestock expressed in

| Year | Cattle | Horse | Pig | Sheep |
|---|---|---|---|---|
| | per 1000 head | | | |
| 1884 | 338 | 121 | 333 | 753 |
| 1895 | 363 | 123 | 402 | 488 |
| 1911 | 336 | 108 | 343 | 418 |

**Table 8.**

standard animal is mainly the result of an increase in the cattle stock. The 1880s and 1890s were the years of the main increase in the cattle stock too; between 1884 and 1911, however, the number of cattle was increased almost exclusively by increases in the cow stock. In the total growth of about 1·4 million that of cows was 1·3 million. This change occurring in the structure of the cattle stock parallel with an increase in number shows the purpose of cattle farming to have changed all over the country; meat and milk production became more important than draught power production. This circumstance changed also the regional distribution of the cattle stock in the Carpathian Basin. While the livestock was earlier concentrated on the wide rich grasslands of the Great Hungarian Plain, at the same time the density of the cattle stock was roughly uniform in the country – as the draught power demand of peasant farms was everywhere the same –, between 1880 and 1910 the centre of cattle farming shifted to the West- and South-Transdanubian areas having good markets and leading in fodder production too, as well as to the southern part of the Great Hungarian Plain. Besides the excellent grazing possibilities they offered, these areas were near to the new industrial centres. On these areas the rearing method changed essentially; cattle breeding aimed at beef and milk production required stabled rearing and field-grown fodders domineering in feeding. On these areas, especially in Transdanubia, grazing served almost exclusively hygienic purposes, as food was provided primarily by field-grown fodders. There was only one region in the country, Transylvania, where cattle breeding continued to serve traditional purposes: ox rearing. It was here that the method of rearing changed the least, grazing remained its principal basis. Nevertheless, the situation, here too, changed inasmuch as while in other parts of the country dairy farming and fattening came into prominence, Transylvanian ox rearing found a new outlet much more important than the former: the large-scale farms of Hungary met their draught animal requirements from that part of the country. So the method of ox rearing in Transylvania did not remain traditional either, although the transformation was somewhat different than elsewhere.

Changes in the rearing method and modifications in the purposes of breeding influenced the structure of livestock as well. The number of oxen stopped increasing, their share in the total number of cattle decreased, while the percentage of cows increased. It was then that a structural modification began in the livestock of Hungary, which produced proportions similar to those evolved in the structure of the cattle stock in developed industrial countries.

Change in the cattle breeds was, however, much more vigorous. It cannot be said that the change of breeds recorded by statistical surveys started and ended in this period, but the principal phase of the process took place between 1884 and 1911. The main point was that the grey Hungarian cattle was replaced all over the Carpathian Basin by various red-spotted breeds of Central and West-European origin. In the course of a large-scale import activity various breeds were introduced into Hungary; intercrossings between them and with the stock of the Carpathian Basin produced in a few decades – a relatively short time in cattle farming – a radical change in the composition of the stock. In 1884, 80·3 per cent of the cattle stock still consisted of grey Hungarian cattle; this proportion decreased to 51·6 per cent by 1895, and to 27·8 per cent by 1911. The rapid transformation consisted, in essentials, of the replacement of grey Hungarian cattle providing draught power and partly meat by more intensive *triple-purpose* breeds *equally* suitable for meat and milk production, and for draught work. The red-spotted (Fleckvieh) breed thus evolved in Hungary, and its local types developing relatively early (their origin and development is, even today, an unsettled question) had extremely good qualities combining the favourable features of the foreign breed (high milk and meat yields) with some advantageous properties of the native stock. These Hungarian red-spotted breeds generally were more easy to fatten than the western breeds, and in milk production competed with them.

Transformation did not, naturally, take place in a single step and was not smooth either. The red-spotted breed – though becoming typical by 1911 – only had a share of 57·7 per cent in the total stock. The joint share of the other coloured breeds of foreign origin was still 10·1 per cent at that time, as if indicating the enormous extent of mixing caused by the high-rate diversity of imported breeds. Contemporary protectors of the grey Hungarian breed considered this highly varied import of breeding animals carried on by large farms in those decades very harmful. True, the traditional uniform stock was broken up and numerous breeds appeared in the country, but besides its disadvantages this diversity involved great advantages too. Namely, in the attempts made – and which failed – for several decades the only sound, and ultimately realized, way of development spontaneously crystallized. That is why it was so advantageous that the imports of breeding animals were not restricted for decades, until the Ministry of Agriculture set up the breeding districts (1880–88), and that the measures taken – and finally enacted in 1894 – to make breeding work more or less uniform by setting up breeding districts were never applied in practice.

The rules of economy had a much greater effect than any government regulation. Where market possibilities were earlier available, in the western and north-western regions of the country, the wide introduction of dairy farming induced a spontaneous change of breed much sooner. The grey Hungarian breed of cattle amounted to more than 80 per cent of the cattle stock even in 1884, while western breeds made up already 40–44 per cent on these areas. Then, as the possibilities of dairy farming increased and new outlets opened up, western breeds spread further. By 1911, 91–94 per cent of the cattle stock in Transdanubia and Csallóköz* consisted of red-spotted breeds (!) indicating that it was in those regions that dairy farming took the largest share in agricultural production. On the area enclosed by the rivers Tisza and Maros too, the ratio of the red-spotted breed was above 72 per cent. Change of breed was much less extensive in the Great Hungarian Plain; the red-spotted breed was only represented by some 20 per cent, and an overwhelming part of the stock – nearly 59 per cent – still consisted of

* Area between two branches of the Danube.

grey Hungarian cattle. The Danube–Tisza Interfluve and the eastern part of Upper Northern Hungary occupied an intermediate place; some 54 per cent of the stock consisted in these regions of red-spotted western breeds. The grey Hungarian breed and the buffalo together made up about 57 per cent even in the most traditional parts of Transylvania.

This transformation of breed character cannot be separated from the modification of production and establishment of social organizations intended to increase the possibilities of production and marketing. In connection with this it must be emphasized, however, that on account of the specific Hungarian conditions the functions and social role played by the primarily marketing organizations introduced into Hungary on Western European models were in many respects different from those in Western Europe. The fact that the first co-operatives established in Hungary in the middle of the 1880s were located in Transdanubia, and that later on when at the end of the nineties the co-operative movement expanded, most co-operatives were concentrated in Transdanubia again, may be an indicator of the local character development of dairy farming. However, the co-operative movement was not only an indicator but also a typical means of small-scale dairy farming in Hungary. The first co-operatives based on Danish models initially drew large farms together. However, these were very few in number; in 1885 only 7, and in 1890 18 co-operatives functioned in the country. Owing to their large dimensions the large-scale farms of Hungary were in no need of the co-operative form, their production possibilities were from the beginning much better than those of small farms. The dairy co-operative created opportunities and provided essential means for the small-scale peasant dairy farms. The decisive change occurred in 1895 when the small peasant farms of Transdanubia began to organize co-operatives. The number of co-operatives functioning mostly in Transdanubia, and to a lower extent in the Tisza–Maros region(32) was 146 in 1898, 246 in 1900, 452 in 1902 and 651 in 1907. In other parts of the country their number was negligible. The rapid progress of the co-operative movement was not welcomed by the owners of large estates who believed their monopolies to be threatened by it. They made their dislike felt ever so often.

This is quite understandable if we know the Hungarian conditions of those times. Marketing did not mean any difficulty for large farms, as they only changed over to dairy farming where adequate market conditions had been set up, and their large volume of products easily found their way to the market. The situation was not the same with small holdings and peasant farms which could not compete with large-scale farms either quantitatively or qualitatively, although a larger part of the cattle stock (as of the whole livestock too) in Hungary was owned by small holders. In 1895, 77, and in 1911, 79 per cent of the cattle stock were reared in farms smaller than 60 ha. The value of the higher cattle density of small farms was, however, offset by the about 30 per cent lower body weight of cattle, and 50 per cent lower milk yield of red-spotted cows compared with the large farms (Table 9). The difference in milk yield(33) (data from 1895) was, however, much greater than that, because in the large farms cows were regularly milked all round

| Breed | Small-scale farm (below 60 ha) | Medium-scale farm (60–600 ha) | Large-scale farm (above 600 ha) |
|---|---|---|---|
| Grey Hungarian | 747 | 833 | 959 |
| "Mokány" and "riska" (reddish) | 832 | 1 159 | 1 219 |
| Red-spotted | 1 135 | 1 394 | 1 726 |
| Badger-coloured | 1 104 | 1 625 | 2 181 |
| Other coloured | 990 | 1 297 | 1 630 |

**Table 9. Annual milking averages (in litres of regularly milked cows in various farm size groups) (1895)**

the year, while in the small farms a considerable part of the cattle stock – especially cows of grey Hungarian breed – were still not regularly milked. Hence it follows that the national average of milk yield per cow was extremely low – about 808 litres – in 1895. The replacement of breed promised, however, radical changes in this field too(34).

The adverse conditions of small farms could only be alleviated through the activity of the co-operative system, since the difference between large- and small-scale farms under Hungarian conditions was extremely great, much more than in Western Europe. At the same time the extension of dairy farming in peasant holdings was unfavourable for large farms which were ready to purchase animals for fattening and well-yielding cows from peasants. The owners of large farms thought these possibilities to be threatened by the spreading of dairy co-operatives, therefore they took measures against them wherever possible.

Large-scale farms made use of other advantages of theirs too, such as their favourable position concerning breeding animals. No proper balance of dam and sire could be established since the mid-fifties, the financial means of breeders usually were completely exhausted by increases in the cow stock, which in turn involved a reduced supply of sires (in 1884, 57·9 while in 1911, 59·5 cows fell to one bull on a national scale). This ratio was – of course – much more favourable in large farms where the proper ratio of sires and dams was practically always ensured. It can thus be imagined what the conditions of the peasants' stock were like in this respect(35). The government made efforts to provide sires, in 1894 it established a fund for this purpose which practically meant that sires were either purchased from abroad or raised in Hungarian large farms. The government measures were not, however, able to fill the gap(36), and small farms were financially at the mercy of large farms for decades when they wanted to buy sires.

In short, cattle farming in Hungary underwent radical changes. The dominant breed of red-spotted cattle – as we saw – produced more milk and meat. In 1895 the average weight of red-spotted cows was 337 kg compared to the 287 kg weight of grey Hungarian cows. If we consider, in addition, that red-spotted oxen were slaughtered when four to five years old, while in the 16th–18th centuries the grey Hungarian oxen were slaughtered at the age of 10–12 only, we can understand that significant changes occurred in the output as well(37). The increase of yields considerably exceeded the demands raised by the increasing number of inhabitants.

This was the reason why a cattle stock reduced relative to the number of population made not only a higher domestic consumption possible but increased exports too.

Regional differences must be mentioned separately. In that period Transdanubia became the centre of cattle breeding. There the stock showed the highest density and the change of breed was in the most advanced state. This had an extremely favourable effect on the whole structure and production technique of agriculture in Transdanubia, and served in this respect as a kind of model for other parts of the country too.

Changes occurred in pig farming too, and were of decisive importance for the whole livestock. Around the turn of the century pig farming became the second most important branch of livestock husbandry in Hungary, and it was then that pig fattening developed into a separate industry more or less independent of the farm conditions. Characteristic of Hungarian conditions, this enormous change in pig farming took place in such a way that while the whole structure of pig farming underwent transformation, and fundamentally new forms of management developed, the old patterns survived unchanged. Among urban workers and in petty bourgeois strata pig breeding based on purchased piglets and similarly purchased feedstuffs, or on dish-wash, and mainly serving the purpose of consumption, remained in practice. The peasantry, that is the small farms, switched over to fattening pigs in pens, sometimes grazing them in herds; they fed their own-bred animals partly on pig-wash, but mostly on fodders produced by the farm. A part of these farms put their pigs on the market. By the turn of the century large-scale farms too developed up-to-date piggeries built partly on meat processing. In the 1850s and 1860s large-scale farms raised small numbers of pigs in general, but as the grain crisis arose their interest in pig keeping grew, as it required less investment and offered a more rapid return than cattle breeding did.

When comparing the beginning and end of the period we find the increase in the number of pigs not very considerable. In 1870 there were some 3·57 million pigs in the country; this number rose to 6·31 million by 1911. However, if we examine the development during these forty years in detail we find it to have been very substantial. According to data of Table 6 showing the number of livestock the rapid increase in the number of pigs fell within the decade from 1884 to 1895; the 1884 pig stock of 4·80 million grew to 6·43 million by 1895; this number even exceeded the 1911 figure! Did that mean that by the turn of the century the pig stock of Hungary attained the level it could no longer surpass? This would not have been the case even if we had not spoken of pig farming becoming an independent industry, and of agricultural production and commercial fattening making rapid progress in those very decades. It is only that the swine-fever that had been causing great losses in America for nearly forty years reached Hungary in 1895. The swine-fever first spread in the 1860s to England, then to Denmark and Sweden and later to Germany, and appeared on the large Hungarian pig market of Kőbánya* in 1895. It was a great blow to Hungarian pig farming,

* A district of Budapest today.

since it paralysed the earlier so important exports of live and slaughtered pigs; pork could be sold on foreign markets in a processed form (fat, bacon, salami) only. As an immediate effect, however, the plague took its tithe of the livestock. From 1895 to 1899 more than 1·8 million, from 1900 to 1904, 0·75 million, from 1905 to 1909, 0·94 million while between 1910 and 1914, 0·92 million pigs died or were slaughtered, that is more than 4·45 million in twenty years(38). This enormous loss is reflected by the figures when, at the same time, we find the number of pigs to have stagnated in Hungary between 1895 and 1911. The increase in the number of pigs during the forty years – which, taking the damage by the pest into account, was considerable in spite of the losses – was sufficient to make pig breeding independent of imports. In the seventies of the 19th century a fairly large number of pigs were imported, mainly from Serbia, parallel with the export. By the beginning of the 20th century this import decreased significantly not only on account of the reduced exports caused by swine-fever, but also because increases in the stock rendered imports superfluous.

As a consequence of the swine-fever, at the turn of the century increase in the number of pigs more or less stopped. This did not, however, prevent the stock from improving in quality. As we have already mentioned, it was, in fact, then that the easy to fatten, high lard producing "mangalica" breed became dominant. In 1884 almost 90 per cent of the pig stock consisted of lard-type pigs, mainly of mangalica. The mangalica breed became dominant first of all in the Great Hungarian Plain, the South (the main maize zone of the country) and in the hilly regions. The mountainous border lands were still hardly penetrated by this breed, as the extensive conditions of grazing and management did not meet the high requirements of mangalica rearing; in those regions the former rough-haired breeds remained dominant. The dominance of the mangalica breed involved the transformation of rearing conditions, and grazing was restricted to these mountainous areas. The 10 per cent non-lard type pigs recorded in the statistical surveys were not meat type pigs in the modern sense of the word, but partly "szalontai" and "bakonyi" breeds native in the Carpathian Basin, which never were regularly bred on any larger area, and partly those derived from crossing meat type pigs imported from Western Europe with mangalica.

A qualitative improvement of breeds was brought about by the spread of the modern meat type pig. The dumping of American lard ousted the Hungarian lard from the European markets, and – as a result of an increase in the production and consumption of milk – the demand on lard dropped anyway. Breeding and rearing of meat type pigs were promoted also by developments in cattle breeding and dairy farming (through the by-products) where it was managed on a farm-scale. So it was not accidental that the English meat type pigs were first introduced in the same parts of the country where the dairy farms had spread, and where more favourable markets were available. In the fifties and seventies of the 19th century, at the western border, in the Sopron district, the English (large-white, middle-white, berkshire, yorkshire, poland-china) breeds called meat type pig in Hungary of which the parents had been purchased at the international exhibitions in Vienna in 1853 and 1873 were widely introduced by the large-scale farmers setting up dairy plants in the vicinity of Vienna. Pure-bred meat type pigs were found nowhere else in the country at that time, and even later spread, but slowly, always in districts outstanding for cattle breeding too. Hence the statistical data showing that in 1895, 15 and in 1911, 20 per cent of the stock consisted of meat type pigs are not reliable, since an overwhelming part of the stock described as meat type consisted of crossed half-bred or quarter-bred pigs. However, we cannot speak of any wider spread of the modern meat type pig since the above mentioned English pig breeds considered in Hungary to be of meat type were registered in England as lard pigs. However, since the output ratio of meat/lard was with these breeds much higher than in the case of mangalica, they were raised as meat type pigs in Hungary. No doubt, however, that the appearance of these western – first of all English – breeds in Hungary at the turn of the century was the first step toward the systematic development of meat type pig breeding. We can thus witness, in pig breeding too, the phenomenon of a breed hardly becoming dominant when another one begins to spread. This was the case with mangalica too, which needed to be protected against more prolific, more profitable meat type pigs even before it could have ousted the former breeds. Meat type pig was undoubtedly the thing of the future.

As we have mentioned changes in the breeds involved the qualitative adjustment of the management method in pig breeding too. Rearing pigs by grazing was almost completely discontinued, and pigs were kept in pens and fed on field grown fodders on peasant farms as well. Modern pigsties and farrowing pens were built, first of all on larger estates, but in many small peasant farms too. Large-scale pig fattening became an independent industry. The largest fattening plant that supplied almost the whole country was the one established near the capital, at Kőbánya (now a district of Budapest) in 1869. It made a rapid progress: by the nineties it occupied an area of about 100 ha, and in 1894, within a single year, received more than 622 thousand pigs. Some one-third of this number was consumed in the capital, the rest was exported(39). The swine-fever – although setting back the production of the Kőbánya fattening plant to a great extent – could not stop the industrial fattening activity. While Kőbánya could never regain its former importance after the plague had been checked, up-to-date fattening plants of smaller capacity were established in other places of the country too, first of all in connection with large estates, whose fodder crops provided a sound basis for fattening. These fattening plants were set up partly at the western frontier, in export market districts: Sopron, Győr; further in the vicinity of larger towns like Pécs, Szabadka, Szeged, Debrecen, etc.(40). This phenomenon, no doubt, contributed to stabilizing the activity of breeding.

In spite of all this the small peasant way of rearing remained the dominant form of pig farming. Increase in numbers appeared first in small farms, large farms endeavoured in the first place to improve the quality of the stock. In 1895, 75·2 per cent of the stock was to be found in farms smaller than 60 ha; this proportion grew to 79·8 per cent by 1911, since due to the swine-fever large farms reduced the number of their stocks. This fact was taken into account in the fattening industry too, since its activity was mostly built on animals purchased from peasant holdings.

The change of breeds and the improvement and intensification of the method of management resulted in a powerful increase of output in pig breeding. As we have seen pig farming was the only branch of livestock farming where the numerical increase could keep pace with – and in that period even exceeded – the increase of population. Beyond an increase in the number of pigs per 1000 head, in the second half of the 19th century also the output per pig grew considerably; pigs of the mangalica breed were more liable to be fattened than the traditional pig breeds of the Carpathian Basin, so the average weight of pigs practically redoubled by the end of the period. As for fertility, on the other hand, mangalica did not bring any favourable change, as it only farrowed once a year, and then maximum five to six piglets. Significant changes were anticipated in this field too at the end of the period, in the first decades of the 20th century, with the appearance of western pig breeds. Although they did not weigh, when fattened, as much as mangalica did, but developed rapidly and were much more fertile. The main cause of their rapid spreading was, however, the transformation that the demands of foreign markets had undergone, which sooner or later called for a change of breeds in Hungary too. Hence a new upswing was expected in the output of pig breeding too.

Considering the second half of the 19th century as a whole, a remarkable increase is found in the number of *horses* too. The bulk of increase occurred in the fifties and sixties, from which the least statistical data are available. This can be explained with the transformation having taken place in the social and production structure of Hungarian agriculture after the abolition of serfdom. The system of detached farmsteads that evolved subsequently as a result of the cereal boom involved not only the areal extension of the ploughing operation but also the multiplication of transporting tasks, and was thus predestined to broaden the use of horses. The cultivation of light, sandy soils did not require as strong a draught animal as the ox, and the conveyance of produce too could be solved by horsepower. Hence the horse stock showed an intensive increase in the Great Hungarian Plain, while in other parts of the country the change was insignificant. Ploughing was thus performed in two different ways: on the heavier sticky soils of Transdanubia with oxen, and in the Danube–Tisza Interfluve and the Great Hungarian Plain mainly with horses. When in the Great Hungarian Plain the number of horses attained the level determined by the requirements of cereal production, the horse stock of the country practically stopped increasing; the numerical increases between 1895 and 1911 (ca. 30 thousand horses) resulted exclusively from increases in the army's and constabulary's horse stock.

All this determined the distribution of horses among the farms. An overwhelming part of the horse stock was found in small farms as peasant property. More than 86 per cent of the stock was owned in 1895 and 1911 by peasants. The great majority was used, accordingly, for draught work. About one-third of the total stock was gelded, indicating that horses mostly were used for draught work. For breeding purposes (mainly for export or for the army) horses were seldom maintained in peasant farms; this task was undertaken mainly by large farms.

Even if there were no essential changes in the number of the horse stock at the turn of the century, the qualitative changes were all the more important. At the beginning of the 20th century hardly any trace was found of the small, large-headed, grey-brown horses with bushy mane that were the progenies of an old horse breed in the Carpathian Basin. Horse farming starting in the first half of the 19th century, after 1867 an upswing transformed the total horse stock of Hungary. Besides the requirements of agriculture, the military interests of the government – in accordance with the contemporary strategy – demanded a large number of horses of excellent calibre. For this very reason horse breeding of all branches of livestock farming was what the government paid the greatest attention to and did its utmost for.

The four state-owned horse breeding establishments (Kisbér, breeding exclusively English thoroughbreds; Bábolna specialized in English and Arab horses; Mező-hegyes, breeding English and English-Arab hybrid horses; Fogaras, with Lippizan horses) as well as the four stud-farms supplied high quality horses not only for the state, but through several hundreds of breeding stations (972 in 1912) improved the whole stock of the country. There were, in addition, private studs too, which – while working first of all for export – contributed to the general improvement of the horse stock. This two-way improvement, though still not able to ensure the necessary number of stallions, produced significant results. The state-owned and private horse-breeding establishments were only able to cover 35–40 per cent altogether of the requirements for mating. This made it possible to keep stallions without permission, and no strict measures could be taken against it either, since the state-owned and licensed private breeding stations could not satisfy the demands. Exclusively, only high quality horses were bred for export and other commercial purposes, but the horse stock used by the peasantry was extraordinarily mixed. Many local types developed, and any improvement was extremely difficult, especially on areas of detached farmsteads in the Great Plain. It was only in the 1930s that a crucial change occurred here in horse breeding. Horses used in trade were, on the other hand, thoroughbred animals that won fame both at home and abroad, and made the horse stocks of certain state-owned or private stud-farms much sought-after. Parallel with the growth in number and horse stock of state owned and private horse breeding establishments the export increased in this period. The number of horses exported from Hungary increased from 4 000 in the sixties of the last century to 41 000 in 1895 and more than 62 000 by 1911(41).

*Sheep farming* in Hungary showed an unambiguous setback. Surveys made in the second half of the 19th century revealed that sheep farming as a whole was declining in Hungary, as all over Europe. When comparing the number of sheep in 1911 with that in 1850 we find a remarkable decrease; even in comparison with the 1870 conditions the stock was reduced by some 45 per cent. However, between 1884 and 1911 the decrease was not nearly as great as in the developed industrial countries of Europe (except France). This relatively moderate decrease can be explained by the fact that the conditions of sheep farming were not controlled exclusively by considerations of profitability, but also by the existence of large pastures, especially in the eastern part of the country and in the mountains, which could only be utilized by sheep farming. In addition, the function of sheep breeding on the peasant farms – first of all in the above mentioned regions again – showed hardly any change compared to previous decades. The sheep were raised first for milk, partly meat and wool, but mainly for hide. In most peasant farms the bulk of the stock consisted of racka and cigája breeds. On the central areas of the country, in the first place in Transdanubia and the Danube–Tisza Interfluve, part of the peasant farms changed over to rearing merino sheep, especially in the 1870s and 1880s. As a consequence the number of sheep belonging to the racka and cigája breeds decreased from 9·7 to 4·3 million between 1870 and 1895. However, in the same way as the number of the whole sheep stock stopped decreasing between 1895 and 1911, no further reduction in the breeds racka and cigája was found either, moreover, their number increased by 0.2 million. This shows that in these two decades the number of sheep decreased mainly in large-scale farms. The number of merino sheep fell from about 6·2 million in 1870 to 2·4 million by 1911. These figures indicate the position of sheep breeding in Hungary at that time, and the decline of the wool boom, the separation of the Hungarian sheep breeding from the Austrian-Bohemian textile industry made their effects felt first in the decrease of large-scale sheep stocks. It had an influence also on the distribution of the sheep stock in the different groups of farms. The majority of sheep was in the possession of large farms. By 1895 this proportion decreased to 53·4 per cent of the total stock; that was the amount owned then by farms larger than 60 ha, and even this continued to decrease. The rapid liquidation of the sheep stock of large-scale farms at the turn of the century resulted in a mere 40·2 per cent of the total stock remaining in the large farms by 1911.

We shall present here some details on the areal distribution of the sheep stock. Before 1850 a major part of the stock was to be found in Transdanubia, and it was there too, that the merino breed became dominant. At the turn of the 19th early 20th century in this region, and gradually in the central part of the country too, traditional breeds were replaced by merino sheep in peasant farms as well. The racka and cigája breeds became restricted partly to the Great Hungarian Plain, but mainly to the border areas, the alpine pastures of the Carpathian Mountains and Transylvania; in 1911, 3 million of the 4·5 million racka and cigája sheep were found in Transylvania and in the Carpathians. An overwhelming part of the sheep stock in these regions was owned by peasants, large estates engaged in sheep breeding were mostly found in the central areas of the country.

The regional distribution of sheep farming was modified by increasing difficulties in marketing, namely the marketing conditions of other livestock branches – especially of cattle rearing based similarly on grazing – improved at the expense of sheep breeding. Due to more favourable marketing conditions, on areas where the pastures were better, cattle farming began to push sheep farming into the background. The reduced grazing area and bad marketing possibilities did not lead to the introduction of more developed feeding methods but, rather, the centre of sheep farming was transferred to the eastern part of the country, where the poor alkaline pastures could only be utilized by sheep farming. On these areas the sheep stock remained thus intact, while in the western part of the country the number of sheep was sharply reduced; so within the sheep stock a considerable shift of proportion was caused in the regional distribution.

In connection with this, the new phase of development in European breeding sheep for meat had not appeared in Hungary then. With the import of overseas wool the fine-wooled stocks were replaced by sheep for meat all over Europe, as wool production was no longer profitable. The relatively low rate decrease in the number of sheep in France e.g. was a consequence of the introduction of various sheep bred for meat. At the time of the fall in wool prices France developed higher body weight merino types yielding both excellent quality meat and valuable wool: consisting of the English Dishley merino, the Charmoise sheep and a quickly growing type called merino-precoce. In Hungary, on the other hand, the production of sheep for meat could not be realized. Owing to an aversion shown by the population to mutton its consumption did not increase, and the exports for which France would have been the largest market were reduced by customs limitations. The volume of mutton consumed by the population in Austria and Bohemia did not increase either, so the export of Hungary was hard hit when in 1877 France raised the customs duties of live sheep and mutton. Hungarian exports were then reduced by half. Yet, there were certain changes in this field. In 1911 more than 9 per cent of the sheep stock of about 7·6 million consisted of meat type sheep. So the first steps toward the transformation of sheep farming were taken with the view of compensating for the permanent decline in wool prices.

Besides large animals livestock farming in Hungary was characterized by a number of small animals reared and bred too. From an economic point of view *poultry farming* was the most important of them. Poultry was always maintained in Hungary, but as for the number of fowls extremely contradictory data and opinions were published. The poultry stocks of farms were first registered in 1884 when the number of fowls was found to be 32·3 million of which 66 per cent (some 21·7 million) were hens. The total poultry stock of Hungary was first taken in 1895 when 29·3 million fowls were registered in the country (the fallback in numbers is illusory, registration in 1895 took place at a later date of the year than in 1884, and a large part of the stock had already been consumed). Most of them were hens. There were typical regions of poultry breeding e.g. the Danube–Tisza Interfluve, the southern parts of the Great Hungarian Plain as well as the area enclosed by the Tisza and its eastern affluents (Kőrös, Maros), where stock density was higher than average. Yet, the density of stock was more or less uniform in the country, although on the central areas grazing conditions were more favourable than elsewhere. But since most—more than 90 per cent—

of the stock was kept on peasant farms (smaller than 60 ha), the overall density of the poultry stock was fairly even.

Poultry farming had not attained yet the farming level of large animals at that time. The traditional view of poultry breeding not being equal to other branches of livestock farming predominated until the 1890s. Poultry farming was considered to be a secondary branch of farming, a work to be done by women, which in a large-scale farm where certain particular tasks would have to be carried out by paid workers was not profitable. Naturally, the situation was not the result of subjective considerations alone. The small peasant farm having many members in the family—i.e. unpaid—labour, and where adequate household refuse was available, was the ideal framework for the extensive poultry farming that took place in Hungary at the turn of the century. Similarly large numbers of poultry were maintained by the servants of large farms. Poultry reared in this way was very cheap, and breeding at that price level was not profitable for a large-scale farm.

The largest part of the poultry stock consisted of traditional Hungarian breeds. In the first half of the period in question, hardly any breeding task was solved. Eggs, feather and poultry meat were produced in sufficient quantities, and there was no governmental or social organization engaged in studying the questions of poultry breeding with any intensity. Due to the limitations of transportation, feather followed by live poultry were the most important export products at that time. Neither slaughtered poultry, nor eggs could have been exported in larger quantities owing to the given technical conditions, moreover, their market was not wide enough. It was around the eighties early nineties that the market of eggs and slaughtered poultry expanded, placing the egg and meat yield of the native Hungarian hen stock in the forefront. It was then that experts realized that the Hungarian dunghill hen—excellently adapted to the extensive rearing conditions in Hungary and which was given grain feed only now and then in winter, while in other parts of the year lived on grass around the house, on insects, grains scattered about in the field and farm-yard, or on household refuse—produced low yields and, in addition, as a result of several centuries of inbreeding both egg and meat production declined. The way out of this situation may have been partly by selection, partly by crossing. Both activities were started quite extensively. In 1891, then at the turn of the century again, the Ministry of Agriculture organized an exchange of breeding animals, purchased an improved stock from abroad and attempted an exchange of breeds between regions distant from each other. Accordingly, the improvement of Hungarian barnyard fowls was carried out in two ways, partly with foreign breeds, e.g. the Plymouth breed was introduced in Hungary in 1880–90, the Orpington at the turn of the century(42). A control exercised by the state from 1891 accelerated the process. Between 1897 and 1914 an exchange of poultry was carried out in the course of which 150 thousand imported cocks were distributed in return for barnyard cocks(43). The idea was fairly good but its execution not in the least. The distributed amount could not be enough to transform the enormous stock of poultry, and the breeds

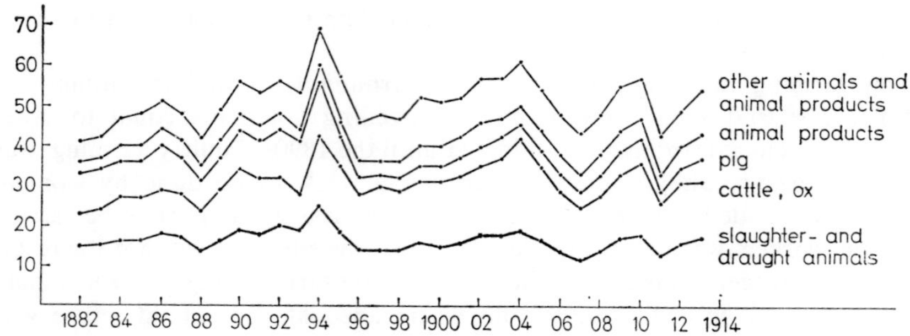


**Fig. 11. Share of livestock in the total export, 1882–1913**

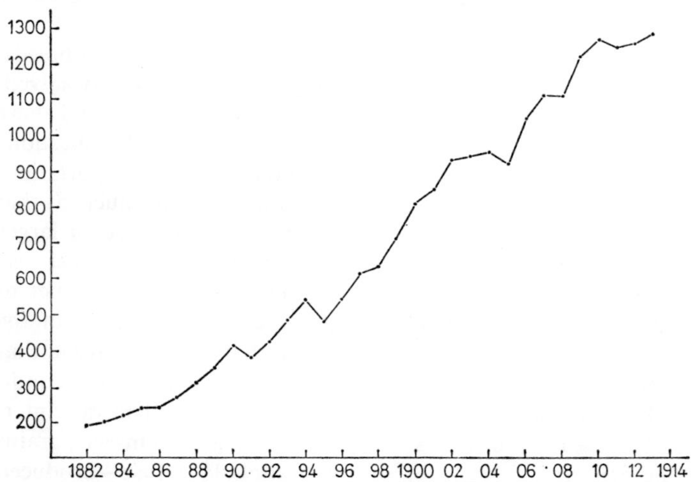


**Fig. 12. Export of animal products (1000 q) 1882–1913**

**Fig. 14. Cattle export (1000 animals) 1882–1913**

were changed according to the frequently changing fashion. As a result in many places extremely mixed breeds developed, which did not mean real improvement. Nevertheless, poultry breeding, as a whole, still showed some progress.

The result of this activity was positive inasmuch as the export of slaughtered poultry and egg increased considerably. At the turn of the century, by the 1910s the export pattern was completely transformed. True, Germany, the largest foreign market, hindered the Hungarian export by various sanitary measures aimed primarily at protecting the poultry breeding of Germany and improving its marketing conditions, but the western part of the Monarchy created such a high demand that could not even be fully satisfied by the Hungarian poultry breeding. Feather which had represented about 60 per cent of the exports was replaced in the structure of export by eggs and slaughtered poultry; the export of live poultry remained roughly at the same level, and so did feather(44), Hungarian poultry farming joining the international trade rather quickly, under the very influence of the market slowly advanced toward transformation. Around the turn of the century large-scale rearing methods began to develop as a response primarily to all foreign, and Hungarian town markets. In accordance with the contemporary conditions in Hungary under which the price level was determined by small peasant farms putting large volumes of poultry on the market at a very low price, these methods were primarily aimed at modernizing the marketing system rather than establishing large-scale production. In certain larger towns of the Great Hungarian Plain, e.g. Kecskemét, Kiskunhalas, Szentes, Orosháza, Szabadka, etc., that is, in the major towns of a poultry district, commercial fattening plants were set up where poultry purchased from peasants at the neighbouring markets were fattened for 8–10 days, then marketed. Large-scale methods were of interest mainly in slaughtering, plucking, drawing, packaging, cooling and transportation. A plant usually kept 20 thousand fowls at a time. Moreover, they even imported poultry for fattening from Romania and Serbia(45).

Development of livestock husbandry in that period is shown also by the data on *export*. The demands of developing industrial areas on livestock husbandry are reflected in these data. Since 1882 regular statistical surveys have been made concerning the export, and the data on the period between 1882 and 1913 give account of essential developments(46). Exports of slaughter and draught animals ranged approximately between 0·9 and 1·13 million a year at that time. The cattle export grew from 84–90 thousand animals to 444 thousand by 1904, then in subsequent years ranged from 300 to 400 thousand. At the turn of the century the export of beef-cattle redoubled (increased from 112 to 255 thousand). Exports of draught oxen and breeding animals too increased rapidly, especially in the 1910s. The export of oxen grew at a rather uniform rate from 75–82 thousand to 301 thousand by 1904. This was followed by a slight fallback; around 1910 it was about 200 thousand. Bull export too was multiplied; the annual 300–500 bulls exported regularly in the early 1880s amounted to 2300–2500 by the beginning of the 1890s. Then the growth of exports accelerated, the number of bulls exported exceeded 19 thousand at the turn of the century culminating with 39 thousand in 1913. The export of cows increased by similar proportions, from 1800–2000 to 6000 by 1893, exceeding 56 thousand in 1904–5 and culminating with 80 thousand in 1910. The number of steers and heifers exported in the early 1900s ranged between 15 and 20 thousand, sometimes rising above 50 thousand. It was similarly in 1890–1900 that the export of calves younger than one year grew, although fluctuation here was, of course, rather high, since the changes in market conditions affected first of all the young animals. The volume of cattle export at least doubled in these three decades, and in certain groups was even higher than that.

Beside an intensive fluctuation *sheep export* showed an essential decrease from the middle of the 1890s. From an annual 200–240 thousand the export fell to 100–130 thousand by 1910, and sometimes was even 30 per cent below this level. *Pig export*, on the other hand, made a substantial progress up to 1895, when the swine-fever appeared in Hungary too. Between 1882 and 1894 exports increased from 600 thousand to 1·3 million, then in the second half of the nineties and at the beginning of the 20th century fell back to 3–400 thousand. Some increase started around 1908, the export was then 5–600 000 a year, and in 1913 almost reached 900 thousand. The causes of this fallback are generally known: the swine-fever was responsible for it, which not only decimated the stock but also almost stunted exports.

The export of horses showed a considerable quantitative increase too, rising from 9000 in the early 1880s to 18–19 thousand by 1896; from then on it was regularly above 30 thousand a year, and as a result of this even growth, attained 52–62 thousand in the first decades of the 20th century.

The export of poultry and poultry products assumed considerable dimensions too. During the three decades the export of live fowls grew about threefold or sometimes even fourfold. Still greater was the increase in the export of slaughtered poultry, which rose from an annual 10 thousand q in 1882 to 135–145 thousand q by the early 1910s. Hence it was in that period that the export of slaughtered poultry became important.

The export of livestock products likewise showed a growth, from 186–200 thousand q to 1·25–1·29 million q. Increase, here too, was thus extremely important. The growth of exports was especially outstanding in milk and dairy products, eggs, raw hide and fats as well as in fresh meat. Some role was played in this by the fact that – as we saw – the export of pigs fell back at the turn of the century, and that of ham, salami and processed meat grew instead. Exports of feather and some other products (e.g. honey) remained more or less the same.

The exports of animals and livestock products increased thus in very large proportions. We have seen the numerical data, and find a similarly outstanding growth when examining the value of export too. The export value of animals and animal products increased from 102 million crowns in 1882 to 575 million crowns by 1913, while its share in the total exports grew from 20·38 to 30·18 per cent(47). Livestock breeding became thus a very important factor in the economic life of Hungary.

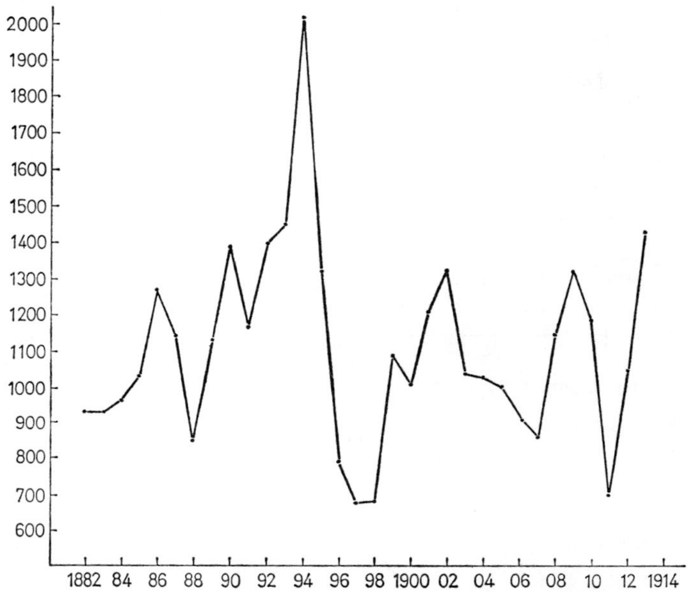


**Fig. 13. Export of slaughter and draught animals (1000 q) 1882–1913**

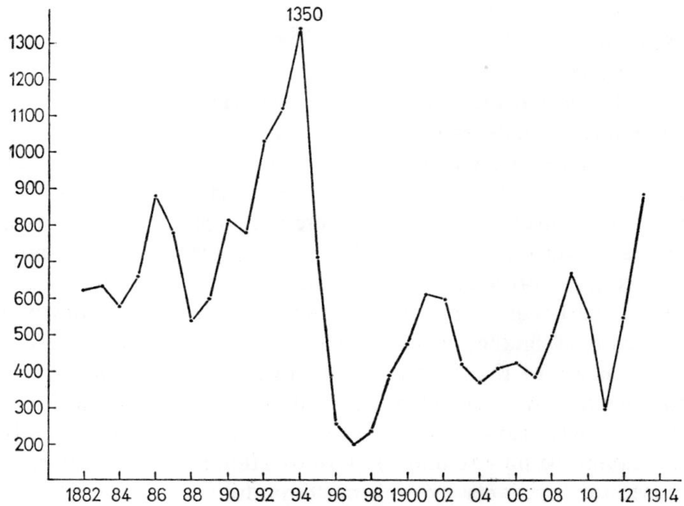


**Fig. 15. Pig export (1000 animals) 1882–1913**

X

**Fig. 16. Poultry export 1882–1913**

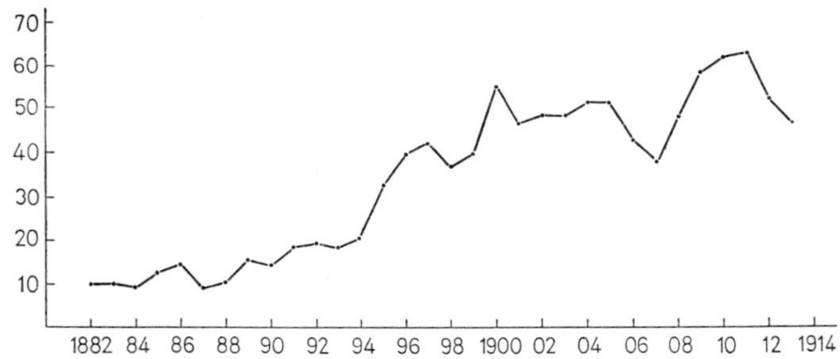


**Fig. 17. Horse export (1000 animals) 1882–1913**

In the period examined the western part of the Monarchy became the main outlet for animals and livestock products too. Generally 90–95 per cent of the export and in certain cases almost the total export found markets within the boundaries of the Monarchy. With some products, on the other hand, we can witness just the opposite process; the increasing volume of exports decreased the share of the western areas of the Monarchy, because Austria and Bohemia could not receive more products in these branches. Such were e.g. the sheep export, to some extent the horse export, and also the exports of live poultry, eggs, raw hide and especially of feather and other small volume commodities, for which the absorbing capacity of the Austrian and Bohemian areas was exceeded by far by Hungarian exports. These products found outlets in the industrially developed countries of Central and Western Europe, and some of them even in France, although the latter – being itself an exporter – attempted to block its markets from the Hungarian products by high customs duties.

One should not think by any means that a country like Hungary exporting such large volumes of animals had hardly any import of these products. Even if the increase of imports did not keep pace with the expansion of the export, there is no doubt that up to 1906 imports of most products were growing. Of the countries surrounding Hungary, from Serbia and Romania as well as from the Balkan territories of the Monarchy huge animal imports were realized(48). These animals were fattened in Hungary and expedited to the western part of the Monarchy. One must not think, however, that this import of animals could reduce the volume of Hungarian livestock export to any extent. It had only a supplementary part in the export; the kind and number of the imported animals were primarily determined by their availability in Hungary, mainly when for some reason production in Hungary decreased, or its increase could not keep pace with the expanding demand. The livestock export of Hungary to the Monarchy was only a part of the import carried on at that time by the Monarchy as a whole, and was highly advantageous for the agriculture of Hungary, as by means of this the import fodders could be marketed, etc. How independent the volume of Hungarian exports was from this import is shown by the fact that the increase in exports regularly exceeded the growth of imports, and that, when after 1906 the import of animals and livestock products was radically reduced as a result of a considerable rise in customs duties, Hungarian livestock breeding made up for the losses, from one day to the next and the absence of imports did not cause any difficulty.

The other component of imports was that of animals from Central and Western European countries. Imports from this direction had quite a different role from that played by Balkan imports. Even their volume was only a fraction of the latter, and in practice meant exclusively the import of breeding animals. As we said before, it was at that time that an extensive change of breeds took place in Hungary in almost every field. New, more intensive breeds were introduced, and the import of breeding animals was one of the main approaches. This import—when examined quantitatively—was not significant, but its implications were all the more important. During the 19th century Hungary too became a part of the powerful historical process by which the more intensive Central and Western European breeds entered the countries of Eastern Europe and transformed the pattern of livestock breeding there. The figures on livestock imports from Central and Western European countries show the realization of this process.

As we have mentioned, animal imports from the Balkan countries, Romania and Serbia suddenly stopped, when the increased agricultural customs duties introduced by a law decree in 1906 and enacted in 1907 rendered any further import impossible. Increased protective tariffs are worth being discussed separately, as they reflect the typical situation agriculture and livestock breeding in Hungary got into around the turn of the century.

The gigantic development of agricultural production and livestock husbandry within, it which characterized the turn of the century, did not take place at the same rate in the different regions of the country. It was, naturally influenced by farm conditions too. The development of livestock husbandry, the intensification of the whole agricultural production was felt as a tendency all over the country, but the individual regions gave different responses to the changes. On areas nearer to the industrial centres of the Monarchy, e.g. in Transdanubia, and especially in its western half, in Csallóköz, etc., it was more intensive than elsewhere. To give a rough characterization of the situation, the proportion of more intensive animal species (cattle, horse) and breeds (red-spotted cow, pig for meat, etc.) was much higher in Transdanubia than in the central and eastern parts of the country; in Transdanubia these intensive species and breeds (and accordingly crop production too) were in a more advanced phase than in the Great Hungarian Plain. In Transdanubia cattle began to push sheep out of the pastures, that is, the centre of sheep breeding started to shift to the central and eastern parts of the country, while Transdanubia took the lead in cattle density. There were essential differences in the distribution of breeds too. In Transdanubia spotted cattle, while in the Great Plain grey Hungarian cattle were dominant. Meat type pigs played, likewise, a much more important role in Transdanubia than in the Great Hungarian Plain, etc. The region stretching from the western frontier to the Danube line was thus ahead of the areas east of the Danube by one phase of development, and differences were even accentuated by the more intensive character of agriculture.

Farmers did not respond in the same way to the consequences of the grain crisis. The peasant farms generally increased the number of their livestock. These farms had a considerable surplus labour to be employed in tending animals and working in the field where the sowing area of grain and roughage crops increased parallel with the expansion of livestock breeding. The peasant farms took part in the development of livestock husbandry all over the country – though at a varying extent and level. In the western part of the country where market possibilities had even earlier attracted dairy farming, peasant farms developed first cow raising, then pig rearing based on the latter, while in the central and eastern parts of the country pig and poultry raising were first promoted, although the cattle stock of peasant farms undoubtedly increased in these regions too. Peasant farms were engaged first of all in livestock rearing and partly fattening. Livestock husbandry in the larger farms was not so uniformly dominant. With the exception of large-scale farms in the western part of Hungary, which produced for Austrian and Bohemian markets, cereal production continued to play a leading role in the management of large estates. Namely, these farms lacking sufficient capital were prevented from changing over to livestock breeding in a few decades. Those farms, on the other hand, starting intensive dairy farming and pig fattening were pioneers in the qualitative improvement of livestock breeding. They introduced new breeds, cows of high milk yield from the west, meat type pigs, etc. and offered an example of improved rearing conditions, more intensive management to peasant farmers. To sum up the tendencies of development: by a quantitative increase of livestock the majority of peasant farms shifted to the more intensive production branch of livestock husbandry, while most large estates (especially in the central and eastern parts of the country) adhered to the extensive branch of cereal production and tried to improve it.

It was, in fact, the demand of these grain producing large estate owners that manifested itself in the request of raising the agricultural customs duties in the

Monarchy. Competition by the cheaper overseas, Romanian and Russian grain crops and the cheap Balkan pork landed these farms – and naturally through them the whole of agriculture – in a difficult position. Their claim strengthened parallel with the competition of overseas products. That it was a claim of large farms alone was confirmed by the fact that the increase of egg tariffs was hardly ever mentioned among the requests, although Russian eggs meant a keen competition for Hungarian producers; but because egg was a typical product of small peasant farms, marketing difficulties were of no importance for the agrarian movement. The interest of grain producing large farms lay thus in raising the customs duties. By the turn of the century the stiff resistance of the industrial circles of the Monarchy (whose interest was to keep food at a low price level) induced these strata to exaggerate the problems of nationality, that is, their fight assumed the form of national policy. That is why the economic agreement with Austria to be renewed every twelve years was postponed in 1897, and an independent customs area was demanded (in which some role was given to representatives of the Hungarian small-scale industry and of certain neglected industries – e.g. textile industry). The attack made in a wide coalition was finally successful. After ten years of ardent political fighting the large estates won; the government party representing the interests of industrial circles and backing the given form of Austro-Hungarian compromise failed at the elections of 1905. Although the coalition of the opposition parties gave up its political claims (essential modifications in the form of the compromise), it did so only when the increased customs duties were put into force in 1906 and enacted in 1907. It is interesting to compare this situation with conditions in England where the much more developed bourgeois strata won in 1846 in the issue of grain tariffs. The divergent results of the fight reflect the difference between the two countries in the development level of economy and, accordingly, of society.

The increase in customs duties – raising the price returns of agriculture by an average of 30–50 per cent – was considerable. The per quintal tariff of wheat, so important for large estates, was raised from 3·57 crowns in 1887 to 6·30 crowns(49). The higher customs duties ensured the total market of the Monarchy for the agriculture of Hungary protecting it from the overseas, Balkan, and Russian agricultural produce. This is reflected in the tables containing data on animal imports, where an extremely great decrease is shown after 1906. The rise in customs duties – which resulted in an intensive increase of agricultural prices – was followed by an upswing in agriculture remembered even today as the "happy times of Franz Joseph" in the memory of the oldest generation. The effect of this increase in customs duties has been much discussed by the historiography of Hungary; it is a positive fact, however, that the annual growth of agricultural production ranging earlier from 1·3 to 1·8 per cent attained 4 per cent between 1906 and 1914. The rise in food prices, on the other hand, caused a considerable strike movement whereby workers achieved an adequate increase in their wages. The demand of agriculture for industrial products grew substantially; machines, fertilizers flowed into agriculture at a much higher rate than before.

# X

The reliable market of the Monarchy as well as the expansion of this market and increase of buying capacity in Austria and Bohemia rendered a development similar to that in Western Europe possible for the agriculture of Hungary in 1880–1910s. In the second half of the last century, but mainly in the 1880–90s, competition by the overseas grains shifted the emphasis in the agricultural development of Western Europe towards livestock husbandry, vegetable growing, orchard plantation and flower production. These countries laid stress primarily on meat, milk and dairy production, vegetable, fruit and flower growing; cereals as well as certain fodders were imported by them. Hungary had considerable amounts of grain surplus, a much higher proportion of the population was engaged in agricultural work here than in the Western countries, so the above described development would not have taken place here – or at least would have reached a much lower level – if the economically more developed areas of the Monarchy had not played the same role the increasing urban population – that is the inner market – had in the countries of Western Europe. Introduction of protective tariffs was one of the signs indicating that the economic level of the Monarchy as a whole had attained that of the Central and Western European countries which also introduced high customs duties to protect their agriculture (e.g. France). All this could not have happened if food requirements in the western part of the Monarchy had not grown at such a fast rate as they did in the second half of the 19th and at the beginning of the 20th century. In Hungary the same process of agricultural intensification – and especially improvements in livestock breeding – was due to the developed industrial areas of Austria and Bohemia which, owing to the uniform customs area, provided a sound market for Hungary. As a result of all this, however, the level of agriculture in Hungary was determined *in this respect* by the developed industrial part of the Monarchy, so it did not depend in the first place on the economic growth of the country. All this was, naturally highly favourable for agriculture – and indirectly for industry too.

Mainly this situation was responsible for the level of development of Hungarian agriculture exceeding so substantially the level of agriculture in Russia, Romania and the Balkan countries at the end of the last century. The latter countries had to tolerate the disadvantages of protective tariffs introduced in the Western European countries against the overseas competition (except those parts of Poland that belonged to Germany, because agriculture here was backed by the German protective tariffs), while Hungarian agriculture, due to the protective tariffs of the Monarchy, could make a progress, its market was more or less ensured. Additional investments involved by intensification, higher production costs were covered by agricultural prices, which under the influence of protective tariffs were much higher than prices on the world market. Before the First World War agriculture was characterized by an accelerated growth and increased intensification in Hungary too. All this was upset for a long time by the First World War.

**Notes**

(1) The press and economic literature of the early 19th century is full of references to the subject. In his memorandum submitted to the monarch on 4 May 1808, Joseph, Palatine of Hungary, pointed out the dominance of sheep breeding and the lapse of the other branches of livestock farming. S. Domanovszky: József Nádor iratai. (The writings of Palatine Joseph). Budapest, 1935. III. 177.
(2) See again the reports of Palatine Joseph (e.g. on 23 March 1804 he analyses the causes of high meat prices, and later refers again to such phenomena. Ibid. 653.) On meat shortage in the 1810–20s see E. Éber: A magyar állattenyésztés fejlődése (Development of livestock husbandry in Hungary). Budapest, 1961. 163–166.
(3) For summarizing data on price ratios see: Éber: op. cit. 117–118.
(4) For data on the extension of sheep stock on large estates, and on the growth of the sheep stock at the expenses of other livestock branches see: Éber: op. cit. 120–123; L., Gaál: A magyar állattenyésztés múltja (The past of livestock husbandry in Hungary). Budapest 1966. 288. As for the occupation of common pastures by the sheep stock of land lords and its effect on the serfs the statement of M. Táncsics, the famous contemporary politician of serf origin, is cited by Éber: op. cit. 123.
(5) In Hungary, like in all Eastern European countries, the size of landed property was a determinant of social class and strata. In Western Europe the production level of farms was primarily determined by the invested capital rather than by the land. In these countries difference in the production methods no longer existed between peasant and manorial farms in the 19th century, since the latter had been liquidated in some form or other during the previous centuries and was only found in traces. Economic development made the peasant farms equal in rank. In Eastern Europe—as in Hungary too—, on the other hand, the great difference between the manorial large farms (usually larger than 100 ha, sometimes even many thousand ha in size) and the small farms (below 60–100 ha) owned almost exclusively by peasants remained unchanged. There was also an enormous social difference between peasants and landlords which appeared in the whole pattern of their lives, from clothing to eating and other habits. Such great differences were already unknown in Western Europe. And this difference manifested itself in the economic activity, the production of farms too. Only an extremely low number of peasants had sufficient capital to modernize production. Therefore when we speak of small farms it is always about peasant lands, and by writing about large farms we always mean former seignioral (i.e. *by no means* peasant) farms.
(6) Numerous examples of management modernized with the development of sheep breeding in view are cited by Gy. Mérei: Mezőgazdaság és agrártársadalom Magyarországon (Agriculture and agrarian society in Hungary). Budapest, 1948.
(7) Serfs pushed out of the common pastures, and fight for pasture between serfs and landlords, see in Mérei: op. cit. 195–208.
(8) Emphasized by Gaál: op. cit. 265.
(9) Export data summarized by Éber: op. cit. 132–133. For the decade of 1831–1840 see Mérei: op. cit. 30–32.
(10) Éber: op. cit. 171.
(11) For the contemporary situation of livestock farming see Éber: op. cit. 125–130, 136–144, 148–159, 163–172, 175–181; Gaál: op. cit. 256–262, 268–343 and Mérei: op. cit. 24–29, 161–164.
(12) T. I. Berend–Gy. Ránki: Közép-Kelet-Európa gazdasági fejlődése a 19–20. században (Economic development of Central and Eastern Europe in the 19th and 20th centuries). Budapest, 1969. 88–90.
(13) For the export structure of the 1910s see P. Gunst: A mezőgazdasági termelés története Magyarországon 1920–1938 (History of agricultural production in Hungary 1920–1938.) Budapest, 1970. 58.

(14) A Magyar Szent Korona Országainak külkereskedelmi forgalma 1882–1913 (Foreign trade of the countries of the Hungarian Holy Crown in 1882—1913). Budapest, 1923. Magyar Statisztikai Közlemények. New series. Vol. 63.
(15) For the extension of arable areas at the beginning of the 19th century see: Közgazdasági Lexikon Budapest, 1898. I. 689; for the 1860s: Die Boden Kultur-Verhältnisse Österreichs. Wien 1868. For the evaluation of data see Éber: op. cit. 208.
(16) On the basis of data from Die Bodenkultur-Verhältnisse Österreichs, Wien 1868.
(17) Éber: op. cit. 204.
(18) These are approximative data, since we do not know what the hl weight of grain could have been at the beginning of the 19th century. Considering, however, that the improved wheats were widely introduced only from the late 1860s, hl weight can be regarded as having roughly been the same so far. For data referring to the early 19th century see Közgazdasági Lexikon I. 692; for the 1860s: Die Bodenkultur-Verhältnisse Österreichs.
(19) On the basis of data from Die Bodenkultur-Verhältnisse Österreichs. See further: Éber: op. cit. 207, 238–239, 252–253.
(20) For the beginning of the 19th century see: Közgazdasági Lexikon, Vol. I; for the 1860s: Die Bodenkultur-Verhältnisse Österreichs, Wien 1868. The data are interpreted in the same way by Éber: op. cit. 208–209. For the conditions and yields of pastures see: H. Ditz: A magyar mezőgazdaság (Hungarian agriculture). Pest, 1869.
(21) For the demand of coarse wool see: Gaál: op. cit. 418–419 and 424; for the economical production of coarse wool: Éber: op. cit. 244; for the export data: Die Bodenkultur-Verhältnisse Österreichs, Wien 1868. See further: Éber: op. cit. 248–249.
(22) For the price trends of wheat see: Árstatisztika 1867–1911 (Price statistics 1867–1911.) Magyar Statisztikai Közlemények. New series. Vol. 44, 14* and 15*.
(23) Ibid. 17*.
(24) Ibid. 15*.
(25) Ibid. 18*–19*.
(26) For the data see: A Magyar Szent Korona Országainak 1901–1915. évi mezőgazdasági termelése (Agricultural production in the countries of the Hungarian Holy Crown in 1901–1915). Magyar Statisztikai Közlemények. New series. Vol. 66. Budapest, 1924.
(27) Ibid. 44*.
(28) A magyar mezőgazdaság árhelyzete az utolsó évszázadban (1867–1963) (Price conditions of Hungarian agriculture in the last century 1867–1963). Budapest, 1965/6. (Statisztikai Időszaki Közlemények. Vol. 73). 10.
(29) Price statistics p. 27*.
(30) As a further reason, a part of the sheep stock owned by the peasantry continued to serve for the fulfilment of the producers' own requirements (hide, milk, meat). See Gaál: op. cit. 415.
(31) Data of official livestock registration made by the Central Statistical Office.—The documentary value of surveys is analysed in P. Gunst: Livestock Husbandry in Hungary from 1848 to World War I. Agrártörténeti Szemle 1972. Supplement. 26–28.
(32) B. Tormay: Egy fejezet hazánk mezőgazdaságának történetéből (A historical phase of Hungarian agriculture). Budapest, 1901. 22, L. Für: Az állattenyésztés szerkezeti átalakulása a századfordulón (Structural adjustment of livestock husbandry at the turn of the century). A Magyar Mezőgazdasági Múzeum Közleményei 1969–1970. Budapest, 1970. 277; Éber: op. cit. 313 and Gaál: op. cit. 408.
(33) On the basis of registration data from 1895.
(34) The national registration of 1895 estimated the amount of milk produced to be 1 443 million litres. The reason why the average per cow is so low (808 litres) compared with the data of Table 9 is that the latter only contains the data of regularly milked cows, while the amount of 808 litres is the average of all cows. Accordingly, a considerable proportion of cows—mainly those of Hungarian breeds—were not even in 1895 regularly milked.

(35) According to some data from 1881 bulls were 6 338 fewer in number than required for commercial production at that time. In certain counties the ratio of bulls to cows was 1 : 120–150. Éber: op. cit. 308.

(36) Government activity on a larger scale began at the beginning of the 20th century. In 1903, 4 263, in 1913, 8 953 bulls (of which 7 460 were red-spotted bulls of Simmenthal character) were distributed in the country. Éber: op. cit. ibid.

(37) Lecture delivered by János Pirkner at a national conference on livestock breeding in 1910.

(38) Éber: op. cit. 345.

(39) B. Tormay: Sertéstenyésztés. Magyarország földművelése (Pig breeding. Agriculture in Hungary). Budapest, 1896. 256–265.

(40) Ibid.

(41) On the basis of data from the publication: A Magyar Szent Korona Országainak külkereskedelmi forgalma . . . (Foreign trade in the countries of the Hungarian Holy Crown in . . .).

(42) Z. Mártha: A magyar tyúk nemesítésének első időszaka (The first period of Hungarian hen breeding). A Magyar Mezőgazdasági Múzeum Közleményei 1962. 69–73.

(43) Ibid. 77–80.

(44) For statistical data see: A Magyar Szent Korona Országainak külkereskedelmi forgalma . . . (Foreign trade in the countries of the Hungarian Holy Crown . . .). The structural adjustment of the export is analysed by Éber: op. cit. 363.

(45) E. Hreblay: A baromfi hizlalás és a hízott baromfi értékesítése (Poultry fattening, and marketing of fattened poultry). Budapest, 1900. 8.

(46) See the publication: A Magyar Szent Korona Országainak külkereskedelmi forgalma. . . (Foreign trade in the countries of the Hungarian Holy Crown . . .). Data presented in P. Gunst: Livestock Husbandry in Hungary . . . 42–43.

(47) Ibid.

(48) Data ibid.

(49) Price statistics . . . 18*.

# XI

# Agricultural Exports in Hungary (1850–1914)

The revolution and war of independence in 1848/49 was the overture of a new era even in the field of Hungarian agricultural exports. Though the structure and the volume of agricultural production could not be changed in a moment the former conditions were rearranged radically in many respects as regards the possibilities. The changes made their influence – felt in a short time – both in promotion and intensification.

1. The system of the Austro-Hungarian economic relations was established on new foundations. Apart from the political problems the change that came into being on the 1st October 1850 was of great importance as regards Hungary's foreign trade connections: the customs frontier between the hereditary provinces and Hungary came to an end.

So, not only was a retarding technical hindrance of the Hungarian economic development removed from agricultural exporting but a totally new situation came into existence in quality. Austria and Hungary became a unified customs area which lasted until 1918. After the Treaty of 1867 the question of an independent Hungarian customs area regularly emerged at the economic meetings held every 10th year between the two countries, and it must be admitted that the number of those people who wanted the cancellation of the unified customs area increased gradually, but until the end of World War I, the collapse of the Austro-Hungarian Monarchy did not threaten the existence of the customs union of the Dual Monarchy.

The customs union meant a unified customs area of Austria and Hungary defended by a customs frontier against other countries. Within the Austro-Hungarian Monarchy there were no customs duties or fees. The customs tariffs were unified.

Due to the customs union and the liberal economic policy realized within the scope of this union those branches of the economy which had comparative benefits either on the world market or on the Austro-Hungarian market, proved to be more profitable than the average, could mutual participate in the markets of the other party. For example the Austro-Czech textile industry depressed the Hungarian one for the whole period, and the same happened with the Hungarian agriculture or a few of its branches which left the Austro-Czech agriculture and some branches of the food industry far behind.

These features which provided comparative benefits for the union of customs areas were quite indifferent to the Hungarian agriculture at first and had only the advantage that in the event of a bountiful harvest or vintage Austria could not limit the imports of Hungarian agricultural products; and in the event of a poor crop it could not limit the Hungarian export over the customs frontiers in favour of Austro-Czech customers as the Austrian offices had usually done before 1848. Those Hungarian products which were sold in foreign markets were bought either by Austria and Bohemia or by the South-German states or ships carried them overseas. It is a fact that during the centuries the rate of hereditary provinces in the Hungarian agricultural export market had gradually increased but the customs frontier played an important part only in the increase of state incomes. As long as the customs frontier between Hungary and the hereditary provinces existed a unified internal market of the whole Monarchy could not have been considered and a great quantity of the Hungarian agricultural exports was disposed of over the borders of the Empire.

*Table 1*

*Average prices of corn**
(crown/q)**

| | Hungary | Austria | France | Germany | England |
|---|---|---|---|---|---|
| 1867–70 | 21.26 | 25.06 | 24.48 | 22.10 | 25.76 |
| 1871–75 | 25.22 | 27.92 | 25.20 | 21.44 | 25.22 |
| 1876–80 | 22.58 | 25.24 | 23.52 | 19.02 | 21.82 |
| 1881–85 | 20.62 | 22.12 | 20.86 | 19.06 | 18.50 |
| 1886–90 | 16.12 | 17.66 | 19.38 | 15.66 | 14.50 |

* Magyarország története 1848–1890. (History of Hungary between 1848 and 1890) p. 1057.
** Forints before 1892 are converted into crowns here and further. (1 forint = 2 crowns)

But this initial period ended in 1878. The appearances of the overseas corn in the European markets caused a lasting fall in prices from 1873 on; in fact it happened only to the grain crops[1] (Table 1). With regard to the Hungarian growing of corn it became important at which markets the Hungarian corn-surplus would be put up for sale. And at this point the unified customs area of Austria and Hungary had a role of prime importance. The protective systems of the Monarchy at last after minor or greater debate protected the price of the Hungarian corn. In consequence of the customs union the total territory of the Monarchy functioned as an internal market for the Hungarian corn and other agricultural products as a whole. Here the Hungarian corn

[1] For the process taken place in agriculture see: L. Gaál–P. Gunst: Livestock Husbandry in Hungary from 1848 to World War I. *Agrártörténeti Szemle*, 1972. Supplementum, pp. 7–48.; L. Gaál–P. Gunst: *Animal Husbandry in Hungary in the 19th–20th Centuries.* Budapest, 1977. pp. 11–63. For the whole Hungarian economy see *Magyarország története 1848–1890* (History of Hungary between 1848 and 1890) Volume 6. Ed. by Endre Kovács, Budapest, 1977. and *Magyarország története 1890–1918.* (History of Hungary between 1890 and 1918) Volume 7. Ed. by Péter Hanák, Budapest 1978. Also see I. Berend T.–Gy. Ránki: *A magyar gazdaság 100 éve* (A Hundred Years of the Hungarian Economy) Budapest, 1972; and I. Berend T.–M. Szuhay: *A tőkés gazdaság Magyarországon 1848–1944.* (The Capitalist Economy in Hungary between 1848 and 1944.) Budapest, 1973.

and the surplus of the whole Hungarian agriculture was sold at a higher price than it was in the world market. The whole territory of the Monarchy provided to as expending and increased degree benefits for the whole of the Hungarian agricultural production, which would not have occurred if there had been independent customs areas. It has to be taken into account that in the industrialized western part of the Monarchy the demand for agricultural products showed an upward trend which meant an *extending*, *stable* market for the Hungarian agriculture during the whole period, which would also guarantee higher prices than the world market ones at the same time.

In consequence of all this more and more Hungarian agrarian exports were taken to the markets of the Monarchy. The Hungarian exports could not supply the total amount of consumption of the Dual Monarchy from the middle of the 1890s and that is why the unified customs area became very important for the Hungarian agricultural production as it protected the Hungarian agrarian exports against the high pressures coming from the lower prices of foreign corn and flour and so a higher price for them could be guaranteed for several decades from 1878–80 to 1914 but especially from the end of the 1890s.

Other consequences of the transformation of the Austro-Hungarian connections after 1848–49 may be mentioned here. Besides the unified customs area the two countries had and maintained a common currency system – Austrian forint was used and later, after the change – over to the gold standard it was replaced with the crown and there was only one common issuing bank for them. Certain economic matters namely excise duties, inland revenues, postal and telegraph service, railway system, system of weights and measures, patent rights, qualification of noble metals, etc. were arranged in the same way on both sides of the Monarchy and in these respects there was a uniformity in practice all over the Monarchy. The homogeneous tariff system of the hereditary provinces and Hungary was based on a homogeneous and common currency system, with the result that the economic power of the developed and industrialized western parts provided an opportunity for Hungary to join the money-markets of Western Europe. Overall it ensured better possibilities for the import of capital supporting economic development than if Hungary had been economically independent. The Austro-Hungarian Monarchy had the reputation of being a good debtor and both the state and private loans of Hungary were enjoying the benefits of the fact that looked at over the whole period there was a continuous and (though showing a declining tendency) an active foreign trade balance of the Monarchy (Table 2). The common currency system was in practice the guarantee of the Hungarian demand for loans. All these had beneficial effects on the increase of the Hungarian agricultural production, the modernization of its structure, and the development of its whole production level.

*Table 2*

*The foreign trade balance of the Austro-Hungarian Monarchy**
(million crowns)

Excess of exports = +
Excess of imports = –

| | |
|---|---|
| 1840–1847 | – 15.4 |
| 1851–1855 | + 30.4 |
| 1856–1860 | – 40.2 |
| 1861–1865 | + 112,2 |
| 1866–1870 | + 99.6 |
| 1871–1875 | – 232.6 |
| 1876–1880 | + 185.8 |
| 1881–1885 | + 214.2 |
| 1886–1890 | + 318.8 |
| 1891–1895 | + 209.4 |
| 1896–1900 | + 126.6 |

* Magyarország története 1848–1890. (History of Hungary between 1848 and 1890) p. 991.

2. The possibility of realization of the Hungarian agricultural export was established on new bases. The changes that took place after 1848–49 are out of all proportion to the initial stages of building a network of railways though they coincided and in the end the influences of these two independent factors were interwoven and they strengthened each other. The building of the main railway lines changed fundamentally the technical possibilities of the agricultural export. In the Middle Ages only goods of high value could be taken out of the country (e.g. wine of quality) to western markets or else animals which could get there on foot. The Hungarian cow could get to the markets of Northern Italy and Southern Germany (as far as Strasbourg). Mass products mainly corns could be transported to foreign markets only to a minimal extent. For example Austrian towns situated on the border of Hungary and Austria regularly bought the Hungarian corn.

In the middle of the 18th century, long before the railway building, the improvement of the technical conditions of corn export started. Above all the building up of the military roads improved the possibility of exports in certain regions. The corn transport to Vienna on the Danube against the current of the river was also important. But these possibilities applied to a considerably smaller part of the country, until 1848. To a greater extent the region between the northern side of Lake Balaton and the Carpathians was concerned where during the 18th century a corn growing seignorial estate system based on socage developed. At the turn of the 18th and 19th centuries the boom due to the Napoleonic wars gave the extension of corn growing an advance mainly along the Danube and on Tisza from Pest to Szabadka (Subotica). However, in most parts of the country corn growing could not develop due to the lack of appropriate transport possibilities and in these territories several forms of extensive grazing husbandry had existed up to the building of the railway system. (Only the first decades of the 19th century brought about some changes, e.g. as a consequence of the development of the Austro-Czech textile industry there was a demand for wool because it was more valuable and transportable than corn. In this way even new regions such as the southern part of Transdanubia etc. could be involved in the agricultural commodity production.)[2]

All these changed after the building of the railway network. The first shorter railway line (a little part of the Vienna-Pozsony (Bratislava) – Pest main line) was opened in 1846. The traffic between Pest and Vienna started in December 1850 and then a great number of main lines were opened in rapid succession.

So the possibilities for the growing of corn for sale on a large scale were established. Even in the Great Hungarian Plain corn in demand in world markets could have been produced because in this way it could be transported. The structure of the Hungarian agricultural production changed very rapidly. The extensive husbandry based on pasturing was replaced with the growing of corn and it became widespread all over the country. Most of the meadows and grazing lands were broken up – and peasants took the place of shepherds. More and more corn and flour were carried out of the country not only to Western Europe but to the overseas countries, e.g. to Brazil, too.

3. Some other elements also forced these changes to come about. The contemporary economy developed totally new economic conditions due to the abolition of serfdom, to the abolition of immunity from taxes of the nobility and the introduction of new, modern forms of taxation (e.g. property-taxes). Taxes had to be paid on grazing lands cultivated extensively, so the income coming from husbandry sometimes did not cover the new taxes. Ploughing of grazing lands, and the start of corn growing on these lands were imperative economic necessities. At the same time the building of the railway network made the transport possible. The start of corn production could be realized without any great outlay and this branch of agriculture needed the least capital investment and it is not a negligible point. It must be noted that the reasons for the prosperity in corn production were brought about by the effects of several elements.

The sudden and radical changes transformed the Hungarian agricultural production rather rapidly. These increased the volume of production beyond the requirements of the home country and changed the structure of production, while low prices provided an opportunity to improve the level of production.

That is exactly the most important period of transformation (from 1850 to 1870) for which there are no authentic data and this also applies with equal force to the agricultural production and foreign trade of these two decades. As far as the latter is concerned the situation is even worse, because there are

[2] See P. Gunst: Die technische Entwicklung der ungarischen Landwirtschaft und die Hindernisse dieser Entwicklung. *Zeitschrift für Agrargeschichte und Agrarsoziologie*. 1975. pp. 59–70.

continuous data referring to export trade only from 1882. There can be found rather incidental data of the three previous decades of which documentary values have been strongly questioned. But this situation is not quite hopeless if the main tendencies of development are required in outline.

The statistics of the Austrian Empire are inadequate to furnish data with reference to the Hungarian agricultural production (with the exception perhaps of the animal-registration in 1857), for they do not contain any data of the Hungarian export and import trade separately as they refer to the Empire as a whole. So there are only rough data of the export of corn, flour, animal products, etc. (see Table 3) but in practice they do not give us information as the volume of the Hungarian export cannot be separated from the whole. It is quite certain that most of the corn, flour and animal exports were taken to markets over the borders of the Empire from Hungary. However, the Hungarian agricultural export trade was much greater than that as the considerable part remained inside the Empire entirely in case of a poor crop. The first data given by the Hungarian Central Statistical Office established after 1867 cannot help much in this case, though as it appears to me data coming from literary sources with reference to mass products (mainly corn, flour, meat, wool, wine) may not be wrong, at least they may not be worse than those of later times which regarded them as generally reliable. The winding up of the tariff walls between the hereditary provinces and Hungary after 1850 was the reason for the unrealiability of statistical records as later on only goods carried by train were registered in customs statistics, these were taken directly abroad

*Table 3*

*Foreign trade of the Austrian Empire (1850–1865)**
(1000 crowns)

| | 1850 | | 1851 | | 1852 | | 1853 | |
|---|---|---|---|---|---|---|---|---|
| | Exports | Imports | Exports | Imports | Exports | Imports | Exports | Imports |
| Sum total: | 317910 | 209694 | 301094 | 260046 | 398722 | 372980 | 465590 | 498032 |
| From this: Field crops and garden plants | 29024 | 8666 | 27932 | 12192 | 38160 | 10382 | 43158 | 12208 |
| Animals | 20830 | 6058 | 34006 | 11852 | 39370 | 13630 | 40776 | 20698 |
| Animal products | 2170 | 6352 | 1290 | 4160 | 2000 | 4634 | 2462 | 5524 |
| Fat and oil | 25082 | 40 | 32056 | 1214 | 24384 | 1372 | 28276 | 1750 |
| Wheat and spelt (1000 cnt) | – | – | 687 | 247 | 1263 | 188 | 1574 | 66 |
| Rye and mixture of wheat and rye (1000 cnt) | – | – | 580 | 437 | 2866 | 402 | 3011 | 260 |
| Maize (1000 cnt) | – | – | 908 | 98 | | | | |
| Flour (1000 cnt) | – | – | 70 | 67 | 79 | 115 | 95 | 165 |
| Oxen (1000 head) | – | – | 71 | 30 | 80 | 32 | 74 | 42 |
| Pigs (1000 head) | – | – | 408 | 46 | 548 | 79 | 601 | 124 |
| Wool (1000 cnt) | – | – | 90 | 68 | 135 | 113 | 140 | 226 |

* Source: Tafeln zur Statistik der Österreichischen Monarchie für die Jahre 1845–1865.

| | 1854 | | 1855 | | 1856 | | 1857 | |
|---|---|---|---|---|---|---|---|---|
| | Imports | Exports | Imports | Exports | Imports | Exports | Imports | Exports |
| Sum total: | 417456 | 436046 | 472928 | 465016 | 573714 | 502720 | 558086 | 461644 |
| From this: Field crops and garden plants | 49786 | 14508 | 38110 | 25644 | 27278 | 40172 | 24694 | 40718 |
| Animals | 36550 | 9812 | 37734 | 10282 | 35216 | 11160 | 27140 | 13474 |
| Animal products | 11554 | 8938 | 13868 | 8902 | 14302 | 10694 | 13978 | 13236 |
| Fat and oil | 29230 | 1428 | 32878 | 2044 | 36590 | 2484 | 28774 | 3600 |
| Wheat and spelt (1000 cnt) | 2097 | 289 | 1554 | 369 | 685 | 1081 | 621 | 1607 |
| Rye and mixture of wheat and rye (1000 cnt) | 3910 | 702 | 2536 | 1826 | 1629 | 2877 | 1386 | 884 |
| Maize (1000 cnt) | 120 | 106 | 138 | 242 | 122 | 303 | 156 | 614 |
| Flour (1000 cnt) | 56 | 24 | 49 | 29 | 61 | 26 | 48 | 35 |
| Oxen (1000 head) | 636 | 90 | 735 | 75 | 611 | 92 | 400 | 106 |
| Pigs (1000 head) | 291 | 157 | 222 | 203 | 184 | 233 | 236 | 186 |
| Wool (1000 cnt) | | | | | | | | |

| | 1858 | | 1859 | | 1860 | | 1861 | |
|---|---|---|---|---|---|---|---|---|
| | Imports | Exports | Imports | Exports | Imports | Exports | Imports | Exports |
| Sum total: | 616570 | 551198 | 538040 | 585358 | 491348 | 652770 | 496844 | 651770 |
| From this: Field crops and garden plants | 29852 | 32526 | 29846 | 34906 | 24002 | 73728 | 24362 | 86818 |
| Animals | 33176 | 12772 | 30354 | 13510 | 24114 | 15272 | 35580 | 18880 |
| Animal products | 13100 | 11362 | 12190 | 11250 | 24572 | 12176 | 30082 | 10654 |
| Fat and oil | 37388 | 3010 | 26736 | 4912 | 23062 | 6198 | 27226 | 7060 |
| Wheat and spelt (1000 cnt) | – | – | – | – | 446 | 2861 | 485 | 5829 |
| Rye and mixture of wheat and rye (1000 cnt) | – | – | – | – | 1271 | 2420 | 1363 | 1668 |
| Maize (1000 cnt) | – | – | – | – | 255 | 623 | 273 | 797 |
| Flour (1000 cnt) | – | – | – | – | 60 | 47 | 86 | 47 |
| Oxen (1000 head) | – | – | – | – | 326 | 128 | 540 | 241 |
| Pigs (1000 head) | – | – | – | – | 218 | 247 | 225 | 221 |
| Wool (1000 cnt) | | | | | | | | |

| | 1862 | | 1863 | | 1864 | | 1865 | |
|---|---|---|---|---|---|---|---|---|
| | Imports | Exports | Imports | Exports | Imports | Exports | Imports | Exports |
| Sum total: | 526152 | 651142 | 569614 | 643452 | 545074 | 702638 | 557730 | 730262 |
| From this: Field crops and garden plants | 25970 | 85266 | 28660 | 58014 | 36146 | 68000 | 28890 | 99116 |
| Animals | 32750 | 17022 | 29470 | 16458 | 24002 | 16230 | 25712 | 20378 |
| Animal products | 24840 | 9818 | 23228 | 14936 | 21376 | 17338 | 22930 | 16458 |
| Fat and oil | 29896 | 5238 | 34490 | 6216 | 26332 | 9308 | 30644 | 11124 |
| Wheat and spelt (1000 cnt) | 446 | 5051 | 713 | 1878 | 1004 | 2445 | 599 | 4968 |
| Rye and mixture of wheat and rye (1000 cnt) | 1673 | 1413 | 1018 | 1441 | 1957 | 887 | 1431 | 2476 |
| Maize (1000 cnt) | 178 | 880 | 323 | 735 | 391 | 811 | 343 | 1183 |
| Flour (1000 cnt) | 83 | 39 | 62 | 35 | 57 | 43 | 38 | 66 |
| Oxen (1000 head) | 464 | 187 | 522 | 137 | 350 | 73 | 486 | 108 |
| Pigs (1000 head) | 214 | 327 | 214 | 357 | 251 | 367 | 219 | 374 |
| Wool (1000 cnt) | | | | | | | | |

over the frontiers of Hungary. At the same time many products were carried by ship or cart and a great deal of animals were driven on foot even at the end of the 1860s or the beginning of the 1870s. The statistics do not contain the data of the products exported in this way. That is why the statistical data of agricultural exporting between 1850–1875 were considered to be unreliable. Moreover between 1876–82 there was no publication of data at all.

Apart from the diversity of statistical surveying and other difficulties coming from data processing taking the period as a whole and looking over the agricultural export trade we may say that between 1848/49 and 1914 the common Austro-Hungarian customs area and the possibility of railway transport accelerated the processes in connection with the Hungarian agricultural exports which were present even in the 18th century and at the beginning of the 19th century. Above all the volume of agricultural exports increased rapidly. The value of the total amount in terms of money does not show this definitely (Table 4) however, the data referring to the amount of exports show this process more positively. The increase of exports accelerated especially at the beginning of the period in the 1850s and partly in the 1860s which between 1845 and 1868 exceeded 5% a year relying on constant prices. This decreased to 2.5% a year in the 1870s and then increased to 4% again in the 1880–90s though sometimes it also reached 5%. A considerable part of the exports derived from agriculture (80–85% in about 1845, later 65–70% and in the 1900s it was still 60%), so the volume of the Hungarian agricultural exports increased rapidly in the years for which we have no separate data referring to them.[3]

*Table 4*

*Foreign trade of Hungary between 1868 and 1874*
(million crowns)

| | Imports | Exports | Excess of exports (= +) Excess of imports (= –) |
|---|---|---|---|
| 1868* | 639.40 | 660.00 | +20.60 |
| 1869** | 817.94 | 659.50 | –158.40 |
| 1870 | 688.14 | 685.74 | –2.40 |
| 1871 | 944.62 | 715.14 | –229.48 |
| 1872 | 976.28 | 616.16 | –360.12 |
| 1873 | 913.56 | 600.18 | –313.38 |
| 1874 | 904.76 | 577.84 | –326.92 |

* Károly Keleti: Visszapillantás közgazdaságunk egy negyed évszázadára. (Review of Hungary's 25 year-old economy) Budapest, 1878. p. 21.
** Referring to 1869–1874. Magyar Statisztikai Évkönyv (Hungarian Statistical Annual), V., Kereskedelmi Forgalom (Trade) 1874–1889. pp. 2–3.

[3] *Magyarország története 1848–1890.* (History of Hungary between 1848 and 1890.) p. 994.

In fact, the earlier tendencies appeared in the transformation of the agricultural export structure, too. While in the Middle Ages Hungary exported cattle and it was during the 18th–19th centuries that for the first time the export of pigs became also a dominant factor. But the more important change in structure was that the export of corn gradually increased from the second half of the 18th century. The exports of wool and the rapid increase of its volume transformed similarly the traditional structure of exporting.[4] In the second half of the 19th century these structural changes continued and other elements had influences only to a lesser extent e.g. the export of food products, sugar and flour, are the most important among them which will be mentioned later in detail. Summing up of transformation of the agricultural export structure in general it can be said that while about one-third of the agricultural export was corn and the other two-thirds were animals earlier, in the 1890s this rate was reversed completely and the volume of the Hungarian agricultural exports multiplied. The collective labeling of agricultural products cannot conceal the important structural change in the export of plant and animal products. Among the plant products, wheat and maize but mainly flour had become an important part in export and among the animal products the export of pigs and later poultry nearly reached the importance of cattle; egg and leather took the place of wool which had been supplanted by the second half of the 19th century. The structure and the components of the Hungarian agricultural exports became significantly modern.

The analysation of each component may begin with an examination of the volume of exports. The volume of the most important products (corn, flour, fruit, vegetables and sugar) increased considerably between 1882–1911. This increase was more than 40% in the case of corn and the increase of flour exports was more than 100% while the export of vegetables increased by 250% and the export of sugar also increased ninefold (Table 5). If we compare these with the period of 1848/49 we can see that the export of these products increased to an even greater extent, though here we have neglected the exports of animals and animal products. Nevertheless the exports of cattle between 1882–1913 increased by 250% and the exports of pigs by 50% at least.

[4] In the Hungarian exports livestocks mainly cattle and wine played the most important role until the middle of the 18th century. Even in the middle of the 18th century cattle formed the 34–43% and wine the 12–21% of exports. Corn could hardly reach 5–17% , and wool 1–6% of the whole export. See Gy. Ember: Magyarország külkereskedelmi áruforgalma a XVIII. század második harmadában. (The Hungarian Foreign Trade in the Second Third of the 18th Century.) *Századok*. 1975. pp. 796–896. By the beginning of the 19th century the structure of exports changed considerably. Between 1819–1829 14.9% was livestocks, 11.84% was wine while corn formed the 12.4% of exports, and wool became the most important article (42.20% !) Tobacco also appeared here (4.2%). See Gy. Mérei: A Magyar Királyság külkereskedelmi piaci viszonyai 1790–1848 között. (The Foreign Trade Markets of the Hungarian Kingdom Between 1790–1848.) *Századok*. 1981. p. 484.

With regard to the value the situation is somewhat different. The price structure referring to basic commodities was modified significantly so that as a consequence of the overseas competition there was a remarkable decline in prices of corn and flour in the 1880s and after all this decline in the price of meat was not felt to such a degree. The rate of decline in price of cattle reached that of corn at the turn of the century but the price level of pigs remained the same during the whole period and it grew rapidly in the first decade

*Table 5*

*The main articles of the Hungarian exports**
(1000 tons or 1000 heads)
From these

| | Corn | Flour | Slaughter and draught animals | Cattle | Pig | Animal products | Sugar |
|---|---|---|---|---|---|---|---|
| 1882 | 1578.1 | 289.1 | 929.3 | 84.3 | 618.5 | 186.1 | 19.0 |
| 1883 | 1531.9 | 354.0 | 933.8 | 90.3 | 633.9 | 203.7 | 20.2 |
| 1884 | 1378.2 | 349.3 | 958.5 | 91.8 | 583.5 | 215.6 | 23.2 |
| 1885 | 1623.2 | 349.9 | 1034.3 | 99.5 | 657.3 | 243.2 | 28.0 |
| 1886 | 1560.5 | 353.9 | 1273.5 | 115.3 | 875.9 | 239.7 | 20.8 |
| 1887 | 1615.0 | 371.8 | 1141.4 | 126.5 | 778.1 | 270.1 | 27.0 |
| 1888 | 2084.5 | 475.5 | 854.8 | 127.3 | 542.0 | 306.4 | 21.1 |
| 1889 | 1766.0 | 461.8 | 1029.1 | 151.4 | 601.5 | 347.7 | 30.1 |
| 1890 | 2102.8 | 446.8 | 1388.7 | 210.0 | 814.1 | 410.6 | 34.0 |
| 1891 | 2089.5 | 481.2 | 1169.4 | 172.6 | 778.1 | 381.5 | 40.4 |
| 1892 | 2049.3 | 497.2 | 1398.4 | 146.6 | 1031.7 | 422.0 | 40.4 |
| 1893 | 2214.4 | 557.7 | 1451.0 | 119.6 | 1116.0 | 480.1 | 65.1 |
| 1894 | 2037.6 | 596.0 | 2018.7 | 245.1 | 1354.9 | 540.9 | 63.9 |
| 1895 | 2031.6 | 644.5 | 1319.7 | 247.1 | 707.6 | 484.1 | 66.6 |
| 1896 | 2714.2 | 718.9 | 793.8 | 238.4 | 255.7 | 536.4 | 87.0 |
| 1897 | 2132.1 | 575.3 | 681.7 | 247.6 | 200.3 | 614.3 | 103.8 |
| 1898 | 1854.9 | 486.0 | 676.1 | 255.3 | 236.7 | 630.8 | 124.8 |
| 1899 | 2239.3 | 566.9 | 1093.1 | 294.2 | 391.2 | 705.0 | 135.6 |
| 1900 | 2648.6 | 686.2 | 1005.4 | 321.5 | 484.9 | 808.3 | 172.9 |
| 1901 | 2403.4 | 708.0 | 1211.6 | 326.3 | 611.2 | 849.9 | 188.8 |
| 1902 | 2633.6 | 709.2 | 1320.6 | 366.8 | 604.0 | 934.8 | 173.6 |
| 1903 | 2665.4 | 771.4 | 1044.3 | 391.2 | 413.1 | 935.1 | 213.5 |
| 1904 | 2181.0 | 719.3 | 1032.4 | 444.5 | 372.9 | 948.6 | 154.9 |
| 1905 | 2339.6 | 712.0 | 1003.1 | 374.6 | 408.3 | 921.2 | 162.5 |
| 1906 | 2785.7 | 790.8 | 910.0 | 295.8 | 425.1 | 1049.7 | 140.1 |
| 1907 | 2892.0 | 797.7 | 859.6 | 264.6 | 392.3 | 1109.8 | 142.0 |
| 1908 | 2396.2 | 675.2 | 1148.3 | 368.7 | 504.4 | 1110.5 | 211.0 |
| 1909 | 2268.5 | 661.8 | 1324.5 | 431.5 | 674.5 | 1216.4 | 162.0 |
| 1910 | 2377.1 | 636.8 | 1186.3 | 422.3 | 550.7 | 1266.3 | 200.9 |
| 1911 | 2726.3 | 748.3 | 702.4 | 256.9 | 301.7 | 1251.0 | 179.7 |
| 1912 | 2497.8 | 828.7 | 1052.7 | 340.7 | 547.6 | 1259.0 | 356.9 |
| 1913 | 2375.6 | 813.3 | 1426.0 | 347.3 | 893.1 | 1294.6 | 422.3 |

* On the basis of data published in A Magyar Szent Korona Országainak 1882–1913. évi külkereskedelmi forgalma. (The Foreign Trade of the Hungarian Holy Crown Countries between 1882 and 1913.) Budapest, 1923. Magyar Statisztikai Közlemények, Új sorozat 63.k. (Papers in Hungarian Statistics. New Series, Vol. 63.)

of the 20th century (Table 6). That is why it was unfortunate that swine-fever kept the Hungarian agriculture from taking advantage of this large-scale prosperity. As far as the value of exports is concerned its growth rate does not show significantly the rapid increase of the Hungarian agricultural exports. The reason why we do not mention a long-lasting fall in the rate of exchange for Hungary is because the price level of imported basic commodities also decreased considerably in these decades.

*Table 6**

*Change of export-prices (q or heads/crown)*

| | Average of 1882–86 | % | Average of 1887–91 | % | Average of 1892–96 | % |
|---|---|---|---|---|---|---|
| Corn | 18.20 | 100 | 16.05 | 98 | 15.33 | 84 |
| Flour | 28.33 | 100 | 26.84 | 92 | 23.25 | 82 |
| Cattle | 470.- | 100 | 425.- | 90 | 419.- | 89 |
| Pig | 118.- | 100 | 120.- | 102 | 118.- | 100 |

| | Average of 1897–1901 | % | Average of 1902–1906 | % | Average of 1907–11 | % |
|---|---|---|---|---|---|---|
| Corn | 18.02 | 99 | 17.03 | 94 | 23.49 | 129 |
| Flour | 26.61 | 94 | 25.06 | 88 | 33.69 | 119 |
| Cattle | 391.- | 83 | 447.- | 95 | 487.00 | 104 |
| Pig | 127.- | 108 | 137.- | 116 | 162.00 | 137 |

* A Magyar Szent Korona országainak 1882–1913. évi külkereskedelmi forgalma. (The Foreign Trade of the Hungarian Holy Crown Countries between 1882 and 1913.) p.3.

The value of the Hungarian foreign trade between 1882–1913 grew significantly, the exports doubled and the imports went up by more than 120% (due to the increased consumption and investments of the last years of peace). In the course of the 32 years between 1882–1913 the country had excess of exports in 15 years altogether, but in the other 17 years the imports were greater, and finally the balance of foreign trade of these three decades was passive at 635 million crowns (the steady trade balance of 916 million crowns between 1909–1913 was essential in this case because there was an active balance in the previous decades) (Table 7). In spite of the quantitative records the steady trade balance – mentioned above – was due to the fall of prices in agricultural products and above all corn, on the one hand and the serious damage to agriculture after 1895 (swine-fever, phylloxera) on the other.

Agricultural products were more than half of the total Hungarian exports and about 60% including export of wood. Taking only the five most important

*Table 7*

*Development of the Hungarian foreign trade*
(million crowns)*

| Average of the years | Imports | Exports | Excess of imports (= +) Excess of exports (= −) |
|---|---|---|---|
| 1882–1885 | 918.8 | 842.9 | − 76.9 |
| 1886–1890 | 896.9 | 902.1 | + 5.2 |
| 1891–1895 | 1050.4 | 1058.7 | + 8.3 |
| 1896–1900 | 1141.5 | 1160.6 | + 19.1 |
| 1901–1905 | 1242.7 | 1338.9 | + 96.2 |
| 1906–1910 | 1685.7 | 1625.6 | − 60.1 |
| 1911 | 2082.2 | 1830.4 | − 251.8 |
| 1912 | 2212.1 | 1962.8 | − 249.3 |
| 1913 | 2075.3 | 1904.7 | − 171.6 |

* A Magyar Szent Korona Országainak 1882–1913. évi külkereskedelmi forgalma. (The Foreign Trade of the Hungarian Holy Crown Countries between 1882 and 1913.) p. 3.

*Table 8*

*The shares of the most important agricultural products in Hungarian exports* (per cent)*

| | Corn | Flour | Corn and flour together | Slaughter and draught animals | Animal products | Sugar | Together |
|---|---|---|---|---|---|---|---|
| 1882–91 | 21.5 | 11.9 | 33.4 | 16.6 | 3.7 | 1.3 | 55.0 |
| 1892–1901 | 19.2 | 13.4 | 32.6 | 17.1 | 4.5 | 2.8 | 57.0 |
| 1902–1911 | 17.4 | 13.7 | 31.1 | 15.9 | 4.8 | 3.1 | 54.9 |
| 1912 | 15.9 | 13.5 | 29.4 | 15.5 | 1.5 | 5.7 | 55.1 |
| 1913 | 13.7 | 13.5 | 27.2 | 17.0 | 5.1 | 5.6 | 54.9 |

* A Magyar Szent Korona Országainak 1882–1913. évi külkereskedelmi forgalma. (The Foreign Trade of the Hungarian Holy Crown Countries between 1882 and 1913.) p. 20.

agricultural groups of products into consideration the exports of these were about 55% of the total amount (Table 8). Only the shave of corn and flour reached and went beyond the one-third of the whole exports and in this proportion flour went on growing even after 1882. The structural division of the total export value of wheat and rye for bread and flour shows fairly well that in the last decade of the period the value of flour exports grew to more than the 60% of the total bread-crops and flour exports. It was as a result of this that in the 1880s and mainly in the middle of the 1890s the exports of Hungarian corn to the markets over the frontiers of the Austro-Hungarian Monarchy practically came to an end. There was a growth of demand for corn in the well-developed regions of the Monarchy as a result of which the customs area became clearly an import region in which German and French protective duties played a prominent part. These countries kept the interests of their own milling industry in view so that the Hungarian corn and flour were excluded from these countries. This happened also in Great Britain but the reasons were different here. In English markets free trade was encouraged both in theory and in practice so the Hungarian flour was both saleable and marketable there as long as its price corresponded to that of the world market or its quality was better. The only reason why the Hungarian flour could keep its position in English markets from the 1880s in consequence of the price competition of the American wheat was its good quality. When the American flour made this grade it replaced the Hungarian flour because it was the same, or nearly the same in quality, but it was sold at a lower price.[5] So the Hungarian corn and flour were excluded from the markets of Western Europe by the middle of the 1890s. But at that time there was an extension of the market in the western part of the Monarchy which could absorb the Hungarian corn and flour exports. There is an example that is characteristic of this period: between 1882–1913 the exports of the Hungarian flour to the hereditary provinces increased fivefold! Between 1882–1886 the 59.6% of flour exports were sold in the Monarchy but between 1907–1911 the percentage was already 96.4% (Table 9).

Maize production was a rather new branch of the Hungarian corn growing and its rapid development was closely connected with the disintegration of the three course rotation system. Though maize exports produced a changing

*Table 9*

*The structural division of the total export value of bread crops and flour* (per cent)*

| | From the total export value of wheat, rye and flour | | |
|---|---|---|---|
| | Wheat | Rye | Flour |
| 1882–1891 | 44.3 | 9.0 | 46.7 |
| 1892–1901 | 30.6 | 11.4 | 58.0 |
| 1902–1911 | 26.6 | 12.6 | 60.8 |

* A Magyar Szent Korona Országainak 1882–1913. évi külkereskedelmi forgalma. (The Foreign Trade of the Hungarian Holy Crown Countries between 1882 and 1913.) p. 20.

[5] After a time as a result of the influx of overseas products the price of flour and corn became cheaper in Great Britain than it was in Hungary. In the 1880s the London price of corn was somewhat higher than it was in Budapest, and the difference decreased very fast. From 1892 it became smaller and remained so every year until World War I. See Árstatisztika. (Price Statistics) Budapest, 1913. (*Magyar Statisztikai Közlemények*, Új sorozat, 44. k. Papers in Hungarian Statistics, New Series, vol. 44.) p. 18. The same can be seen in the Belgian markets where there was no duty on corn. For this see K. Rege: *A magyar búza áralakulása és termelési költsége 1820-tól 1930-ig.* (The Price and Production Costs of the Hungarian Corn from 1820 to 1930.) Budapest, 1931. p. 19.

picture the export possibilities contributed to its production in every way. In some years great quantities were exported but sometimes there was an excess of imports. In practice the foreign trade in maize depended on the changes in pig breeding. If the pigs decreased in number there was no need of so much corn (e.g. at the time of swine-fever) the export market became important. But when the pig production increased the exports of maize decreased simultaneously and in some cases imported maize was needed (Table 10). (The common customs area of the Monarchy needed imported maize continuously between 1850–1914.)

*Table 10*

*Foreign trade of maize* (1000 tons)*

| | Exports | Imports |
|---|---|---|
| 1882 | 97.7 | 102.3 |
| 1883 | 153.2 | 47.0 |
| 1884 | 93.0 | 52.1 |
| 1885 | 105.8 | 115.3 |
| 1886 | 140.0 | 20.0 |
| 1887 | 84.5 | 16.8 |
| 1888 | 114.6 | 8.6 |
| 1889 | 201.0 | 5.1 |
| 1890 | 180.1 | 25.5 |
| 1891 | 235.4 | 19.6 |
| 1892 | 357.4 | 3.4 |
| 1893 | 255.0 | 17.5 |
| 1894 | 159.0 | 62.6 |
| 1895 | 114.7 | 78.5 |
| 1896 | 311.1 | 31.8 |
| 1897 | 354.1 | 71.2 |
| 1898 | 237.0 | 281.8 |
| 1899 | 299.1 | 49.0 |
| 1900 | 269.7 | 39.5 |
| 1901 | 325.5 | 77.2 |
| 1902 | 416.0 | 41.4 |
| 1903 | 255.4 | 100.3 |
| 1904 | 224.3 | 114.2 |
| 1905 | 90.4 | 192.2 |
| 1906 | 222.1 | 73.3 |
| 1907 | 433.1 | 18.0 |
| 1908 | 391.3 | 7.7 |
| 1909 | 378.9 | 21.2 |
| 1910 | 436.1 | 29.2 |
| 1911 | 512.3 | 46.4 |
| 1912 | 201.8 | 268.4 |
| 1913 | 173.5 | 224.8 |

* On the basis of data published in A Magyar Szent Korona Országainak 1882–1913. évi külkereskedelmi forgalma. (The Foreign Trade of the Hungarian Holy Crown Countries between 1882 and 1913.)

The same change took place in the structure of the export of beef cattle and to some extent of draught animals. The share of exports of animals was generally 15.5 – 17% of the total exports in which the proportion of beef cattle increased from 33.3% to 58.7 though at the same time there was a decrease from 55.2% to 28.5% in the case of pigs. It was the swine-fever which stopped abruptly and retarded the rapidly growing export of pigs. The change taken place gradually in cattle breeding from the 1880s also played an important part in the changes in proportion. It was mainly due to the spread of western species which made the Hungarian cattle marketable outside the Monarchy. It explains why between 1882 – 1886 96.3 thousand head of cattle were exported every year on average; (compared with the exports of the 1850s and 60s this meant a considerable increase) it increased on an average to 348.8 thousand head of cattle between 1907 – 1911. (In fact the increase was somewhat less because at the beginning of the 1880s driving on foot was still important which, of course, was not shown in the Hungarian statistics.) The exports reached the highest point in 1904 when it was 450 thousand head of cattle which compared with the beginning of the 1880s meant at least an increase of 180% all things considered.

The Hungarian cattle were sold in bulk at the markets outside the Monarchy. The gradual growth of the exports to Austria meant business on commission in general; in this way the Austrian middlemen could keep the trade well in hand and most of the animals having been taken to the St. Mark's markets of Vienna were transported further on to Germany and Switzerland. There was a considerable excess in exports outside the Monarchy beyond the statistics. It has to be said that after 1904 a rapid decrease of animal exports to the markets outside the customs areas took place. It was only Italy where the Hungarian exports of animals increased, the Hungarian beef, cattle and draught animals – mainly cattle – were gradually driven out of the important Western European markets, France, Germany and Switzerland as a result of the overseas competition.

To a certain extent the situation was different in the case of the Hungarian pig exports. It increased rapidly in the decades previous to the swine-fever: it grew from 618 thousand head to 1.3 million between 1882 – 1895. The exports to Germany only increased threefold between 1892 – 94. But it fell back very quickly due to the swine-fever, and in 1897 it was only 200 thousand. It was only at the end of the first decades of the 20th century that it reaches the volume of the 1890s again. Consequently Hungarian pigs were driven out of the European markets to the ones inside the Monarchy. In German markets it was caused by an increased protection of the native production on the one hand and by the competition of Polish, Russian, Danish and American pigs on the other.

Gradually new products replaced the traditional goods (corn, flour, livestock) in the Hungarian agricultural exports to the markets outside the Monarchy and the rapid increase of these exports compensated partly for the shortage for traditional goods. Among the new products sugar, wood, poultry, eggs, feather, and certain manufactured goods such as salami, ham, butter and cheese, etc. were important, but sugar was the best market of all.

The Hungarian sugar industry could not match sugar consumption of the country until the beginning of the 1880s. In 1888 only 11 factories were working, the other ones closed down because of the disadvantageous taxation system and its consequences. In 1888 it came to a critical point as the consequence of the Act of 1888 XXII, and the revision of tariff inseparable from that. In connection with this taxation of the end-products at the place of production was introduced. The reduction in charging for transportation essentially went a long way to a tendency for growth in production and in this way it increased the area of sugar-beet and sugar production by sugar factories because it made possible that for-off parts should be connected to sugar production as well.[6] On the strength of these there were 28 productive factories in 1913 and the production of 30 thousand tons in 1889 grew to over 200 thousand tons by 1900.[7] Most of the production was sold outside Hungary. The Hungarian sugar went to the Austro-Czech markets first and in the first half of the 1880s it was 18.6 thousand tons a year on average. The volume of exports grew rapidly. In 1890 about 10 thousand tons of Hungarian sugar was exported to countries outside the Monarchy. In 1913 the Hungarian sugar exports amounted to 409.4 thousand tons. At that time 37.5% of the total sugar exports of the Monarchy came from Hungary (Table 11).

Great Britain and Italy were the most important sugar markets – the latter up to 1896, but it then considerably improved its sugar industry. The first sugar exports to India took place in 1898 and in the first decade of the 20th century India and Turkey became the main export markets. As the result of the loss of Cuban sugar production due to the Spanish–American war, Hungarian sugar was shipped to America as well. The exports were promoted in general by the Brussels sugar agreement passed in 1902 by the claims of Great Britain, which proved to be advantageous to the exports outside the Monarchy. It was rather disadvantageous to the Austro-Hungarian market as it made the imports of Austro-Czech sugar to Hungary easier but nevertheless it forced the Hungarian sugar industry to enter into competition and from this point of view it had not an entirely negative influence on the Hungarian sugar production.

The export of other goods also increased. From 1897 the export of living and slaughtered poultry increased. At that time 5 million living poultry were exported; of this one million were taken to Germany. Export to Germany grew

[6] See in detail V. Sándor: *Nagyipari fejlődés Magyarországon 1867–1900.* (Development of large-scale Industry in Hungary between 1867 and 1900.) Budapest, 1954, pp. 101, 117, 354–355 and 448–456.

[7] I. Berend T.–Gy. Ránki: *Magyarország gyáripara az imperializmus első világháború előtti időszakában 1900–1914.* (The Manufacturing Industry of Hungary in the Age of Imperialism before the World War I from 1900 to 1914.) Budapest, 1955, pp. 256–263.

*Table 11*

*The export and import of sugar**

| | Exports | | Imports | |
|---|---|---|---|---|
| | volume (1000 tons) | value (million crowns) | volume (1000 tons) | value (million crowns) |
| 1882 | 19.6 | 12.3 | 34.4 | 28.0 |
| 1883 | 20.2 | 13.3 | 32.8 | 26.1 |
| 1884 | 23.3 | 9.8 | 35.1 | 23.9 |
| 1885 | 28.0 | 11.4 | 31.6 | 20.3 |
| 1886 | 20.8 | 9.1 | 36.2 | 24.0 |
| 1887 | 27.0 | 10.6 | 30.6 | 20.0 |
| 1888 | 21.1 | 9.6 | 31.8 | 22.1 |
| 1889 | 30.1 | 14.0 | 38.5 | 25.6 |
| 1890 | 34.0 | 13.9 | 43.4 | 23.4 |
| 1891 | 40.4 | 16.5 | 36.0 | 19.9 |
| 1892 | 40.4 | 18.2 | 31.5 | 18.2 |
| 1893 | 65.1 | 29.4 | 35.9 | 25.4 |
| 1894 | 63.9 | 22.8 | 42.4 | 21.5 |
| 1895 | 66.6 | 18.4 | 48.4 | 22.0 |
| 1896 | 87.0 | 28.4 | 38.7 | 22.3 |
| 1897 | 103.8 | 30.4 | 38.5 | 22.9 |
| 1898 | 124.8 | 38.2 | 39.6 | 23.0 |
| 1899 | 135.6 | 38.2 | 45.4 | 24.7 |
| 1900 | 172.9 | 46.8 | 42.4 | 18.1 |
| 1901 | 188.8 | 47.8 | 40.1 | 17.6 |
| 1902 | 173.6 | 35.6 | 48.3 | 18.7 |
| 1903 | 213.5 | 40.6 | 49.2 | 15.4 |
| 1904 | 154.9 | 42.5 | 31.0 | 9.2 |
| 1905 | 162.5 | 47.2 | 33.1 | 8.5 |
| 1906 | 140.1 | 35.0 | 45.8 | 9.4 |
| 1907 | 142.0 | 36.6 | 46.9 | 13.7 |
| 1908 | 211.0 | 57.2 | 49.5 | 13.5 |
| 1909 | 162.0 | 46.2 | 44.5 | 13.8 |
| 1910 | 200.9 | 64.2 | 40.1 | 14.9 |
| 1911 | 179.7 | 57.1 | 36.6 | 13.3 |
| 1912 | 356.9 | 111.0 | 33.3 | 15.5 |
| 1913 | 422.3 | 107.5 | 38.9 | 13.9 |

* On the basis of data published in A Magyar Szent Korona Országainak 1882–1913. évi külkereskedelmi forgalma. (The Foreign Trade of the Hungarian Holy Crown Countries between 1882 and 1913.) p. 20.

fast and between 1902–1904 it reached 4 million. Germany was good market for slaughtered poultry and eggs, but Vienna was the most important outlet for eggs. The developed and industrialized part of the Monarchy needed a considerable volume of imported eggs. In the animal production fats and bacon played a considerable part for which Germany was the main outlet beyond the Monarchy, but the presence of the cheaper American bacon and fats caused considerable competition here.

The other significant items of the Hungarian agricultural exports fluctuated from time to time and in some cases the import of these products was greater than their export. This happened even to the traditionally important wine. The Hungarian wine export took the advantage of the situation that in Western Europe in the 1870–90s phylloxera caused the rein of grapegrowing, and so considerable volume could be exported to France, Switzerland, Italy and Germany. But in the 1890s phylloxera appeared in Hungary as well and ruined the Hungarian viticulture as a consequence of which the country imported wine in large amount mainly from Italy.

The volume of imported raw hide corresponded to its export in general. Hungary would have been self sufficient in this point of view but the export of livestock (mainly cattle) decreased considerably the number of available animal skins, moreover, the bad way of currying (for this the Hungarian hides were sold at a price of second and third class products) marking of animals by embossing and the cutting of hides at flaying added to this.

In the whole period the export of wool was among the traditional export goods continually falling off. The rivalry of the overseas wool was very strong in the 1880s as a result of the reduction of transport prices, so the Hungarian export of wool dwindled rapidly (Table 12) but the imports increased. There was a traditional fault which deepened this process, namely the Hungarian wool was inadequate to manufacture all kind of goods from because of its poor quality. That is why the export of wool could be maintained only to Austria and Bohemia.[8]

During the whole period the outlays of the Hungarian agricultural exports did not run into difficulties. Practically the main Hungarian export goods, corn and animals, could be sold unrestrictedly in the European markets between 1850–1878. The low prime cost of the overseas corn production forced prices down abruptly from 1878 on and it caused a crisis in price all over Europe only but did not result in stagnation or restriction of market. On the contrary, the market potentials extended continuously even in the last third of the 19th century and in one and half decades previous to World War I and as it has been already mentioned it was also valid for the whole economy of the Monarchy. Previous to the 1880s the market of the Hungarian corn grew rapidly also beyond the Monarchy but the customs duty on corn enacted after 1878 in France and later in Germany made the increase of the Hungarian export practically

[8] The imports of agricultural products were not significant with the exception of those articles which were needed by the business interests of manufacturing industry, e.g. corn was imported in great volume. In 1898 Hungary imported more than 250 thousand tons corn and it was 488 thousand tons in 1909. But the import corn did not reach 100 thousand tons in general. The livestocks also were regularly imported until 1906. It was 100–200 thousand pigs and several thousand head of cattle. From 1906 it decreased rapidly as a consequence of the decrease of Serbian imports of cattle. The value of the imported agricultural goods was not significant, it was about a few million crowns (with the exception of 1909 when the value of the imported corn was 111.2 million crowns).

*Table 12*

*The export and import of wool**

| | Exports | | Imports | |
|---|---|---|---|---|
| | volume (1000 tons) | value (million crowns) | volume (1000 tons) | value (million crowns) |
| 1882 | 12.5 | 64.7 | 1.4 | 7.4 |
| 1883 | 12.5 | 64.6 | 4.3 | 22.3 |
| 1884 | 11.4 | 18.3 | 4.1 | 6.6 |
| 1885 | 11.4 | 24.9 | 5.0 | 7.6 |
| 1886 | 14.5 | 47.4 | 2.2 | 5.9 |
| 1887 | 9.8 | 31.1 | 4.4 | 10.2 |
| 1888 | 11.3 | 29.4 | 2.1 | 4.2 |
| 1889 | 13.7 | 39.2 | 1.5 | 3.2 |
| 1890 | 10.4 | 28.1 | 1.3 | 2.5 |
| 1891 | 9.2 | 23.2 | 1.1 | 2.1 |
| 1892 | 9.2 | 20.6 | 1.2 | 2.0 |
| 1893 | 11.2 | 21.2 | 1.1 | 1.2 |
| 1894 | 10.1 | 22.8 | 1.3 | 2.1 |
| 1895 | 8.3 | 17.6 | 1.6 | 2.8 |
| 1896 | 7.8 | 17.2 | 1.5 | 2.7 |
| 1897 | 7.0 | 14.3 | 1.7 | 2.5 |
| 1898 | 7.0 | 15.7 | 1.8 | 2.5 |
| 1899 | 9.3 | 25.2 | 2.1 | 3.4 |
| 1900 | 6.3 | 13.8 | 2.1 | 3.5 |
| 1901 | 7.1 | 15.1 | 2.0 | 3.3 |
| 1902 | 9.4 | 23.7 | 2.3 | 4.1 |
| 1903 | 8.8 | 22.5 | 2.4 | 4.5 |
| 1904 | 7.9 | 19.9 | 2.4 | 5.0 |
| 1905 | 9.3 | 23.8 | 2.7 | 5.7 |
| 1906 | 9.3 | 25.1 | 2.8 | 7.1 |
| 1907 | 8.0 | 23.7 | 2.7 | 7.1 |
| 1908 | 7.8 | 18.5 | 2.7 | 6.2 |
| 1909 | 7.6 | 19.3 | 3.5 | 10.0 |
| 1910 | 7.5 | 19.6 | 3.9 | 10.3 |
| 1911 | 6.6 | 16.3 | 3.8 | 10.5 |
| 1912 | 7.0 | 16.6 | 3.8 | 11.3 |
| 1913 | 6.5 | 16.3 | 3.4 | 10.2 |

* See the note of Table 11.

impossible, moreover regressed it. In this way the Hungarian corn and flour were gradually supplanted to the customs area of the Monarchy. Namely the demand for corn and flour in the hereditary provinces grew to such an extent that by the turn of the century more and more overseas corn was imported which could depress prices more forcefully. That is the reason why the problem of customs duty on corn grew more pointed at that time. However, all these meant that further on no difficulties in selling the Hungarian corn and flour had to be counted on.

The crisis in price did not influence other products of the Hungarian agricultural exports. At that time the overseas competition did not still endanger the prices of meat and meat products, poultry, eggs, feather; not only could these goods be sold in foreign markets but they could fetch favourable prices simultaneously.[9] Thus, the meat production of Hungary was coming more firmly into prominence from the turn of the 1870s and 1880s. There was an increase in exporting of cattle again and the export of pig developed at a good pace, and so did the production and export of poultry, eggs and feather. Besides these only sugar had an important role. Then the structure of the Hungarian agricultural exports was undergoing a change again. The rate of corn and flour in the exports stagnated and fell back and the importance of meat, animal products and sugar came gradually to the front.

The gradual increase in the volume of agricultural exports made the proportion of certain goods fairly stable taken the Hungarian exports as a whole. The agricultural exports formed a slowly decreasing part of the total export value but in terms of money it did not only form the greatest part, but it exceeded the 60% of the total export value. Taking this into consideration it was of great importance for the economic life of the country. Between 1850–1914 the influx of foreign capital was permanent and importing the necessary capital to the industrialization Hungary's balance of payments became naturally passive. This was partly poised by the considerable volume of exports (only partly, even in case of active foreign trade balance).[10]

[9] The prices of animal and wool between 1867–1910 (q/crowns)*

| | cattle | calf | pig | sheep | wool** |
|---|---|---|---|---|---|
| 1867– 70 | 47.49 | 92.36 | 109.37 | 68.40 | 315 |
| 1871– 75 | 49.36 | 108.36 | 117.70 | 81.17 | 348 |
| 1876– 80 | 48.15 | 92.10 | 96.00 | 77.70 | 319 |
| 1881– 85 | 51.46 | 92.58 | 98.37 | 84.23 | 294 |
| 1885– 90 | 48.76 | 90.94 | 89.10 | 73.69 | 277 |
| 1891– 95 | 53.12 | 96.14 | 93.28 | 69.09 | 239 |
| 1896–1900 | 57.59 | 94.27 | 94.19 | 72.62 | 274 |
| 1901– 05 | 65.44 | 105.01 | 103.50 | 77.64 | 305 |
| 1906– 10 | 75.39 | 117.24 | 124.75 | 94.67 | 328 |

* Prices of St. Mark's market in Vienna. They had an influence on the Hungarian one, as well. More than the 60% of animals sold there came from Hungary.

** The prices of wool are given with a year's delay. The basic years are 1867/71. From then the five-year averages up to 1907/11.

[10] F. Fellner: *A nemzetközi fizetési mérleg és alakulása Magyarországon*. (The Hungarian International Balance of Payments and Its Change) Budapest, 1908. pp. 168–175. He refers to the fact that the excess of agricultural exports is not sufficient to compensate to the steady trade balance itself and an active trade balance could have been set up only by the means of a considerable industrial development.

The common market of the Austro-Hungarian Monarchy became more and more important in the development of the Hungarian economy. From the turn of this century customs abroad had a role only when there was a surplus of the Hungarian agricultural products and the market of the Monarchy was not able to take it up. Though all kinds of articles were regularly taken to the markets of customs abroad, namely outside the Monarchy, but it may be said in general that only certain animal products (meat, fat, poultry, feather, eggs got to the markets beyond the Monarchy's frontiers). Between 1880–1914 the mass products of the Hungarian agriculture which had been taken to South-German–North Italian, French or English markets earlier were practically banished from them. Just then these products remained the main export articles of Hungary even in later times.

In the second half of the 19th century and at the beginning of the 1900s the Hungarian agricultural exports (apart from some products of less importance) were driven back to the customs area of the Monarchy. It was the protective line of the customs area which maintained the price level at which the production was profitable under the given Hungarian production conditions.[11] The customs area resulted simultaneously in a new division of labour between Hungary and the hereditary provinces. It would seem as if the unified market of the Monarchy had preserved the traditional structure of the Hungarian agricultural production as a result of the fact that it promoted the Hungarian agriculture providing outlets for its products and protecting its price level against the overseas dumping prices. But it was not the case.

Austria and Bohemia, the well-industrialized territories of the hereditary provinces were coming to play greater and greater part in the Hungarian exports, for the economic interdependence of Hungary and the provinces was intensified definitely and markedly in the last third of the 19th century. The struggles taken place between the agrarian and merkantilist representatives of the leading circles of the Monarchy meant only the surface of the process. The economic division of labour, the historic tradition of which had gone back at least to 150 years gradually increased and it reached a new level of quality in the last decades of the century. Within this there was only a debate on the rate of profit distribution between the main tendencies of economics. But due to the considerable increase of agricultural duties it changed in 1906 when the conflicting tendencies came to an agreement at last for a probable longer historic period. All these did not refer to the Hungarian agriculture as a whole but only to those large estates which produced mainly corn in a more extensive way (estates of 100–1500 hectares in the Great Hungarian Plain are spoken of mainly) for the peasant farms and the real capitalist farming on a large scale which were able to adopt more intensive methods could change in

[11] Corn was tax free article to import to the customs area of the Monarchy until 1881. Customs duty on corn was introduced in 1882 which was 1.19 crowns per q. In 1887 it was increased to 3.57 crowns. These were equivalent of the contemporary German ones. There was a greater increase in 1906 when it was increased to 6.30 crowns per q.

time and keep abreast of the current requirements. Overall it meant that the whole Hungarian agricultural production would have been capable of developing without the increase of agricultural duties. The increase of duties was taken in the favour of landowners who were great in number but economically unimportant (it is another problem that these people held important offices mainly in the eastern part of the country, so they were politically important, which was seen at the elections in 1905 and with course of the following political events which led finally to the increase of agricultural duties). Though the earlier development of the Hungarian agriculture shows quite well that it could keep abreast of the Western-European agricultural development by the means of well-paid protective markets of the Monarchy.

We have seen the increase of export volume and the structural change in agricultural exports between 1850–1914. How, in which ways did the agricultural exports influence the economy of the country at that time?

It is obvious that it was one of the greatest *tensile forces* of the economic development and it contributed significantly to the general economic development and industrialization, thanks above all to the development of agricultural production. The outlets, which were at disposal in the course of the whole period, and the fairly high prices on the protected markets of the Monarchy in three decades when the economic development of other East-European exporting countries was stopped or hindered by the long-lasting fall in corn prices could intensify the development of the Hungarian agricultural production and were beneficial to the growth of volume and improvement of its level. In Hungary the territory involved in agricultural production grew considerably and the development of intensive branches accelerated. The cultivatable land was expanded due to drainage in accordance with which the grazing lands were broken and became lands in tillage. Within the field growing of plants the territory of corn production grew first, then in the decades of the fall in corn prices the number of live-stock increased and the quality improved. The territory of both fodder plants and industrial crops production was expanded to a high pitch, that is to say, the range of more valuable goods production was remarkably expanded[12] (Table 13).

The favourable conditions of production also made the change of technics and technology rapid. Fallow was reduces, the territory of the three-course rotation system contracted and simultaneously the change-over to a more up-to-date crop rotation became faster. The enclosure (commassation) of peasant holdings also started even if the results had not been significant. Manufactured articles were replacing the tools made by local smiths or the home-made

[12] For the agricultural development see the articles of A. Vörös and L. Für in: *A magyar mezőgazdaság a XIX–XX. században (1849–1949)* (The Hungarian Agriculture in the 19th and 20th Centuries (1849–1949) Budapest, 1979. pp. 11–152, 155–274. (*Agrártörténeti tanulmányok 4.*)

*Table 13*

a) *Distribution of land area* (in %)

| Year | Total (in mill.ha) | Arable | Garden | Meadow | Vine-yards | Pasture | Forest | Other |
|---|---|---|---|---|---|---|---|---|
| 1851 | | 29.8 | ? | 10.7 | 1.3 | 12.7 | 28.7 | 16.8 |
| 1867 | | 34.9 | ? | 13.4 | 1.2 | 14.9 | 28.3 | 7.3 |
| 1873 | 27.8 | 34.7 | ? | 13.3 | 1.2 | 14.8 | 28.2 | 7.8 |
| 1883 | 28.2 | 41.0 | 1.2 | 10.6 | 1.3 | 13.1 | 26.9 | 5.9 |
| 1895 | 28.1 | 42.8 | 1.3 | 10.2 | 1.0 | 13.0 | 26.6 | 5.1 |
| 1913 | 28.2 | 45.5 | 1.3 | 9.2 | 1.1 | 11.8 | 25.8 | 5.3 |

b) *Number of livestock (in 1000 pieces)*

| Year | Cattle | Horse | Pigs | Sheep |
|---|---|---|---|---|
| 1857 | 4775.0 | 1769.3 | 3499.0 | 10261.0 |
| 1870 | 4496.9 | 1819.7 | 3573.3 | 13760.7 |
| 1884 | 4879.0 | 1748.9 | 4803.6 | 10852.1 |
| 1895 | 5829.0 | 1972.9 | 6436.6 | 7813.1 |
| 1911 | 6184.4 | 2001.4 | 6416.4 | 7697.7 |

ones, so ploughs, most of the basic implements were manufactured. New machines also appeared in agriculture, the use of threshing and seeding machines spread quickly (threshing was motorized in 1880s), and at the end of the 1850s steam-ploughs were already used in large estates, tractors and other electric motors (e.g. crushing-mills, etc.) started to spread at the turn of the century. Mills appeared in most peasant farms. From the 1860s the use of fertilizers can be traced – first only in large estates or in case of sugar-beet growing, but later, at the turn of the century they were used in sowing areas of sugar beet in well-cared peasant holdings, too. The increase of animals in number raised the volume of manure and consequently the retrieval of producing capacity of soil improved which promoted the decrease of fallow-lands. The considerable increase of average yield was a consequence of all these (Table 14) and in the years previous to World War I the average yields of the Hungarian agriculture exceeded significantly those of the eastern and south-eastern countries (comparing to the Hungarian agriculture these had been underdeveloped even before 1850, or rather, Hungary kept extending this advantage over the yields of these countries) and they came to the lowest Western-European ones, e.g. the yield of corn production was comparable to that of the French one. In some cases the Hungarian average yields could overtake the lowest levels of the Western-European countries (Table 15). This improvement can be seen well especially between 1907–1914 when as a result of the increase of corn duties by 30–50% subsequent capitals came to the Hungarian agriculture and number of machines and other modern tools used in agriculture grew abruptly. The yearly increase of the Hungarian agricultural production was as

*Table 14*

*Yields of some plant products in Hungary (q/ha)*

| Year | Wheat | Rye | Barley | Oat | Maize | Potatoes | Sugar-beet | Cattle-turnip |
|---|---|---|---|---|---|---|---|---|
| 1871/75 | 6.13 | 6.11 | 7.37 | 5.42 | 7.40 | 22.97 | 123.49 | 83.90 |
| 1876/80 | 8.24 | 7.12 | 8.76 | 6.76 | 10.98 | 36.81 | 167.90 | 159.66 |
| 1881/85 | 11.03 | 9.73 | 10.75 | 8.48 | 13.38 | 63.94 | 190.04 | 240.27 |
| 1886/90 | 11.95 | 9.82 | 9.92 | 7.96 | 12.23 | 55.21 | 170.61 | 210.46 |
| 1891/95 | 12.79 | 10.79 | 11.78 | 10.34 | 15.31 | 64.13 | 177.87 | 226.55 |
| 1896/1900 | 11.36 | 10.50 | 12.13 | 11.07 | 14.61 | 80.10 | 209.80 | 254.26 |
| 1901/05 | 12.08 | 11.24 | 12.29 | 11.00 | 12.36 | 77.77 | 205.32 | 232.97 |
| 1906/10 | 12.01 | 11.35 | 12.49 | 10.91 | 17.26 | 79.67 | 228.67 | 277.28 |
| 1911/15 | 12.39 | 11.51 | 13.63 | 11.75 | 17.15 | 83.39 | 246.56 | 295.83 |

*Table 15*

*Yields of wheat (q/ha)*

| | 1891–95 | 1903–12 |
|---|---|---|
| Denmark | 23.6 (1) | 27.6 (1) |
| Great Britain | 19.9 (2) | 21.4 (4) |
| Belgium | 17.2 (3) | 24.2 (2) |
| The Netherlands | 13.4 (4) | 23.3 (3) |
| Germany | 14.5 (5) | 20.2 (5) |
| Hungary | 12.8 (6) | 12.3 (8) |
| France | 12.5 (7) | 13.7 (6) |
| Romania | 11.8 (8) | 11.6 (9) |
| Austria | 11.6 (9) | 13.4 (7) |
| USA | 9.3 (10) | 9.6 (10) |
| Italy | 7.9 (11) | 9.4 (11) |
| Spain | 7.3 (12) | 8.9 (12) |
| Russia | 7.0 (13) | 6.6 (13) |

great as 4% in these years. Moreover, taking the whole period or its greatest part into consideration (1867–1913) the growth rate of agricultural production remained favourable and yearly it was about 2% on an average.[13]

The large-scale agricultural exports could be shown not only in the modernization of agricultural production and the raise of producing level but in the raise of the living standards of the peasantry as well. The possibility of the increase in production and the expanding market made their influences feel both on the peasantry's income and the increase of their consumption. At last it reacted upon the industrial development for it enlarged the internal market and

[13] L. Katus: Economic Growth in Hungary During the Age of Dualism (1867–1913). A Quantitative Analysis. In: *Social-Economic Researches on the History of East-Central Europe*. Bp. 1970. pp 50–51. (*Studia Historica* 62.)

increased the demands for manufactured goods. But all these happened under rather limited conditions as neither the growth rate nor the degree of the Hungarian industrialization was satisfactory and above all, it was just shown in the process that the peasant population was still growing in number rapidly (but its rate to the whole population decreased rather quickly under Eastern-European circumstances!).[14]

However, when we speak of the economic importance of agricultural exports we have to stress these mentioned above. Much as we consider the contemporary Hungarian economy be underdeveloped comparing to the Western-European development in this respect we have to point to the fact that the living standards of the Hungarian peasantry were higher than those in the Eastern-European countries – and taking the living standards of Russian, Rumanian, Bulgarian, Serbian peasantry, or the Polish living in the Russian Empire, into consideration in Hungary it was higher and between 1850–1914 this difference markedly grew for the good of the Hungarian peasantry.

The great increase of agricultural exports had a good effect on the influx of foreign capital to the Hungarian economy, and agriculture both in direct and indirect ways. It also promoted the growth of capitalistic lease as well as investments of capital to agriculture by raising mortgages. It could be true that a part of loans was not used for direct agricultural production, but for buying lands or supplying consumption and luxury needs, but finally the great value of foreign and Hungarian capital having come to agriculture contributed to cover the required capital of the country. The import of foreign capital and its investments in the Hungarian economy are provable, in consequence of which the production capacity of the country became stronger and the infrastructure of economy (road making and railway construction, regulation of riverways, etc.) improved. This process would have been slowlier and would not have transformed the economy to such an extent if the rapid development of agricultural exports had not provided any good investment possibilities for foreign capital either in infrastructure promoting the agricultural exports directly or in production by the means of mortgage loans. Between the increase of mortgage loans and the development of agricultural production there is a rather close connection and it is not by chance that the sums of loans increased 11 times between 1867 and 1900, and it duplicated again between 1900–1913 (that is when the Hungarian agricultural production and exports grew rapidly[15]) (Table 16).

[14] The proportion of agricultural workers in the whole employees (per cent)

| | | | | | |
|---|---|---|---|---|---|
| Germany | 1907 | 33.1% | Hungary | 1910 | 64.5% |
| France | 1906 | 42.5% | Russia | | |
| Austria | 1910 | 42.3% | Romania | | |
| Bohemia | 1910 | 38.1% | Bulgaria | | |
| | | | Serbia | | |

[15] I. Berend T. – Gy. Ránki: *A magyar gazdaság száz éve*. (A Hundred Years of the Hungarian Economy) Bp. Kossuth – Közgazdasági és Jogi Könyvkiadó, 1972, p. 40.

*Table 16*

*The change of loans on mortgage**
(million crowns)

| | | | |
|---|---|---|---|
| 1866 | 84.8 | 1890 | 938.6 |
| 1867 | 170.0 | 1895 | 1386.4 |
| 1870 | 253.0 | 1900 | 1924.6 |
| 1875 | 410.8 | 1905 | 2535.1 |
| 1880 | 488.4 | 1909 | 3225.2 |
| 1885 | 675.4 | 1913 | 3800.0 |

* Magyarország története 1848–1890. (History of Hungary between 1848 and 1890.) p. 974; I. Berend T.–Gy. Ránki: A magyar gazdaság 100 éve (A Hundred Years of the Hungarian Economy) Budapest, 1972. p. 40, and A magyar mezőgazdaság a XIX–XX. században. (Hungarian Agriculture in the 19th and 20th centuries) (1849–1949), Budapest, 1976. p. 164.

Among the agrarian countries of Middle- and Eastern Europe it was only Hungary's agriculture which had got a rapidly expanding *internal market* during the whole period, with protected price level against the price-cutting tendencies of world market. As Austria and Bohemia functioned as internal market for the Hungarian agricultural exports, so it could contribute considerably to the ever increasing export of manufactured agrarian goods. The protected market of the Monarchy guaranteed Hungary an exceptional position among other countries exporting agricultural goods. As a result of this position Hungary could export the increasing part of its exports in the form of food-industrial goods. Especially the rapid development and the important position in the Hungarian industrialization of two branches of food industry – milling and sugar industry – were due to this special market position. There is no doubt that other branches of food industry also developed rapidly from the turn of the century mainly as a result of the considerable exports to the markets of the Monarchy, namely distilling industry, salami and ham production, several kinds of canning factories above all developed from the turn of the century, paprika mills, dairies were founded (butter and cheese export), etc. In general the development of food industry accelerated. But the sugar and milling industry remained the two most important branches of the Hungarian food industry later on as well – though their importance was reversed.

The development of milling industry was closely connected to railway construction. The fact that GANZ works produced the world-famous roller-frames and chill casting railway wheels at the same time points beyond its symbolical importance, too. The development of the Budapest centered milling industry went on rapidly and the quality of the Hungarian flour kept the first place in world market for about two decades. Besides the advantageous export possibilities, the spread of modern technics and their further improvement, the business strategies (permission of the so called "grinding trade" up to 1900) it was the unified customs area of the Monarchy which played the very important role and made the influx of Hungarian flour to the markets of Austria and

Bohemia easier consequently the influx of capital to milling industry became advantageous.

The big commercial mills (that is the modern industrial ones) were founded and developed in Budapest first and in the country only from the turn of the century. The mills realized remarkable and continuous concentration of capital and its rate was gradually increasing. The 10 big Budapest mills had the greatest trade invariably (Table 17) but at the same time the lifting of "grinding trade" in 1900 (that is repayment of customs duties on imported corn in case of flour exports to customs abroad) meant an overture of a new period in the Hungarian milling industry. By that time the foreign especially the American milling industry developed technically which after expiring the Hungarian licences kept up with the times by taking over these inventions and drove the Hungarian flour out of the world markets. It is true that the markets of the Monarchy were still existing but were not able to ensure the exploitage of the total capacity of big mills. Then the main task of cartel was to form the grinding gaps in milling industry. But all these cannot minimize the importance of

*Table 17*

*The flour production of mills in Budapest*
(1000 tons)*

| | Wheat-grinding | | Flour production |
|---|---|---|---|
| 1864 | 46.6 | 1880 | 279.8 |
| 1865 | 53.1 | 1881 | 303.8 |
| 1866 | 60.5 | 1882 | 356.0 |
| 1867 | 108.7 | 1883 | 417.4 |
| 1868 | 145.0 | 1884 | 404.5 |
| 1869 | 223.6 | 1885 | 434.4 |
| 1870 | 266.7 | 1886 | 380.7 |
| 1871 | 252.7 | 1887 | 394.7 |
| 1872 | 239.8 | 1888 | 475.7 |
| 1873 | 227.7 | 1889 | 445.7 |
| 1874 | 237.8 | | |
| 1875 | 290.3 | | |
| 1876 | 308.2 | | |
| 1877 | 372.5 | | |
| 1878 | 426.5 | | |
| 1879 | 429.6 | | |
| 1880 | 354.2 | | |

* Vilmos Sándor: Nagyipari fejlődés Magyarországon 1867–1900 (Development of large-scale industry in Hungary between 1867 and 1900) Budapest, 1954. pp. 67 and 340.
The total grinding output of the ten biggest mills in Budapest was 767.3 thousand in 1912.

*Table 18*

*Roller-frames – sale of GANZ Works**

| | Number of sold roller-frames | | Sold in Hungary (per cent) |
|---|---|---|---|
| 1875 – 1879 | 3660 | | |
| 1880 – 1884 | 7967 | 1875 – 1885 | 18 % |
| 1885 – 1889 | 5570 | 1886 – 1895 | 34.3 % |
| 1890 – 1894 | 4185 | 1896 – 1900 | 57.8 % |
| 1895 – 1899 | 3321 | | |

* Vilmos Sándor: Nagyipari fejlődés Magyarországon 1867 – 1900 (Development of large-scale industry in Hungary between 1867 and 1900) Budapest, 1954. p. 470.

the Hungarian milling industry in the Hungarian industrialization process.[16] The Hungarian mills provided stable market for Hungarian machine industry, mainly for GANZ works which had become one of the best factories of the Hungarian industrialization by producing a leading technical invention in mass which was of world level at that time (Table 18) – in addition it was the first product in the history of the Hungarian industry which was a maximum output and could be sold in world market without having rivals for a long time.

While Hungarian capital had the leadership in milling industry, in the Hungarian sugar industry the Austro-Czech manufacturers took the first steps. Both raw material and labour power were cheaper in Hungary. A new system of taxation was introduced in 1888 and the tariffs were modified as a consequence of which the Hungarian sugar industry began to develop rapidly. A lot of new factories were founded, the showing area of sugar-beet increased and the production prospered. Sugar consumption from the low level of the 1880s grew to 7.8 kgs per head by 1913 (though it was a great growth, but it did not reach of the Western European countries) but the most sugar was sold in outer markets, in Austria and in the countries of customs abroad. The agreement which was concluded in 1902 in Brussels and forbade to premiate the exports, did not throw an obstacle in the way of this process. The Hungarian sugar exports declined to the Austro-Czech markets in part but spread in the markets of India, Turkey, the Balcans, Great-Britain, etc. even more faster. Sugar industry was modernized in a quick bar too, and we could be the witnesses to the introduction of the most up to date methods in Hungary at least twice between 1888 – 1914. Therefore, the Hungarian sugar factories, which had already reached higher concentration of capital by that time than their one-time masters, the Austro-Czech sugar factories had had a rather considerable effect on the Hungarian machine industry and contributed to the Hungarian industri-

[16] For all these see: V. Sándor Ibid.; I. Berend T. – Gy. Ránki: *Magyarország gyáripara...* pp. 250 – 255.

alization.[17] At that time distilling industry also developed rapidly by means of a partly renewed technology.[18]

The prosperity of the Hungarian sugar and milling industry and the development of other departments of food industry influenced favourably the improvement of the Hungarian machine industry. Food factories proved to be a good market for machine production while the constant modernization of certain branches of food industry (milling and sugar industry), newer and newer investments had positive influences on the Hungarian machine industry as a whole and contributed to its development. These branches of food industry gave the machine production a good chance to produce machines in appropriate series. It is valid for the total agricultural production, as well. The modernization of the agricultural production (even its slower timing comparing with the Western European one) formed a good market for the agricultural machine production which got important orders – especially after the large-scale rise of agricultural customs duties in 1906. The fact, that in the second half of the 19th century large estates preferred foreign – German and English – products of agricultural machine industry partly modified the situation. By the end of the 19th century the Hungarian agricultural machine production developed considerably and increased its share in the Hungarian markets. At the same time the exports of these machines to Russia and the Balcans grew. But in export increase the rapidly widening internal market played an important role, which afforded a good background for the production of appropriate great series.[19]

Besides all these the agricultural exports, the prosperity of agricultural production and the rise of living standards of agrarian population had roles in industrial production as well. The modernization of agricultural production demanded new buildings, farm railway lines, access roads, vehicles of transport, etc. which contributed to the development of certain branches of building industry and machine production. Building, transformation of furniture (e.g. spread of craftsman-made furniture in peasant families), and the changing living standards of peasantry in general also influenced the development of Hungarian industry even with case when the market grew for the favour of rural and town craftsmen.

Agricultural exports had far-reaching considerable effects on the whole Hungarian economic life. There is no doubt about its favourable contribution to the acceleration of the industrialization process. Then it had a direct part in establishing the preliminary conditions, of industrialization. The Hungarian agricultural exports covered partly the considerable part of imports. On the other hand it improved the financial balance of the country. The balance of payment of Hungary in the whole period was inactive, even besides the imported surplus of foreign trade. It could not have happened in another way

[17] Ibid. pp. 256–263.
[18] Ibid. pp. 263–265.
[19] Ibid. pp. 211–213.

for the reason that the industrialization took place by means of import of foreign, mainly Austrian and West-European capital and it could not be modified by the fact that the proportion of foreign capital in investments gradually decreased after the turn of the century. Still, the rapidly increasing and improving organic composition of agricultural exports – besides the increasing cash remittances sent by emigrants from the turn of the century – offered a guarantee for foreign capital to consider its Hungarian investments favourable. (It is another problem, that the passivity of the Hungarian foreign trade increased so abruptly which marked that the Hungarian economic development had come to its turning-point as it had not been able to keep abreast of the needs of increasing exports any longer.[20]) It is the case even if it is very difficult to determine the measures of all these concretely. The common customs area (no to forget about the active trade balance of the whole period which had fairly good effects on the Hungarian economic development) and common currency system of the Monarchy made really advantageous conditions for the Hungarian import of capital.[21] It is still undeniable that in the respect of the whole economic development of Hungary the agricultural exports were of great importance.

[20] It must be mentioned that the foreign trade balance of the Austro-Hungarian Monarchy turned to be steady from 1907. Though in 1907 and 1908 there was not a considerable excess of imports (44.7 million, 142.8 million, resp.) but in 1909 and 1910 it reached 400 million crowns a year. Between 1911 and 1913 it was 780–800 million a year. It clearly shows that *structural* changes of economy could not be avoided. It needs a more thoroughful study.

[21] Before 1909 the financial balance of the Monarchy was steady only to a lesser extent. See Fellner: Ibid. pp. 178–179.

# XII

# Agrarreform und industrielle Revolution in Ungarn

Welcher Zusammenhang besteht zwischen der ungarischen Bauernbefreiung und der industriellen Revolution? Inwieweit war die Durchführung der Agrarreformen, die mehr oder weniger konsequent erfolgte Beseitigung der feudalen Verhältnisse in der Landwirtschaft die Voraussetzung für die Entfaltung der industriellen Revolution, des Kapitalismus? Fragen, auf die wir seit dem Ablauf der erwähnten Prozesse die Anwort zu wissen meinen. Dabei könnte die Antwort bei weitem nicht so eindeutig sein, wenn wir alle Umstände beachten würden, die irgendwie in dem Prozeß eine Rolle gespielt haben.

Hier und jetzt kann es lediglich unsere Aufgabe sein, die Verbindungen zwischen den Agrarreformen und der industriellen Revolution in Ungarn innerhalb der uns zur Verfügung stehenden Rahmen in Betracht zu ziehen. Gleich im voraus müssen wir also klären, daß die ungarische Geschichtsschreibung unter Agrarreformen die Bauernbefreiung versteht, d.h. den Prozeß, in dessen Verlauf die persönliche Abhängigkeit des Bauern vom Grundherrn aufhörte und jener zugleich das ihm zustehende Land als ausschließliches, frei verfügbares Eigentum erhielt. Wir können darunter also auch die Trennung, die Separation des grundherrlichen Landes vom bäuerlichen Land verstehen. Zur gleichen Zeit haben die Zeitgenossen und auch die ungarische Geschichtsschreibung der Abschaffung der Avitizität, das heißt der Ermöglichung des freien Verkehrs, des Kaufs und Verkaufs, der Veräußerung des Bodens, der Garantie aller jener Voraussetzungen, die gemeinsam das freie bürgerliche Bodeneigentum bilden, große Bedeutung beigemessen. Die Beseitigung der feudalen Eigentumsverhältnisse ist also — bildlich gesprochen — in der gemeinsamen Realisierung dieser zweifachen Ereignisreihe, in der Gesetzgebung der Revolution vom Jahre 1848 verkörpert.

Diese beiden Faktoren aber betreffen nicht in gleicher Weise, nicht einheitlich die industrielle Revolution, allgemein die Industrialisierung. Die Avitizität erschwerte es dem Adel, an äußere Kapitalquellen zu kommen, Kredite aufzunehmen, insofern es unmöglich machte, die Güter zugunsten des Kreditgebers zu veräußern. Theoretisch konnte es dazu nicht kommen, in Wirklichkeit aber fand in ungarischen Adelskreisen ein bedeutender Geldverkehr statt.

Heute wissen wir, daß die Avitizität in der ersten Hälfte des 19. Jahrhunderts den örtlichen Geldverkehr praktisch nicht mehr behinderte, das heißt, die Kredite, die die Adligen einander gaben oder aber die, die andere Elemente, Kaufleute, Pächter den Adligen gaben. Allerdings machte die Avitizität die Einbeziehung ausländischen Kapitals in derartige Kreditgeschäfte unmöglich. Ausländischer Kredit stand in der ersten Hälfte des 19. Jahrhunderts nur den reichsten ungarischen aristokratischen Familien zur Verfügung, ausländische Bankleute gaben ausschließlich ihnen Kredit. Diese Familien verfügten nämlich über die nötige Immobilien-Deckung, damit die ausländischen Kreditgeber sich sicher fühlen konnten.

Die damaligen feudalen Verhältnisse schlossen natürlich die Bauernschaft insgesamt vollkommen aus dem Kreis der Kreditvergabe aus. Die Bauern waren praktisch auf Wucherer angewiesen, ganz gleich ob ihre Kreditgeber Kaufleute, Wirtsleute, Mühlenpächter oder wohlhabendere Bauern waren. Es stimmt allerdings, daß das adlige Bodeneigentum nicht unbegrenzt war, denn viel Land (vor allem Weinkulturen und zum Teil Rodeland) waren auch für die Bauern frei verfügbar, aber die Hofstelle und ihre Appertinenzien (die zugehörenden Ackerstücke, Wiesen, Weiden, Waldstücke, usw.) konnten keinesfalls in diesen Verkehr einbezogen werden. Der bäuerliche Bodenverkehr war auf den bäuerlichen Boden außerhalb der Hofstelle beschränkt.

Den ersten bedeutenden Eingriff in die Beziehungen zwischen Bauern und Grundherrn ging stattlicherseits von Maria Theresias Regierung aus. Kleinere Eingriffe hatte es auch schon früher gegeben, die aber hatten die grundlegenden Beziehungen nicht berührt. Um die Mitte des 18. Jahrhunderts aber waren die Beziehungen Bauer–Grundherr so kompliziert geworden, daß selbst schon der klare Überblick über die Lage irgendeine Regelung erforderte.

Der Reichstag vom Jahre 1514 hatte den Freizug der Bauern aufgehoben, das Bauerntum rechtlich an die Scholle gebunden. Diese Bestimmung war zwar einige Jahrzehnte später (1556) aufgehoben worden, aber wesentliche Bestimmungen waren in Kraft geblieben. Vom Ende des 17. Jahrhunderts ab aber begann in den von den Türken befreiten Gebieten die Ansiedlung von Bauern aus Deutschland. Dadurch entstand neben Bauern in „ewiger Untertänigkeit" die breite Schicht der Siedler–Bauern mit Kontrakten, die das Recht an Freizug hatten. Gesteigert wurde der Wirrwarr dadurch, daß auch von den früher „ewig untertänigen" Bauern viele zahlreiche Erleichterungen erhalten hatten, manchmal persönlich geadelt worden waren oder aber umgekehrt: auf adliges Land übersiedelten, wo sie weiterhin Bauer blieben. Dies alles brachte die Lage gründlich durcheinander, machte die enge Verflechtung der bäuerlichen Verpflichtungen unübersichtlich. Der Hof in Wien aber hätte gern klare Verhältnisse gehabt, damit die bäuerlichen Lasten offenkundig wurden.

So kam es im Jahre 1767 zur zentralen Regelung der urbarialen Verhältnisse. Maria Theresias Verordnung klärte den rechtlichen Charakter der Böden, indem sie den Grund und Boden praktisch in zwei Teile aufteilte: das von den Bauern genutzte Land erhielt urbarialen Charakter, das vom Grundherrn bewirtschaftete, von ihm unmittelbar genutzte Land erhielt „allodialen" Charakter. Nach dem urbarialen Land schuldeten die Bauern dem Grundherrn Dienstleistungen und Steuern (Zensus, Zehnt, Fron), daneben zahlten sie natürlich auch der Kirche und dem Staat Steuern. Für das allodiale Land zahlte man keine Steuern, denn der Adel und das adlige Land war steuerfrei. Der Grundherr zahlte dem Staat für dieses Land auch dann keine Steuern, wenn es in Wirklichkeit von Bauern genutzt wurde, die vertraglich an den Grundherrn gebunden waren. Vom Ende des 17. Jahrhunderts ab wurden das ganze 18. Jahrhundert hindurch auf vielen allodialen Ländereien Bauern angesiedelt, oft ganze Dörfer. Hier konnte der Grundherr mehr Steuern verlangen, denn für dieses Land führten die Bauern keine Steuern an den Staat ab.

Dar Urbarialpatent teilte also den Boden rechtlich deutlich in zwei Teile, in vom Grundherrn und in vom Bauern bewirtschaftetes Land. Diese Aufteilung, die zugleich den Grundherrn daran hinderte, dem Bauern als urbarial eingestuftes Land wegzunehmen und zu Allodialland zu machen, ja ihn selbst nach dem Aussterben der Bauernfamilie verpflichtete, auf dem Urbarialland eine neue Bauernfamilie anzusiedeln, schuf im Prinzip auch die Grundlage für die spätere Befreieung: im Jahre 1848 kam das Urbarialland eindeutig in den Besitz der Bauern, während das Allodialland Eigentum der Grundherrn wurde.

Das Urbarialpatent war selbstverständlich nur der erste Schritt bei der Regelung der Beziehungen zwischen Grundherrn und Bauern. Obwohl der Bauer in Ungarn nie in seiner Person an den Grundherrn gebunden war (auch früher nicht „leibeigen" gewesen ist), stellt die Herrschaft Josephs II. auf diesem Gebiet dennoch eine deutliche Zäsur dar.

Die persönliche Unabhängigkeit des Bauern vom Grundherrn wurde mit Josephs II. Untertanen — Verordnung und mit der im Jahre 1787 zur Zügelung der Mißbräuche des Patrimonialgerichts und der adligen Komitate herausgegebenen Verordnung über die Regelung der Prozeßverfahren vor dem Patrimonialgericht zum großen Teil verwirklicht. Die Verordnung vom Jahre 1785 strich die Bezeichnung „leibeigen", die Bindung des Bauern an die Scholle und gewährleistete den Freizug des Bauern. Noch im Jahre 1783 erließ der Herrscher die Verordnung, in der er die freie Heirat des Untertanen erlaubte, die Verfügung über seine bewegliche Habe und die freie Berufswahl. Sie verbot die Vertreibung des Bauern von seiner Hofstelle und den Gesindezwangsdienst. Im Jahre 1787 erlaubte der Herrscher das ganze Jahr hindurch den bäuerlichen Weinausschank, womit er das System der adligen Monopole zerbrach. Alle diese Verordnungen, die auch ihre Gültigkeit behielten, nachdem Josephs II. System zusammengebrochen war (der Herrscher zog sie auch auf dem Sterbebett nicht zurück), wurden vom ungarischen Reichstag 1791 zum Gesetz erklärt (so der Freizug und auch, daß der Bauer seinen Prozeß mit dem Einspruch bis vor die Königliche Tafel bringen konnte, usw.).

Von den dreißiger Jahren des 19. Jahrhunderts ab rückte die Frage der Beziehungen Grundherr–Bauer wieder in den Vordergrund des politischen Lebens. Der Reichstag vom Jahre 1832–36 erklärte die Zehntfreiheit der Brache zum Gesetz (womit die Entwicklung der landwirtschaftlichen Produktion gefördert wurde), ermöglichte es dem Bauern, sein Land auf Grund gegenseitigen Einverständnisses zu kommassieren, seine Weide abzutrennen, und, wenn er es wollte, seine jährlichen Lasten in einer Summe abzulösen. Auch der Verkauf der Nutznießung der Hofstelle wurde möglich. Das Recht des Bauern, Land zu erwerben (und zu vererben) billigte der Herrscher nicht, so konnte es nicht in Kraft treten.

Nach 1836 nahm in den Reihen der Bauern das Streben nach Befreiung zu, nach der Abschaffung der Fron, der Zensus-Verpflichtungen und auch nach dem freien Land. Sie forderten auch die Ausweitung der Selbständigkeit der bäuerlichen Gemeinden. Der Reichstag von 1839–40 nahm schließlich die freiwillige Erbablöse an, aber unter Beibehaltung der grundherrlichen Gerichtsbarkeit und regelte auch die Erbfolge des Bauern-Untertannen. Der Reichstag von 1843–44 nahm das Recht des Landerwerbs der Nichtadligen an und im Prinzip auch die allgemeine Steuerpflicht. Letztere ging aber noch nicht in die Praxis über.

In Ungarn entwickelte sich die Lage sehr merkwürdig. Während der Wiener Hof die Reformen in der zweiten Hälfte des 18. Jahrhunderts in Gang setzte, änderte sich die Situation nach 1789 grundlegend. In den Jahren der Französischen Revolution und der napoleonischen Kriege hatte sich zwischen dem Hof und dem ungarischen Adel eine Einheitsfront zur Unterdrückung der Auswirkungen der Revolution, zur Verhinderung der Ausbreitung ihrer Ideen gebildet. Diese auf konservativen Grundlagen beruhende Einheitsfront zwischen Hof und ungarischem Adel war aber nach 1825 zerbrochen: von da ab wurden die progressiven Elemente des ungarischen Adels und der Aristokratie die Initiatoren und Erbauer des Weges zu einer bürgerlichen Umgestaltung, während die konservative Mehrheit des Adels und der Aristokratie in der Hoffnung auf die Unterstützung des Hofes auch weiterhin entschlossenen Widerstand leistete. Bisweilen aber schlug der Hof, aus taktischen Gründen, um die Opposition zu spalten, selbst Reformen vor, in der Hoffnung, die zerbrechliche Einheit des reformorientierten Adels zu brechen, was öfter auch Erfolg hatte. Insgesamt aber war die den kleineren Teil des Adels darstellende adlige Opposition in den Jahrzehnten vor 1848 die führende Kraft der auf die bürgerliche Umgestaltung hinwirkenden Reformen.

Die Möglichkeiten des Reformadels waren natürlich beschränkt und bis 1847–48 sichtlich erschöpft. Auf dem Reichstag vom Jahre 1847 schlugen die Anhänger der Reformen die verbindliche Erbablöse (mit der Entschädigung der urbarialen Verhältnisse) dort vor, wo mehr als 50% der Einwohner der Gemeinden darum ersuchten, außerdem die Aufhebung der Avitizität. Die allgemeine Steuerpflicht, die Gleichheit vor dem Gesetz und die Beteiligung der nichtadligen Klassen am Munizipalrecht bildeten ebenfalls einen Bestandteil des Programms des Reformadels. Auf dem Reichstag stießen diese Reformen aber auf Widerstand, und der gesamte Reformprozeß schien ins Stocken zu geraten, als die Kunde von der 1848er Pariser, dann der Wiener Revolution die Reformen endgültig den toten Punkt überwinden ließ. Nach dem 15. März 1848 nahm der Reichstag mit stürmischer Eile die noch fehlenden Gesetze der Umgestaltung an, die der Herrscher am 11. April sanktionierte. Damit war der Reformprozeß im wesentlichen abgeschlossen (selbst dann, wenn die Regelung zahlreicher Fragen für die folgenden Jahre, ja Jahrzehnte blieb und der letzte Akt erst 1896 erfolgte).

Die 48er Gesetzgebung strich das Urbarialrecht und alle Dienstleistungen, die auf Grund von Urbarien ersetzenden Erbkontrakten erbracht werden mußten, das heißt, sie hob das feudale Grundeigentum an den Hofstellen der Bauern auf. Sie strich auch den Zehnten für die Kirche. Die Entschädigung der Grundherren übernahm der Staat, die Dienstleistungen pro Hofstelle als 5%ige Zinsen ansetzend. Die Gesetze schafften die Institution der Patrimonialgerichtsbarkeit ab, erklärten die allgemeine Steuerpflicht, die Steuerfreiheit des Adels wurde also gestrichen. Abgeschafft wurde die Avitizität und damit wurde der freie Verkehr des Bodens möglich. Das alles zusammen bedeutete, daß die Hindernisse für kapitalistische Verhältnisse in der Landwirtschaft verschwunden waren.

In den folgenden Jahrzehnten wurde die Entwicklung der Landwirtschaft im Grunde von diesem Prozeß bestimmt. Aber wir können auch andere Faktoren nicht außer acht lassen, die gemeinsam mindestens von solcher Auswirkung auf die Umgestaltung der Landwirtschaft waren wie die Abschaffung des feudalen Systems.

Wir dürfen nicht vergessen, daß die Bauernbefreiung im großen und ganzen mit der grundlegenden Umformung des Verkehrs zusammenfiel. Noch am 2. August 1844 fand der erste Spatenstich für die Eisenbahnstrecke Pest–Vác statt, am 15. Juli 1846 begann der Verkehr auf dieser Strecke. Am 1. September 1847 wurde auch die Strecke Pest–Szolnok in Betrieb genommen und etwa anderthalb Jahre später sollte die Hauptlinie Wien–Pest eröffnet werden (deren Teilstrecke die Verbindung Pest–Vác war). Die Revolution zog den Bau etwas in die Länge, aber auch so konnte die Eisenbahnstrecke Wien–Preßburg–Pest am 16. Dezember 1850 eingeweiht werden. Damit war der Anschluß der ungarischen Landwirtschaft an den Weltmarkt möglich geworden. So wie die Nord-, Ost- und Südgebiete durch Verbindungslinien an die Hauptstrecke Wien–Pest angeschlossen wurden, so wurde die landwirtschaftliche Produktion verändert. Bis dahin hatte nur das Lebendvieh der wichtigste Exportartikel sein können, denn es wurde ja auf die Märkte getrieben. Getreide konnte nur aus dem westlichen und nordwestlichen Grenzgebiet mit dem Wagen auf die österreichisch–böhmischen Märkte gebracht werden. Der Ausbau der Eisenbahnlinien aber schloß bis zum Anfang der 1860er Jahre sehr weite Gebiete des Landes an den Weltmarkt an. Diese Wende ist von mindestens solcher Tragweite wie die Bauernbefreiung selbst.

Hier erwähnen wir auch, daß nicht allein der Eisenbahnbau die modernen Verkehrsformen schuf, wenn er auch von der größten Bedeutung war, sondern auch der Straßenbau und die Flußregulierung. Diese Tätigkeiten wurden in der zweiten Hälfte des 19. Jahrhunderts immer wichtiger und trugen ebenfalls zur Umformung der landwirtschaftlichen Produktion bei.

Mit dem Prozeß der Bauernbefreiung war eine andere Veränderung verbunden, die die Entwicklung der landwirtschaftlichen Produktion ebenfalls grundlegend beeinflußte: am 1. Oktober 1850 wurde die Zollgrenze zwischen den Erblanden und Ungarn aufgehoben. Das können wir auch anders formulieren: das Habsburgerreich (nach dem Ausgleich von 1867 die Österreichisch–Ungarische Monarchie) wurde zu einem einheitlichen Zollgebiet und blieb es bis zum Zerfall des Reiches im Jahre 1918.

Anfangs brachte das einheitliche Zollgebiet keine konkreten Vorteile für die ungarische Landwirtschaft, es waren lediglich die Beschränkungen gefallen, die früher die landwirtschaftliche Produktion der Erblande vor der ungarischen Konkurrenz geschützt hatten (bei guter Ernte Einfuhrverbote usw.), und daß die Pflicht der Zollentrichtung an der ungarischen Grenze aufgehört hatte. Die außergewöhnliche Bedeutung der Maßnahme vom 1. Oktober 1850 erwies sich erst drei Jahrzehnte später, als der Wettbewerb mit der überseeischen Getreideproduktion die meisten europäischen Staaten zwang, sich von den anderen abzuschließen, das heißt von 1878 ab. Danach wurde das ungarische Getreide zunehmend von den französischen und süddeutschen Märkten verdrängt, Ungarn konnte dagegen aber — dank des gemeinsamen Zollgebiets — seine Produkte unbeschränkt in den österreichisch–böhmischen Ländern absetzen. Österreich und Böhmen waren für die ungarische Landwirtschaft bis zum Ende des ersten Weltkrieges so gut wie ein Binnenmarkt. Das bedeutete in diesen Jahrzehnten praktisch unbeschränkte Unterbringung auf dem Markt bei wesentlich höheren Preisen als auf dem Weltmarkt.

Neben dem einheitlichen Zollgebiet waren noch andere Faktoren von Bedeutung: an erster Stelle muß hier das gemeinsame Zahlungssystem erwähnt werden. Als Finanzeinheit bot die Österreichisch–Ungarische Monarchie Ungarn und auch der ungarischen Landwirtschaft zahlreiche Vorteile, besonders bei der Entwicklung des modernen Kreditsystems und auf dem Gebiet der Finanzierung der landwirtschaftlichen Investitionen. Das war natürlich nicht in erster Linie für die Landwirtschaft von Bedeutung, es ging vielmehr darum, daß Ungarn als Teil der Monarchie an den Vorteilen der schnellen Entstehung eines relativ fortgeschrittenen Geldsystems teilhatte und das wirkte sich zum Beispiel auch auf das Kreditwesen in der Landwirtschaft aus.

Ähnlich förderlich für die Entwicklung des Landes im allgemeinen, und innerhalb derselben auch der der Landwirtschaft war die Verwirklichung des einheitlichen Maß- und Gewichtssystems und der Arbeitsprinzipien von Eisenbahn und Post — mit einem Wort, alle die zum Begriffsbereich der allgemeinen Modernisierung gehörenden Faktoren, über die wir im allgemeinen wenig sprechen, die aber im Modernisierungsprozeß von Bedeutung sind.

Durch all diese Faktoren gemeinsam schaltete sich die ungarische Landwirtschaft innerhalb der kurzen Zeit von ein-anderthalb Jahrzehnten eng an den Weltmarkt an und das veränderte schon an sich das Produktionsgefüge in grossem Umfange. Die große Getreidekonjunktur, die vom Beginn der 1850er Jahre bis zum Ende der 1870er Jahre für die Weltwirtschaft bezeichnend gewesen war, hatte auch ihre Wirkung auf Ungarn gehabt. Parallel zum Ausbau der Eisenbahnstrecken wurden die Weiden umgebrochen und ihr Großteil in Ackerfelder umgewandelt. Die extensive Viehzucht übergab ihren Platz immer mehr dem intensiveren, an sich genommen aber ziemlich extensivem Getreideanbau.

Das hatte natürlich auch andere Gründe. Es handelte sich um einen zwangsweisen Prozeß, um einen Prozeß, dessen Wurzeln auch in vielfacher Hinsicht mit der Bauernbefreiung verbunden waren. Nach der Bauernbefreiung mußten auch für das Allodialland Steuern gezahlt werden, und selbst die niedrigste Bodensteuer war höher als der Nutzen aus der extensiven, auf dem Weiden basierenden Viehzucht. So war es ein wirtschaftlicher Zwang, der den extensiven Getreideanbau, so extensiv er auch war, statt des Weidegangs einführte.

Andererseits hatten die grundherrlichen Güter, die von der Arbeitskraft, dem Zugvieh und den Arbeitsgeräten ihrer ehemaligen Untertanen getrennt worden waren, nicht genügend Kapital, um sich in unbeschränktem Umfange eigenes Zugvieh und eigene Arbeitsgeräte zu beschaffen, sie waren gezwungen, mit dem relativ geringsten Kapital das relativ höchste Einkommen zu erzielen. Diese beiden Faktoren, die Steuer und der Kapitalmangel gemeinsam zwangen die Güter mit elementarer Kraft, den Getreideanbau auszudehnen, denn hierzu waren die geringsten Investition und das wenigste Anlagekapital (Gebäude usw.) erforderlich. Das Ergebnis war innerhalb von zwei Jahrzehnten das Zusammenschrumpfen der Weidegebiete und die rapide Ausweitung des Getreideanbaus und der Ackerfeldproduktion. Parallel dazu ging der Viehbestand zurück, vor allem die Rinderzucht, dessen Auswirkungen sich vor allem auf den großen Auslandsmärkten zeigten (so entstand in Wien öfter Fleischmangel, dem auch steigende Fleischpreise nicht abhelfen konnten).

Die praktische Durchführung der Bauernbefreiung wurde natürlich nicht von einem Tag auf den anderen verwirklicht, ihre Durchführung war ein längerer historischer Prozeß. Im großen und ganzen nahm die Abwicklung der praktischen Aufgaben anderthalb Jahrzehnte in Anspruch. Nach dem Scheitern der Revolution führte der Absolutismus die unmittelbare Aufhebung durch. Die Verordnungen vom 2.–3. März 1853 (Urbarialpatent) führten die Entschädigung im einzelnen aus und regelten die Methoden der Separation. Zwischen Grundherr und Untertan erfolgte die Separation, die Abtrennung des Bodens, im allgemeinen vor dem Gericht. Im ganzen Land war die Separation der grundherrlichen und der bäuerlichen Böden im großen und ganzen bis zum Ende der 1860er Jahre (1868) abgeschlossen. Die Separation aber bedeutete nur die Aufteilung des Bodens unter die beiden Parteien und war nicht automatisch gleichbedeuten mit der Zusammenlegung, das heißt, das von den Bauern genutzte Land wurde weiterhin im Rahmen der Dreifelderwirtschaft bebaut. Die Flurbereinigung war eine gesonderte Frage und fand nur dort statt, wo die bäuerliche Gemeinschaft diese besonders forderte. Da die Flurbereinigung für die bäuerlichen Wirtschaften ziemlich hohe Lasten bedeutete, braucht man sich nicht zu wundern, daß noch im Jahre 1945 bei einem Sechtstel der landwirtschaftlich genutzten Fläche keine Flurbereinigung durchgeführt worden war (bei insgesamt 1860 Gemeinden). Ein besonderer Nachteil war, daß gerade in den intensiver bewirtschafteten Gebieten die meisten nicht bereinigten Flächen lagen. Dabei hätte die Flurbereinigung eine bedeutende Ertragssteigerung zur Folge gehabt, nach zeitgenössischen Angaben stiegen die Erträge allein durch die Flubereinigung im allgemeinen um etwa 18–20%.

Die Separation der bäuerlichen und der grundherrlichen Böden nahm also insgesamt anderthalb Jahrzehnte in Anspruch, bedeutend länger aber dauerte die Regelung der weiteren Probleme aus der Bauernbefreiung. Die Gesetze von 1848 (diese betrachtete die Gesetzgebung des Absolutismus ebenso als Grundlage wie die souveräne ungarische Regierung nach dem Ausgleich vom Jahre 1867) nahmen nämlich Maria Theresias Urbarialpatent zur Grundlage. Danach wurde das Land, das in bäuerlicher Nutzung war, den Bauern gegeben, während das Allodialland in den Händen des Adels blieb. 1767 aber galten viele Böden als Allodialland, obwohl es von Bauern bewirtschaftet wurde. Neben den auf Allodialland angesiedelten Dörfern gab es noch zahlreiche bäuerliche Schichten, die auf *rechtlich* dem Grundherrn gehörendem (allodialem) Boden lebten und arbeiteten (Tabak-, Melonengärtner usw.), wenn auch nicht in größeren Niederlassungen, aber verstreut im Lande. Ihre Zahl war nicht niedrig und — ebenso wie auf die auf Allodialland angesiedelten Dörfer — erstreckte sich auch auf sie die Bauernbefreiung nicht.

Im Absolutismus gelang es nicht, ihre Probleme zu lösen, denn es fand kein gesetzgebender Reichstag statt. Erst nach 1867 konnte es zur gesetzlichen Regelung aller jener Fragen kommen, die die zu summarisch gefaßte Bauernbefreiung von 1848 offengelassen hatte. Zwischen 1868 und 1873 wurden die meisten Angelegenheiten geregelt, allerdings dauerte die Bereinigung der strittigen Fragen der Befreiung bei einigen Schichten auch bis 1896.

Einfach war der *Weinzehnt*, den die Bauernbefreiung nicht geordnet hatte. Hier entschied das Gesetz von 1868, daß die Bauern den Weinzehnt selbst unmittelbar ablösen mußten. Ähnlich wurde das Problem der Industriafelder (Rodungsfelder, Extirpationsfelder) gelöst. Die einzelnen ehemaligen Untertanen mußten solche Felder außerhalb der Hofstette (des Hofbestandes) ebenfalls selbst ablösen. Das Ausmaß der Ablöse richtete sich in beiden Fällen nach der Summe, mit der die mit der Hofstelle verbundenen Dienstleistungen abgelöst worden waren, nur daß dies in diesen Fällen ohne die Übernahme der Lasten durch den Staat geschah, die Bauern mußten den von den Gerichten festgestzten Zahlungsverpflichtungen selbst genüge tun.

In der gleichen Weise wurde bei den *Neusiedlerdörfern* vorgegangen, dort also, wo die Untertanen nach dem Ende der Türkenherrschaft im Rahmen einer Gemeindeorganisation angesiedelt worden waren. Solche sogenannten Taxalisten-, Kontraktual-Siedler-, oder Gedingedörfer standen mit ihren Grundherren in einem privatrechtlichen Vertragsverhältnis. Ihr Land galt rechtlich als Allodialland, sie hatten also früher keine Steuern an den Staat gezahlt. Deshalb bekam der Grundherr von ihnen gewöhnlich höhere Leistungen. Im Jahre 1873 bestimmte ein Gesetzesartikel (XXIII.), daß die Bauern dieser Dörfer ihr Land und ihre Dienstleistungen selbst ablösen sollten. Natürlich nur die Dörfer, die Verträge vorweisen konnten. In vielen Fällen also (wo sie aus irgendeinem Grund keinen Vertrag vorlegen konnten) verloren die Bauern nach dem Gesetz ihr Land beziehungsweise den größten Teil davon.

In ähnlicher rechtlicher Lage waren im Grunde genommen auch die sogenannten *Gutshäusler* oder Kurialsassen. Das waren Bauern, die nicht nur Allodialland als Ackerfeld, Wiese oder Weide nutzten, sondern deren Haus und Garten sich ebenfalls auf Allodialland befand. Sie waren vor 1848 in den Augen des Grundherrn Häusler ohne Besitz (solche Bauern, die nicht einmal die kleinste Hofstelle hatten), aber in den Augen der auf dem Urbarialland lebenden Häusler galten sie eigentlich als Land besitzende Bauern, denn sie hatten größere Ackerfelder als die damaligen Kleinhäusler. Die Gutshäusler galten eigentlich als Pächter auf dem Allodialland. Unter ihnen waren auch Bauern mit größerer Wirtschaft, die meisten aber hatten 0,5–1 Hektar Ackerland. Rechtlich befanden sie sich in einer komplizierten Situation. Ein Teil von ihnen bezahlte dem Grundherrn nur den Zensus, sie hießen die Zensualisten. Andere waren ihrem Grundherrn durch Kontrakt verbunden, das waren die Kontraktualisten. Andere gaben dem Grundherrn ein Fünftel, ein Sechstel oder ein Siebentel der Ernte. Noch andere lebten auf „Industriafeld" und zu ihnen gehörten auch die schon erwähnten Siedlungsdörfer. Die Lage dieser Siedlungsdörfer regelte ein Gesetz aus dem Jahre 1873. Die Bauern hier bauten vor allem Tabak an.

In den Jahrzehnten nach 1848 verloren sehr viele der Gutshäusler nach und nach ihr Land. Auf unterschiedlichen rechtlichen Wegen erreichten die gewesenen Grundherren, daß diese Bauern gezwungen waren, ihr Haus und ihr Land zu verlassen. Die Lage der übriggebliebenen wurde 1896 geregelt und zwar auf dem Wege der Ablöse. Sofort nach Erlaß des als Grundlage der Maßnahme dienenden Gesetzes begannen die gerichtlichen Verfahren. Diese Prozesse zogen sich lange hin, und eigentlich legte erst 1914 die Gesetzgebung die Grundprinzipien des gerichtlichen Verfahrens fest. Im Weltkrieg ruhten die Verfahren. Schließlich löste die Bodenreform vom Jahre 1920 die Frage der restlichen Gutshäusler. Es ist kein Wunder, daß die vielen Gutshäusler die Kategorie der Bauernschaft bildete, die auf dem Altar der „Großzügigkeit" der Bauernbefreiung von 1848 zerbröckelte.

Für große Massen der Bauernschaft aber war die Bauernbefreiung, die Art ihrer Dürchführung eine Wohltat. Das Land, das vor der Befreiung in ihrer Hand war, von ihnen genutzt wurde, blieb ihnen im allgemeinen auch nach der Befreiung. Die zu zahlende Entschädigung belastete zugleich die Bauern nicht. In Ungarn gab es nämlich schon viel früher den entsprechenden Geldverkehr, und beim Adel, aber auch bei den Bauern hatten sich die entsprechenden Geldsummen angehäuft. Nicht zuletzt übernahmen auch die Bauern den entsprechenden Teil im Ware–Geld–Verkehr. Verglichen mit den deutschen Gebieten sagt das alles nicht viel, scheint es natürlich, wen wir aber die Umstände des rumänischen oder russischen Bauern betrachten, so scheint es schon ein grundlegender Unterschied zu sein. In den rumänischen Fürstentümern belasteten die Ablösesummen die Bauernschaft so sehr — vor allem, weil der Ware–Geld–Verkehr noch minimal war —, daß schon wenige Jahre nach der Befreiung die Verschuldung der Bauernwirtschaften begann, der Wucher die Bauern aussaugte. Ähnliche war die Lage in Rußland und allgemein überall dort, wo der Ware–Geld–Verkehr nicht auf dem entsprechenden Niveau stand, nicht den entsprechenden Umfang hatte. In Ungarn aber verursachte die Bauernbefreiung in dieser Hinsicht keine Wirren, die Bauernwirtschaften konnten ungestört arbeiten, empfanden vor allem die Vorteile der Veränderungen.

Es ist schon erwähnt worden, daß sich die direkte und indirekte Auswirkung, die die Bauernbefreiung auf die ganze ungarische Wirtschaft, inbegriffen auch die landwirtschaftliche Produktion gehabt hat, sehr schwer bestimmen läßt. Wenn wir aber einen längeren historischen Abschnitt untersuchen, sagen wir die Industrialisierung in den Jahrzehnten zwischen 1850 und 1914, die ganze wirtschaftliche Entwicklung, so ist das leichter lösbar.

Vor allem müssen wir daran erinnern, daß gleichzeitig die Wirkung mehrerer Faktoren auftritt, damit der Kapitalbedarf der gesamten Wirtschaft, inbegriffen die Landwirtschaft, befriedigt werden kann. Gefördert wurde dies in erster Linie durch den freien An- und Verkauf der Grundbesitze, denn in Form von Hypotheken floß sehr viel Kapital in die Wirtschaft (nicht unmittelbar in die Landwirtschaft!). Das hing besonders mit der Abschaffung der Avitizität zusammen, wodurch der Weg für Kredite frei wurde. Aber natürlich trugen dazu auch in großem Maße die Umgestaltung des Verkehrs, die Verlegung der Eisenbahngeleise und auch die Konjunktur auf dem Weltmarkt bei (speziell auf dem Gebiet der Getreideproduktion), deren unmittelbarer Einfluß auf die landwirtschaftliche Produktion in Ungarn nicht geleugnet werden kann. Die Entwicklung der Produktionstätigkeit auf den Gütern, die Bereitstellung der notwendigen Investitionen war vor allem die Folge der Verwirklichung des freien An- und Verkaufs des Bodens, da dies alles bei der Entstehung wirklich kapitalistischer Großbetriebe eine bestimmende Rolle spielte.

Die Veränderung des Verkehrs, der Hochwasserschutz (durch die Flußregulierungen wurden sehr große, früher unter Wasser stehende oder vom Wasser überflutete Flächen der landwirtschaftlichen Produktion zugeführt), der Strassenbau — dies alles zusammen spielte eine Rolle bei der Veränderung der Produktionsstruktur, bei der Vergrößerung der Anbaufläche und der Ertragssteigerung. In den drei auf die Bauernbefreiung folgenden Jahrzehnten können wir Zeugen einer erstaunlichen Zunahme der Getreideproduktion sein. Die Ackerfläche war größer geworden und darauf die absolute Fläche und der Anteil des Getreideanbaus, die Saatfläche der Getreidearten, vor allem des Weizens war ausgeweitet worden, die Erträge, vornehmlich der Ernteertrag des Getreides hatte erstaunlich zugenommen. In der zweiten Hälfte der 1870er dann wurde die Wirkung der Getreidekrise spürbar: das Sinken der Preise für die Getreidearten. Danach begann dann allmählich in der landwirtschaftlichen Produktion eine Art Strukturwandel: die Anbaufläche und die Ernteerträge beim Getreide stagnierten, demgegenüber entwickelte sich sichtbar die Viehzucht, in erster Linie die Schweine- und Rinderzucht. Daneben gewann der Feldfutterbau schnell an Boden und vom

Beginn der 1880er ab auch der Anbau von Industriepflanzen (an erster Stelle der Zuckerrübe).

Die Auswirkung der Bauernfreiung auf die industrielle Revolution war ohne Zweifel erfolgversprechend, wenn dies auch nicht unmittelbar nachgewiesen werden konnte. Indirekt aber waren die beiden Prozesse durch zahlreiche Bande miteinander verknüpft. Die Bauernbefreiung und die Abschaffung der Avitizität ermöglichten die Vergabe von Hypotheken, damit floß Kapital in die Wirtschaft, das wiederum industrielle Investitionen beschleunigte: das ist lediglich das eine Verbindugssystem zwischen den beiden Erscheinungen. Zur gleichen Zeit forcierte die Veränderung der landwirtschaftlichen Produktion direkte landwirtschaftliche Investitionen und die Nachfrage nach neuen Geräten, Maschinen, nach Eisenpflug und Eisenegge, nach Sensen und kleinen Maschinen stieg schnell.

Der Strukturwandel in der landwirtschaftlichen Produktion, die Inbesitznahme des gesamten Zollgebiets der Monarchie durch den ungarischen Agrarexport zwischen 1850 bis 1914 brachte dem ungarischen Außenhandel eindeutig eine positive Bilanz. Der Exportüberschuß war — abgesehen von den letzten vier bis fünf Friedensjahren, in denen die Exportbilanz zunehmend passiv wurde — in vollem Maße eine Folge des Agrarexports, die Ausfuhr von Industrieartikeln, Rohstoffen, Halbfertig- und Fertigwaren überstieg weit die Einfuhr von Halbfertig- und Fertigwaren im gesamten Zeitraum. Der ungarische landwirtschaftliche Export aber sicherte der gesamten ungarischen Außenhandelsbilanz einen so bedeutenden Überschuß, der es für ausländische Investoren eindeutig erscheinen ließ, daß ihre Investitionen und ihre Kapitalforderungen entsprechende Deckung hatten. Dem ansehnlichen ungarischen Exportüberschuß stand zwar im ganzen Zeitraum eine negative Zahlungsbilanz gegenüber, deren Grund gerade in den ausländischen Krediten und Tilgungen lag, aber diese negative Zahlungsbilanz wurde gleichsam in der aktiven Zahlungsbilanz der gemeinsamen Wirtschaft der Monarchie „aufgesogen", auch diese begann lediglich in den letzten Friedensjahren anhaltend negativ zu werden. Dies alles zusammen machte Ungarn zu einem anziehenden Investitionsmarkt, ein Umstand, dessen Vorteile sich in ausländischen Kapitalanlagen und als deren Folge in der Beschleunigung des Industrialisierungsprozesses zeigte.

Auf die Industrialisierung aber übte die Veränderung in der Landwirtschaft eine weit größere Wirkung aus: der schnelle Anlauf und die günstige Lage der auf den gesamten Markt der Monarchie aufbauenden ungarischen landwirtschaftlichen Produktion machte innerhalb des gemeinsamen Zollgebiets die schnelle Entwicklung verschiedener Nahrungsmittelzweige möglich. Die schnell Weltniveau erreichende ungarische Mühlenindustrie, die Budapester Großmühlen entstanden zur Befriedigung des Mehlbedarfs der ganzen Monarchie, was nicht zuletzt zu großangelegten Investitionen beitrug. Auch die ungarische Fleisch- und Konservenindustrie produzierte für die Märkte der Monarchie. Dasselbe galt auch für die Brennereien, vornehmlich aber für die Zuckerindustrie. Die ungarische Zuckerproduktion zeigte von 1880er Jahren ab einen stürmischen Aufschwung, sie setzte ihre Produkte vor allem in Österreich und in Böhmen ab, aber auch auf dem Weltmarkt (in England, Italien, dann in der Türkei und in Indien). Der größte Teil der ungarischen Zuckerproduktion wurde also auf dem Weltmarkt abgesetzt.

Die Entwicklung der Nahrungsmittelindustrie, dabei die der beiden führenden Industriezweige, der Zuckerherstellung und der Mühlenindustrie, wirkte nicht nur auf die landwirtschaftliche Produkton zurück, sondern war auch mit der Entwicklung der Industrie verknüpft. Das eklatanteste Beispiel dafür liefert die Mühlenindustrie. Die schnelle Entwicklung der ungarischen Großmühlen bot mit der Weiterentwicklung einer Erfindung der Ganz-Fabrik der ungarischen Maschinenindustrie neue Möglichkeiten. Den Schalenguß hatte die Ganz-Fabrik schon früher bei der Herstellung von Eisenbahnrädern patentieren lassen. Diese Technologie probierte man sehr bald — und zwar erfolgreich — bei der Fabrikation von Walzstühlen aus. Die neue Methode ermöglichte die Herstellung von viel feinerem Mehl und von bedeutend mehr Feineinstellungen bei der Mehlproduktion. Das Weltpatent der Ganz-Fabrik für diesen neuen Typus des Walzenstuhls trug wesentlich zum Fortschritt der ungarischen Industrialisierung bei und schuf zugleich ein volles Vertikum in der Produktion, vom Weizenanbau über die Mehlproduktion hin bis zur Mühleneinrichtung.

Im großen und ganzen eine ähnliche, wenn auch nicht so bedeutende unmittelbare Wirkung zeigt sich auch in der Zuckerherstellung. Die ersten ungarischen Zuckerfabriken wurden von österreichischen und böhmischen Kapitalisten gegründet, unter Verwendung von deutschen Maschinen. Bei den in den 1880er Jahren eingerichteten ungarischen Zuckerfabriken wurde das frühere Produktionsverfahren verbessert, die bei der Zuckerherstellung verwendeten neuen Maschinen und Geräte waren viel effektiver als die in den früher in Ungarn eingerichteten Fabriken. Ja, es begann sogar der Export ungarischer Zuckerfabrikeinrichtungen nach dem Balkan und zum Teil auch nach Rußland. Hier entstand also auch mehr oder weniger das ganze Vertikum, von der Produktion der Zuckerrübe bis zur Fabrikation von Zuckerfabrikeinrichtungen. In den übrigen Zweigen der Machinenindustrie ist eine solche Erscheinung in viel geringerem Umfange zu beobachten.

Die angedeuteten Tendenzen verraten, daß die Möglichkeiten der landwirtschaftlichen produktion auf gewissen Gebieten auch die Industrieproduktion veränderten, das heißt die Umgestaltung der ungarischen landwirtschaftlichen Produktion hatte Einfluß, und zwar direkten Einfluß auch auf die Umgestaltung der Industrialisierung des Landes. Das war ohne Zweifel eine der größten direkten Auswirkungen der kapitalistischen Veränderung der Landwirtschaft auf die Industrialisierung. Trotzdem sehen wir nicht hierin die wichtigste Wechselwirkung zwischen Agrarumgestaltung und industrieller Revolution, sondern darin, daß die Landwirtschaft fähig war, ihren feudalen Charakter mit Hilfe von Reformen zu wandeln und sich zumindest soweit zu verändern, daß diese Veränderung an sich die Garantie dafür bot, daß die ungarische Landwirtschaft über eine ganze historische Epoche hindurch, von 1850 bis 1914 für die ganze Wirtschaft des Landes die für die Investitionen, für die Industrialisierung erforderliche Kapitalaufnahme nicht behinderte, sondern im Gegenteil, förderte.

Kehren wir zurück zur unseren Grundfrage: welcher Zusammenhang besteht zwischen dem Bauernbefreiungsprozeß und der Industriellen Revolution in Ungarn? So formuliert erhalten wir keine deutbare Antwort. Die Bauernbefreiung ging dem Beginn der industriellen Revolution in Ungarn voran und als sich die Industrialisation in Bewegung setzte, wurden schon die wirtschaftlichen und sozialen Erfordernisse geschaffen, ohne die sich der Industrialisierungsprozeß nur begrenzt verwirklichen läßt. In Westeuropa war alles schon viel früher, also noch vor der Industrialisierung abgelaufen und auch in Ungarn verwirklichte sich dieser Prozeß zur rechten Zeit in der Landwirtschaft. Obwohl in der Landwirtschaft Ungarns in der ersten Hälfte des 19. Jahrhunderts eine direkte Notwendigkeit die Umgestaltung noch nicht unumgänglich machte. Ein großer Teil der Reformpolitiker erkannte aber (mit Hilfe westeuropäischer Beispiele), wohin die Weiterentwicklung führt. So geschah, daß die industrielle Revolution in Ungarn nicht in die Hindernisse des feudalen Agrarsystems stieß, was überall der Fall war, wo die Umgestaltung des Agrarsektors synchron (paralell) mit der Industrialisierung ging.

# INDEX